D1267222

The
Positive
Thinkers

Donald Meyer

The Positive Thinkers

Popular Religious Psychology from Mary Baker Eddy to Norman Vincent Peale and Ronald Reagan

REVISED EDITION
WITH A NEW INTRODUCTION

Wesleyan University Press
Middletown, Connecticut

This book was originally published in 1965 by Doubleday & Company, Inc. as *The Positive Thinkers: A Study of the American Quest for Health, Wealth and Personal Power from Mary Baker Eddy to Norman Vincent Peale*. It was republished in 1980 by Pantheon Books as *The Positive Thinkers: Religion as Pop Psychology from Mary Baker Eddy to Oral Roberts*.

Grateful acknowledgment is made to the following for permission to use copyrighted material from these publications:

Abingdon Press, from *You Can Win* by Norman Vincent Peale; Back to the Bible Broadcast and Moody Press, Chicago, from *Nervous Christians* by L. Gilbert Little; The Bobbs-Merrill Company and Mrs. Ralph Waldo Trine, from *The Best of Ralph Waldo Trine*. Copyright © by The Bobbs-Merrill Company, Inc., reprinted by permission of the publisher; D. Van Nostrand Company, Inc., from O. Hobart Mowrer's *The Crisis in Psychiatry and Religion*. Copyright 1961, by D. Van Nostrand Company, Inc., Princeton, N.J.; McGraw-Hill Book Company, from *Peace of Soul* by Fulton J. Sheen. Copyright 1949 by McGraw-Hill Book Company. Used by permission; Mrs. Grace Hyde Trine, from *The Land Of Living Men* and *In Tune With the Infinite* by Ralph Waldo Trine; Unity School of Christianity, from *Prosperity* by Charles Fillmore, and *The Science of Being and Christian Healing;* Willing Publishing Company, from *How to Attract Money* by Joseph Murphy; The World's Work Ltd., and Simon and Schuster, Inc., from *Love or Perish* by Smiley Blanton. Copyright © 1956, 1957 by Smiley Blanton, M.D.

All inquiries and permissions requests should be addressed to the Publisher, Wesleyan University Press, 110 Mt. Vernon Street, Middletown, Connecticut 06457

LIBRARY OF CONGRESS CATALOGING-IN-PUBLICATION DATA

Meyer, Donald B.
  The positive thinkers:from Mary Baker Eddy to Ronald Reagan/ Donald Meyer.—Rev. ed., Wesleyan ed.
    p. cm.
  Bibliography: p.
  Includes index.
  ISBN 0-8195-5160-0 ISBN 0-8195-6166-5 (pbk.)
    1. United States—Church history—19th century.   2. United States—Church history—20th century.   3. Peace of mind—Christianity—History of doctrines.   4. Spiritual healing—United States—History of doctrines.   5. Wealth—Religious aspects—Christianity—History of doctrines.   I. Title.
BR517.M48   1988
277.3′082—dc 19   87-34521
                                                                         CIP

Manufactured in the United States of America
First Wesleyan Edition, 1988
Wesleyan Paperback, 1988

For my mother and father

"And so," said over his shoulder Comrad Ossipon, who sat on the chair behind,—"and so Michaelis dreams of a world like a beautiful and cheery hospital."

"Just so. An immense charity for the healing of the weak," assented the Professor, sardonically.

"That's silly," admitted Ossipon. "You can't heal weakness. But after all Michaelis may not be so far wrong. In two hundred years doctors will rule the world. Science reigns already. It reigns in the shade maybe—but it reigns. And all science must culminate at last in the science of healing—not the weak, but the strong. Michaelis wants to live—to live."

"Mankind," asserted the Professor with a self-confident glitter of his iron-rimmed spectacles, "does not know what it wants."

—Joseph Conrad, *The Secret Agent*

INTRODUCTION TO THE
WESLEYAN EDITION

For this new edition of *The Positive Thinkers*, I have contributed a chapter focused almost entirely on the latest, and one of the most remarkable, conjunctions of religion and politics in recent American history, the campaign of Ronald Reagan for reelection in 1984. For their part, Mr. Reagan and his political operatives explicitly affirmed that their new "conservative" majority must be openly religious. At the same time, the fundamentalist clergy whom they wooed explicitly welcomed an openly political expression of their faith. Cries from both political and religious opponents that this campaign was breaking down walls of separation between church and state went unheeded. Protests that a kind of civic peace based on pluralistic toleration was being jeopardized were dismissed. Yet the novelty in the campaign of 1984 lay not in some fusion of political and religious forces. Jimmy Carter had linked his own evangelical values with his political campaign of 1976, and historians can point to numerous episodes over the previous two centuries when alliances between politics and religion flourished. The novelty of 1984 consisted in the way the political and religious Reaganites defined their opponents.

The fundamentalists' political agenda comprised "social issues": aversion to abortion, to the Equal Rights Amendment, and to homosexuality; demand for a return of prayer to the schools, of "moral values" to public life. Those opposed to the fundamentalists were regarded not simply as religious opponents but as adherents of a philosophy hostile to religion itself: "secular humanism." Economic issues, on the other hand, had dominated the President's first term: supply-side tax cuts, cuts in welfare spending, squeezing out inflation by weathering through a recession. There was no obvious congruence between these two perspectives. The President, however, offered his own basic aim as in itself moral: the reduction of government. The reduction of government, moral in itself, then carried economic rewards. It would induce a return to prosperity and the long postwar boom, so badly interrupted in the seventies. The fundamentalists' alliance with economic Reaganism bespoke the needs of a group already leaving its own past of poverty and marginality behind. The transformation of Oral Roberts's depression-hardened Pentecostalism into Tulsa's gleaming modernities symbolized the transformation of a whole popular culture. The flourishing TV ministries of the seventies further confirmed it. Reaganism would revive the expectation of a folk that virtue would be rewarded. Whether this would prepare the way for still another revival of popular psychology in the form of positive thinking remained to be seen. But mind cure and positive thinking had always been less a by-product of some decay in liberal Protestantism than testimony to the inability of liberal Protestantism to convert more than a minority to its views. Positive thinking had always demonstrated the existence of masses of individuals no longer secure in old faiths of folk and tribe but unequipped with the strengths of liberal and pluralistic culture.

My discussion of the campaign of 1984, then, is postulated on the guess that the alliance of fundamentalist and economic Reaganites followed from an attempt to revalidate a society in which material wealth and psychological security were assumed to be within the reach of anyone willing to think the right way, willing to "believe." Does this imply that Ronald Reagan himself was—is— a positive thinker? Not in the sense traced in this book. Indeed, Reagan's imagination, like that of most of his fundamentalist troops, ran to a Manichean view of the world, often as lurid as theirs, a view insisting upon the presence of powerful forces of evil, the presence of Satan. In the traditions of mind cure and positive thinking, such notions were thought negative indeed. Part of the anesthesia to social reality found in positive thinking had had as one of its reasons the elimination of any need to grapple with negation, want, confusion, evil. But the meaning of dualism in Reagan's imagination was not as clear as some of his formulations of it. And the same was true of the political cohorts of the Moral Majority. "Secular humanism" was a suspiciously protean Satan, a peculiarly unformulated enemy, and a spectator might wonder whether it existed more in the need of its accusers than in any perception of reality. If their political crusade succeeded, their need might evolve. Still, it is my impression that the changes that overtook the American economy in the seventies were sufficiently deep as to render any widespread revival of positive thinking unlikely, no matter how earnest the effort. Ronald Reagan's sunny optimism may have charmed multitudes, but that optimism was neither an economic nor a religious substitute for realism and hard work.

Donald Meyer
1988

CONTENTS

Part Two: Peace in the System: Sociology as Psychology

A Conclusion

PREFACE TO THE SECOND EDITION: 1980

FIFTEEN YEARS AGO, when this book was first published, it seemed within the bounds of caution to offer, at the end of Postscript II, some modest predictions. None has been borne out. "Perhaps among Catholics the Presidency of John Kennedy and the Papacy of John XXIII and of Paul VI would soothe agitated souls." Instead, American Catholics find themselves confronted with questions not of their place in the nation, for that is now secure, but of their place in the church. What are they to do with popes who refuse to concede the merit of their own moral culture? "Perhaps among Jews further assimilation might seem compatible with stable identity." But "further assimilation" has paled into irrelevance in face of another outside crisis: the challenge, since 1967, to the survival of Israel. "Perhaps among Protestants, the emergence of a postwar generation of tough-minded young theologians and intellectuals and urban-oriented pastors, plus the racial challenge to integrity, might mean reawakening." But within another ten years the hopes for religious meaning in social awakening had faded and a new generation of evangelical Protestant leaders had emerged with different priorities. So much for predictions.

On the other hand, the larger premise of the book has, I think, proved solid. The fate of religious imagination, as a source of vitality and renewal in a secular democratic society, can hardly be decided elsewhere than where that society itself is at its strongest—that is, where "individualism," individual ambitions, primary groups, education for self-improvement, and the will to insist that "institutions" serve individuals, not vice versa, all flourish most fully—in short, among middle classes. Here, contrary to what De Tocqueville predicted 150 years ago, the surest field for widespread democratic initiative and vitality has proved to be precisely that of religion. Politics might harden, the economy rigidify into command-oriented bureaucratic hierarchies, science itself become an orthodoxy, while American religion proved, generation after generation, a realm open to free individual private enterprise. "There is more to human life than meets the eye. More to oneself; more to one's neighbor; more to the world that surrounds us.... And the further we probe, men have always found, the deeper the mystery, or the reward, or the involvement. It is this 'more,' perhaps, that provides at least one of the bases of human religion."[1] In America, large numbers of people have been peculiarly free to probe the "more" in themselves. The special danger followed from the special opportunity: religious freedom could be wasted in religion as therapy, as cult of reassurance, as psychology of peace and positive thinking. That is the danger I investigated in the book.

For what it is worth, I offer the modest speculation that the grounds for positive thinking have been reduced during the fifteen years since 1965. "Harsh reality" has made certain illusions more difficult to sustain. The "individualization" of Catholicism has, of course, swelled the precincts of basic middle-class life immeasurably. The safeguards against "culture-religion" that once were impacted in sheer "ethnic" and "minority" identity have thus been disintegrating, despite efforts to defend them. But precisely in the vitality of justifying a new morality against old rules of their church, individualized Catholics, for all the pain and anguish of their situation, have enjoyed at least temporary escape from the swamps of religion-as-therapy. The same logic no doubt applies to American Jews: so long as Israel remains at hazard, what danger can there be of an uncritical assimilation?

The decisive stage remains Protestantism. The declining membership of the mainline denominations, where positive psychology most flourished, has been matched by a "rise" of evangelicalism. This might be interpreted—and evangelicals themselves want to interpret it that way—as a protest against the mainline denominations' soft liberalism, their openness to every fad of culture, their vulnerability to "narcissism" and self-seeking therapy, and, thus, as a "restoration" or "revival" of old, hard, fundamental Protestantism, at once suspicious of the "world" and capable of dominating it.

I have offered my own estimate of these Protestant things in a new final chapter. Still persuaded, as I was in the book, that not only can religion not be understood, it cannot even be securely identified as religion, except in its relationship to power and culture, I have not tried to provide anything like an appreciation, let alone a portrait, of the new evangelicalism, but rather to indicate some of its intersections with politics and culture. To do so I have used two individuals, Jimmy Carter and Oral Roberts, as symptomatic rather than representative or prophetic. I have used one collective figure whom I regard as both symptomatic and prophetic: the new woman minister.

—Donald Meyer
Middletown, Connecticut
November 1979

INTRODUCTION

This is a book about popular psychologies aimed at health and wealth and peace of mind. In studying popular ideas one rarely has a neatly defined beginning, climax and end. It is obvious that popular psychologies aimed at good things are to be found through the centuries and probably are as old as man. I am interested in the ideas I discuss for themselves, but famous exponents of popular ideas are usually most intriguing because of their fame. They won audiences. Thus, if my terminal heroes are, respectively, Mary Baker Eddy and Norman Vincent Peale, this is because of their stature, not in "intellectual history" but in the "social history of ideas." If I begin when I do and not earlier, despite the spiritualists and phrenologists and mesmerists long antedating Mrs. Eddy and her late nineteenth-century peers, this is because I am interested in the evidence linking my particular popular psychologies with pervasive disturbance in the capacity of established ideas and institutions to satisfy.

Being practical, popular psychologies promise power. The largest power of all being God's, it is no accident that the first psychology I examine was also a theology. After noting some secular diagnoses of psychological ill-being in post-Civil War America, I shall devote Part One to the teachings of what can be gathered under the label "mind cure." Not all those professing these teachings accepted the term and some repudiated it; yet, if only on the authority of an eminent observer of the scene, William James,[1] it seems to me useful and I use it deliberately. "Mind cure," I propose, was a distinguishable ideology entailing a distinguishable way of life. Emerging self-consciously from and against the old Protestant tradition, particularly of New England, mind cure in its official, organized, institutional life never did finally shake off all traits of the cult and never won truly impressive numbers of technical adherents. But it had a larger life than the life of its churches, as its literature shows, and it registered tensions in its parent culture. It attracted both men and women, but I shall emphasize the fact of the special attraction of mind cure's psychology for certain sorts of women. Historians generally write about one minority of people—adult males. Someday, when they learn to expand their focus and include women, along with children, the aged-retired and the usual neglected out-groups, they will find it helpful to understand the psychology of people whose relationship to the standard powers of the world is that of weakness. In Part One I try to move a step or two in this direction.

In the two succeeding sections I turn to developments opening the door wider to mind cure after 1900, and to psychologies structurally identical with that of mind cure. Part Two deals with ideas about industry and businessmen. I do not intend to discuss businessmen so much as ideologies about them. I am sure that, just as in late medieval times there were avant-garde Renaissance men, and in Renaissance times lingering medieval men, so in modern American corporate business life men of the old style persisted among the new organization men. But, to the best of my knowledge, the drift of popular psychology for the businessman streamed away from an old style toward a new. After discussing some ideas which failed to shape the new industrial world and thus narrowed the choice of new psychological styles, I proceed to the psychologies themselves. In the erosion of the old "Protestant ethic" into incoherence, what seems eminently intriguing is the spread of new ideals structurally identical with, sometimes actually indebted to, the mind cure psychology pioneered strongly by and for women. Again, just as one cannot be sure that the ladies who bought mind-cure books led mind-cure lives, so one cannot be sure the men who read Frank Haddock or Dale Carnegie or Elton Mayo lived by their word. But these were ways men were being told to think about themselves, means of self-conception, and worth understanding. I conclude this section with a chapter suggesting how, as a function of the new psychologies, people more at large could come to think about the new economy in the religious spirit of mind cure.

In Part Three I draw on the demonstrable rise of a preoccupation with therapeutic psychology among the old-line Protestant churches after World War II. Here psychology was welcomed on its own terms and in fact often inspired theology. I assume here a fusion of the problems of specifically feminine and masculine identity sketched in the two previous parts, relying upon analysis of the most popular of all popular therapists, Norman Vincent Peale, to show that the issues were general. If it is true that the churches have become progressively less stimulating and progressively more reflexive institutions in our society, certainly this trend has links with the rise of psychological therapy toward the center of their attention.

If religion in one form and another figures throughout this book, it is not because of any argument that religion has first rank in causing anything. I take it just that in the religious extensions of their thoughts people reveal more of what they thought of themselves than we would know without them. As to the problem, how to read back and forth between self-concepts and God-concepts, between psychology and theology, there is no formula, except perhaps the formula that to think there is no relation is always mistaken. I have tried to let the record speak for itself. Also, this narrative is not in- tended to imply any general evaluation of "religion." As to that, my view goes with William James: religion has been creative and stimulating, religion has been inhibitory and debilitating, and it is well to tell the difference. Nor do I imagine the history I tell here characterized "Protestantism" in America. As for mind cure among Catholics and Jews, I confine myself to a second postscript. I am concerned to illuminate one evolution, one tendency, one style, not a panorama. I would not have been drawn to do so had it not seemed to me a fascinating one, and then, more gradually, an important one because it has not been grasped. But clearly, it is one among many other spreading adaptations to the unprecedented intimidations of a new world not yet recognized in its promise of psychological as well as economic abundance.

Thirty-five years ago Paul Tillich, writing from European experience, warned that "the disintegration of the consciousness-centered personality is now proceeding on a terrifying scale."[2] Since then, and especially since 1945, a good many Americans have, in effect, repeated the same alarm. David Riesman won fame for describing the shift from inner-directedness to other-direction. C. Wright Mills described the difference between the "old" middle class and the "new" middle class. William Whyte, Jr., Vance Packard, Martin Mayer stand out among a small battalion of able popular sociologists detailing the evidence for Tillich's theme in American life. I hope this book recalls such men to its readers. At the same time I hope its special note remains clear. What Tillich, Riesman, Mills and others have described in their sociological histories were vast cultural and economic changes to which people adapted psychologically in ways which were unconscious and unaware as often as not. From Tillich's comment one can infer that people aware of the disintegration to which he refers would resist it. In the popular psychologies I discuss, I mean to illuminate some deliberate, conscious, systematic participation in that disintegration.

Some final comments seem in order despite their somewhat technical bearing. Unlike scientific psychologists, popular psychologists were not much concerned about terminological exactitude. I intend to be clear, but I cannot pretend to clarify issues of terminology. For instance: the psychologies I discuss promoted the tactic of deprecating what might as well be called forthrightly "ego resources." The debate over the degree to which "ego processes" are "unconscious" as well as conscious is one which popular psychology has not appeared to make crucial, and I shall take it that their references to the "larger powers" of "superconsciousness" and to the "subconscious," "unconscious," and so on refer beyond the jurisdiction of ego—or whatever one wishes to call the process that constitutes an individual irreducibly an individual. I do take it for granted that human individuality has such an irreducible, "ultimate" character. I take it for granted that individuals cannot finally be explained in terms of biology—"id," "impulses," "drives"—or of sociology—"roles," "superego," "situation"—or by any combination of the two. Since the theme of the status of the individual has been important in popular psychology, it seems well to make this clear. In her essay "The Ultimate Unit" (in *Philosophical Sketches*[3]), Susanne Langer has mustered some of the arguments convincing to me on this ancient issue. Moreover, I assume not only the correctness of this assumption but its use as a measure of psychological well-being. Assuming that historians can judge without distorting their understanding, I have judged that more consciousness is better than less, greater ego-power is better than reduced ego-power. Readers who like to begin with a conclusion might read first what I have placed last, Postscript I on William James, who seems to me to have embodied this judgment.

Finally, this book has much to say about the words "sickness" and "health." A neat and narrow definition is possible: sickness is malfunction, health is normal function. But when it comes to minds and selves and souls and egos, definitions blur. If the heart's normal function is plain, what is the normal function of a soul, or, to move to the middle ground of mystery, of a brain? These words have become metaphors, similes, analogies, party cries and moral labels. One of my aims is to observe precisely this inflation of usage, and some of its problems. Ours has been called a "hospital" culture, its institutions geared more and more toward taking care of people rather than facilitating people's self-exploration. Gerald Kennedy, a leading Methodist bishop, included the churches in his recent castigation of "mass adjustment to the invalid psychology."[4] I aim to narrate a way of thought in which people have construed themselves as patients, have collaborated willingly in the process of self-disintegration, under the highest of auspices, God.

PART ONE

Peace in God: Theology as Psychology

CHAPTER I

THE DISCOVERY OF THE "NERVOUS AMERICAN"

SICK PEOPLE call on doctors—but not always. Sometimes they call on priests. One hazard of twentieth-century sophistication is the difficulty of knowing when to call on which. In simpler ages through most of history the problem hardly existed. Doctors were not very successful. Besides, doctor and priest might be the same. But in the Western world of science and reason they had been separated and by the nineteenth century were jealously distinct. One of the keys to our story was their excessive apartness, a rivalry reflecting not just science, but deeper schisms in the cultural heart. The dumb sense of millions might feel something wrong with a culture that had so complacently compartmentalized life: doctor for this, pastor for that; body is this, soul is that; men are one sort, women another; and business is business. With devastating simplicity, Mary Baker Eddy said that life is One.

One of the more intriguing examinations of the cultural body of post-Civil War society was one medical man's diagnosis of a malady which he himself indicated carried a religious charge. Dr. George Beard was a neurologist in New York City in the eighteen-seventies, eighties and nineties. Neurology was only just then maturing as a field of detailed empirical—rather than speculative—

specialization, and there was much enthusiasm among neurologists. Dr. Beard felt it. In fact he had a sense of mission. In the late seventies he had summed up his early work in a study entitled *Nervous Exhaustion*. Though not the first to use the word, he more than any other doctor was responsible for the word "neurasthenia" entering the fashionable vocabulary of Americans from the eighties through the age of Progressivism. Not long after Beard's book appeared, an English doctor referred to it in a volume of his own which he, the English doctor, entitled *Slight Ailments*. Beard did not like this. He was sure he had to do with no "slight" ailment.

"As compared with politics," he granted, "a topic like this must seem, and especially in a land like ours, very small indeed. . . ."[1] But this mere "seeming" had to be changed. Not only was "nervousness" a widespread ailment. It had cultural and in fact world-political significance. "The philosophical study of the several branches of sociology, politics, charities, history, education," Beard urged, would never become precise or complete until it absorbed the problem of nervousness—especially "in a land like ours." The crucial feature of nervousness, Beard had discovered, was that it had to do with particular times and places. It had to do with the United States. Far from disordering the race at large, it was a malady of pointed national frequency. This Beard announced in his more sensational book of 1881, *American Nervousness*.

George Beard was hardly the first to call Americans nervous. Viewing the national psyche some fifty years earlier, De Tocqueville, too, had found it a nervous sort.[2] But Beard did not mean what De Tocqueville had noted fifty years before. Like most things he saw in America, the youthful Frenchman had explained nervousness as a result of equality. With general equality men felt the excitement of opportunity on the one hand; on the other hand they felt the stress and anxiety of universal competition. Facing both promise and peril, they responded with movement, agitation, aggressiveness, a mood of almost phosphoric intensity, never resting, incapable of peace. What De Tocqueville observed amounted in effect to a kind of super-mobilization of energy, the jittering of diffuse but omnipresent ambition.

Energy and activity: these became items in the self-admiring image of nineteenth-century Americans. Benjamin Franklin, in the eighteenth, had taught straightforward secular and psychological rules for mobilizing and multiplying personal energy, and the nineteenth-century Protestant churches had reabsorbed them painlessly. Ever since Crèvecoeur observed that there was a "new man" at large, without identifying him exactly, the quest for American identity had assumed that that identity was to be found in purposes, aspirations and achievements, and further, that whatever these purposes were, they were served by energy-packed questing individuals.

The national style of sickness

Dr. Beard's diagnosis suggested something different: the national character might be defined by its afflictions rather than by its achievements. It might be defined not by its style of health but by its style of sickness.

By "nervousness" Beard meant not hyperactivity but depletion—nervous exhaustion. "Nervousness is nervelessness—a lack of nerve force."[3] Just what he meant by "nerve force" was not crystal-clear. Neurologists were still groping. Various fluids, animal magnetisms and, in Beard's day, electromagnetisms, were hypothesized to explain the action of nervous tissue. What depletion meant for the afflicted was clear though. Nervous exhaustion was peculiar to "nervously organized" people. Such people had a larger endowment of neural equipment, and therefore a larger capacity for experience. At the same time, this greater capacity meant greater vulnerability. Beard noted that Americans could not drink as much as formerly, or as much as most Europeans still could. They could not take as large doses of medicine as others.

There were certain puzzles in all this. Yet, obscurities aside, Beard was pointing directly enough at a sad phenomenon. People were leading less of a life than they were capable of.

In confronting the symptoms of nervousness themselves, Beard drew up a long and depressing list which I drastically condense:

. . . insomnia, flushing, drowsiness, bad dreams, cerebral irrita-
tion . . . neurasthenic asthenopia . . . atonic voice . . . nervous dyspepsia . . . sweating hands and feet . . . fear of light-
ning, or fear of responsibility, of open places or of closed
places, fear of society . . . fear of fears . . . fear of everything
. . . lack of decision in trifling matters . . . pains in the back
. . . cold hands and feet . . . a feeling of profound exhaustion
unaccompanied by positive pains . . . vague pains and flying
neuralgias . . . involuntary emissions . . . dryness of the
hair. . . .[4]

Surely these were unfortunate symptoms, but though from the
standpoint of the doctor accustomed to diseases that hospitalized
and immobilized, wasted and racked, crippled and killed, some
were no doubt "slight ailments," yet the doctor and the patient do
not necessarily share perspectives.

Actually, of course, Beard was discussing symptoms that within
thirty years were to seem to doctors themselves far from slight.
Beard was no psychiatrist, but he had taken a decisive step: he had
admitted into the list of legitimate medical symptoms a whole set
of experiences, forms of behavior and states of mind that medicine
had not accepted. As a diagnostic category the word "neurosis" had
appeared no later than 1798 in the studies of insanity by the inspired French doctor Phillipe Pinel, but Pinel's "neurosis" was not
the modern concept, for it referred directly to some impairment of
the neural equipment itself. Beard too, in thinking of nervousness,
remained "materialistic," in that he conceived a lack of "nerve force"
as a lack of something in the nerves themselves and not as something psychic or psychological. But he was pointing at factors that
linked such neural weakness with minds, emotions, character. In
this he was pointing toward a revolution that ran beyond medicine.

Throughout medical history doctors could be found attributing
various afflictions of mankind to mental, moral, emotional and even
spiritual factors, echoing though rarely improving upon moralists
and priests. Occasionally some verged upon sociology, blaming ill-
nesses upon conditions in society. And practicing bedside doctors
had always, depending upon the common sense of the race, ap-

preciated that some of their patients' woes were "imaginary." But the cutting edge of modern scientific medicine lay elsewhere, especially with science's emergence from the medieval unities. Sickness, by the standards of the modern medicine of the nineteenth century, was basically an intrusion. Something happened to or penetrated its host as an outside force in itself quite indifferent to its host's character. The body was "put upon." In the phrase of a later psychology, sickness was "ego alien." Pasteur's sensational demonstrations of bacterial infections seemed to confirm this model. Germs were obviously something which invaded, and the invasion befell without reference to minds, emotions, wills, psyches, souls, morality or anything else having to do with character. Medicine's own struggle for freedom from the entangling alliance with "orthodoxy" in thought tended to intensify this view of things. This medical materialism was one of the great triumphs of modern science, nor was its harvest of fruits remotely complete in the nineteenth century. But it had been won at a price: the isolation of medicine from the human sciences—psychology and sociology. Beard was in the process of ending the isolation. Nervousness was not ego-alien intrusion. On the contrary, as a sickness it directly expressed the nature of those who were sick. It was a function of mind, no matter how obscure the connection.

Beard offered social rather than psychological descriptions of the connection. His correlations with America were explicit. Not that he had any real sociology: the factors he chose to emphasize added up to a somewhat untidy impressionism. Noise, railway travel, buying on margin, liberty, rapid turnover of ideas, climatic variations— all made for nervousness. Some had been blamed before; others were his own additions. At any rate, when all was said and done, he summed up his eclectic list under one heading, one "predisposing cause" and one alone constituting the "necessary condition" for nervousness. This was no less than "modern civilization." America led the nations in nervousness because it led the nations in modern civilization. Though Beard offered no stable abstract definition of modern civilization, one can see what he meant by his criteria: steam power, the periodical press, the telegraph, the sciences and—"the mental activity of women." These represented, in effect, more power of communication. Modern civilization meant expanded opportunities for experience. Logically enough, then, Americans suffered differentially, a "few millions" more than others. These few millions were found more typically in the North and East than in the South and West, among professional and business classes than among farming and working masses. In short, nervousness beset the most advanced people, the successful people, the people who most fully indulged modern civilization. Evidently they were the victims of their own creation. Henry Adams would be saying much the same in a few years, as, in a different vein, Walt Whitman already had, but neither so clinically.

Search for a cure

A book written by a doctor, especially one written—as was *American Nervousness*—for lay readers, ordinarily includes some talk of a cure. To a degree, however, Beard had locked himself into a necessary pessimism by implying an inherent tension between human neural apparatus and modern society. He used an analogy precious to late nineteenth-century neurology:

> Edison's electric light is now sufficiently advanced . . . to give us the best possible illustration of the effects of modern civilization on the nervous system. . . . The force in the nervous system can . . . be increased or diminished by good or evil influences . . . but nonetheless it is limited; and when new functions are interposed in the circuit, as modern civilization is constantly requiring us to do, there comes a period, sooner or later, varying in different individuals, and at different times of life, when the amount of force is insufficient to keep all the lamps actively burning; those that are weakest go out entirely, or, as more frequently happens, burn faint and feebly—they do not expire, but give an insufficient and unstable light—this is the philosophy of modern nervousness.[5]

Life was overloaded.

Confronted by an imbalance between two terms, one could modify one or the other, or both. Maybe something should be done about modern civilization. Beard was capable of formulations anticipating the Freud of *Civilization and Its Discontents:* "One cause of the increase of nervous disorders is that the conventionalities of society require the emotions to be repressed."[6] But not for a moment did he mean to be attacking civilization. He drew no romantic inferences. He had no political or social therapies to propose. In effect, Beard assumed that "modern civilization" was what it was; nothing was to be done about it. In this tacit isolation of therapy from society, of health from politics, he was offering nineteenth-century individualism one of the major lines upon which it could fall back in its twentieth-century retreat.

If not civilization, then, perhaps "the force in the nervous system could be increased." And indeed, popular pseudo-sciences directed to increasing nervous energy were to proliferate, over them all looming the figure of William James, prophet of "the energies of men." Dr. Beard was less helpful. True to the dominant metaphor of his generation, he looked to automatic evolutionary progress. "In the near future," a new sort of man would evolve, a "typical American of the highest type," interestingly uniting solidity, fire and delicacy. Given Beard's physicalist outlook, presumably this new man would be new not just psychically but also neurologically, in the very physical qualities of his neural system. With this equipment, presumably, he would be adapted to civilization, capable of keeping "all the lamps actively burning." Thus, in medicine, as in economics, sociology and religion, the wise man might abide in evolutionary optimism.

But things were not quite this easy. Though promising rapid progress in neurology, and in fact himself responsible in coming years for exploring medical uses of electricity, as well as for research into "sexual neurasthenia," Beard doubted that such progress guaranteed fundamental relief. New advances in medicine and civilization, he warned, would no doubt be accompanied by new nervous disorders. Moreover, observed more closely, the evolutionary route itself did not seem particularly inviting. Before the "re-deeming forces that are in a measure to neutralize" nervousness got into full swing, it appeared, not only would nervousness itself intensify and spread, but such woes as greater "inebriation," consumption of opium, and, more dimly, confusions and turmoils remarkably like class war could be expected. This made it difficult to think that the future was, after all, "near." As if this was not enough, Beard's vision of the redeemed future itself contained features that might have been dismaying to some. Apparently the Americans of the "highest type" were not to be typical of all Americans—and even these were not to come unanimously into the ultimate inheritance. Beard had spent one long section of his book pondering the reasons for the longevity of great men who worked with their brains; at the end, he predicted the appearance, from among the new highest type, of the truly highest type of all, a "limited order of philosophers," who would, in a fashion unprecedented in history, think for themselves "as though the gods were blind."[7]

That the final cure of modern nervousness would be found in a limited number of possibly impious superminds was an idea hardly likely to elevate Beard's evangel alongside the multitude of therapies—social, economic and political as well as medical—that had begun to swarm in late nineteenth-century imagination. These were democratic. And they were also pious. If Beard's diagnosis was correct, it was likely that other therapies than his own would be required. The people whom he was diagnosing were not submerged masses or lowly classes for whom the edifying message of patience and evolutionary heaven by and by might have had appeal, nor pilgrims on this earth guided by stoicism and detachment. They were people who had expected things here and now. They were the successful, believers in this world, expectant of happiness, not neurosis. The therapy they would demand would be therapy for the here and now.

Was Beard, a somewhat eccentric doctor after all, and somewhat messianic, correct in his diagnosis that nervousness was an especially modern and American pathology? It is at least intriguing that Sigmund Freud cited Beard as evidence for the pathology of American conditions. But possibly this was only one more sample of that conditioned reflex of many European intellectuals—to find in America the confusion of European dreams; Freud certainly was one of the less well-traveled travelers in America. Earlier than Freud, earlier than De Tocqueville, another famous diagnostician of culture had sketched somewhat the same clinical picture. Americans, Stendhal wrote, in, significantly enough, his book *On Love,* "are just and they are rational, but they are not happy." But if Freud had visited the patient at least once, Stendhal had not found it necessary to take any personal history at all before setting down his wit. Would one wish to say that George Beard did not know Americans, however? If his portrait was at odds with the self-image of the Age of Enterprise, it should be remembered what he was: a doctor. Minds may lie, even to themselves, but the body finds it hard to lie. Men strong in the eyes of their publics and their historians betray their dyspepsias, their cold hands and feet, their "fear of fear" and their "fear of everything" in the examing room. If Beard was rare among doctors for suggesting that bodily symptoms were a language saying something about character, many others were soon to follow him.

The discerning eye of William James

In any case, it did not take a doctor to discern the worm of weakness in late nineteenth-century energy, although, interestingly enough, William James had been trained as a doctor, too. But it was with a moralist's eye that James discerned loss of force in the national psyche. As a youth, in 1867, while visiting the Amazon with Louis Agassiz, James had contemplated the "sleepiness, laziness and stolidity" of the Brazilian Indians, and responded in a standard fashion, praising the "real greatness of American energy." James was to compare American energy favorably with European stagnation too, and more than once in coming years. But in later years James undercut this conventional, highly Protestant perspective to point out that the vaunted American type, with its hustle and bustle, its tension and efficiency, was too taut. Why else did Americans suffer so often from nerves? One might, he suggested, speak fairly of "Yankee feebleness and inefficiency, and inability to do anything with time except to waste it." James's feelings here were instructed by his lifelong familiarity with the Puritan style, dedicated to control, discipline, self-containment and will—the style that had won the center of the stage of Success. It had come to be self-defeating, he argued. Americans were getting in their own way.

Naturally, one can argue that James, like Beard, was a missionary, not a cool observer. Then what about statistics? Statistics on the incidence of psychoses in nineteenth-century America have been assembled,[8] but of course Beard was hardly talking of psychoses. Statistics on nineteenth-century neurosis do not exist, for the very good reason that the concept did not exist, in anything like the modern sense, as a diagnostic category. Statistics on the incidence of psychosomatic woes did not exist for two very good reasons: the diagnostic concept did not exist, and besides, no one knew —or knows today—just what woes belong under it. Statistics on the incidence of diffuse dissatisfactions, unfixed discontent, vague depletion and free-floating unhappiness do not exist. The somewhat touching lust of various social scientists for quantities cannot then be satisfied.

Yet there is no need to argue that the testimonies of Dr. Beard and William James must stand in lieu of statistics, nor even of calling upon additional judiciously chosen witnesses to echo them. Though extremely improbable, it is possible that what Beard called nervousness had always afflicted—and will always afflict—a more-or-less standard fraction of any population. Somewhat more plausible would be the argument that, while indeed a social variable, nervousness was common over a larger time-space than Beard imagined, in, say, the West at large over the past two hundred years. What interests us is not incidence, but attention; if there was as much nervousness in late eighteenth-century America as in late nineteenth-century America, it did not lead to as much. It provoked no new religion.

The most telling feature of the sickness Beard analyzed was its paradoxical character. Though attacking those of the most advanced character, yet neurasthenia reflected upon the character of those it tainted. It implied a therapy directed not at some outside, ego-alien forces, but at the patient. It implied a form of conversion. Moreover, it suggested what form this conversion might take. In sickness what is sought is health. Health is ordinarily regarded— when it is "regarded" at all, for ordinarily the point of being healthy is to be able to forget about it—as a means to other things; healthy men are those able to pursue their ends. But the people identified by Beard had pursued their ends; they were the beneficiaries of modern civilization. Their situation suggested an alternative: health might come to be an end in itself. A new style of man might emerge: he who lives to avoid affliction.

Despite the unsatisfactory nature of Beard's own answers to the blight of nervousness, there was one part of his answer subject to pleasing amendment. It was evident that the number of super-philosophers capable of displacing the gods would be limited. But why was it not possible for practically anyone not to think "as though the gods were dead," but to think God's thoughts? Presented with this open door to hope, faith and health, patients if not doctors were not likely to hesitate. To think God's thoughts was to reform one's neurasthenic consciousness, for surely the mind of God be-trayed no nervousness.

CHAPTER II

NEW SHELTERS FOR TROUBLED SOULS

In 1892, in a commencement address entitled "The Gospel of Relaxation," William James commended to the attention of the graduating class of the Boston Normal School of Gymnastics a current best-seller, *The Power of Repose,* by a lady named Annie Payson Call. Miss Call, respectable Back Bay Bostonian, sister of a respectable Boston lawyer, unmarried, was one of numerous straightforward secular exponents of nerve therapy. Since in her book she had recommended bicycling, tennis and skating among other physical means, the gymnasts were no doubt appreciative. But at the same time Miss Call sensed limitations in her physiological approach: could soma truly be the access to psyche? She pressed on. In her second book, *As a Matter of Course,* she dwelt heavily upon emotional therapy, subordinating her original physiological, gymnastic emphasis for good. Through a long series of later tracts, beginning with *Nerves and You* and culminating with her wartime *Nerves and the War,* she purveyed a psychological therapy.

Yet was this enough? Having concluded her instructions for battlefield serenity in *Nerves and the War,* Miss Call appended a short section entitled "The Heart of Good Health."[1] Having already published this essay some ten years earlier, plainly she regarded it as a kind of capstone on her teaching. In this little statement a new dimension was added: the spiritual. Miss Call invoked a magic name: Emanuel Swedenborg. In Swedenborg's esoteric wisdom she found the outlines of a religious physiology. What we are doing when we practice relaxation and repose is to open ourselves to divine life.

. . . We learn how to allow the body to be perfectly passive so that it may react to the activity of the mind; and thus the mind itself should know how to be passive in order to react to the activity of the Divine mind.

This revelation of the religious potential in simple therapy was, of course, by the time Miss Call offered it, widely familiar. So was her use of Swedenborg, the eighteenth-century Swedish ecstatic-mystic. And the name Swedenborg suggested that this was not exactly one of the familiar forms of faith of the nineteenth century. Miss Call was, in her honest, modest, unevangelical fashion, trying to service needs that standard Protestantism had not yet appreciated. Perhaps some intellectual delicacy, possibly some inward shrinking restrained her from claiming the charisma of religious leadership herself, but nonetheless she was in the stream of religious revolution.

Phineas Parkhurst Quimby

Its immediate fountainhead was a specialist in nervousness, a self-made specialist, appropriately, as this was to be a self-made religion. It should be noted at the start, however, that P. P.—for Phineas Parkhurst—Quimby, too, had a certain touching modesty about him, wishing no credit for inventing dogma or passing miracles. To some of the more eager of his followers Quimby felt obliged to address "A Defense Against Making Myself Equal with Christ," a disclaimer his most famous patient and pupil was never quite able to issue.[2]

A simple, self-educated handyman from Belfast, Maine, who repaired clocks, Quimby, like many ordinary New Englanders in the eighteen-twenties and thirties, spent much time off work attending esoteric lectures and brooding on private notions. He had the chance to hear of spiritualism, hydrotherapy, mesmerism and various other psychological exotica of the times. Notably, he heard of hypnotism from a French lecturer, Charles Poyen, visiting Portland in 1827. In this same period, over a number of years, in his own thirties, Quimby experienced the symptomatic trauma of the new faith, a bout of, to use the term George Beard was to make famous, neurasthenia. Quimby was in fact for a time a semi-invalid. In 1838 he began to try himself as a hypnotist. Within a few years he had cured himself. By the sixties he had become well known in the Portland neighborhood as a healer.

Quimby had real powers of observation and reflection. After some experience in his practice he realized that certain of his patients were responding just as well to cheap and simple remedies as to expensive complicated ones. This led him to conclude that not the material remedies, but his patients' belief in the efficacy of the remedies played the decisive role. The healing was mental. This induced him to give up hypnotism in favor of mental suggestion plain and simple. He cultivated the power of mind or thoughts. Then he went further, extending his reflections upon the healing process into metaphysics. After his death in 1866, his notes, never to be published until 1921, became the center of acrimonious controversy between competing circles of the new religion, the crux of which concerned the credit Quimby deserved as founder and "discoverer." Important for the morale of the various new groups, the debate was not important with regard to the nature of the new religion as a whole: it repeated and elaborated Quimby's original inflation of practical healing into a psychology and then into philosophy and religion.

The first mind-cure books

One of Quimby's patients was the Reverend Warren Evans of Boston, an ex-Methodist who had fallen to the lure of Swedenborg. In 1869 Evans published the first of several books, *The Mental Cure*, which was also the first published volume of the new religion, and it was under the label "mind cure" that the new faith was popularly known. As is often the way with popular labels, "mind cure," suggesting as it did a technique of mental manipulation, and hence of simple pragmatics, undercut the claim to extra-pragmatic truth. Evans' first book was in effect a protest against the popular realism, for its point was that cures were not mental, at least insofar as "mental" referred simply to the human mind. Making Quimby's unpublished speculations more explicit, Evans argued that healing, far from being the fruit of finite human thoughts, was spiritual, the fruit of what Swedenborg had called "divine influx," "love" and "the Christ." This was the leap of faith in the new religion, from therapy to theology. In later books Evans reworked his ideas in less Swedenborgian language, endeavoring, as he thought, to bring them more in line with the more respectable Idealism of the great Europeans after Kant.

Another of Quimby's patients was Julius Dresser, also of Boston, who, with his wife Annetta, tended Quimby's notes and name after his death, and passed the torch on to his son, Horatio Dresser, who proved to be prolific of philosophical expositions on into the nineteen-twenties. The drift toward philosophy was cultivated in the eighteen-seventies during what was known as "the Boston craze," by the Boston Metaphysical Club, made up of local ministers, some of them Swedenborgians like Evans, businessmen, lawyers and Boston ladies. It anticipated in a general way one branch in the later history of the mind-cure movement.[3]

This began to take some definite form in 1892 with the formation of the International Divine Science Association, gathering up local groups in New England and, by then, across the country (though rarely in the South) that had repeated the local beginnings of the Boston club. Actually national, not international in scope, this body succeeded in holding five national conventions, but in little more. An International Metaphysical League followed. Its second convention, in New York in 1900, drew individuals such as George Herron, late of Grinnell, Iowa, and social-gospel fame, who spoke of "The Nature of Power," and the eclectic New York intellectual John Jay Chapman. This was to forsake any real coherence for general intellectual laissez-faire, and another try had to be made. Final success dated from 1906 with the National New Thought Alliance (so-called only from 1908), renamed the International New Thought Alliance in 1914, an organization active and flourishing to the present day.

New Thought

The New Thought Alliance did not break with its origins in Quimby's healing, that is, with applied therapeutic religion. Though himself an author of remorseless abstractness, Horatio Dresser urged in 1919 that New Thought's "practical, clearcut and specific" features be stressed. He had titled one of his own books *Human Efficiency*. At the same time, however, the hope of the alliance was that philosophy, its new philosophy, might become the context and nourishment for the new life. In 1916 it adopted a statement of purposes:

> To teach the infinitude of the Supreme One; the Divinity of Man and his Infinite possibilities through the creative power and constructive thinking in obedience to the voice of the Indwelling Presence, which is our source in Inspiration, Power, Health and Prosperity.[4]

This was frame enough for identity, and within its outlines there was room for variety. It was in New Thought circles, for instance, that anything like regular infusions from the mystic East colored mind cure. Swamis might appear at New Thought conventions, and an occasional adept learn yoga or even become a yogi. But New Thought was native. Himself noting some resemblances of New Thought to Hinduism in 1919, Horatio Dresser firmly rejected anything like real cousinship. The East shimmered in circles beyond our ken, among theosophists, Vedantists, followers of Swami Ramakrishna. Breaking free of old creeds and dogmas, New Thought expressed no instinct to embrace still older ones. It was to be kept new by continual exploration of the possibilities of mind.

Still, the promise went unfulfilled. As early as 1919 Dresser was complaining of philosophic decline, by which he meant that the "practical application" he himself urged had become all too standard in its concern for health, then for "power" and prosperity. The most noted new figure after World War I, Ernest Holmes, founder of the Church of Religious Science in Los Angeles in 1923, had no pioneering thoughts to offer, only more techniques. In 1944, when the Alliance published a kind of symposium group-portrait, the philosophy remained what it had always been. Philosophy had become technique, incantation.[5]

The New Thought Alliance was not a new religious denomination, not even a sect or a cult. It simply federated, or better confederated, an array of small groups and separate churches—Unity Centers, Divine Science and Religious Science congregations, Churches of the Higher Life, etc.—which, though claiming an identity of their own, did not claim exclusiveness. This looseness served the ambivalence of an important impulse. Mind cure registered desires to escape older authority, and these desires found outlet in the new bodies. At the same time, by their nature these desires were not free of anxiety, and the Alliance was also geared to attract those not yet prepared to actually leave their old Methodist or Baptist or Presbyterian or Episcopal—or even Catholic or Jewish—affiliations.

Enter Mary Baker Eddy

But of course where religious ferment was abroad a sharper organizational identity was likely. So also was the emergence of a new prophet, giver of laws, organ of God, a new authority. Mary Baker Eddy's followers never received the caution Quimby addressed to his own against making their teacher equal with Christ. Eventually they engaged in the familiar process of constructing a biography flawlessly consistent with the logic of their faith rather than with the abundant evidences of their leader's life, and, as other piety had done, succeeded only in substituting a sentimental for a dramatic odyssey. Edwin Dakin, author of the most acute of her biographies —and one which her church sought implacably to suppress—wrote quite without condescension of "the illimitable resources of one of the most gallant and infinitely pathetic figures in modern times,"[6] and went on to document amply the resources, the gallantry and the pathos.

Born in a New Hampshire village in 1821, of uncertain health as a girl, the young Mrs. Mary Baker Glover was tragically widowed, by yellow fever, at twenty-three, hardly more than a bride, far from home, with an unborn baby in her womb. For years she passed a delicately poised life back in her family, now and then rocked in a cradle cleverly devised by her sister against the occasions of her nervous attacks. With Dr. (of dentistry) Daniel Patterson, whom she married in 1853, she moved from one small New Hampshire village to another, slipping into isolation and invalidism. The doctor was not a success; in 1862 he got himself captured in the war. Previously he had written Phineas Parkhurst Quimby, of whose remarkable cures he had heard, asking help for his wife. In 1862 Mrs. Patterson herself went to Portland to meet Quimby—and her destiny.

Quimby cured her, and Mrs. Patterson enthusiastically undertook to be his disciple. She studied his notes. She spread his reputation. She was well. Her father died in 1865. Quimby died in January 1866. In February 1866 Mrs. Patterson—back with her husband in Lynn, Massachusetts, now—fell, becoming "the helpless cripple I was before I saw Dr. Quimby." According to her memoirs, she then "discovered the Science of divine metaphysical healing," and cured herself. Dr. Patterson left her in 1866; later they were divorced. (He died in 1896 in the poorhouse.) Between 1866 and 1875, in circumstances of poverty and loneliness, Mrs. Patterson lived with the tenacity of fixed purpose—to write her book. When it appeared, in 1875, it won scant attention, but by then Mrs. Patterson had gained the personal strength of mission, had begun to teach and had begun to attract students and an entourage. More editions would soon appear, revised and rewritten. In 1877, aged fifty-six, she married Asa Gilbert Eddy, forty, a student, not unlike Quimby in being small and mild. (He died in 1882, of mesmeric poison.) By then the first gathering of followers had occurred, and the first chartering of a Church of Christ (Scientist), in 1879.

The story of Mrs. Eddy's church, like the story of her life, has been told and retold—founding of the Massachusetts Metaphysical College in 1881, the National Association in 1886, the visit to Chicago in 1888, the early schisms, the trust deed of 1892, on through the building of the great edifice, to the prolonged struggle over power after her death in 1910, ending in 1921 in the definitive victory of the absolute centralized rule of the Board of Directors.[7] In Mrs. Eddy's obituaries, estimates of Christian Science membership ranged from eighty-five thousand through hundreds of thousands to millions, the modal guess being that mystic statistic of American success, a million even. This was testimony to fascination, not research. Like the ancient Jews, Mrs. Eddy did not want her flock numbered, and in accord with her edict Christian Science has always been chary about divulging membership. Actually, 85,000 was the figure listed in the Census of 1906 which, obviously, only a few of the obituary writers had troubled to consult. Her death, although Mrs. Eddy had indicated that ideally death like other woes was unreal, did not check the growth of her church. The plainest figure was to be that given by Christian Science leaders themselves in speaking for their allotment of chaplains during World War II: 268,915. The steepest slope of this growth had probably been passed during the nineteen-twenties, when the Census indicated 202,098 American Christian Scientists. Since World War II nothing indicated that the growth of the church was more than "natural," following the growth of population, if indeed it matched that. By mid-century there were around 2300 organized Christian Science churches and societies in the United States, around 10,000 practitioners of Christian Science therapy, hundreds of reading rooms. But these are only denominational statistics.[8] Mrs. Eddy's influence did not stop with the members of her church, nor were all her followers in it. There were schisms, and there were those who practiced "science" without leaving their Congregationalist or Methodist or other home.

Christian Science was from the beginning mind cure's "hard," fully and tightly organized, exclusive denomination. Mary Baker Eddy combined what among the Mormons had been split between Joseph Smith and Brigham Young, charisma as author of a holy book and brilliant talents as organizer and administrator, and she chose successors who administered her organization tirelessly. This hard orthodoxy also was a natural precipitate of mind-cure atmosphere, where the emptiness of old homes made sharp the yearnings for a new, where the hollowness of old words made sharp the listening for new, where not only new techniques but intense new identities would be gratifying to some significant fraction of the seekers. From the beginning Christian Science lived on dogma, the very words of Mrs. Eddy herself jealously guarded not only against change but even against interpretation. If such authority was repugnant to those in the New Thought Alliance, for others it could confirm and deepen a sense that, while old dogmas had come to sound toneless, yet Truth endured, unshakable, beyond relativities and humanisms. Finally, as I trust discussion will explain, it was no accident that the one triumph of authority in the new teaching was that of a woman.

The Unity School

As a hard organization, jealous in the preservation of its outlines and its methods, Christian Science was to remain the most immediately conspicuous form of mind cure, but in the long run it was far from the most pervasive. Other groups, and above all the scores of independent writers and preachers and practitioners, were freer to adapt and extend and apply method and philosophy as they chose. The most striking and successful organized proselytizing agency was the Unity School of Christianity in Kansas City, Missouri.[9] Like dozens of others in the last fifteen years of the nineteenth century, Charles Fillmore and his wife Myrtle commenced teaching as a small family enterprise, bringing out the first issue of a magazine called *Modern Thought* in April 1889. There were already others like them in Kansas City. The Fillmores had been initiated into mind cure in Christian Science classes taught there in 1887, though neither joined Mrs. Eddy's church. Mrs. Fillmore, long a sick woman, was healed. Charles Fillmore, a semi-invalid himself, was also just suffering the deflation of the

Kansas City real-estate bubble of the late eighties, in which he won, then lost, a small fortune. Eventually he, too, regained his health. Both, with Mrs. Fillmore the more urgent, did more studying with Mrs. Emma Curtis Hopkins in Chicago, Mrs. Hopkins being one of the many talented women—Mrs. Elizabeth Stuart, Mrs. Ursula Gestefeld, Mrs. Augusta Stetson, etc.—who broke with Mrs. Eddy to teach on their own.

From as early as 1891 the Fillmores conceived their work as that of expounding a "practical" Christianity to people of all denominations. Thus Unity was to be a "school" and not a new church. During the early years Unity grew slowly but steadily, under various names and through various journals, plus an invention of Mrs. Fillmore, the Society of Silent Help, later called the Society of Silent Unity, offering people the aid of long-distance prayer. Basic Unity principles were soon crystallized by H. Emilie Cady, a homeopathic doctor in New York, who wrote a series of lessons in 1894–95, later collected as *Lessons in Truth*, Unity's elementary textbook.

Through its magazines, but perhaps most of all through Silent Unity, the school's audience expanded. From 1890, at nine o'clock each night, the Fillmores and a few helpers met in silent prayer, joined by dozens, then hundreds, soon thousands of followers across the Midwest, eventually across the country. In 1906 there were 15,000 members. In that year the Fillmores bought new, larger quarters, which were expanded in 1910, then again in 1920 and 1928. In 1906 Unity severed connections with the New Thought Alliance; rejoining in 1919, once again in 1922 the Fillmores disaffiliated, this time for good. In 1920 they began buying land outside Kansas City at Lee's Summit. Eventually a spread of over twelve hundred acres, it was to become modern headquarters. During the twenties new magazines were started, including *The Christian Businessman*, later called *Good Business*. After some depression doldrums, construction at Lee's Summit was resumed in 1940, the final transfer being completed in 1949; the old quarters in Kansas City were taken over by the Salvation Army. Mind cure had gone to the suburbs.

It is difficult to find a word that tells exactly what it is. It is the center of a big publishing business. It is a place of prayer. . . . It is a garden community. . . . It is a recreational center. . . . It is a school and a retreat. . . . It is a farm . . . it is a place of God. . . .[10]

As of 1954, *Weekly Unity* claimed 200,000 subscribers; Silent Unity processed 600,000 requests for prayer a year through the agency of 120 workers at headquarters; *Wee Wisdom* entered 200,-000 homes. Altogether Unity claimed to reach a million homes a month with its eight magazines and its hundreds of pamphlets and scores of books at low prices. Fillmore's own production over a long life was considerable—*The Science of Being and Christian Healing, The Twelve Powers of Man, Jesus Christ Heals* and *Prosperity* being four of ten volumes all carried through many printings, as were the books of a large stable of other writers. The success of this literature justified expensive recent anthologies— *The Unity Treasure Chest* (1956) and *The Good Business Treasure Chest* (1958).

Long since, the Fillmores had yielded on the principle of working only within existing churches. This they continued to do, but at the same time the early Kansas City meetings held at three o'clock Sunday afternoons were changed to the standard—and competitive—Protestant 11 A.M. Hundreds of Unity congregations were organized over the country, with their own Unity preachers. Daily Unity broadcasts were to be heard from more than fifty radio stations. Charles Fillmore, who, somewhat like Mrs. Eddy, had surmised that death too might yield to thought, died in 1948, aged ninety-four; Myrtle Fillmore had died seventeen years earlier at the age of eighty-six; but their sons—Lowell Fillmore primarily— had already assumed direction of a thoroughly established organization. Unity had emerged as mind cure's leading wholesaler.

The flood of books and magazines

New Thought Alliance, Christian Science, Unity: important as these were, they, along with still other organized groups, were only special instances of mind cure; it was not remotely necessary to belong to any of them to learn the word. The evangel was carried on a small flood of books and magazines promoting no institutional interest at all. Books and magazines were in fact a significant social index of mind cure: it was a religion of people who could financially, would culturally, and did in fact spend money for reading. Mrs. Eddy's habit of releasing new editions of *Science and Health* did not escape the notice of such of her critics as Mark Twain. It was an independent, Prentice Mulford, inspirational writer, director of the popular White Cross Library, who gave popular currency to the mind-cure phrase "Thoughts are things" (anticipated by Theodore Parker) before his death in 1890. Julia Anderson Root's *The Healing Power of Mind,* published in San Francisco in 1884, and Helen Bigelow Merriam's *What Shall Make Us Whole, or Thoughts in the Direction of Man's Spiritual and Physical Integrity,* published in Boston in 1888, were other examples of early free-lance mind-cure writing. They anticipated a torrent, feeding and feeding on the churches. Henry Wood and the vastly successful Ralph Waldo Trine began to publish in the nineties, followed by a geyser in the first decade of the new century, powered by scores of authors: Trine, Charles Brodie Patterson, James Allen, Frank Wilson, Helen Wilman, Julia Seton, and so on. All these were popular writers in the sense that they made no effort to argue their case beyond the argument that if one believed, one's belief would work. Many were concerned simply with technique, not philosophy. And many decisively enlarged what had begun in Quimby as a focus on health in its narrow sense, into a promise unlimited. Trine's subtitle for *In Tune with the Infinite,* one of mind cure's all-time best-sellers, summed it up: *Fullness of Peace Power Plenty.*

Several score, possibly over a hundred, magazines and papers had been started by 1910, some quickly dying, some enduring longer. Helen Wilman, whose *Conquest of Poverty* (1901) was widely read, edited *Freedom* in Florida; in New York, Charles Brodie Patterson edited the New Thought *Mind;* Mrs. Kate Atkinson Boehme published *Radiant Centre* in Washington, D.C.; and in Chicago Sidney Flower's journal ran through several names before settling on *Journal of Magnetism and New Thought*. One of the most successful was *Nautilus,* founded by Mrs. Elizabeth Towne in Holyoke, Massachusetts, in 1898, destined to last till the late twenties. Boston, Hartford, Kansas City, Denver, Los Angeles, San Francisco all had their local organs. Few survived the First World War. Some were absorbed into stronger papers; all were affected by an expanding Unity School aiming at nationwide audiences. Here as elsewhere local enterprise gave way to national.[11]

There was never an end to the production of new mind-cure tracts. After World War II they poured forth again: Hilde Black Shaffer's *The Eternal Miracle* (1954), Joel Goldsmith's *The Spiritual Interpretation of Scripture* (1947), Gardner Hunting's *The Word beyond Words* (1953) and Frederick Bailes's *Human Power for Human Problems* (1957). And of course the mind-cure churches flourished. But by the twenties, mind cure faced a new situation. The old-line Protestant churches themselves were beginning to respond, and to compete. From the twenties they began absorbing a new therapeutic psychology as part of their own armamentarium. Here and there "healing" began to concentrate imagination. By 1937 Norman Vincent Peale had organized his Religio-Psychiatric Clinic on New York's lower Fifth Avenue. Here and there, ministers of the old-line churches deliberately and explicitly imported mind-cure notions into their presentation of the faith, as in Lewis Dunnington's *Handles of Power* (1943) and *The Inner Splendor* (1954) and Marcus Bach's *The Will to Believe* (1955). More generally, like the two major parties the old denominations began absorbing the issues raised by the "third-party" mind-cure groups, and mind cure, only approaching mass success in its own cults, found its larger destiny. By Peale, a Methodist-ordained minister serving a historic Reformed Church, it was made useful not simply for the narrow concerns of its first believers, but for the anxieties of modern man.

By 1955 Peale's influence provoked something of a crisis in Protestant leadership, with national mass-circulation magazines, church journals, books and even local congregations given over to soul-searching and defense. It was evident that Peale had managed to tap wide audiences formed by prolonged changes in the tone and morale of American society, for whom the coherence of Protestantism even as late as the early twentieth century was not enough. His attackers did not fall short of declaring his Protestantism non-existent. Peale survived. As he himself recounted it, he found himself stunned by the attacks. Troubled, even considering the virtues of resigning his post, he entered his season of withdrawal. There he found his answer. His father assured him he must go on. Was he not, after all, helping millions? Besides, it was unheard of in a democratic society for a man to believe his lonely critics when millions had approved. And so he returned. *How to Stay Alive All Your Life,* Peale entitled his next book; what else was George Beard's neurasthenia but a form of half-living? Finally, in consistent exemplification of the logic of the new religion, Peale proved he was right as well as helpful by publishing the testimonies of those declaring that for them positive thinking had indeed worked.

There was no particular reason to doubt them.

CHAPTER III

THE TROUBLED SOULS OF FEMALES

IN MOST contagions there is a focus of infection. Then the contagion spreads.

Among several conspicuous features, perhaps the most obvious in the evangel of mind cure was the ubiquity of women. Not only was its most famous exponent a woman; scores of its lesser exponents were women, as founders, writers, preachers, teachers, healers. Mind cure gave jobs to women by hundreds and thousands. The clear majority of Christian Science practitioners were women. The majority of preachers in the proliferating Unity churches were to be women. Mind cure had higher proportions of women in its congregations than the old churches. Women bought its books heavily. Was there something wrong with women?

Annie Payson Call thought so. Miss Call knew George Beard's work, and like Beard she fancied herself examining the national psyche as she examined nerves. Nervousness was "americanitis," she agreed, adopting the diagnosis offered by still another doctor—this one a German visiting the country not long after Beard's book had appeared. But Miss Call made Beard's sociology still more specific. For whom, after all, were her prescriptions of bicycling and looser clothes primarily intended? "The nervous strain of sham

emotions, it must be confessed," Miss Call confessed, "is more common to the feminine nature."[1] As she progressed through her
nerve books, urging calm emotions and a passive mind, she taught
wives how to deal with irritable husbands, women how to deal
with "dear but irritable" (female) friends, women how to work
equably beside "the woman at the next desk." Perhaps the very
"mental activity" of women, regarded by Beard as one of the
criteria of "modern civilization," was bad. More than rarely, the
respectable middle-class magazines of the late nineteenth century
printed solemn ponderings by doctors (male) on the rigors of female education: something had to be causing, they knew, the de-
plorable incidence of nervous disorder among genteel young
ladies. Also, young ladies seemed to be suffering, with surprising
frequency, from ulcers.

The nineteenth century in the United States was a great age
for men. Men were in short supply everywhere. De Tocqueville's
portrait was that of a society where every (white) man fancied
his life in terms of his "chances," and these were real. Once industry put down lasting roots and urban life began to spread, after
1830, practically every head and hand found welcome. There were
opportunities for all sorts of businesses. Mechanics were needed,
artisans, machinists and engineers. Men learned on the job. Most
of the railroads were built sloppily, partly because of the priority
of profit-lust, but partly because of the shortage of skill. Foremen
were needed, and clerks. And expanding businessmen gradually
realized they needed offices: managers, executives, administrators
—and even salesmen—were needed. This was the dizziness of freedom, the dizziness of that mobility so impressive to European vis-
itors. Banks sprang up like weeds. As agents and shepherds of every
substantial interest, lawyers swarmed. A remarkable array of new
identities, well-defined in terms of capital, skills, energy, role, ad-
vancement, presented itself everywhere. And incredibly, there were
plenty of chances to drift, to float, to recover anonymity and start
again, to escape, or at least to indulge the fantasy of escape. The
whole nation was a West.

All this had been new. For most men, even into the early years of the nineteenth century, it had still been true that they knew themselves according to their place in a scheme of things, that of the village, of the parish, of the craft, overarched with appropriate cosmological myths. There was a whole of which they were a part, and the part found definition and integral standing in the whole. The new way, for the men of the nineteenth century, was to know oneself as potency, as power. A man was real to the extent that he moved, for motion registered his self-impulsion. One of the features of the age was the crumbling of old concepts of the whole. If there was a "scheme of things," it was much cloudier and less explicit than the schemes of the past. The immense self-consciousness that colonial Americans had invested in re-creating around themselves in an empty land the security of a stable solid social order was translated into the intense self-consciousness of individuals forging themselves as embodiments of Will. Excitement, clamor, room for aggression, a multitude of hard realities with which to grapple—men had these to enjoy.

Women in the nineteenth century were not so lucky.[2] Some were not lucky at all. Of course, for the large majority of women life remained, almost through the century, reasonably close to what it had been. A woman's duties on the farm remained clear—though even farm women began to suffer: mechanization of farm work, for instance, was in the first place mechanization of the man's work more than of the woman's; and, by comparison with the new urban glamour, the farm woman could come to feel herself doomed to lonely drudgery. Were Grange socials enough? Still, in countless small towns women continued to exercise all-round craftsmanship. And in both scenes, there were hardly more confusions in the roles of wife and mother than had always haunted these supremely subtle destinies.

But the women of the future were the women whose men were caught up in the new world of motion. The situation such women faced had its frustrating simplicity. The more their men succeeded, the less they were needed. The more their husbands worked, the less they had to work. In an age of vast demands upon manpower, a small but growing quantity of womanpower was neglected. The farmer and his wife had been a work-team; so also the wife and her husband in the self-sufficient monopolistic small towns. But just what did the middle-class female contribute?

The busyness of the Victorian housewife

One solution to underemployment was make-work. Compared to the efficient simplicities of older abodes, the middle-class home took on complication. Those older simplicities often enough testified to a plain—though relative—poverty, which a seasoned asceticism took in stride. Yet, one of the telling things about the new affluence was that it did not after all achieve comfort. Instead, from the eighteen-thirties and then blatantly in the Victorian household of the postwar generation, the domestic environment grew crowded, stuffed with a welter of furniture, each piece itself curled and carved, with folds and hangings and ruffles appended everywhere. Everything caught a great deal of dust—and then had to be dusted. The various theaters of male existence—office, courtroom, factory, livery stable—got no cleaner; some were willfully dirty. Cleanliness meant home. The nineteenth-century Protestant estimate of cleanliness as next to godliness reflected something more than an appreciation of the new scientific hygiene; it reflected a search for something to do. The woman who kept busy keeping her home clean worked hard, but the meaning of the work was veiled. Besides, with supplies of Irish, then Swedish and German and other immigrant girls abundant, often enough it was the maid who dusted anyway.

Simply to know what sofas, what tables, what lamps and hangings and *objets d'art*, what silver to buy was a job, naturally. Indeed, simply to know how to go about practically anything became a matter for a higher level of awareness and study. How to dress, how to eat, what to eat, what to read, what to feel, how to behave at parties, what styles and—soon—what brands to buy: such nagging uncertainties supported a genre of books, manuals, newspapers, magazines, almanacs. Clearly indebted to the Puritan determination to be disciplined and under control in all things, in the nineteenth century this quest for advice broke free from Puritan motives in favor of new ones.

They were complex, these new motives. The use of styles and manners to exhibit one's elevated status was hardly disguised, and the career of that conspicuous consuming made notorious by Thorstein Veblen had entered its democratic phase, confined no longer (as Veblen never thoroughly realized, his capacity for revulsion being only human and therefore limited) to the distinctly predatory. Though Veblen indicated that the purpose of conspicuous displays was to display one's freedom from the servitude of work, one must observe against him that few men—few males, that is— actually did stop work. Work—in the twentieth century it was to be called a "game"—had become an obsession. As for women, conspicuous consumption, whether on the level of the most marginal or on that of Fifth Avenue, occupied them closer to the heart. If it in one way signaled a woman's freedom from one sort of labor, it also gave her another job. The career of the woman whose busyness is shopping had begun. Man earns, woman spends.

Changing virtues

In earlier times the basic virtues praised and rewarded by the community, in the voice of its Protestant conscience, had been acceptably distinct. Following the more precisely religious qualities of humility, a repenting heart, subscription to various theological truths, and often some charity, these virtues had included the useful traits of the Protestant, Calvinist, Puritan ethic: diligence, frugality, honesty. These had been incumbent upon everyone; that is, they were expected of man and woman alike. For both, they were advantageous, serving as a sufficiently complete portrait of basic character on the frontier, on the farm, in the villages and towns still unchallenged by change, machines and mobility. Between the farmhouse and the fields, between the shop and the home, there obtained no functional contrast in styles of human being. As throughout history, men were more various than women to the superficial behavioral eye, but they both hung on the same coordinates. The new sort of job being done by the new sort of woman, however, expressed and evoked new dimensions.

Nonetheless, if in the gratuitous complication of the female's domestic world one finds compensation for something being lost, one also discerns a deeper pulse. No matter how assured and sufficient the older role of hard and essential worker had been, it had partaken overwhelmingly of "necessity," and the new conditions opened the potentials for liberty. In all the quest for advice about practically everything, response to such potentials was not absent. How many of the domestic practices in new-style homes before the Civil War manifested, however tentatively or awkwardly, some true pioneering in taste and imagination? We are already familiar with the rebelliousness of certain women in matters of dress. It could hardly be otherwise among women trained with their men in the psychological self-inspection mankind owed to God. The "how-to" books on domestic and social technique repeated in intimate and private terms some of the aspirations aimed explicitly at liberty in the larger social-reform movements of the day. However, hardly less than the more compensatory did these exploratory impulses promote characterological differentiation by sex.

The revolutionary potential proved itself most vividly in the first woman's rights movement. The preoccupation of only a few (men as well as women), the woman's rights movement failed of its purpose if only because, in the high tide of visionary masculine democratic morale, it won only a few. More fundamentally, it was to fail because it lingered in retarded self-consciousness. Yet the handful of articulate women did manifest a profound alarm. In the new culture, home and family were supported by a man making money. Money was translated into possessions. The woman, at home, making no money, ran an obvious danger. Woman herself might become a possession. One can find in the biographies of eminent female reformers evidence of their instinct to escape possession on most intimate levels—in their debt to emancipated fathers, in their marriage to younger men, in their not marrying at all, in their criticism of wifehood and motherhood, even in an unconventional occasional reversal of the order of marriage and

motherhood. Not to become reflexive, not to be simply the object
and evidence of wishes outside themselves—this was a distinct concern. As a leading daughter of good old Puritan Connecticut put
it:

> Another error is that it has been made the first object in educat-
> ing our sex to prepare them to please the other. But reason and
> religion teach, that we too are primary existences . . . the com-
> panions not the satellites of men. . . . The taste of men, what-
> ever it might happen to be, has been made a standard for the
> formation of the female character.[3]

The danger of enslavement

"Issues" in history have rarely presented themselves in neat pack-
ages. Historians have yet to exploit one of the richest veins of
pre-Civil War complexity: the link between the anxiety to abolish
slavery and the anxieties of women (though William Taylor has
made a splendid raid into the territory). Abolitionist tracts did not
fail to dwell lingeringly upon the figure of the female slave—practically always a mulatto—helpless in the hands of her captors. In
the greatest tract of all, Mrs. Stowe—a woman, after all—portrayed
in scene duplicating scene the ultimate horror: the victimized possession of the slave woman, as mother first of all, and then as wife
and as female flesh. Behind the manifold indictments of the slave
system, there flickered, dim, fascinating and horrifying, the fact
of the slavery of women. Black women, but white women too.
Through comparative studies of Southern American with the rest
of Western Hemisphere slavery, historians have come to highlight
the fact that only in the United States did the legal code deny
slaves family existence and protection against sexual violence.
American slavery was a sexual segregation of Negro men from
white women echoed by sexual integration between white men
and Negro women. Two myths emerged, that of the Negro male,
sexually menacing, and that of pure white Southern womanhood,
sexually helpless, the most purely a possession, the most purely
passive of all.

What had begun, as Catharine Beecher wanted it, as a demand

for equality, evaporated into something else. Their usefulness having become ambiguous, women faced the danger of being turned into possessions, hence enslaved and passive. The escape that took form as a leading model for female existence for some forty years tried to finesse the danger. Women were superior. A female existence radically different from that of men, different in its inner organization, its refinement, its transcendence above the hard materials of the world, became a style for those who could afford it. In its prewar naïveté, full of romantic sensibility, it had the virtue of being new at least, hence something yet to be explored; in its postwar routine of respectable gentility, it bred exhaustion. To obey these ascriptions of special qualities, women had more to do than just accept tradition. They had to forget and to pretend. They had to convince themselves, to will themselves to be creatures without will.

The primary arena of decision was obvious. For thirty years before the Civil War, discussion had swirled around the family in all its aspects—kitchen, nursery, sitting room, clothes closet, and of course bedroom. Not that such self-consciousness was new. The earliest Puritans landing on American shores had been forced to sharp awareness of the family order, but this had been part of a general awareness and anxiety. In order to avert disintegration in the wilderness they had had to calculate policy for everything, church and state, economy and education, and leisure as well, the family drawing no especially obsessed attention. In the nineteenth century the family did draw particular regard.

It seemed possible that the family might prove to be the central bulwark of stability and values. Not the family but everything else was disintegrating and the family therefore at all costs must hold. This sense was particularly evident in the old denominations of classic Puritan descent. Protestantism itself appeared to be disintegrating into a welter of sects; religious authority crumbled; the prestige of the ministry crumbled. In the accelerating democratization of society, established economic and social and political authority crumbled, and political struggles to save them seemed

doomed. Upon the family, then, let trust for stability in the flux
be loaded. Puritanism had never dreamed of entrusting it so much.

This intensified responsibility, moreover, ran in the face of the
continuing assumption by outside agencies of old duties of the home.
The nineteenth century saw the spread at last of a public school
system. Factories were beginning to produce what had commonly
been made at home. Popular reading and entertainment were beginning to supply what the family circle had long supplied. Becoming more specialized, the family at the same time was expected to become more influential.

And then, assigned the job of sustaining moral order, in its very
cultivation of its own intensified purity the family tended to intensify the sense that the "world" was in truth essentially alien, a
realm of dangers, disorders and demoralizing temptations. Here
and there, where old Calvinist authority still worked—voiced often
by Scottish and English divines imported for the purpose—the logic
foundered in dilemma. In *Home, A Book for the Family Circle*,
published in America in 1874, the Reverend W. K. Tweedie expounded the family's exalted responsibilities at great length and in
the severest terms. For Tweedie, in fact, religion *was* family life,
so much so, that to "leave home" was to plunge into the unworthiest
perils. The world was a wilderness. It was hard to see how one
could safely leave home at all. This was unsatisfactory. It would
do no good for the family to conserve an ethic so exquisite it
unfitted its members for society.

The ideology of mother

What really mobilized the logic of the saving family was not in
truth this moral mission. Rather the logic was the context for the
more specialized ideology of mother. Tirelessly celebrated in New
England and the East before the Civil War, mother was revealed
as the key figure in civilization. Holy being of total virtue, calm
and elevated substance, and perfect comprehension of her children, mother constituted a role in obvious compensation for losses.
Though fewer than those of her predecessors, the tasks of the new-
model mother were more intense. In order to radiate the high moral

and psychological traits entrusted to her for inculcation, she had to enjoy a higher estimate of her meaning. In order to specialize in psychological affairs, she had to become a more purely internal creature.

When integrated into a spreading liberal Protestant preoccupation with love as the supreme expression of religious reality, and with "personality" as the highest form of existence, this re-evaluation of mother secreted genuine potentials for an emotional generosity and a fine carelessness in life which the old faith and the old culture had rarely stressed and frequently suppressed. But these potentials found precious little expression, for the way the job was conceived carried its obvious corollary. Women were to be segregated. Ideal mother simply intensified the notion of a normative female character generated in the new classes, and taken over from England, which always meant that that character required its special circumstances, its carefully defined environment, its strict boundaries, that it might flourish.

In this ideology success bred failure. The very virtues of the ideal woman and mother unfitted her for one of her jobs. Upon half her children her influence could have been suitable—upon her girls. But for preparing her boys she was incompetent, assuming that her boys were in fact to "leave home." Protected from the world precisely in order to conserve her special attributes, she knew nothing of it. Boys raised by pure women might never gain competence in the world of hard knocks. In *Lectures to Young Men*, first published in 1844 when he was still in Indianapolis, then republished in 1872 after he had moved to Plymouth Church in Brooklyn, Henry Ward Beecher, the most authoritative moralist of the respectable congregations after the war, revealed the imagination that defined this puzzle. In these immensely cautionary discourses, Beecher, too, worked with the image of a dangerous, temptation-fraught world. But against this world he did not range the family. He assumed that it was in the world that real moral drama occurred, and he undertook to prepare the young men in the fashion of the old-style preacher who had something to say directly, man to man. Whereas Horace Bushnell in his famous *Christian*

Nurture was saying in effect that the preacher and church should work to prepare the family to prepare its children, Beecher evinced the old direct authority. His advice was predictable enough: he praised the classic secondary virtues of industry, frugality, seriousness, perseverance. His argument was perfectly pragmatic: these virtues worked, though of course Beecher assumed they were also pleasing to God. Implicit in all this was Beecher's assumption that a kind of personal hardness was required in the face of the world—and this hardness had no coherent place or source in the new-model, mother-centered, Christian family circle. It was only his own conventionality that inhibited Beecher from noting still other traits that also might be useful to aspiring young men—certain sorts of intelligence, certain complex skills, sheer aggressiveness, perhaps plain emotional zest, even gaiety and delight in the conflicts and grapplings of work—but these were perhaps even less likely to be engendered in the sentimental family.

Popular social myth reflected this maladaptation of the moral middle-class family well on into the twentieth century. The boyhood appropriate to the man who succeeded in the world of hard knocks remained that of the older world of the farms and the small towns, as though only here, not in the comfortable-uncomfortable gentility of respectable urban-suburban families did the male gain that fundamental conditioning he needed. Contrary to the notion of mother as cause, the man of success vaunted himself as his own cause; he "made" himself; he was the "self-made" man of endless fraternal oratory.

The fatherless best-sellers

The undercurrent of sentimental culture after the Civil War was, naturally enough, aggression against the male (an aggression, not too surprisingly, by no means confined to women, as the instance of Anthony Comstock evinced). Consigned to segregated delicacy, women consumed—and hence inspired—a vast literature for women, by women, about women. Long neglected as innocently trivial fodder for innocently private lives, this literature yields, upon inspection, somewhat unnerving contents. Reading through from

Susan Warner's *Wide Wide World* of 1850, to such best-sellers as Eleanor Porter's *Pollyanna* of 1913, including, Louisa May Alcott's *Little Women* of 1868, and Kate Wiggins' *Rebecca of Sunnybrook Farm* of 1903, one is, if attentive, somewhat puzzled by a consistent vacuum. Father is missing. He is missing psychologically because he is inept, not a father at all, as in *Little Women*, or he is lost, or he is dead. Evidently, for the female authors to present their female readers an image of the independent, self-responsible girl (such as the charming Jo), the presence of the generative male had to be dispensed with. As for other levels, Beatrice Hofstadter, recently rereading more of the impeccably moral lady-novelists of the age,[4] has clearly shown the underlying wish of so many delectable heroines. Once she has identified the man she means to marry, the heroine turns to making him over (as, appallingly, father could not be made over). He must be tamed. He must be, as the heroine of Augusta Evans Wilson's novel *St. Elmo* (1867) sets out to assure, emasculated. In these phantasmic basements of popular culture, one finds opposites meaning the same thing. In *Virgin Land*, Henry Nash Smith has described the transvestite appearance, from the seventies, of the lady gunmen in dime Westerns, shooting, swearing, smoking, drinking—and worse.

It is hard to be surprised. The repression being imposed in the fifties and nailed down in the seventies was a special pathology, not the discipline of a long-seasoned long-practiced style but a defensive, emergency, improvised ideology. Women, as the old Puritan refusal to preach any less severe a doctrine to women and children than to men recognized, had a life in the real world. How could the instinct for reality be repressed? In her ideal guise, all the woman's special attributes, all her assignment to her special sphere, bespoke one thing: she was weak, standing in this weakness at the furthest remove from the basic image of male existence as potency and power, self-sufficiency and will. Men had their own passion, and at the prospect of emancipated women recoiled with that fright special to those addicted to an obsession. Not a single reform, not even the obviously humane progress of medicine, failed to evoke male hysteria, often that of ministers themselves. Anesthesia in childbirth was "against nature," female education was against nature; bloomers—pre-Civil War slacks—were against nature. Natural, normative, respectable female existence decreed the passivity and weakness of women. In that event, where was salvation but in demanding a world for the weak? Weak, women could not maintain themselves in their own proper image even when (and this was probably most of the time) they wanted to. Things began to go wrong with them. What then if passivity could be strength?

Naturally there were many paths. Nor could the segregated enjoy an undisturbed fruition. Supposedly both exalted and weak, some women, an adventurous few, might insist that elevation deserved strength, and go into charity and social work. Fewer might deny the myth of two realms altogether, entering the male's world of careers, or even of free imagination. Others might find in woman's world the ferocities of "Society" slaking competitive energies as surely as the economy, or a renewed realism about the family circle itself, about children, and about men and women together. And there were plenty of signs of impatience, toward the end of the nineteenth century, with narrowness of life, among men as well, free enough, imaginative enough, strong enough to wish for variety, new things, new devotions. The gay nineties could not, after all, have been so gay had not the essentials of its gaiety been ready—men and women both, boys and girls together.

Through the history of the race, deeper in time than historians usually tell, one thing most of all has offered relief from dilemmas: keeping busy. But among all mothers, among all women, some especially were badly off. Life as mother was short. As fewer children were born, as medicine added years, the job of processing children comprised a smaller and smaller fraction of the lifeline. What happened when a woman was fifty-five? Or fifty? Or forty-five? In the old days old age still had its family place. In the old family even the occasional spinster, just as the widowed grandmother (or grandfather), still worked and ruled. With the new ways of mobility a new organization of age had evolved: each generation for itself. The measureless and dreadful loneliness of senior citizens, retirement, biological and familial superannuation, portended. For women it arrived first and worst. Forty-five or fifty was not so old; a woman might be at the peak of her personal (as distinguished from her biologically maternal) powers. Men were supposed to be at that age. What filled the void? "Sham emotions," as Miss Call called them, were alluring. And through these sham emotions a woman could get sick. She could make herself sick. Though she was exalted, something was wrong; but though something was wrong, she was weak. To be sick was a route for the pure but weak, neither the masterful, aggressive reform of reality by the strong nor the anarchic selfish rebellion of the weak and impure. To make oneself sick was an escape, for it invited a project which at the same time did not require one to wrestle with the world. Perhaps the world meant no malice. Perhaps the world, despite one's own debility, was friendly. Perhaps it was only the faulty imagination within oneself that inhibited one's enjoyment of a harmonic universe. The project of getting well could be pursued entirely within oneself.

CHAPTER IV

PASTORS AND DOCTORS WHO DIDN'T HELP

BUT COULD NOT the churches help? "The ideas of the Christian churches are not efficacious in the therapeutic direction," William James observed in 1902, speaking at Edinburgh, "whatever they may have been in earlier centuries."[1] Though not pressing the distinction here, James was aiming his remark, as usual, at that Protestant culture of his typical audiences, those of the North and East, of the professions and academies and business, those diagnosed by George Beard. That this respectable Protestantism of Puritan descent had indeed neglected "therapeutics" no one rose to dispute. That it had at first regarded the rising practice of mind cure as disreputable had been obvious.

Measured against the history of the race, this neglect of healing was strange. In primitive religions the priest had regularly doubled as magician and physician both. Through centuries European Christian culture had included religious healing as a matter of course, mixing demonology and charms, relics and shrines, exorcists and saints and thaumaturgic kings, plus an intuitive psychological medicine ordinarily associating sickness with sin. In Catholic Europe this practice remained; Lourdes was earning its fame. Moreover, Luther, at the Protestant fountainhead, had been a man richly appreciative of the interplay between health of body and mind; he himself had not hesitated to heal his famous friend, Philipp Melanchthon. And in America, where life could regress on many frontiers, revival sects found in healing and cures evidence of the presence of the holy spirit on into the twentieth century.[2]

But Protestants, in their original impulse itself, in rejecting all they regarded as magical, rejecting healing amulet and relic as well as sacrament and priest, instantly narrowed any practice of religious healing, lifting it above the psychological pragmatics of popular religion everywhere.[3] At its purest the drive of Calvinist and Puritan piety was to know God's will in all events without exception. "Enjoying" God consisted in just this perception. Hence, in their search for "explanations" consistent with God's absolute sovereignty, Puritans intensified the argument that sickness was linked with sin, a form of malingering, a sign of debilitated or undeveloped will. In one direction, Puritan determination to hold God first led logically to a willingness to be sick, just as to the famous formula of the Edwardsean Samuel Hopkins—a "willingness to be damned." We do not know if such stoicism, medically speaking, was more or less effective than the magical medicine it supplanted; probably the question would resist answering. But far more important was the logic in the opposite direction. Let men exert themselves still more, let them mobilize every possible resource and energy to eradicate sin and, by becoming creatures of will power themselves, glorify God in imitation.

Not that this worked. Morally disciplined will did not prevent sickness and death. But it helped define a new line of attack and a new distinction. Generated in its own bosom, the attack upon Puritanism argued that God surely did not elect to damn men. And God surely did not elect to make men sick. Good and respectable persons could expect something less arbitrary from God than events in no correlation with goodness and respectability. On one side this attitude simply impelled a Puritan outlook further. The eighteenth-century merchants, the good Unitarians of the early nineteenth century, the newly self-confident masses, the new science-minded men who rejected the Calvinist God were not doing so because they felt themselves weak. Theirs was a positive argument: strong men, honest men, good men would not be damned, for this would be unjust. The parallel in matters of sickness was exact—almost. Sickness—psychological sickness—was simply a fault, a sign of sin, of weakness; people who suffered from it had only themselves to blame. Nineteenth-century post-Calvinist liberal religion was no more drawn to sympathetic exploration of neurasthenia, or of psychosomatic woes, or of neuroses than had been Puritanism itself. In fact, it was less drawn, since it emphasized the project of "making men," of mobilizing moral will into "character," even more than had Puritans. Piety was being succeeded by "moralism," to use Joseph Haroutunian's phrase, and the moralistic approach to sickness could often enough be more severe than that of pious stoicism.

Exaltation of science

And yet, there were facts to be faced—facts that *could* be faced more squarely than before. Men and women did get sick, suffer wounds, die, in no visible correlation with their characters. Saints fell to the plague; rascals survived. What might this be due to, if not to God? Obviously, to "matter," to the material, to nature, which had nothing to do with morality. The obvious imperative followed: nature was to be mastered and "conquered" by men. Confronted by storms and droughts, by fevers and infections, men were to respond not in helpless piety but in manly struggle. Knowledge is power. Piety is action. With the attack on Calvinism, and the emergence of a God consistent with the highest human morality, science became the partner of will. Of course, Puritanism itself had secreted its own drives toward science. While still defending the old theology with vehemence, Cotton Mather had put together his *Angel of Bethesda,* a scientific medical volume, the earliest from an American, and this treatise was as expressive of Mather as his theological tomes. Within Puritanism science might be primarily a route to piety, a new and refined way to know God, but this could include application also. The religious roots of science in the West are slowly coming to be understood, but whatever the lines of descent, in Protestantism they ended in a kind of doctrine of two worlds. In the lingering debates over God in old New England, scandalized defenders of orthodoxy saw that the new-model piety of liberal religion granted God only a partial jurisdiction. He was interested only in moral events, not brute events. As there were two worlds, so there were two kinds of sickness, and so, two kinds of treatment.

The most resonant voices of nineteenth-century American Protestantism resisted such dualism. In Emerson, Thoreau, Melville and Whitman, Nature evoked a mystical identification; calling his own pure researches "science," Thoreau explicitly distinguished his science from the science working for mastery in gratification of unreconstructed human ego-needs. In quite a different spirit, William Graham Sumner insisted man must submit to a one-ness with nature, which was not something he could change and reform to his wish. And finally, among several others, Chauncey Wright, Charles Peirce and Josiah Royce all exalted a pure method of science, free of the warping, narrow, divisive individual ego, pursuing truth on its own disinterested logic, concretely embodying loyalty, community and love, not "power" and "mastery." But, whatever their long-range influence, these were voices either lost or distorted in the winds of mobility and democracy. The two-headed practice of moralism and power-oriented science defined the pursuit of Success.

The quest for self-control

Discarding the figure of the Virgin Mother, discarding the saints —among whom there had been women—discarding the religious orders—which had invited women too—Protestantism had embarked upon a rigorous discipline aimed at self-control. The effect was to enforce ever more sharply a split between two sorts of affliction, the first that vague, undramatic, subtle disability of tone, of feeling, of morale held accountable to a deficient inner control, the second the gross, obvious, external afflictions of infectious epidemics and crude violence, the fault of no one. In popular Catholic culture the Virgin Mother, along with certain of the saints, had traditionally been the object of supplication—one to whom one could bring one's weakness and fears and longing rather than to an already overburdened Son or an overawing Father. She was the true mediator, on the simply human rather than the awesomely theological level, in whose presence one's dependency did not mean shame.

Calvinists tried to live in the naked glare of the Father alone, but their liberal critics rejected this as itself too dependent a relation, and turned toward the Son. Nothing needs to be inquired after more acutely than this early approach to Jesus, for it evidently concealed under its wish for intimacy a demand for liberation. Intensifying the sanction for strength, effectiveness, purpose, will, the liberal faith promoted these into male monopolies. And after all, were women to become self-made men?

In popular late nineteenth-century Protestant culture some of the old mediatorial qualities crept into the liberal Jesus, generating the pale, soft, sentimental figure of the Sunday-school oleographs. But such a figure could only have been ambiguous, provoking more problems than it solved, for Jesus was after all a man. And while it would no doubt have been a prodigious achievement for an Anglo-Saxon stock to come to suspect that male existence could well include some of those qualities of mercy, sensitivity and care that had been segregated as "feminine," still it would be dangerous to infer weakness in the very essence of Being itself. We have no evidence that the late nineteenth-century "religion of Jesus" was helpful therapeutically. When, in 1888, Mrs. Hannah Whitall Smith published her highly successful little tract *The Christian's Secret of a Happy Life* and addressed herself to dispelling the burden of "duty and doubt" evidently crushing her (heavily female) readers, she was not able finally simply to tell them that Jesus would bear and care; in a final decay of the old piety, in a muffled anticipation of mind cure, she had to tell them to solve the problem themselves by refusing to think about it.

If not the churches, then could not medicine itself help? Unfortunately, if twentieth-century sophistication was to make it difficult in certain cases to know whether to consult doctor or pastor, presumably this was an improvement upon the predicament of those who could find help from neither. It was a predicament common in the nineteenth century. Stoicism had faded before science could take charge. And this was true in both the realm of "psychological" and of "physical" sickness, of "inner" and "outer" affliction.

The slow advance of medicine

The plain fact was that medical science lagged in delivering the goods.[4] Between expectations and practice a gap yawned. True, Henry James did not err in causing his Dr. Sloper to move in the highest social circles before the Civil War in *Washington Square*, for the practice of medicine had become eminently respectable; but this status, as through ages, derived heavily from the wish for doctors' services—or rather, the wish that their services work. But there were no sensational breakthroughs in practice. Probably advances in health were owed more to early hygiene-minded engineers and statisticians bemused by the new cities than to doctors. Practical medicine during the Civil War remained a butchery.

Certainly nineteenth-century doctors had freed themselves rather largely from the theories of their predecessors, who had talked in terms of various medical "systems," all of them essentially speculative in character. Repeating the history of scientists in other fields, they wanted more facts. They wanted to be empirical even at the cost of over-all philosophy. But more facts did not mean better treatment, at least not immediately. Better diagnosis, perhaps, and more intellectual satisfaction for the doctor, but not necessarily a cure. The "cures" associated with the older medicine had amounted to little more than ponderously rationalized use of ancient, folk-tested techniques—bleedings, purgations, warmings, chillings, leechings, and assorted dosings usually as familiar to primitives and to midwives as to trained professionals. In 1747 John Wesley published his *Primitive Physic* as a guide to humble family practice, and this text, popular for more than a century, no doubt served as well as doctors. Perhaps the chief early benefit of the new empiricism was the skepticism it promoted of these often drastic measures, not in favor of new methods but in favor of no method at all, a policy allowing a revived appreciation of the healing powers of nature—*vis medicatrix naturae* (a notion that could blend comfortably into contemporary romantic attitudes toward "Nature" generally, as the embodiment of the divine). But no one had the idea that things had decisively improved. Epidemic diseases—smallpox, diphtheria, scarlet fever and even yellow fever —remained lethal, and common, especially among children. Tuberculosis, pneumonia and intestinal afflictions remained dangerous. So did childbirth. (Oliver Wendell Holmes's insight, in the forties, that puerperal fever was spread by doctors was not appreciated for a good many years.) As for gross injuries, infections always threatened and surgery remained appalling. Anesthesia began to spread slowly only after 1846. Years went by before antisepsis appeared. Doctors were not truly scientific heroes. They knew too little. They were only, here and there, heroes invented by the wish.

With religion contracting before science flowed in, the need to rationalize could strike lugubrious chords. Around tubercular maidens romance wrapped the winding-cloth of deathly purity; tears refracted child-death into scenes of sentimental innocence. But no matter how rationalized, there is no reason to doubt that these woes always had been woes. Yet for growing numbers of people the woes of the flesh were becoming more woeful. Sickness had new impact in view of new expectations. Was it a question of psychological or of physical, of outer or inner, affliction? It made no difference. For people no longer disciplined to life and death by orthodox stoicism, no longer hedged narrowly by close economic and rigid social circumstances, life ought to display a more immediately obvious logic. There ought to be a closer correlation between wishes and reality.

Let, then, politics, religion, science and the providences of mystery combine to establish such a harmony as the world had never seen. Let the family be pure, the community secure, the society stable, the economy expanding. Still the body · remained vulnerable. Death could strike, as always, along with sickness and pain. Disease, sickness, death, bearing no relation to right moral order, manifesting alien, material, outside forces, defeated wishes unfairly. It was an unfairness, moreover, most conspicuous among the most pure—girls, mothers, women of sensibility, children. Health would complete the magic circle of security for the weak.

Of course, the "gap" between religion and science was as old as history, since science could not eliminate nor religion etherealize the ultimate issue of every logic, death itself. Pseudo-sciences and pseudo-religions, hence, had not failed to flourish everywhere. But they flourished with a peculiar lush abandon in the generation before the Civil War. Sentimentality itself was pseudo-religion in a passive mode. More actively, there proliferated the pseudo-sciences—hydropathies, diet fads, homeopathies, mesmerisms, hypnotisms—along with those curious empiricisms satisfying sheer curiosity about the powers of man for which neither old religion nor new science sufficed: phrenologies, spiritualisms, astrologies.[5]

Soon, however, after the interval of poignant confusion and waiting, medical science did begin to prove its clinical powers, and many were of particular interest to women. Holmes, Sr.'s attack upon infectious obstetrical methods did begin to be heeded. Progress in anesthesia helped. Prenatal care and pediatrics improved. With Pasteur, from the seventies, protection against virulent childhood diseases began to seem promised. No longer was ancient fatalism respecting woman's "burden"—enunciated by men—easily heard. And from the seventies the antisepsis discovered by Joseph Lister vastly improved every sort of medical treatment, reclaiming, together with anesthetics, even surgery from some terror. And with this, the final outlines of modern pathos were drawn. For this progress was selective.

Given such advances in science, there was less reason, medically, somatically, for anyone to get sick, stay sick, suffer and die before the biblically appointed span. For those, then, who nevertheless did get sick, feel sick, stay sick, the poignance was greater. In such cases doctors might well be victims of their own success. In the light of their empirical materialistic science they might be blinded to strangely elusive facts. As it happened, among nineteenth-century doctors "reductionism" was a more potent ideology than for even the most orthodox Social Darwinists "reducing" sociology to biology. Even when conceding they were dealing with psychological woes, doctors tried to locate organic lesions, wounds, malfunctions, as George Beard himself, otherwise inspired in his madness to admit "nervousness" into medical purview at all, could not help doing.

The failure of mesmerism

The situation owed something also to the fact that "psychological" medicine still suffered from dubious antecedents and dubious practice. The career of the strange German doctor-showman-scientist, Friedrich Mesmer, fell like a shadow over nineteenth-century psychiatry. Through spectacular demonstrations in Paris in the late eighteenth century, Mesmer, who never knew himself whether he was charlatan or genius, had aroused wide European interest in something he called "animal magnetism," an empirically elusive medium for influencing both body and mind. But Mesmer, and his magnetism, fell between two stools. His theories seemed to amount to a kind of secular dissolution of the spirit, disturbing to churchmen. And to scientists increasingly wary of all that smacked of magic and the supernatural, he appeared a quack. Mesmer became the creditor for uncounted numbers of amateur psychic practitioners of the nineteenth century, including Phineas P. Quimby —acceptable neither to science nor to church.

The man who might have brought an interest in Mesmer's phenomenon to American scientific attention, Benjamin Franklin, was a member of the French government commission which, in 1784, disposed of Mesmer's theory by declaring that "imagination," not magnetism, accounted for his results. The commission was quite correct. It was a sophistication that had been understood by Paracelsus in the sixteenth century: what a man believes does have effects, whether his belief be true or false. But it was a sophistication that missed the point. There was something to be explained. "Imagination" no more explained anything than "dormitive principal" explained the effects of morphine. "Imagination" was the starting point for science, not the point to stop. Franklin's indifference was typical of his peers. Men of rational intelligence and education, self-created through the sort of calm psychological drill Franklin had imposed on himself, were, naturally, never victims of "imagination." Psychiatry, avoiding "imagination," sought its "facts." This was true of the strongest mind in early American psychiatry, Benjamin Rush, in his *Medical Inquiries and Observations upon the Diseases of the Mind,* of 1812, despite Rush's interesting amalgam of religious with scientific concerns. It was true of the American Psychiatric Association formed in 1844, which in any case, for lack of therapeutic progress, earned its honor simply in humanitarian reform of hospital conditions (brilliantly assisted by Dorothea Dix). Dealing chiefly with patients suffering the crudest violent disturbances, far beyond even the pretended competence of psychic healers or religious counsel, doctors' hopes to correlate symptoms with damage were rarely supplemented with psychology. Hardly more than custodians, they were taking real steps in the painfully retarded effort to extend human rights to one of the most frightening categories of humankind, the insane, but they were far from useful in the subtle twilight of neurasthenia.[6]

Medically, the line that led to modern psychological medicine was a broken one. Charting it from Mesmer, it was interrupted by the frivolous and unscrupulous uses to which his notions were put. It was resumed again in the nineteenth century with the interest of doctors, especially James Braid in England, in what Braid labeled hypnotism, only to be discredited again by misapplication. It was finally resumed for good in the sixties and seventies in France, where Charcot in Paris, and Liebeault, the charmingly modest country doctor of Nancy, explored hypnotism and mental suggestion, particularly with hysterics. After these great-grandfathers, Janet and Breuer became the grandfathers, followed by the father-creator of a systematic therapy postulating a psychological existence susceptible to change and improvement quite independent of physical (surgical, chemical, osteopathic, etc.) intervention: Freud. Of course, Freud recognized his real forebears: the "poets."

Attempts to explain illness

In the United States, William James was acquainted with late nineteenth-century English work, notably that of the non-doctor Frederick W. H. Myers, who had offered his concept of the "subliminal" level of consciousness in the eighties. For years James and Myers shared an interest in the Society for Psychical Research. And for years James was one of a handful of prophets insisting that hypnotic phenomena, the subconscious, mental suggestion and "mental healing" be examined with scientific seriousness, not dismissed in the fashion of Franklin as "imagination." James made it a point throughout his career to lash out at the doctors for their dogmatic determination to explain all mental states—certainly all pathological mental states—as due, in some simple, one-directional, cause-effect relation, to body states. Doctors, he repeated, ought to recognize their own occupational superstitions. As late as 1902 he still found it appropriate to assail "medical materialism."

Plainly in these circumstances there could have been little of psychosomatics. Besides Beard, here and there other medical psychiatrists such as Dr. Hack Tuke in England verged upon it in speculations on the "influence of mind upon body," absorbing into sober science a problem over which Western philosophy and poetry had puzzled for two millenniums. But almost by definition late nineteenth-century psychiatry impeded itself. Like the rest of medicine it sought "specifics," one specific therapy addressed to one specific local damage. Perhaps, though, disease was not so molecular. Perhaps the body still needed to be regarded as a single system, and sickness needed to be comprehended in terms of the total system. Perhaps even in the case of obvious "invasions" from outside, certain internal events might be as crucial as the invasion. Perhaps sickness was not always what it seemed—a disturbance of "normal" function. After all, what was one of the results of sickness in most civilized circumstances? The sick got taken care of. To those who were ill, attention was paid. Was it possible that the patient was looking for such attention? Sickness might be, not ego-alien, but a project of the ego: for people who were underemployed, a form of occupation; for the lonely, a demand for intimacy. Sickness might constitute a means for bringing lives otherwise diffuse to a focus. It might, paradoxically, be an assertion of desire. Medicine incapable of conceiving sickness as a function of the "person," or of the "soul," or of the "self," left untouched all that area where personal "wholeness" was at stake. If, on the face of it, "wholeness" was a field for religion, then medicine had left open the same void which the old religion had left open to medicine. Religious medicine was the logical recourse.

Medicine, in short, could easily seem to be standing athwart moral middle-class logic that the wishes and expectations of good people should come true. If it was easy to spiritualize the biology of evolution into pleasing cosmic drama, as John Fiske did, it was not so easy to spiritualize the biology of medical practice. The more scientific they became, the more doctors might appear to be representatives of sheer mechanical, impersonal, amoral matter. Pasteur's germ theory added vividness to this impression. Germs, morally indifferent outside entities, inexplicable according to any logic of rewards due good character, in their unpredictable visitations seemed to express the old inscrutable God of orthodoxy rather than the new God of love. And germ theory had its sexual associations. Nineteenth-century germ theory resembled Social Darwinist concepts of the struggle for existence between competing organisms, and Social Darwinism was of course an ideology exclusively for men. Women were not expected to have to struggle; then how could they defeat germs?

There was more to the sexual tension. The sexually charged role of doctors, seen clearly by Henry James, won common recognition in twentieth-century popular culture as well as in theories of clinical practice. But while in the twentieth century this charge was suitably contained and even neutralized in the doctor's various disguises as kindly old country practitioner or glamorous young man-in-white or lonely dedicated researcher, in the nineteenth century it could be raw and frightening. Part of the sentimentalization of sickness was the medical modesty of women, a modesty exaggerated by the Victorian mood to the point of betraying itself.

In an earlier era when doctors themselves were little better than midwives and seasoned grannies, this had made little difference, and even doctors might choose—as they did—to praise modesty as of higher importance than getting well. But the progress of medicine, especially in prenatal care and obstetrics, necessarily entailed greater frankness, and this exactly at the time of highest Victorian self-consciousness about the diametrically different styles of feeling between the sexes. The doctor could be seen in his very person as intruder, symbolic of the gross in contrast to the delicate, of the physical in contrast to the spiritual. Nor was this utterly without foundation. The first major psychological syndrome to draw concerted medical attention was hysteria, which by a fallacious, though by no means accidental, etymological association with the uterus and its related organs, doctors commonly presumed to be a disorder limited to females. Not infrequently their physicalist, materialist approach to this disease led them into surgical remedies verging upon sadism. One of the breakthroughs into modern psychological medicine was to be Freud's discovery that hysteria was not a monopoly of women. Nor was the relationship of patient and doctor at all eased through the century by the female ministrations of the doctor's assistant, the nurse. Despite the heroic efforts of some notable women during the Civil War, despite the epic leadership of Florence Nightingale in England, nursing began to constitute a calling for many young women in the United States only at the end of the century.

In a sense that was necessarily obscure, but not less potent for that, scientific medicine could very well seem a male agency, intolerant, as strong men were supposed to be intolerant, of weaknesses, uncomprehending, as the self-made men of the free-enterprise system were themselves uncomprehending, of life in a truly individual mode.

A religious medicine of feminine genesis was the logical recourse.

CHAPTER V

THE THEOLOGY OF MIND CURE

THE POINT of mind cure was to think the thoughts of God. It made some difference, naturally, what God was like. Where did mind cure get its notions?

Horatio Dresser, the historian of New Thought, found it pleasing that Phineas P. Quimby had not really been a philosopher. Apparently Quimby knew little or nothing even of his eminent contemporary Ralph Waldo Emerson. As for Mary Baker Eddy, she herself avowed that *Science and Health* was written under inspiration—direct, final, complete—in this echoing traditional orthodox concepts of a "revealed" Bible. In fact, she relied on Quimby's notes, plus her knowledge of local New England spiritualism, plus gleanings from contemporary wisdom anthologies, plus above all her knowledge of the Bible in its New England reputation. Charles and Myrtle Fillmore, Ralph Waldo Trine, Henry Wood, Prentice Mulford, Charles Brodie Patterson, H. Emilie Cady—these and others after them were ken to no special lore in philosophy or theology beyond their mid-nineteenth-century Protestant heritage.

In 1919 the one man with systematic training, Horatio Dresser himself, who had studied German philosophical Idealism at Harvard, complained of a "philosophic decline" in the New Thought movement since its beginnings. But just what he meant he found it hard to say. Warren Evans' efforts to replace the subjective Swedenborg with the more "objective" Germans bothered him. Urging that New Thought's "practical, clearcut and specific" quality be reclaimed, he explicitly deprecated efforts to explain mind cure "from the point of view either of general curiosity or of an external study of the subject." He wanted "interpretation from the inside, as experienced by the individual." But could this support philosophy, or only the chaos of individual pragmatisms?

Actually, the history of mind cure had not been one of philosophic decline at all, but rather one of consistency with itself. Mind-cure writers did hold implacably to the measure of interpretation "from the inside," never veering toward an "external study of the subject." Their arguments were always "religious," demanding "belief" in a proposition before the proposition could be tested. Yet no chaos of individual subjectivity succeeded. The evangel remained the same in 1965 as in 1875. Writings of this sort were manifestations of local culture, "expressive" first of all, renditions of "experience," perhaps destined never to reach the level of objective logic and external point of view. And these writings expressed a particular local culture. Having listened to a visiting Persian oracle expound mystic wisdom in one of the fashionable drawing rooms on Beacon Hill, the young Anglican seminarian in Arlo Bates's novel *The Puritan* professed confusion: "I couldn't make out what it was for." "For?" came the answer. "To amuse us. We are the children of the Puritans, you know, and have inherited a twist toward the ethical and the supernatural so strong that we have to have these things served up even in our amusements." "Then I think that it is wicked. . . ."[1] Where mere decadence took over, Madame Blavatsky, theosophy and Vedanta did come in to supplement the wisps of Hindoo and Buddha circulating in nineteenth-century avant-gardes since Emerson. But mind cure's satisfaction of the twist toward Truth did not derive from the search for amusement, no matter how amusing Mary Baker Eddy may have seemed on her afternoons in great houses. It derived from need, and it was a fruit of the native ground. When its writers embellished their testimonials with exalted authorities, they quite instinctively turned to American sages—Emerson, and then, later, with delight, William James himself. Norman Vincent Peale was to profess himself a disciple of both. The simple fact of this expressive amateurism in thought rested on an underlying dynamic: far from evincing some bored transcending flight from present scenes and past habits, mind cure wished to fulfill the past in a perfect present. Its ideas of God were generated in American experience. It was an emblem of American culture.

The basic truth

The basic truth upon which mind cure rested can be summed up in its predicates for God[2]—common to Divine Science and Religious Science, Christian Science and Metaphysical Science, Unity and New Thought, Churches of Mind and Churches of Love; to Trine, to Patterson, to Elizabeth Towne, to Emmett Fox.

God was:
Mind (Supreme Mind; Consciousness; Universal Consciousness)
All (infinite; eternal; unlimited; Being; Absolute)
Omnipotence (all-power)
Omniscience (all-wisdom)
Omnipresence (all-presence; indwelling presence)
The Christ
Spirit (Logos; word)
Creator (upholder; unchanging principle; principle; law)
Love
Good
Truth
Supply
Father-Mother

These were not very strange, most of them. Clearly, as Creator, as all-power and as all-wisdom, this God retained features of the orthodox divinity known to Puritans. But did they mean the same? Did these grand attributes still suggest that prodigious sovereignty, trackless and fathomless, immeasurably awful while yet immeasurably sweet, under whose eye Puritans had lived? The function of the orthodox absolute attributes of God in mind cure was rather to avert and outflank the danger that had been opened up in the liberal Protestantism succeeding upon Puritanism. If God was not in fact all-power and all-wisdom, then the consequent voids would have to be filled somehow—by men. There were those, however, whose need consisted in the first place of a void they could not fill. If liberalism was impelled by a spreading sense of personal power and integration, there were those who failed to share it.

The impulse to guarantee God's sufficiency was expressed in another attribute which, no matter how logically it might have seemed to follow from the others, orthodoxy had always regarded with nervous care: His omnipresence (all-presence; indwelling presence). One of the trickier notions of theology, the idea of God's omnipresence was what exposed mind cure to the charge of "pantheism." The horror of pantheism lay in the inference that, if God did dwell everywhere, and indeed was everything, then everything was equal—crocodiles and rabbits, germs and vaccines, dementia and lucidity. It invited claims to immediate, direct intimacy with God; it invited antinomianism, subversive of order. But mind cure's regard for omnipresence bespoke no antinomian ecstasies; omnipresence simply satisfied further the need that nothing be left to sheer existence, nothing be insusceptible to identification with mind.

While preserving God's absolute attributes thus, mind cure sought the closure of absolute assurance. God's face was never hidden. Nothing betrayed this redirection of orthodox theology more plainly than mind cure's invariable omission of the idea of God as Will. Will, or Sovereignty, implied the gap between ruler and ruled, the inevitable danger that the ruled could never succeed thoroughly in searching out the purposes of the ruler. Mind cure's translation of "omnipotence" as "all-power" lacked this essential characteristic of Will—irreducible inward mystery. Will manifested what mind cure wished to expunge—the arbitrary.

Maintenance of the orthodox qualities was protective, defensive, prudential. Mind cure's favorite attribution was more positive. It was the obvious one: God was Mind (Supreme Mind, Consciousness, Universal Consciousness). The crucial aim in this characterization was that it should guarantee a self-enclosed and coherent existence. Life as Will implied an "environment," a realm of action, an arena of events. (And this, incidentally, was the hidden logical flaw in orthodox Calvinist logic: nothing with an environment could be thoroughly sovereign.) Mind was its own order; it was not arbitrary. In a Protestant, Puritan-generated culture, with its long anxiety to seek out inward sins, to inspect impulses, to examine conscience, to let no action pass unchecked, in a culture long intent upon making conscious what in times past had been left to mere instinct or impulse or habit or tradition, Mind was above all the realm in which people might feel that life came finally under control. Weak, one might not be able to master the world, but one could control one's mind; what then if the world was Mind?

Contact with universal knowledge

It was not simply that men could know God as Mind; men were actually individualizations of God. Individualizations of Divine Mind, they themselves were wholly mind. Not that men were God; but they were in no tension with God. It was sometimes difficult to formulate the relationship between divine and human mind; it was not an identity; there were transactions; but nothing limited or distorted communication.

> There is that in man which, when opened, will place him in direct contact with universal knowledge, and enable him instantly and continuously to draw forth anything that he may wish to know.[3]

Puritans, too, had wished to know, but they had expected to spend the years of their lives in exhaustive puzzling, and liberals no less expected knowing to take time—the years of their lives and also the ages of evolutionary revelation, with not only Bible and conscience for guidance but also science and history. Here, in Charles Fillmore's mind-cure terms, was an evangelical fixation upon the Now, "instantly." And mind cure's "direct contact with universal knowledge" offered much more than the purifying grace of the evangelicals' Jesus Christ, for purity was not sufficiency. It offered a total sufficiency of the present, no heaven beyond this present harmony being required.

This availability of knowledge upon demand was one instance of what mind-cure groups commonly called "Supply." The principle was extremely simple: there was always enough. As H. Emilie Cady put it:

> One of the unerring truths in the universe is that there is already provided a lavish abundance for every human want. In other words, the supply of every good always awaits the demand.[4]

No demand can outrun any supply. Upon this equation Norman Vincent Peale was to prop his evangel from the start:

> God will do anything for you that down in your heart you really want him to do. . . . He will actually give you strength, peace, happiness, and boundless well-being if, deep down in your nature, you sincerely want these advantages and desire them enough to take them.[5]

God was unlimited good substance. "He who lives in the realization of his oneness with this Infinite Power," explained Ralph Waldo Trine, "becomes a magnet to attract to himself a continual supply of whatsoever things he desires."[6] The key to the operation of Supply was of course the operation of Mind: one had to "realize," to "understand," to "sincerely want."

Again, no antinomian tendencies toward license were lurking here. Supply did not supply just anything. Dr. Cady, Peale, Trine and the rest were thinking only of certain desires. These were indicated in further predicates for God, such as Love and Good along with Truth. These were subject to elaboration, though, as in the subtitle of Trine's famous tract: to be in tune with the infinite meant peace, power and plenty. I shall have more to say, in Chapter XV, of the literal elaboration of "plenty."

Specifying further that God was All, and, just to be sure, One, only reinforced the circle. All-God retained focus as Supreme Mind, and, as All and One, emphasized the absence of any degree of alien resistance to mind, to love, to good, to truth. Applied to matters of health, the most sensational implication was Mrs. Eddy's insistence that disease simply did not exist any more than did "matter." Both were fictions of blinded minds. The other mind-cure groups preferred to avoid the intriguing logical difficulties Mrs. Eddy incurred by her rigor, without abandoning the main point. One could assimilate the "existence" of "matter" to the notion that All is Mind, and that Supreme Mind is Supply, Love, Good, Truth. . . .

God as Mind was the "Christ"—universal mind in operation, so to speak, especially in its guise as word or spirit. So far as technical dogmatic allegiances were concerned, here mind cure parted most distinctly from the older churches. Neither the sacrificial intercessor of orthodoxy nor the perfect moral preceptor of liberalism, neither God-man nor man-God, "the" Christ, by being a principle, not a man of any sort at all, perhaps most radically shifted religious orientation, by dissolving the sense of time organized around a historical life in favor of a timeless truth. "The" Christ revealed mind cure's non-historical outlook.

What Emerson really meant

"Once inhale the open air . . . and we learn that man has access to the entire mind of the Creator."[7] Ralph Waldo Emerson said this—not Charles Fillmore or Elizabeth Towne or Ralph Waldo Trine. It is important to distinguish the Emersonian from the mind-cure evangel, for, if Quimby did not, certainly Trine was conversant with the seer so admired by his parents. Mary Baker Eddy herself, late in life, held discourse with the most etherealized of the transcendentalists, Bronson Alcott.

Emerson invoked action. Heralding the openness of human mind to divinity, Emerson pursued the complicating internal structure of the supreme experience. Nature was not only symbol of spirit, object of perception, but "thoroughly mediate . . . made to serve . . . until the world becomes at last only a realized will,—the double of the man." Man "is himself the creator of the finite." In later years, once having sung his mystic oneness, Emerson stressed action more than ever, as a means to convert "every jot of chaos which threatens to exterminate us . . . into wholesome force." He had a policy for health: "right drainage destroys typhus. . . ." Moreover, the notorious Emersonian optimism, absorbed into right-thinking, popular, middle-class culture through the later decades of the century, Emerson himself had founded at least partly on what was still in truth the old Calvinist granite. Speaking of health again: what was a man with "sciatica in his loins and cramp in his mind; a club-foot and a club in his wit" to do? "He is to rally on his relation to the Universe," Emerson said, "which his ruin benefits." The old Edwardseans glimpsing ultimate good in immediate evil could hardly have said more. "Leaving the daemon who suffers," Emerson said, "he is to take sides with the Deity who secures universal benefit by his pain."[8] Mind cure's deity straightened club-feet and healed sciatica—killed all pain. The longest chapter of *Science and Health* was the last—"Fruitage," containing "Lameness Cured," "Healed of Hernia and Other Ills," "Cancer Cured," "Awakened to Health and Happiness."

In such passages Emerson was exercising a theory of double consciousness, the consciousness on the one hand of the man standing "against fate," draining swamps, on the other hand that of the man percipient of the swamp's image of the universal beauty. And Emerson did not omit mention of the conditions for the immaculate transcendental illumination: ". . . I become a universal eyeball; I am nothing; I see all. . . . All mean egotism vanishes."[9] Illumination required dissolution of that which had been blind; health, dissolution of that which had been sick. For what had been sick was sick by its nature. Echoing Puritan mysticism, but even more anticipating the mystique of pure science—in Thoreau, Wright, Peirce, Royce—this lyric surrender of the ego embraced truth independent of desire. It embraced it because, known independently of demand, unmistaken as supply, truth was, as poets persistently said, beauty.

That mind cure conventionalized lyric transcendentalism into a prosy pragmatism was apparent. Yet, Emerson's own stopgap notion of double consciousness suggested how difficult it would be—and had always been—to construe a truly unified religious personality.

The pure wish

Mind-cure theology was purely expressive. That is, it was the immediate projection of uninspected wish. Wishes, falling between Emerson's regard for action and will on the one hand, and his regard for selfless knowledge on the other, hung in limbo, powerless. But they could be extruded as metaphysics, and by definition made absolute. In which case all that was needed was some way of denying non-wishful reality. A measure of the urgency of this wishfulness was to be seen in the persistent mind-cure claim to being "science": Christian Science, Divine Science, Religious Science, the science of mind, the science of life. Mind-cure science was not, however, detached from demand. Nor did it devise those scientific tests by which men were joined communally independent of their particular desires and egos. Pure wish was pure weakness; but in its profound unconsciousness of its own nature, mind cure could now and then betray what pure weakness wished for. In the somewhat idiosyncratic terms of a modern exponent, Frederick W. Bailes:

> Since the sufferer is holding a pattern of sickness, the practitioner must hold a pattern of health, and by speaking his words with confidence in the obedience of Universal Subjective Mind he is thereby able to direct the Giant Worker to follow his pattern rather than that of the patient.[10]

If only "you really want him to," God will give you anything. God obeys man.

God was also Father-Mother.

The addition of Mother to God's attributes was mind cure's response to what had undoubtedly been a major repression in Protestant imagination since Calvin. By the nineteenth century Protestantism's attempt to channel the pertinent impulses into the family had come to its half-hysterical climax in the ideology of the genteel family and its concomitant alienation of the sexes—the tragic contradiction of Luther's own original imagination. The precise intellectual parentage of the mind-cure notion is of less importance than its grass roots in an immediate impasse. No one of the exponents of mind cure knew of J. J. Bachofen's speculative discovery of the religion of the Great Mother antedating and underlying the father-and-son gods of later and Western religion. Nor did mind cure draw on Oriental mother-gods, such as the Indian Kali, in whom the destructive as well as nourishing powers of nature (and of mothers) were fused in a way having nothing to do with the schism of Western sexuality. Mind cure's obvious historical hint was due the Shakers, founded by Mother Ann Lee, well known in New England. But it owed most to the self-consciousness induced in a whole class of women in the nineteenth century by the crumbling of traditional identities. In Mrs. Eddy the fixation of that self-consciousness in a new identity lent mind cure a tone and mood it never lost.

If a response, Father-Mother was not a release from repression in the direction of reclaiming intimacy and strength. Among Shakers the elevation of women had gone hand-in-hand with the suppression of sex; in a sense, Shakers eliminated fathers and mothers altogether. But fathers and mothers were useful. In mind cure the operative meaning of Father-Mother was not sexual. Rather, as Supply, as Universal Consciousness (and, hence, awareness of every demand to be supplied), as all-good, all-love and all-power, Father-Mother was the child's wish about his parents, perfect in their gratification of every need, perfect in constituting the sum of reality. Father-Mother was one total environment that by being known only in terms of wish was actually simply the All of which one was an individualization. Father-Mother registered the supreme sway of dependency—which can only wish.

CHAPTER VI

THE PSYCHOLOGY OF MIND CURE

TRUTH WAS TRUTH, but the goal was that Truth be operative. The problem for mind cure was to evict thoughts of untruth, of error. How was this done? The heart of mind cure was its psychology, and the heart of that psychology was its displacement of consciousness. Consciousness could not be trusted.

William James saw this in mind cure, though what he saw drew as much on his own evangelical enthusiasms as upon his scientific observation. "Mind-cure has made what in our Protestant countries is an unprecedentedly great use of the subconscious life."[1] Naturally, awareness of processes beneath the threshold of consciousness was not original to the dawning twentieth century. Priests, oracles, soothsayers, mystics and other beneficiaries of unconscious life, as well as poets, sober philosophers, scientists, doctors and plain folk, had not been lacking to testify to the hidden realms. Yet when James declared that the "discovery" of the subconscious was "the most important step that has occurred in psychology since I have been a student of that science . . . ,"[2] he was referring to a definite breakthrough. At last, the levels beneath consciousness were subjects for systematic scientific examination. It is easy, finding James calling off the names Janet, Breuer, Prince—and Freud—to imagine we know exactly what he was talking about, and to absorb his description of the topic unquestioningly: "whole systems of underground life, in the shape of memories of a painful sort which lead a parasitic existence, buried outside of the primary fields of consciousness. . . ."[3]

This breakthrough challenged "our protestant countries" implicitly, but vitally. Luther had launched Protestantism on the liberating strength of his own sudden and heroic appreciation of buried forces within himself; his revolt registered his sense of a potential personal unity that he knew was unattainable on the basis of works, good intentions, striving and will power. Indeed, all such pretensions became blasphemous. Early Calvinism and the Puritans, too, had hardly lacked appreciation of hidden forces within every individual. But steadily, and, as it seems in retrospect, inevitably, the drift of Calvinist Protestantism was toward categorizing such forces purely as chaos and sin, and mastering them by conscious control and strength of will. The lyric heroes—a Woolman, a Blake, an Edwards, an Emerson, a Whitman—resisted, but they were lonely. The "Protestant ethic" triumphed. Liberal religion fed upon the relative success of this enterprise of will, turning around then to announce that mastery came much more easily than orthodoxy had imagined. Good people simply were not, in their original basic nature, creatures of disorderly, emotional, hidden forces. They were creatures of consciousness and self-control.

Quite unconsciously and unintentionally, it was mind cure in its obsession with health that most clearly exposed the absurdity of this view. Not even Franklin, not even Channing, not even Henry Ward Beecher ever argued that the self-sustaining processes of the body were conscious. Men did not even have to suspect the existence of the adrenals for them to flow, with anger, depression, fear, zest.

Discovery of the subconscious

James was an early spokesman of that modern psychology observing in effect that men were creatures of unconscious depth whether they wanted to be or not. The "subconscious" existed in all men, including those who did not know it and would be dismayed to be told so. Necessarily, this entangled psychology in something more than just a scientific task. Psychology became involved in actively promoting change. It caused men to become aware; where once unconsciousness had been, there consciousness would reign. In turn, this raised the question, just what good was being served, and how might it be systematically pursued? Modern depth psychology originated in personal, clinical rather than in impersonal, laboratory practice. It raised the question, what sorts of people were capable of awareness? James's fascination with the subconscious bespoke his involvement in these existential, therapeutic, "religious" questions far more than his scientist's detachment. With the Puritan New Englander always in mind, time and again he returned to the theme: people limited themselves, they shut themselves up in cages of their own making. This they did by defining themselves according to organized, tidily unified, nicely rational systems of imagination, which in actuality had the function not of providing personal strength but of providing security. They closed themselves to the possibilities for more experience. "There is actually and literally more life in our total soul than we are at any time aware of." "The conscious person is continuous with a wider self," he insisted,[4] this wider self being evident in the subconscious or subliminal. Abundant living depended upon keeping doors open to this dimension.

The Varieties of Religious Experience built upon this psychology. How, James asked, are we to explain such phenomena as mystic raptures, sudden conversions, trances and automatistic behavior? We might well conceive them as subconscious processes erupting to the surface of consciousness, their subject ignorant of where they came from. Scientific psychology should be able to be much more exact in tracking them to their lair.

The question this raised for religion was apparent. The convert himself, or the mystic, believed his experience originated from "outside," in the divine, in God, not in his subconscious. Was he wrong? Was religion then to be "reduced" to psychology? Here was the most notable point at which James invoked the logic of the "will"—or rather, the "right"—to believe. Might not the subconscious be only the channel, not the source, for divine facts? Might not the subconscious be God's passage into consciousness? The "wider self" might be not only the outreaches of consciousness in subconsciousness but the welcome by both to the life of the divine.

James's argument half-concealed one step, one assumption. If invasions from the subconscious were to be conceived as invasion through the subconscious by real "higher powers," it was necessary to think that the subconscious was fitted to serve as such a pipeline. This was how James put it: ". . . Since on our hypothesis it is primarily the higher faculties of our own hidden mind which are controlling, the sense of union with the power beyond us is a sense of something, not merely apparently, but literally true."[5] But what were these "higher faculties"? How did they happen to be part of the "hidden mind"? James did not say. Earlier he had drawn on Edwin Starbuck's *Psychology of Religion* for the same view. Starbuck, noting how conscious will power often inhibits a man's progress toward his goal, argued that in such predicaments the individual ". . . must relax, that is, he must fall back on the larger Power that makes for righteousness, which has been welling up in his own being, and let it finish in its own way the work it has begun. . . ."[6] What was this "larger Power"? Where did it come from? How did it happen to be allied to righteousness? There was no answer.

What was at issue here was not, certainly, the point, known to James as well as to others through ages, that a variety of what could be called problem-solving processes go on unconsciously, and do so much of the time. Some of them could be highly dramatic, experienced by scientists of the first order of rational control as well as by poets, salesmen, lovers and priests. Something else was the issue. Not the existence of levels beneath consciousness, nor even their nature, but their relationship to the conscious was the heart of the matter.

James himself tended to credit the subconscious with semi-magical powers that needed only to be obeyed. Much of his description of the subconscious amounted to no more than a new label for the famous faculty of transcendental reason or intuition celebrated in New England sixty years earlier. In its poetic-philosophic form the transcendentalists' "reason" was naturally unsatisfactory to scientific psychologists; as a concept, the "subconscious" was much more acceptable, less speculative, more open to study and explanation. But the subconscious continued, to be characterized by the traits of the religious faculty: it was a "higher" power, it was "good," it facilitated the individual's fullest, highest, spiritual experience directly. This was a highly American-Protestant response to the first serious wrestles with psychological depth, and it was destined to be echoed in the optimistic, liberal, "American" depth-psychology of the so-called neo-Freudians, as well as in the "non-directive" psychology of Carl Rogers and the "self-realization" principle of Kurt Goldstein. In common to all of these was the cultural, "American" assumption that in "depth" there was nothing inherent to be feared, nothing that made for conflict, for tragedy.

Yet James himself knew that the "subconscious" was not quite so good and convenient an agency as his religious speculation required. His reference to "memories of a painful sort which lead a parasitic existence" came closer to what Freud was beginning to comprehend as the "unconscious" of repression, which was not so promising, perhaps, as a channel for the divine. The subconscious, James also explained,

> . . . contains, for example, such things as all our momentarily inactive memories, and it harbors the springs of all our obscurely motivated passions, impulses, likes, dislikes, and prejudices. Our intuitions, hypotheses, fancies, superstitions, persuasions, convictions, and in general all our non-rational operations, come from it. It is the source of our dreams.[7]

Whatever the underlying pattern of this conglomerate, it would have been difficult to infer its "higher faculties," its "larger Power" that made for righteousness, or its suitability as transmission-belt for divine data.

Aside from James's acculturated tendency to echo Emerson occasionally, as well as his father's Swedenborgianism, it was his eagerness for liberation from complacently formal psychologies that induced his carelessness here. The subconscious was a marvelously useful weapon in his pragmatic insistence upon seeing men in the context of the real problems they faced, his famous pragmatic defense of men's right to believe what might help them in those cases where science, logic and collected evidence came to no conclusion. Yet his enthusiasm for the subconscious reverberated far beyond pragmatism. His whole point about "letting go" into the subconscious, about "opening doors," was that such letting-go refreshened and revitalized consciousness. Such refreshening was its own reward, having nothing to do with pragmatic problem-solving. What James did not do was to explore the capacity to let go as a capacity of consciousness itself, a capacity registering its own confidence in its own strength. The relevant strength was not that which guaranteed sheer "success" or successful problem-solving, for such success was nothing more than to survive as self-enclosed, petrified desire. It was rather the strength to "stand" experience, a strength of intake, a strength to absorb, assimilate and remember more and more of reality. I shall try later to show how James personally did exemplify letting go as a strength of consciousness in one of his own religious experiences. But the fact that he assumed such strength in others meant that he misconceived the logic of mind cure.

Quimby's "spiritual matter"

In mind-cure psychology Phineas P. Quimby, once again, was the pioneer. In conceptualizing regions "below" consciousness his intuitive gifts were again in evidence, for at the time—in the eighteen-sixties—there were no respectable medical or psychological theories compared to which his own might have seemed mere vulgar parodies. Quimby approached things out of his practice. Having healed, first as hypnotist, then by mental suggestion, he had something to explain. How had mind affected body? Groping, he came up with the notion of "spiritual matter," a kind of middle term connecting the two. Healing took place as mind affected this spiritual matter, which in turn affected the body. Obviously this was nothing but verbal play, but it had the merit of trying to isolate phases of a process that did occur. Spiritual matter consisted essentially of a storehouse of past experience: all the thoughts, ideas, beliefs, concepts, notions, fantasies, mental pictures and memory-traces a person had accumulated in his life. This "matter" determined a person's bodily state.[8] Here was a decent enough anticipation of some of James's descriptions of the subconscious.

But as to the use to be made of the subconscious, Quimby was no early James. No one could avoid collecting a store of experience. What one could do, however, was to check it over, reorganize it, and throw some of it out if need be. Exposed to Truth, the erroneous, faulty, disease-producing, worry-inducing items were eliminated. Thereafter, by the use of conscious, deep and correct thinking, and the exercise of mental suggestion, future experiences could be screened before being allowed to become spiritual matter.

Mind cure spoke of man as individualization of the divine, but Quimby by no means equated this divinity with the subconscious—as James verged upon doing. Nor did he argue that the subconscious was the channel open to the divine. In Quimby's view, man's divinity was located in the "soul," and soul ranked "above" mind, so to speak, as "spiritual matter" ranked below it. Quimby sometimes spoke as though all three of these levels were all parts of "mind," the middle level being "conscious mind," "spiritual matter" being "hidden" or "deeper" mind, and soul being that unchangeable part of mind harmonious with divine, universal mind.

Later mind cure perpetuated and intensified this basic structure. Quimby's terms faded in favor of more "scientific" labels; "spiritual matter" (which Warren Evans equated with Swedenborg's "limbus") became the subconscious, the subliminal, even the unconscious, but its role remained the same—reflexive, subordinate, immediately vulnerable to reorganization. What we are to aim for, said Charles Fillmore, is identification of our mind with the God mind; we are to yield in favor of the divine. Did this yielding or letting-go take place through the subconscious? Not according to Fillmore. In his interesting physio-psychology, which located faith in the pineal gland, mental discrimination in the liver, etc., the God mind entered through "the very top of the head," "this higher brain center" known in the Bible as "the upper room."

Fillmore indeed urged "acquiescence" or letting go, but acquiescence "in the logic of the superconsciousness of your own being."[9]

Mrs. Eddy not only did not exalt the subconscious, she did not concede its existence. From time to time in *Science and Health* she suggested a topography reminiscent of Quimby's, as in her reference to diseases that came from "the most hidden, undefined and insidious beliefs," and to "disease as originating in human belief before it is consciously apparent on the body, which is in fact the objective state of mortal mind, though it is called matter."[10] Whatever the mysteries lurking in such examination of what did not truly exist at all, Mrs. Eddy's aim was at the furthest remove from James's. "In persons deep in the religious life," he said, "the door into this region [that is, the subconscious] seems unusually wide open."[11] There was no door for Mrs. Eddy; she in fact denied the "existence" of conscious "mortal" mind as well.

Dominion over conscious mind

In this mind-cure psychology what bore the stigma of inadequacy was not some subconscious; it was "conscious mind" itself, the mind of common sense, rational inquiry, sense experience. Conscious mind was not equipped for the entry and comprehension of divine Truth or for identity with it. Its business was to surrender, to let go, not so that the subconscious could rule, but so that the soul, spirit, superconsciousness, or Mind could. Other religious psychologies through the ages had said as much. But mind cure had not merely to conceptualize man's participation in divinity, but to conceptualize his total participation, including his body, such harmony being evidenced in the fact of healing. Its answer was to downgrade consciousness as the integrating center of the self, for in the partiality of its merely human reason and its dependence upon erratic human experience, human consciousness was faulty, corrupted, fitful and fragmentary, and therefore incapable of wholeness. Only through surrendering its sovereignty was wholeness, that is, health, to be had, and this was surrender to superconsciousness, not to the subconscious. Far from teaching an open-door policy toward the subconscious, mind cure taught absolute dominion over it.

How was this dominion to be established? We can gather the standard method from the mind-cure classic which Henry Wood, an ex-neurasthenic ex-businessman from Boston, published in 1893 —*Ideal Suggestion through Mental Photography, a Restorative System for Home and Private Use*. For restorative home use, Wood gave each of twenty-five pages in the last half of his book to one Ideal Suggestion printed in black block letters: GOD IS HERE; I AM NOT BODY; THERE IS NO DEATH, etc. On the facing page a page-long meditation accompanied each ideal suggestion. Every day, the auto-patient was to retire to a private corner, relax in an easy chair, breathe deeply for several minutes, then "rivet the mind" upon the meditation through several readings. This achieved, he (or she) was to prop up the ideal suggestion "at a suitable distance from the eyes" and fix them (eyes) upon it for "from ten to twenty minutes." Next, eyes closed, twenty to thirty minutes were to be spent allowing the suggestion to permeate the whole organism. During "every wakeful hour of the night" also, the suggestion was to be called back into the "mental vision." There might, Wood allowed, be ups and downs in recovery, but if the method was used sincerely, "ideals will be actualized in due season."[12]

In the preface to his basic text, Charles Fillmore included these cautionary words:

These are not mere lectures, but lessons to be applied as one applies mathematical rules. . . . When a suggestion is made to "hold a thought", . . . the student should stop reading and, both audibly and mentally, do as bid. This will set up new thought-currents . . . and make way for the spiritual illumination. . . .[13]

At the end of each lecture Fillmore supplied statements to be used for "mental discipline":

I am the Christ of God. . . . My perfection is now established in Divine Mind. . . . My doubts and fears are dissolved and

dissipated, and I rest in confidence and peace in Thy Unchangeable Law. . . . I no longer condemn, criticize, censure
or find fault with my associates. Neither do I belittle or condemn myself. . . . I am fearless, powerful and wise in God's
love.[14]

The subconscious did not contain such convictions; it had to be
filled with them.

Christian Scientists did not offer such capsule mental photographs, insisting that they relied upon "understanding" instead. But
Fillmore, too, asked for "understanding," and in any event Christian Science, just as fundamentalist Protestantism, had its One
Book, *Science and Health,* which was the "preacher" read without
comment or interpretation from every Christian Science pulpit. Of
course Mrs. Eddy, like religious leaders before, faced the problem
of translating insights of the spiritual faculty into terms meaningful
to conscious mortal mind, and she exposed her misgivings bravely:

> The chief difficulty, in conveying the teachings of divine Sci-
> ence accurately to human thought, lies in this, that, like all
> other languages, English is inadequate to the expression of
> spiritual conceptions and propositions, through the use of ma-
> terial terms.[15]

Spiritual terms would have been better. Generations of Bible
scholars could have sympathized: which was Truth: Aramaic?
Greek? Vulgate? King James? Douay? or RSV? But in the lack of
spiritual terms, the material English that Mrs. Eddy (and Rev.
Dr. Wiggins) had settled on was not to be tampered with. "A
slight divergence is fatal in Science,"[16] she wrote, and from first
to last she insisted upon meticulous loyalty to the very letter of her
word. Her anxiety for the purity of her language survived her
death. Her very latest apologist, Robert Peel, sensitive with a
scientist's sophistication to the charges brought against mental drill,
nevertheless associated himself with the efficacy of fixed word
patterns:

> The Christian Scientist is constantly on the alert in his mental
> practice to reject the arguments of "personal sense." . . .

Through experience he finds the basic terminology worked out by Mrs. Eddy over many years to be essential to his preserving that razor-edged accuracy of spiritual sensibility that will allow him to discriminate between the suggestions of mortal mind and the impartations of the divine Mind.[17]

The famous "class instructions" by which Christian Science teachers transmitted this razor-edged accuracy of spiritual sensibility consisted totally of painstaking translation of all thoughts and all experience of every patient into Mrs. Eddy's "basic terminology."

Such eminence of the word in mind cure was far from that letting-go into the liberating disorganization of experience James commended. It was fixation, the maintenance of order, the deliberate drill imposed to restrain experience within prescribed formulas. Naturally, for this the authority of superconsciousness was indicated. The meaning of those practices of "relaxing" that intrigued James as so promising a contrast to the rigidity of Puritan and Protestant ethic stood revealed. One relaxed in order that the mental photographs might sink to the level of one's spiritual matter. One "entered the silence" in order to be dominated. One gained "understanding" by repetition of prescribed terminology, designated as "holding the thought." This was how mind affected body, how "thoughts were things."

Far from letting-go into the subconscious, then, in order to escape the cage of consciousness mind cure aimed at still greater control over the subconscious. By "passive relaxation, concentration and meditation," the adept found nothing like the "obscurely motived passions, impulses, likes, dislikes and prejudices" James evoked. James was suggesting that in such letting-go he who relaxed found himself, his "deeper" self. But in mind cure one found the One Voice of the Infinite. The aim was to fill the subconscious so full of suggestion and lesson and science that it would have no life of its own. From time to time James recognized what this process amounted to actually. The teachers of mind cure "have even invoked something like hypnotic practice."[18] Hypnosis, of course, is the surrender of conscious control in favor of external authority. In hypnosis one has indeed surrendered, but not to one's depths, rather to one's weakness, one's will-lessness.

CHAPTER VII

THE PHYSIOLOGY OF FAITH AND FEAR

COULD TRUTH really heal? Could mind cure really work?

As the first wave of mind cure rose, toward 1900, doctors were active in exposing its fallacies. Most obvious were cases where mind-cure methods had simply failed. Patients had not got well. Scandalously, sometimes they had died—been "let" die. Then there were cases of apparent success, only to be followed by the patient's relapse a few days, weeks or months later. But such evidences and arguments were snapping at air. The practitioners of mind cure could always claim, and did, that in these cases the patient had not really mastered mind-cure techniques. Were there never doctors whose patients failed to follow instructions? For that matter, were there no doctors whose patients had died?

More telling was medical attack upon mind-cure diagnosis rather than therapy. How could mind-cure therapists know that the ulcer and lumbago and cancer they claimed to. have healed had been ulcer, lumbago or cancer at all? No doubt they had been just aches and pains, "slight ailments," imaginary. This too left a door or two open, though: since the cases had not been medically diagnosed, doctors could not know for sure either. And sometimes they had been medically diagnosed.

The more subtle argument on which doctors tended to take their stand was that used by Dr. Richard Cabot of the Harvard Medical School in a well-known discussion of 1908.[1] The cures effected by mind cure, he said, were cases of "functional" illness, not of "organic" illness. The distinction between the two was itself a sign of the late emergence of psychological medicine out of nineteenth-century psychiatry and neurology. It was to persist in medical and popular parlance for years to come. But it, too, solved nothing finally: Cabot's approach came close to reasoning in a circle. Medicine was by no means equipped with a long list of functional as contrasted with organic afflictions. Hysteria, the malady stimulating modern psychological medicine due to the work of Charcot and Breuer and Freud, seemed clear enough; and then ulcers did appear to have something to do with mood and mind—but the ulcer itself was organic enough, surely. Actually, Cabot said little more than that whatever mind cure did heal should be called "functional."

Even then the most interesting fact remained: "merely" functional or not, apparently there were cases mind cure could handle. As if to recall the fact that this should not have been as surprising as it seemed to rational-minded people of the time, George Cutten published *Three Thousand Years of Mental Healing* in 1911. Had prescientific medicine been nothing but failure? Had its therapeutic efficacy been scaled to its scientific ignorance? After all, the race had survived. Shamans, sorcerers, exorcists, medicine men, faith healers, quacks—had these professionals never known satisfied clients? Of course they had.

Still, it was not necessary to concede that recoveries over which shamans had presided testified to the truth of shamanism. To what did they testify then? One of the important developments in nineteenth-century medicine itself had been the revived appreciation of the healing processes natural to the body or, as Walter B. Cannon was to put it, "the wisdom of the body." The best of practicing bedside doctors had never ignored this, and in the nineteenth-century one specialty at least, osteopathy, had tried to exploit it systematically. But early osteopathic principles remained highly speculative, to most doctors implausible and no advance either in theory or practice. One of the glories of twentieth-century medical research was to be its deepening comprehension of this amazingly complex "wisdom," to the point, eventually, of inciting various chemical therapies aimed to liberate and strengthen the body's own processes. In short: doctors might do good sometimes by leaving the body alone; and so might shamans.

The birth of psychosomatic medicine

But there was more to it than this. Had it made no difference whether a shaman or exorcist or faith healer had attended or not? One may take the decisive turning-point to have been Walter Cannon's pioneering laboratory research on the autonomic nervous system, the results of which he released in 1915 under the title *Bodily Changes in Pain, Hunger, Fear and Rage.* Herewith, in a kind of dialectical reversal of the course of medical thinking dating in America from Benjamin Rush's *Influence of Physical Causes upon the Moral Faculty* of 1788, Cannon presented empirical foundations for those occasional half-intuitive insights of a few nineteenth-century doctors such as Hack Tuke and, notably, the great Frenchman Claude Bernard, into the influence of mental states, or the mind, upon the body. Psychosomatic medicine was being born.

Twenty-seven years later in 1942, Cannon was to write a dramatic article again putting a firm physiological footing under an especially dramatic instance of mind-body unity, this one with a resonance carrying beyond the clinic into society itself. Anthropologists had long credited a phenomenon known as "voodoo death" among the aborigines of central Australia (as well as elsewhere over the world). They had satisfied themselves it was no trick; its victims did not die by poison, or by any other surreptitious means. Quite literally they died "because" the sorcerer had pointed at them with his magic bone. Cannon explained how this could be. Incited by his fear, the victim's sympathico-adrenal nervous system prepares him for climactic defensive action. But these preparations go unused. Paralyzed by his conviction of his own doom, by his belief, that is, in the power of the sorcerer—reinforced by his knowledge that his fellows, his society, hold the same belief—the victim does not act. Thereupon his defensive mobilizations, in the form of extreme adrenalin production, liberation of sugar, contraction of certain blood vessels, etc., begin to kill him. Sliding into shock, immobilized from taking food and water which would check the process, the victim's body attacks itself. A man is literally killed by a belief.[2]

Here was a straightforward physiological rendition of William James's famous pragmatic insistence upon the "power" of ideas. The important thing about a belief is its consequences, James argued, and to die would seem consequence enough. What about more positive attitudes? Joy is "dynamogenic," said the psychologist George Dearborn in 1916,[3] drawing on his own and Cannon's research; joy and other euphoric moods have definite influence upon arterial pressure and kinesthesia. Over the following four decades there was no one main line of research, there were many. Hans Selye's epochal research in Toronto into what he designated as the "general adaptation syndrome" decisively advanced Cannon's work on the side of physiology, while on the flank of psychology Freud inspired a welter of both speculation and practice. On some fronts, generally backed more firmly by psychology (and, now again, philosophy) than by physiology, the advance went so far as to insist that there was no "mysterious leap" between mind and body at all; the only "leap" was in our language.[4] By 1920 psychosomatic medicine had won its first all-out champion, the German doctor George Groddeck. By 1960 research had not yet defined a center joining the two flanks; psychology could not explain itself physiologically, nor physiology psychologically. In view of modern theories of the operation of the brain, it was quite possible such a center never would be defined, except as that center of unity remained what it had always been, a subject for neither psychology nor physiology but for philosophy. At all events, in psychosomatic medicine the early distinction between functional and organic had begun to erode, and there seemed no way or reason it should not erode further. What illness did not have its "functional," its mental, its emotional, and—hence—its characterological dimensions—and thereby its social, its philosophical, its religious dimensions? Perhaps—just perhaps—"faith" might be relevant—everywhere.

Treatises with such titles as *Scientific Mental Healing, Laws of Mental Medicine* and *Mind-Cure from a Scientific Point of View* were appearing by the time Cannon published his first research. The point of these books was to argue that efficacy was not evidence, that truth and consequences were different. Speaking freely of mental suggestion, of conditioning, and even once again, after long silence, of hypnotism, their authors were saying that mind-cure methods worked (when they worked) independently of mind-cure philosophy. The argument was useful to the old denominations. Put on the defensive by the mind-cure churches, ministers could reject mind-cure theology and, now, early in the twentieth century, begin their tentative assimilation of mind-cure issues. Pastor James Buckley enrolled personally in the ranks of healers, practiced for a time, then released his findings in 1906 under the title *Faith Healing, Christian Science, and Kindred Phenomena*. Mind cure, Buckley announced, was basically hypnotism; it did not depend upon its peculiar religious doctrines.

A new species of popular writing

As a by-product of these developments, a new species of popular writing emerged: tracts by doctors offering advice on how to live life. Psychologists and physiologists joined, William James being the greatest. Of course, doctors over centuries had told their patients to relax, to slow down, to cheer up, but this had been bedside and consultation-room counsel, geared to the pragmatics of a specific trouble. Now they generalized more widely. The famous psychiatrist Abraham Myerson, in *The Nervous Housewife* (1920), sustained one of Annie Payson Call's notable missions, and Miss Call's basic therapy was echoed by Alice Katherine Fallow in *A Talk on Relaxation* (1909) and by Arthur A. Carey in *New Nerves for Old* (1914). Myerson's *When Life Loses Its Zest* (1926), and *The Healthy Mind*, by a symposium of doctors in 1929, were in the genre. Decade by decade the medically sponsored advice continued

—Dr. David Harold Fink's *Release from Nervous Tension* (1943), Dr. John A. Schindler's *How To Live 365 Days a Year* (1954), and Fink's *For People under Pressure* (1956) are popular examples. This amiable psychological advice from doctors had to do with mind and self, soul and spirit, with the "whole man," and with, therefore, that from which scientific medicine had so painfully extricated itself, religion. Doctors were becoming priests again, telling people of ultimate choices. When, in the years after World War II, claims for the power of faith sprang up again in a near-medieval luxuriance, fewer doctors scoffed. Some doctors themselves were ready to "prescribe faith." One doctor in particular worked his way over several decades with the new vision.

Writing before Cannon had published, Dr. William S. Sadler of Chicago, in *The Physiology of Faith and Fear* (1913) and *Worry and Nervousness* (1914), could point to few definite mechanisms by which emotions affected the body, but Sadler was secure in his conviction that they did so. His recommendation amounted to the single imperative: have faith—that is, by a plain inference, have faith in the power of faith. "All faith tendencies are toward mental happiness and physical health. All people, good or bad, get the physical rewards of faith, regardless of whether the objects of their faith and belief are true or false."[5] Impressing itself upon Dr. Sadler as a result of "the accumulating and apparently remarkable cures" wrought by early mind cure, here was the insight of Paracelsus again.

Sadler did not really mean to settle for this. A doctor, something of a scientist therefore, he had some interest in the truth of faith, for he was eager to see "the empiric stage of superstition" yield to science. "Mind cure is now passing as a religion, a cult, or a creed. It is rapidly assuming that scientific role in which it is known as *psychotherapy*. . . ."[6] Evidently that in which mind cure had faith was not acceptable just because its faith worked. But then some complications arose. Proceeding on to Christian Science, Sadler doubled back. The founders of Christian Science, he said—meaning, presumably, Mrs. Eddy—knew well enough that Christian Science was a psychotherapy. Presumably, they (she) had been

shrewd enough to realize many people would respond more easily
to a theology. In this Sadler was mistaken, for it is clear that Mrs.
Eddy, as well as other mind-cure exponents, "believed in" the philosophy and theology they expounded as the basis for their therapy.
But Sadler's point had greater force with his mistake corrected.
Christian Science was actually a form of "nerve training and mind
discipline," yet, Sadler suggested, these alone would not work
nearly as well as when connected with the "great power of religious suggestion—of supernatural authority and of confidence com-
manding possibility."[7] Mind cure would not work known only as
mind cure; it had to be known as religion.

In no sense an exponent of mind cure, since he did not believe
in mind cure's Truth, Sadler nonetheless was treading in a morass.
Intriguingly enough, he ended with a rather conspicuously free-
floating exhortation that faith—which, he had already said, worked
whether true or false—follow the teachings of Christ, and in *Religion, Healing and Health,* a post-World War II survey of the whole
therapeutic scene, James Van Buskirk, fortified by both medical
and theological degrees himself, approvingly quoted Sadler's last
announcement—in the thirties—that sincere acceptance of the teachings of Christ would eliminate half the afflictions of mankind.[8] Justification for faith in the supposedly orthodox Christian contents
was absorbed into medical pragmatism. Jesus Christ was being re-
discovered as the founder of psychosomatic medicine.

In his erroneous notion that Mrs. Eddy knew she was promoting
simple psychotherapy, Sadler was necessarily, and mistakenly, implying a certain opportunism in the mind-cure movement. A doctor, he did not penetrate to the next question. If it was true that
belief and faith had effects, whether true or false, it was true nevertheless that, to have effects, a belief had, after all, to be believed.
Was it possible to believe and have faith because it was efficacious
to believe and have faith? The man whose authority, more than
that of any other, lay behind the swelling appreciation of "faith-
effects" and a spreading eagerness to exploit them, had not been
so uncomplicated in his pragmatism as his popular caricatures ordinarily implied. "Certain men can be influenced," William James

had said, "while others cannot be influenced, by certain sorts of ideas. . . . In general whether a given idea shall be a live idea depends more on the person into whose mind it is injected than on the idea itself. . . ."[9] Anthropologists and physiologists might explain voodoo death, but no modern penologist proposed to entrust the execution of capital sentences to sorcerers.

The problem Sadler wrestled with unsuccessfully was that he and the followers of mind cure were different sorts of persons. The central question raised by mind cure was not, did it work? Often enough it did. "The plain fact remains that the spread of the movement has been due to practical fruits."[10] James was clear about this. It did not always work, but then, neither did scientific medicine, conventional religion, nor anything else. The central question raised by mind cure was, what were people capable of believing? Were there people so fortunate they could believe what it was helpful and healthy and pleasant to believe just because it was helpful, healthy and pleasant? Was there a society so protective that it sheltered them against the blighting refutations of the reality-principle? Could religion become purely the projection of wish, neither humbling the ego nor requiring action to reform the world?

CHAPTER VIII

POLITICAL SCIENCE

MARK TWAIN, in his famous reflections upon Mrs. Eddy's monetary success, highlighted the social stance of mind cure generally.

> No charities to support. No, nor even to contribute to. One searches in vain the Trust's advertisements and the utterances of its organs for any suggestion that it spends a penny on orphans, widows, discharged prisoners, hospitals, ragged schools, night missions, city missions, libraries, old people's homes, or any other object that appeals to a human being's purse through his heart. I have hunted, hunted, and hunted, by correspondence and otherwise, and have not yet got upon the track of a farthing that the Trust has spent upon any worthy object.[1]

The old man's sharpness of eye—and his human sympathies—had not deserted him. He was substantially right. His observation fitted mind cure at large. By comparison with the old Protestant denominations, the new groups organized nothing for the society around them, penetrated nothing, sponsored nothing—with the exception of a good newspaper. In the family of American churches they were from the first the great non-energizers.

The instinct behind this quiescence was not that of hard sectarians, such as Mennonites and the Amish living their lives apart as "peculiar people." Nor was it that of Mormons, organizing a complete new society for themselves. Nor was it that of Lutherans and other foreign-language churches, long anxious to preserve themselves against an "Americanization" which for them at that time often meant Calvinism if not also liberalism. Nor was it that of premillennialists, awaiting the rise of the next world out of the eschatological ashes of this. The quiescence expressed neither quarrel with society nor godly indifference to it. It expressed no tension with society whatever, whether that of fortresses apart or that of mission crusaders.

It might seem that mind cure's quarrel with medicine was an exception, and yet, this general social stance was perfectly modeled by mind cure's therapy. When might people most safely prefer mental techniques to reasonably reliable medical techniques? When might they most reasonably discount inoculation, professional care and a hygiene assuming the reality of germs and the efficacy of drugs, serums and other *materia medica?* Though the failures of medicine to progress in treating many afflictions were numerous, yet the late nineteenth century was not an epidemic-ridden time. Segregation of some of the sick in hospitals was growing; inoculations were spreading; sewage systems and sanitary engineering generally, advanced; standards of civic and personal cleanliness and material hygiene were common. People choosing to ignore them in favor of mind benefited from the environment these established. Mind cure did not win converts in Naples or Calcutta, or in American slums and countrysides. Outside the United States its one appeal was again to people in a community well advanced in modern hygiene—the ladies of the English upper middle classes. In its very core, in short, mind cure manifested an unavowed social dependency.

As if quiescence of outgoing energy were not enough, mind cure displayed internal quiescence as well. In the folk churches, the liberal churches, even the high churches of nineteenth-century Protestantism, the church had been a social center: "socials," suppers, fairs, bees, bazaars, ladies' aid societies, and eventually the ubiquitous youth groups were standard parts of the secondary gain from religious belonging. Here as elsewhere Mrs. Eddy simply defined more sharply a pattern found throughout mind cure: Christian Science was to have little of this. Neither was Unity or Divine Science or New Thought. Some of the early nineteenth-century eagerness for evangelical experience has been explained by social historians as a thirst of frontier gregariousness unslaked by non-existent theaters, popular reading, secular fraternal groups and the sociability of town life. Some of the busyness of the later churches has been explained as an effort to compete with such entertainments as these spread in the secular world. Neither impulse worked in mind cure.

The most characteristic expression of this internal quiescence appeared in connection with mind-cure philosophy itself. An "expressive" body of concepts, composed on the logic of wish, it generated no schools. Since one could know whatever one wished to know "instantly and continuously," there was little need. "Stop reading many books," Emilie Cady urged[2]; use the "short-cut" to the truth you desire, its full revelation in yourself. Actually, of course, mind cure was above all a religion of many books, but books aimed at psychological, not intellectual, effects. This indifference to education could be compared with the tendencies of the two philosophical movements of which mind cure sometimes seemed a parody. Transcendentalism had often inspired summer schools and naturally found its way into the colleges. As for the great late nineteenth-century wave of philosophical Idealism, championed by men such as William Harris and Josiah Royce, the very heart and soul of its purpose was to mobilize the universities as the mind of the community, and, in fact, as successors to the churches, as its spirit. The benefits of philosophy implied full-scale projects for the restoration of cultural, political and economic community. They implied Reform. In this respect, philosophical Idealism represented an effort to recover the cultural energy the churches themselves were losing. But it had not been the cultural apathy of the churches that had impelled mind cure. And patently, mind cure's indifference to schools manifested no baptistic suspicion of learning smothering the spirit. Mind cure's philosophy did not point beyond itself.

Without pushing too hard, one might wonder whether this dependent passivity was not exhibited in aesthetic realms as well. Nineteenth-century Protestantism was not notable for its style by sight or by sound, let alone by more intimate senses. Did mind cure carry this stylelessness further? Speaking only of church edifices, denominations with colonial roots still housed themselves distinguishably. More recently, liberalizing congregations had begun shopping for a historical ambiance which their theology rejected —usually Gothic. Mind-cure churches, however, tended to blend in prosaically with the civic and commercial buildings, libraries and banks of the middle-class urban landscape. Christian Scientists, with more than ordinary financial resources plus the pretensions of a hard organization, resisted little. If the great edifice in Boston, supplementing the original Mother Church, expressed the pretensions with a rather obvious echo, it was also symptomatic that the Scientists did not hesitate in later years to fault the force of their temple somewhat with the utilitarian plant and offices of their publishing company next door. Aside from Bernard Maybeck's noble building in Berkeley and one or two others, the Scientists and mind cure generally embodied in their local temples an aesthetic instinct similar to their charitable instinct: to assume a secular unity and harmony here and now. In their frequent physical resemblance to banks, mind-cure edifices symbolized a standard middle-class wish about the bank—security. The fact that security had been no more the rationale behind many of the banks of the wildcatting early nineteenth century than behind much religion, or than behind a speculative late nineteenth-century Wall Street, was only to testify that in both—economy and religion—the sense of the significance and excitement of risk was withering. Again, though, mind cure was as much a culmination as a disruption of religious history, as well as an anticipation. In aesthetic affairs as elsewhere the Puritan had willfully organized all experience into a system, and while he had shaped the abundance of materials and experience in his tradition with genuine power, he had had no clear sanction for assimilating new materials and new experiences altogether, inviting new style. By mid-twentieth century, churches that once bought Gothic were to be buying modern—no less passively—in a perfect one-to-one echo of their world, shorn even of the tension contained in historic imitations.

Laissez-faire versus Progressivism

What did mind cure look like politically? In New Thought circles around the turn of the century it was common to distinguish those among the leaders who were "individualistic" from those who were "socialistic," just as it was possible to do in many of the old denominations. Yet mind cure had its political tone. Its distinction did not consist of its stronger link with one or the other of the laissez-faire and social-gospel impulses, but rather in assumptions underlying these differences. In this again, mind cure was anticipating attitudes that were to become apparent in twentieth-century Protestantism more largely, ones in which the landmarks of nineteenth-century political positions dissolved. This underlying mood could be seen in two mind-cure writers with contrasting views—the ex-businessman Henry Wood defending laissez-faire and Ralph Waldo Trine celebrating a semi-socialist Progressivism.

Before proceeding, however, I want to stress that most mind-cure writers gave no thought to politics at all. They were not antipolitical; politicians were not like doctors, to be criticized. But politics was irrelevant. Very occasionally a millennial note echoing popular orthodoxy crept into Mrs. Eddy's evangel: "This material world is even now becoming the arena for conflicting forces."[3] In the breakup of "material beliefs," famine, want, woe, sin, sickness and death "will assume new phases, and their nothingness will finally appear." This thread of apocalyptic had the effect of discounting political efforts to deal with want and woe altogether. For a time, early in the century, B. O. Flower, that editor-crusader for all reforms, opened the columns of his activist-minded *Arena* to thought-reform, but no fusion occurred between New Thought and new action.

Henry Wood, having enjoyed his own personal cure from sick-

ness, devoted his post-business career to propagating the philosophy he credited with his recovery. He wrote not only obvious
mind-cure tracts, but a book on political economy, as well as two
novels, the latter the only such products from the prolific pens of
the movement.

Wood's *The Political Economy of Humanism,* first published in
1901 as an expanded version of an earlier work, *The Political
Economy of Natural Law,* was a tract in the manner of the mid-
century clergymen-economists. What Adam Smith had offered in
the eighteenth century as a more-or-less flexible factual demon-
stration of the absurdities of a managed mercantile economy, the
American clerical economists had frozen into a metaphysics: economics was a moral science, its materials the world of natural law
laid out by divine decree, its task the description and defense of
those laws.

For Wood this meant that any problems there might be in the
new industrial society—and he said that none were as serious as
agitators made out—would be solved inevitably, implacably, completely and correctly by, in effect, All-Mind. Like most laissez-
faire economists, Wood did not trust the Creator on an international scale. Tariffs, though perhaps not wholly justified "from a
purely cosmopolitan standpoint," were justified from the national point of view. Otherwise, natural laws would provide. Wood
explained, for instance, how "the silent and unseen forces of *law*"
had brought low the "French Copper Syndicate"; the problem of
the trusts—that is, insofar as it was a problem—would be met by
a silent and invisible winnowing of good trusts from bad. As for
labor unions: "The combination of labor is proper and legitimate."
Unfortunately, Wood was unable to locate any particular combinations that were proper and legitimate. He was not quite willing to
leave their elimination to the mercies of natural law either. As
for poverty: ". . . Intemperance, vice and crime . . . are the true
causes of nine-tenths of [it]."[4]

There is nothing gained in further summation of the economics
of the book. It was a standard treatise of late laissez-faire—when
the sense of providence had become mechanical, the use of natu-

ral law circular, the knowledge of economic practices a generation out of date, and any feeling for a living culture larger than the machinery of the system lost in a mood of stiff righteousness. What needs summation is Wood's coordination of laissez-faire with mind.

The "Established Order" of natural law stood above and prior to mere experience. "Law will not and cannot bend to human caprice, for its lines are immutable. . . . [It] is a ubiquitous and righteous judge. . . ." This would seem unambiguous: eternal norms reign over all, and error, infelicity and failure follow from ignorance or willful disregard of them. But Wood thereupon tried to solve the grand old puzzle of orthodoxy. Was the law—"unrepealable" as it was—uniformly good? From a "material" point of view it appeared not. "But this directly suggests another question: Is man body or mind?" Puritans, in their attempts to justify the ways of God to man, had not used this distinction. The difference between man's measure of the good and divine good was not equivalent to or correlated with the difference between mind and body. Still, Wood might have pursued such a correlation, but something else was involved. "The outward manifestation is only the shadow of the internal substance. All veritable social science is therefore subjective, or in other words, metaphysical."[5] And from the metaphysical point of view the law was as beneficent as it was universal.

But how was the law to be known then? It could not, after all, be discerned in a study of the outward manifestation, in the economy itself. It had to be discerned in the internal substance, and only then in the economy. Or better: it was to be seen subjectively precisely as one gave up all question that there could be any real conflict between the subjective and objective. Hence, although Wood professed to find evidences of the divinity of law in its "uniformity" and "reliability," which might have seemed to sanction plain rational and empirical inquiry for its study, he proposed subtler methods.

> Intellectual logic is inadequate to the delicate interpretation of Natural Law. . . . The intuitive faculty being keener . . . is however able. . . . Intuition alone is able to put its ear to the

ground and distinguish between discordant, even though faint jars, and concordant vibrations.[6]

Economics was rooted in superconsciousness.

Though there were echoes here of the old Puritan assumption that, in order to know God, one must not be blinded by one's own notion of the good, an idea repeated in harsher fashion in laissez-faire Social Darwinism, Wood was not preaching a philosophy of reconciliation, nor of stoic resignation, nor certainly of contrite and grateful subordination of the demands of self to higher "concordant vibrations." He was proposing rather that the crisis of subordination be avoided. The technique by which one appreciated the "laws" was what he offered in *Mental Photography*. "We must refuse mental standing-room to discord. . . . Think no evil, and have eyes only for the good."[7] Laissez-faire was, in effect, a repression of politics, analogous to the repression of negative thoughts and ideas of sickness. Wood's discussion of health in *Mental Photography* was a rather delightful exhibition of mind cure when it did try to deal with the relations between inner and outer, ideas and reality, individual and society:

> It is better to study health than abnormity [sic], because all thought-pictures press for outward expression. To advertise and emphasize disease by dividing, subdividing and multiplying its phenomena, and by giving it formidable and scientific [?] names, is the mistake of the ages. . . . It is a well-known fact that medical students are often subject to attacks of the special diseases which they are studying.[8]

Wood was almost right; it was a well-known fact that medical students were often subject to thinking they had the disease they were studying. Then they generally found out they were mistaken. This notion that the researcher was somehow himself to blame for what he studied was analogous to the moral of Wood's political economy. Men must not doubt that there is a natural law, or that it works beneficently. But did their thinking determine the fact? Did the medical student truly create disease? If not, where did it really originate? At one point Wood was bound to argue that the imagination was decisive:

The kingdom over which human thought is the rightful sovereign is primarily subjective; but through its objective relations its reign is projected outward. Being a positive active force, it shapes and controls matter, which is only passive material, powerless and inert.[9]

Thought determines disease—and the economy. But he had to argue the opposite as well:

The highest and purest human perception is that which sees no evil and understands that all *things*, real entities (for subjective conditions are of our own making), are made by Good, in good and for good. This is self-evident, for the manifestation of God must be universal, else how could He be omnipresent. Subjective thought and experience is [sic] the only lens through which evil can be beheld.[10]

The subjective reigns, therefore it can decide whether evil shall exist; but on the other hand, the subjective should let things reign, for they are made by God in good and for good.

Adam Smith had lent laissez-faire a simple secular sanction: it increased trade, it increased wealth. Protestant laissez-faire added a moral gloss: it tested character. With Wood it became divine, calling for that absolute identification in which the subjective merged itself into the objective. That it was this wish for identification, for a fusion of subjective and objective, a harmony between self and society that impelled his logic, his typically heretical mind-cure autosuggestions showed:

I hold only the perfect, and affirm nothing less. I also claim entire supremacy over intellect and memory. . . . I *create* a harmonious environment. . . . God created all things good, and . . . I will do the same. . . . I am love, and radiate it everywhere. . . . I am spirit, I rule. . . . I am perfect. . . .[11]

Laissez-faire psychology paralleled the psychology of health; rejecting the state as well as medicine, the individual absorbed into himself an image of the whole and called it real.

Trine's land beyond politics

Ralph Waldo Trine's *In Tune with the Infinite,* proving to be a best-seller, inspired Trine to a small flood of books and tracts over succeeding decades. One of these was *The Land of Living Men,* a book "on the conditions that exist among us," published in 1910. If fitted neatly into the Progressive mood—a political book beyond question, almost certainly the most political book ever spawned by mind cure.

Trine wanted reform. He asked for a "people's government" and a "people's society," more specifically, public ownership and control of all public utilities. He praised "the splendid companies of men . . . in our labor unions and Brotherhoods and Federations."[12] An appealing dithyramb, the small volume actually breathed a more generous spirit than many Progressive documents, one such as another Ralph Waldo might have written in the times, since the Progressives could have been thought to unite both the better principles and the better men, as the Jacksonians, Emerson had lamented, had not. Occasionally, as when evoking a future labor party, a vision wonderfully supported by quotation from Whitman, Trine went far indeed. And at least once he issued a dictum that could have fitted into the harsh political realism of Reinhold Niebuhr's epochal *Moral Man and Immoral Society* twenty-two years later: "It has been the history of labor that what it has gained for itself—and it has gained much—it has gained entirely through its own efforts."[13]

On the whole, though, Trine spoke for moderate, not radical, strategy, and for mixed ends. The basic means were Initiative and Referendum, Direct Nominations and Recall—the purified democracy of earlier Progressivism. In effect he was invoking tradition against the novelties of corporate capitalism, and he assumed, as a large wing of the Progressives assumed, that the tradition had a natural majority. The tradition was one of an approximate cheerful equality, without speculative and empire-building urges. Trine displayed no animus against industrialization as such, but his images tended to be drawn from an older world:

It is the laborer with his vine-clad cottage, and sufficient of those things that make for peace and happiness and content in the life of the normal human being, it is a uniformly prosperous common people, that constitutes the really great nation, and not a few castles with their hordes of hirelings about them.[14]

Still, it was easy to take castles and hirelings as symbols for mansions and slums and grant Trine's contemporaneousness. The important thing was the quality of the reformed order Trine yearned toward—and back to.

The aim of his idealism was not to save freedom of opportunity in the face of monopoly and bureaucracy. It was not to save liberal individualism. It was not to save men for their particular purposes, or to save them from authority, for Trine yearned for a self-contained whole. In the land of living men, we are

. . . to open ourselves, our minds and hearts, so that a continually increasing degree of the God life can manifest itself to and through us . . . to understand more and more and come into a continually greater harmony with, the laws under which we live and which permeate and rule in the universe with an unchangeable precision. It is through . . . living out of harmony with the laws under which it is decreed we must live, that inharmony and evil with its [sic] consequent pain and suffering and despair enters [sic] into our lives. There are those who have lived so fully in the realization of their essential oneness with the Divine Life, that their lives here have been almost a continual song of peace and thanksgiving.[15]

This was a land beyond politics. For Trine, politics had no permanent and fundamental existence, grounded in the permanent multifariousness of purposes among men; its function was to eliminate the necessity for politics. The ideal was the fusion of self and society, subjective and objective, personal and economic, in a grand harmony with law rightly understood, as with Wood. In Wood the stress lay more upon mind reaching out to englobe the environment as good, in Trine upon the environment absorbing mind and self in good, but this was one of those contrasts in which opposites melted into each other. Progressivism and laissez-faire could be undergirded by the same wish. In both, politics could be dissolved in a vision of the dissolution of that upon which politics rested—the fact of tensions, the fact of shifts and conflicts of interest to be negotiated, the fact of politics aimed not at a final harmony but at averting those un-negotiated conflicts that shredded community. The difference between the two men was Trine's sense that to place the entire burden upon mind, without touching environment, was schizophrenic. Of course, this sense was totally dependent upon the fact that reform did seem to be in the air. We shall see Trine later, under another fascination, once reform had evaporated.

Moreover, for Wood and Trine alike the significant relationships in the economy and society were not between men, that is, they were not personal, whether in conflict or cooperation. They were between men and the pattern of all things, the laws, the infinite, in more-or-less precise echo of mind-cure philosophy. Here again mind cure parodied ancient tradition, for such divine sociology came down to them from the Puritans and before them from the medieval hierarchies. But of course it manifested no "conservative" harboring of tradition, for like its theology, mind cure's sociology projected a wish about the present, namely, that the present allow itself to be felt exclusively in terms of wish itself—unpolitically. The emergence of modern politics from divine sociology had expressed the emergence of new human viewpoints, expectations and self-confidence; politics was man's confidence in himself. The subsidence of politics reflected exhaustion of this morale.

CHAPTER IX

IMPERSONAL PERSONS

WHAT KIND of person would yield up consciousness to dependence upon the superconscious? Evidently one was the sort of person who yielded up imagination to society as a completed harmonic thing, where neither innovation nor politics would be required. But one can ask again: what sort of person was this? Mind cure's doctrine of personality carries us further. The gist of that doctrine was simple: mind cure rejected personality.

The rejection presumably was rooted in metaphysical logic. God—Divine Mind—was impersonal. Since, "in Science, man is the manifest reflection of God, perfect and immortal mind," the logic was impeccable. Mrs. Eddy did allow that one could define "person" as "infinite spirit" if one wished, and in that case God was personal and so man too. But quite reasonably she found this unsatisfactory.

Person is formed after the manner of mortal man, so far as he can conceive of personality. Limitless personality is inconceivable. His person and perfection are neither self-created, nor discerned through imperfection; and of God as a person, human reason, imagination, and revelation give us no knowledge.[1]

In later mind cure the matter was sometimes dealt with by fiat, as by Ernest Holmes in 1938: "God, or Spirit, is Supreme, Infinite, Limitless Personality."[2] But by then the dangers lurking in the issue had been more fully met. This was the danger of losing the guarantee of absolute security and supply. How could a personal God, a too humanistic image of God, be counted on for certain? One way or another the precariousnesss of existence as a person had to be averted.

What Henry Wood meant by personality was reasonably clear: desires, needs, peculiar wants, a unique inwardness that could not be counted on to fit in with the natural "laws" ruling the world. For Wood, bearing a heavy load of orthodoxy, "personality" threatened order. It suggested fissures, splits, divisions and precariousness within the self—the mere chaos of impulses and desires that was sin—which would prevent any fusion of subjective and objective.[3] In her *Science of Success* (1914), Julia Seton warned of the same thing. "Personality is an unstable thing, and can change from year to year. . . ." It was but the outer man, and our aim must be to bring it under direction: ". . . Our personality will naturally put on a different expression from the individuality when . . . we make our consciousness dependent on external things, instead of controlling and directing all external conditions by the law of life within."[4]

This confronted real issues, for Mrs. Seton sensed a shift in the times as Wood, writing twenty years earlier, had not. She sensed that "character" was no longer the determining power it had been; it was beginning to find its society given it as more or less a system, organized and firm, and this did threaten a split in the self, between inner and outer, private and public, with the outer, "personality," serving, as she put it, as "our introduction to the world," as "our press agent." This suggested the Greek root *persona*, the mask, and masks suggested fission, ambiguity, hypocrisy, disintegration.

This suspicion of personality was no recoil of old inner-directedness from incipient other-direction. It was not a defense of "character" in the old moralistic sense, with all that "character" implied of self-reliance and a more-or-less permanent organization of the self around purpose and will. The rejection of personality was rejection of reliance upon the self in favor of reliance upon the super-self. Walter Devoe, leader of an "Eloist" Ministry in Brookline, Massachusetts, rendered this distinctly in his book of 1904, *Healing Currents from the Battery of Life:*

> The conscious and subconscious degrees of mind constitute the personality, but the soul is the real individual. . . . The conscious and subconscious degrees of man's mind are evolutions from matter; they are highly refined matter, or negative and undeveloped mind. The nature of God is eternal and omnipotent power, the source of all life and being. The soul of man is from above the mortal sphere of mind; it is an individualization of deific consciousness and partakes of the power of Deity; it is the image and likeness of God in man.[5]

"Individuality" instead of "personality"

The mind-cure alternative to "personality" was "individuality," stressed by Unity and Christian Science, by Divine Science and New Thought, and by free-lance prophets alike. Individuality did not mean a center of integration in the individual. It meant reliance upon, indeed identity with, Divine Mind as the only integrating power. It did not mean life defined by the vicissitudes, perils and promises of a unique existence. It meant sharing in a universal essence. It did not mean the unfolding of individual capacities. It meant enjoyment of the capacities of the One. It did not mean the primacy of inner impulse, decision and drama celebrated by William James. It meant alignment with the universal consciousness. No individual was an individual by being unlike other individuals. No one was an individual because of experiences he alone had had. No one was an individual by occupying one unique point in the total organism of being.

The access to the subconscious encouraged by James amounted to an exploration of inner resources all-too-easily suppressed by the overly tight organization of character. But mind cure was by no means ready to "let go" of control. Deriving from egos oppressed by weakness, not strength, it sought control more definitive, more final. As an "individualization" of Divine Mind, one had what one could not have as a mere person:

> When man links his will with the principle of divine force he has superior executive capacity. He swiftly brings forth faculties that, under the slow action of human personality, would take ages to develop. . . . Self-confidence is a virtue when founded on the Truth of Being, but when it rises from the personal consciousness it keeps man from his dominion.[6]

Man's action shall be God's action; his confidence in self shall be perfect because it is not confidence in himself.

But was not God Father-Mother? How then could He be impersonal? This was no inconsistency: Father-Mother was impersonal. The child knows his parents as power, not as Will; he has no notion of their personal, mysterious, arbitrary energy. God's love was not like human love; mind cure rejected the sense of continuity between the two cultivated in liberal religion. Charles Fillmore explained:

> Divine love and human love should not be confounded, because one is as broad as the universe and is always governed by undeviating laws, while the other is fickle, selfish and lawless.[7]

Mind-cure ideas about the life of the family and the rearing of children implemented this outlook. They were far from anticipating the "permissive" theories beginning to take hold in liberal congregations. On the eccentric peripheries of the movement, the repressed origins of the movement kept coming back, in the form of advice for training children by hypnotism and suggestion while they were asleep, or, indeed, still in the womb.

The problem of sex

The mood underlying all other aspects of mind cure might be thought summed up in its attitude toward sex. Given its clientele, sex was, of course, critical for mind cure. If it was a realm ignored by Dr. Beard in his analysis of neurasthenia (although he arrived at it later), then one might argue that mind cure did know more than the doctors.

In 1919 Horatio Dresser had still another complaint to make of the first fifty years of New Thought: it had not developed the early insights of Warren Evans, drawn from Swedenborg, into the intimate association of sexual love with "the inmost life of the spirit," insights which, Dresser said, anticipated and were superior to Freud's.[8] Dresser was perfectly justified in lamenting the failure of sexual imagination to flourish. The eighteen-nineties had seen the beginning of another wave of ideology about sex and women, and mind cure had been part of the ferment. But the key to most revolutions is not so much the freedom they demand as the new limits upon freedom they inspire, and the sexual teachings of mind cure were attempts at limitation.

Mrs. Eddy, in her early writings, disclosed utopian tendencies, in hinting that parthenogenesis would eventually replace physical sexual union. These and other anticipations were subdued in later editions of *Science and Health*—"I discredit the belief that agamo-genesis applies to the human species . . ."—but never wholly sponged away. Modern editions of her scripture continued to teach that "Until it is learned that God is the Father of all, marriage will continue. . . . Spirit will ultimately claim its own—all that really is—and the voices of physical sense will be forever hushed." Mean-while, sexual intercourse, that is, the "material conditions" for prop-agation, "can only be permitted for the purpose of generating."[9]

Mrs. Eddy's chapter on marriage included sharp attacks, exactly in the manner of early women's rights reformers, on civil laws dis-criminating between the sexes. The morale here was that of a special sort of feminism: sexual equality without sexuality.

Charles Fillmore taught to the same effect:

Love is in the world in a diluted form as affection between husband and wife, parents and children, friend and friend, but it can be made manifest in its original strength and purity by each man and woman going to the fountain head, and letting its mighty currents stream forth. Sex lust has diverted the vital forces in the body away from the love center, the *solar plexus*, and it is almost dormant in many men. When a pure-minded woman sends forth her desire for love such men interpret it sexually and are excited to lust. Love is disappointed, and loathing of the ignorant animal eventually follows. *Love is not sex lust*.[10]

Fillmore was not only distinguishing "sex lust" from "sexuality."

So long as your eyes see sex and the indulgence thereof on any of its planes, you are not pure. You must become mentally so translucent that you see men and women as sexless beings— which they are in the spiritual consciousness.[11]

One notes without surprise that, according to Fillmore's curious allegorization of the twelve disciples to parts of the body, the "generative functions" were represented—inevitably—by Judas.

As those exceptions proving the rule, betraying the ferment which helped impel mind cure in the first place, and which it struggled to contain and deny, one notes instances where early mind cure did fuse with a larger sense of freedom. In 1897, in *Idols Dethroned and Dominion over the Animal Kingdom*, Flora Parris Howard, a healer practicing "by the power of the Spoken Word" in Los Angeles, discussed "The Sex Question" in one chapter of her little book, and spoke for "woman's liberation," if not with utter frankness, at least in a manner at odds with that of Mrs. Eddy and Fillmore. Mary C. Ferriter, at the Universal School of Applied Religion and Psychology in Berkeley, explicitly attacked the sexual teachings of Unity, New Thought and Christian Science in her mind-cure tract of 1923, *Truth of Life, Love, Liberty*. Exceptions, these help remind us of the reality of the issue. But the strictest dealing was simply to maintain silence. Females by the scores in cities across the land wrote their essays, poems, tracts and books celebrating a freedom plainly feminist in its promptings, without the flicker of a suggestion that the bodies they wished to heal and the minds they wanted to perfect harbored those impulses of human love that, in their variety, included sexuality. Love was only divine. Like germs, sex did not really exist. The male authors of mind cure were—if that is conceivable—even more "spiritual."

For even the simplest sort of personal relationships, Annie Payson Call had prescribed "distant courtesy" as prophylaxis against
nerves. At a distance one could not be touched, therefore one could
not be troubled.

"Mind your own business after you know what it is," Mrs.
Seton advised. "No matter what anyone else does or does not, it
cannot affect us unless we think it can, and divert our power of
creation and attraction by this thinking."[12] Such distance was obviously a flight, and it is well to appreciate why. The deprecation
of human love was in no way an echo of old orthodox calls for
repentance over the selfishness of allowing one's own feelings to
become one's own center. A flight from feelings in themselves,
above all a flight from dependence upon other people's feelings
into a higher security, the plainest reason for such a flight was that
one could not trust one's own strength to respond. "I have no necessity for controlling people," Fillmore declared. "Events and people
are controlled by divine love."[13] The wish to be impersonal flourished in a prior weakness.

CHAPTER X

MIND CURE AS PATHOS

It was the genius of mind cure to discover how the weak might feel strong while remaining weak. They could get sick, then heal themselves. Becoming healthy became in itself an end, its own world and testimony to the nature of the world. Mind cure's passivity with respect to charity, reform and style, repeated in its psychology, followed by necessity if health was to constitute just this end-in-itself, and not, as ordinarily, simply a condition allowing pursuit of ends and life generally. This met the terms of that paradoxical situation analyzed by George Beard, that those who suffered from the most civilized of all worlds were the most civilized. It met the terms of the symptomatic people, those unhappy middle-class, often middle-aged ladies whose world was complete, and gave them nothing to do. They were powerless to change it, not so much because they were prevented by various outer forces as because it was their world, complete by their own reckoning. What mind cure offered by way of action was precious because it was action, and at the same time action not touching the world. Feelings of strength were induced that never had to be tested against other strength. It was strength that did not have to overcome dependency. There was nothing strange in the fact that these equa-

tions of strength and dependency, health and passivity were bought
at the price of withdrawal from consciousness, self and impulse.
Whatever price was paid was perhaps less than the price paid for
a futile maintenance of self through projects of nervousness and
getting sick. Dependency and passivity allowed the self to be
diffused, in religious vocabulary given over to Divine Mind, and
in its social correlates given over to a society in which charity, reform, education and imagination were no longer necessary.

> Personally [Mark Twain said], I have not known a Scientist
> who did not seem serene, contented, unharassed. I have not
> found an outsider whose observation of Scientists furnished
> him a view that differed from my own. Buoyant spirits, comfort
> of mind, freedom from care—these happinesses we all have, at
> intervals; but in the space between, dear me, the black hours!
> They have put a curse upon the life of every human being I
> have ever known, young or old. I concede not a single excep-
> tion. Unless it might be those Scientists just referred to.[1]

This was the sort of testimony offered by mind cure itself for its
faith. Yet Mark Twain was not really envious, and it is not hard
to see why. Serenity might well be possible when one found no
causes to inspire care. But perhaps causes should not inspire care.
Even so, it was well to be a self that could care in the first place.

In its imagination of a time beyond troubles, of experience
undivided against itself, of sufficiency unhumiliated by purpose,
mind cure now and then effloresced into those fantasies of the world
as love, beyond revenge, beyond hysteria, upon which all lesser
realisms even in the West have fed for whatever they have achieved
of true happiness. Charles Fillmore saw them fulfilled:

> When men understand each other, love increases. This is true
> not only between men, but between men and the animal, and
> even the vegetable worlds. In Yellowstone Park, where protec-
> tion of the animals has been commanded by our government,
> grizzly bears come to the house doors and eat scraps from the
> table, and wild animals of all kinds are tame and friendly.[2]

One recalls Elias Hicks's "The Peaceable Kingdom," a painting that in its gently unembarrassed Quaker Utopianism reminds us that there are media for expressing unhindered love despite the hampers of even so pervasive a social inhibition as language itself. Americans have not lacked such unchecked love, as perhaps the history of the love-affair between the bears and the tourists in Yellowstone, however punctuated by disillusion, might witness. Could one date the spread of a popular yearning for a world tame and friendly from the act of Congress in 1872 establishing that the Wyoming wilderness was really a park—not quite the year of the first edition of *Science and Health?* Closed against aggressive, masterful, obsessive, male, Protestant transformations, the "wilderness" was not in fact meaningful just as excitation of Will, but a manifestation in its untouched innocence of the self-enjoying exuberance of All.

Regarded from one certain vantage-point, mind cure was deeply revelatory of the constricting obsessions from which, like the butterfly from its claustrophic case, it sought to free itself. From an asceticism that had no idea what it was denying itself for, it extricated its wish for "plenty." Beyond megalomaniac ideologies of self-help, self-sufficiency and self-made manhood, it openly projected dependency. From the tunnel-vision of a straining male world of ego, it reached out for what was freely and generously available. Against mechanical specialized physiologies and psychologies and sciences, it posed its wish for wholeness. Beyond anthropomorphic limitations of God to the dimensions of a person, it discerned dimensions upon which personhood itself depended. And in its choice of "health" as its first focus, it dignified sickness as an expression, not of failure, but of the unconscious courage of all existence to abide in life, not against it, to love it, not master it, for sickness self-induced registered the wish for greater harmony, not greater power.

If one takes at all seriously the developing present-day analysis of the fallacies of Western ego and will concepts, of bodyless reason and ascetic technology, then one can only look back upon mind cure as a touching premonitory fluttering of liberation. That, against

the efficiency and violence of the West, a female-oriented unconscious should protest is hardly surprising.

Miracle, however, remains miracle—the invasion of the perfectly
arbitrary and uncontained. Mind cure was contained by its rejected
origins. In its post-ascetic visions of Supply its desires remained
submissive. In its dependency, it projected upon that, on which it
was dependent, the same closed self-sufficiency it dared not claim
for itself. And in its triumph over sickness it gained a health that
had no ends. For survival, the weak propitiate; in the case of mind
cure, that which it propitiated was its superconsciousness, and this
meant just one thing—its sense of American society as a completed
and self-sufficient world.

Writing on "The Influence of Democracy on the Action of Intellect
in the United States," Alexis de Tocqueville had forecast something
like this conclusion. What philosophy was "most fitted to seduce
the human mind" in a democracy? Pantheism. Mind cure came as
close to pantheism as it is possible to come without making philosophy useless as a social ideology. Pantheism became attractive, De
Tocqueville argued, when "each individual man becomes more like
all the rest, more weak and insignificant. . . ." This induced a habit
of "overlooking individuals, to think only of their kind," which in
turn induced men to consider "that all things material and imma-
terial, visible and invisible, which the world contains are . . . only
as the several parts of an immense Being, who alone remains eternal
amidst the continual change and ceaseless transformation of all that
constitutes him. . . ." Such a conception, "although it destroys the
individuality of man, or rather because it destroys that individuality,
will have secret charms. . . ."[3]

De Tocqueville's insight was to see that this "immense Being"
would be American society itself. The charm of pantheistic idoliza-
tion of the society was that it got rid of an individuality that was
only a source of anxiety, since it was weak and insignificant. Mind
cure replaced this individuality (equivalent in its own vocabulary
to "personality") with a sense of being an "individualization" of
God.

The spread of basic mind-cure imagination—whether so-called or not, whether religious or not—depended upon the spread of conditions evoking its reflexive and passive, rather than its spontaneous and Utopian, tendencies. Suppose the multiplication of environmental "homes," within the confines of which, no matter how narrow, individuals might feel the security as well as the superintendence of Father-Mother-Supply? The rise of bureaucratic corporations with their rather rapid absorption of techniques for psychological seduction was already under way. The emergence of the giant consumers' bazaar impended, a salesman-patrolled enclosure the abundance of whose objective goods absorbed subjective energy. Private wish was tamed in the glare of advertised longings. With the spread of the suburb, the less-than-city—"sub" urb—a society less than whole became the ideal for more and more, in more-or-less deliberate withdrawal from spontaneous variety in favor of prescribed, preformed, self-containment in superconsciousness.

As shifts in the decisive stages of life, these developments invited the feminization of American life. Men would become more like mind-cured, late-nineteenth-century women, creatures of pure wish, without power, without politics, their egos individualizations of an omnipresent and omnipotent All, a manufactured way of life. In the popular ideology of nineteenth-century male life, there had been no "way." Any "way" remained to be blazed. Of course, many nineteenth-century Americans, including very many women, had been made extremely anxious by this future-drunken, past-dissolving energy. And, as William Taylor has shown in *Cavalier and Yankee*, many of them tended to resolve their anxieties in fantasies romanticizing—slave society.[4] The immense irony of mind cure was that, yearning to put off the constricting asceticisms of "character" and "will," it prefigured an ideology by which both men and women surrendered themselves to a new romantic captivity—the "way" of prosperity. As will be shown in the section to follow, efforts would be made to induce in men the autohypnotic persuasion that they still amounted to self-made men, but these very efforts were destined to draw them deeper into self-surrender.

PART TWO

Peace in the System: Sociology as Psychology

CHAPTER XI

THE HOUSE THAT TITANS BUILT

To FALL BACK out of the cloudy and somewhat humid world of mind cure into the more bracing realms of business is certainly to re-enter the world of men.

That business life in the late nineteenth century was unusually unrestricted and hardy there seems little reason to doubt. That it offered an unusual arena for the trying and testing of character seems certain also; rarely in our national life has quite so much exhortation toward the cultivation of that dimension, "character," been displayed. By all odds the chief model for character was that of the Protestant ethic in all its sober and rather grim and intense energy.

The Protestant ethic, supplementing the standard "religious" virtues of faith, hope, charity, etc., with the "secular" virtues of industry, thrift, honesty, practicality, rationality and the like, was not a direct emanation from Protestant theology. Luther was not an ascetic, emotionally drilled man. Of course, once again one must beware the hazards of associating what men think about their God and what they think about themselves. In the case of the mind-cure groups I have proceeded on the basis of their own explicit avowal: men are "individualizations" of God. But ordinarily, theology and psychology have not abided in such oneness.[1]

In Anglo-Saxon Protestant history there is evidence of considerable force that the relation has been that of dialectic rather than that of identity. In the first place, with Luther and Calvin Protestants exalted the God of Will, absolute Sovereign, never caught, contained and organized in any system, not even a religious system. At this point, man was what God was not, utterly dependent, his relation to God that of faith and faith alone. In the stage following, Protestants undertook what appeared perfectly consistent with the faith—to do God's will. This contained the seeds of ultimate reversal, for the effective meaning of such an effort was an attempt to be like God, logically implying a succeeding stage. Men who were beings of will could not conceive of themselves as beings of no will; hence they could not conceive of a God of absolute will. They began to revise their ideas of God. God had to be rethought to accord with their ideas of themselves. Thereby, it became progressively easier to be like God.

The logical culmination of this process remained dialectical: men who have become like God do not really need God. They need not deny His existence, they can simply cease imaginative reliance upon Him for much of importance. The knowledge is usually scanted that in the United States a number of remarkable men arrived exactly at this position by the last decades of the nineteenth century. In many ways Benjamin Franklin had anticipated them, but as in so much else, here too Franklin had been an avant-garde of one. In the late nineteenth century, men such as Chauncey Wright, Oliver Wendell Holmes, Jr., Charles Eliot Norton and William James were practical agnostics—intellectuals all, and all, notably, in the New England Puritan mainstream of culture. Here it was, if anywhere, that the psychology of energetic individualism really flowered into achievements of pioneering imagination.

The anxious businessman

Among businessmen things were quite otherwise. The dialectic never reached its climactic reversal. True, the most articulate of the titans, Andrew Carnegie, was agnostic, as was William Graham Sumner, the professor-preacher of self-sufficient Social Darwinistic competition. But the businessmen as a whole did not radiate titanism. They radiated anxiety. Studying late nineteenth-century business men, in *Dream and Thought in the Business Community, 1860–1900,* their most sensitive analyst, Edward Kirkland, found not ebullient, enthusiastic Faustians but men harassed in mind and spirit, full of care, groaning under the burdens. These men were haunted and frightened, and angered by specters of opposition and stupidity, inertia and chaos on every side.[2] To themselves they seemed locked in a mighty struggle for, in the final reckoning, not freedom, but order and security.

By 1900 and shortly thereafter, concretely in the form of the astonishingly rapid series of corporate consolidations, their anxieties were appeased. Wringing monopolistic security out of the confusions of the early days in oil, iron, steel, railroading, milling, mining, manufacturing, merchandising and, of course, with J. P. Morgan, banking, they achieved a seventh day of rest, having wrought a cosmos.

But why had they built this cosmos? What purpose was it to serve? Fifty years later the purpose was to seem obvious: abundance and national defense. But neither of these had filled the minds of the master-builders. In late nineteenth-century business circles, and political circles too, the economic theories of a Simon Patton, visualizing industry from the side of consumption as well as of production, went neglected. A John Bates Clark might gild the argument for laissez-faire with promises of a rising standard of living for all, but such ideas then simply seemed one more threat to the job of establishing industrial discipline. Here and there a new-model boss might anticipate a later appeal, such as the businessman-politician Mark Hanna with his "full dinner pail" campaign. But in business ideology, warnings against the spiritual corruptions attendant upon higher wages, shorter hours, greater leisure and abundance, continued to echo, from Chambers of Commerce and the National Association of Manufacturers, on into the twenties, in secular declension from the original Protestant ethic.

As for national defense, in 1900 what was heard of was imperialism, which was not what had been intended, and was not in the first place a businessman's idea anyway.

The fact was, the men who had built the great new system had created not only cosmos but crisis. Like artists, they had simply done what it was in their art to do and that was the sum of it. Wherewith, the sons of men whose basic time-space had been the future found themselves surrounded by the immense structures of a past. What had been still in 1860 a myriad of local centers of trade, production, finance and communication had by 1900 become the skeleton of one economy, national in scale, standardized throughout. By 1920 its modern communication network, its neural system, was in place, linking ever more intimately every office, every town, home, heart. A "system," one system, embraced more and more with its power to convert every man into a function and a part. The "man-machine" complex became the model for the economy at large. How could the sons be the men their fathers had been?

The pathos of the Protestant ethic

Hardly had the crisis defined itself before the German sociologist-prophet Max Weber wrote what has remained probably the most penetrating summary of this pathos of the Protestant ethic:

> The Puritan wanted to work in a calling; we are forced to do so. For when asceticism was carried out of the monastic cells . . . it did its part of building the tremendous cosmos of the modern economic order. This order is now bound to the technical and economic conditions of machine production which today determine the lives of all the individuals who are born into the mechanism . . . with irresistible power.

Piling up his rhetoric in implicit parody of the old Calvinist vocabulary dwelling upon God's rule—"forced," "bound," "determined," "irresistible"—Weber concluded:

> In Baxter's view the care for external goods should lie on the shoulders of the saint like a light cloak, which can be thrown

aside at any moment. But fate decreed that the cloak should become an iron cage.[3]

It is entirely possible that the history Weber here distilled was but a particular case of a general human tendency. One who thought so was Ralph Waldo Emerson, certainly a man who exalted process over order, creation over the products of creation. "Every spirit makes its house," Emerson observed, "but afterwards the house confines the spirit."[4] An unhappy dialectic, yet the logic Emerson noted implied one route of escape. Since the house had been built by spirit, what would be more natural than to claim that the house was spiritual? Living in the house spirit built would be to live by spirit. Iron cage could be construed as heavenly mansion. Freedom could be won by an adjustment in thinking.

But even should it be agreed that human, as distinguished from divine, creativity ends in self-confinement, it is well to recall that historians can never argue that any particular case of such contradiction was absolute. In the United States, the first prophet of a great industrial and commercial future, the non-Puritan, semi-agnostic Alexander Hamilton had been quite explicit and self-conscious in formulating the purpose which industrial growth and organization was to serve. After him, so too had been such men as John Quincy Adams and the anti-Jacksonian political economist Richard Hildreth. For these men the industrial system was to have been a utility, not a cosmos, a form of policy, not an exercise in psychological self-expression. But in the United States industrialization did not follow the lead of this sort of Federalist-Whig planned state capitalism. From the time of the Jacksonians, it proceeded much more as the emanation of the kind of hyper-intense, obsessed psychology analyzed as early as 1831 by De Tocqueville as a function of democratic equality, and idealized in terms of the religious ethic. The economy became a realm of search for signs, proofs, confirmations.

In the standard mid- and late nineteenth-century ideology of success we have the purest testimony to the psychology of self-entrapment.[5] One trait above all others counted, without which all others failed. This trait was "perseverance." Indefatigable industry, "plodding" persistence, repeated effort, unremitting labor, dogged resolution—Samuel Smiles's famous *Self-Help* (1860) demanded these over and over, and American exhorters echoed the Englishman faithfully, including the somewhat atypically picaresque Horatio Alger. The echo of *Pilgrim's Progress,* with Christian's journey cutting through even the very hearts of wife and children, could hardly have been more perfect. Perseverance was the formula for self-sufficiency, self-enclosure, self-containment. One never recalculated goals. One was already set, pre-programmed to press on, endlessly.

The significance of this stress upon perseverance become plainer as it was linked with a deprecation of "talent." "Quickness of parts," Smiles warned, could easily be a handicap. It might lure young men into thinking doggedness unnecessary. Franklin had catered to this notion, declaring that anyone could imitate him, since he, too, had been just average. Franklin knew better, but later writers —William Makepeace Thayer and Russell Conwell, Henry Ward Beecher and Horatio Alger, even the professors Mark Hopkins and Noah Porter—perpetuated the theme in earnest. Talent distorted equations between efforts and rewards. Protean and innovative, talent disrupted settled channels for hard and methodical work. Talent implied that men could never finally "make" themselves, grasp themselves, complete themselves. Talent implied variety. It was better to persevere, to press on, to keep on doing what one had done before. But the principle of perseveringly pressing on offered no escape from the iron cage.

The fears of universal freedom

That the United States had generated a crisis in its affairs was widely recognized by 1900. For the next fifteen years the national life was to be dominated by efforts to meet it, efforts loosely if fairly gathered under the label Progressivism. The essential question was, would the crisis be seen in terms technological and organizational, or psychological and intellectual, indeed, even "spiritual" and "religious" in a sense far deeper than attempts to "apply" religious morals in business? For perspective, it is fascinating to recall that the notion of a specifically Protestant incompetence in industrial society had been raised, not once but twice, and with melodramatic force, fifty years before.

George Fitzhugh, son of a tattered Virginia tidewater, is conveniently classified as one of the most resourceful apologists for Southern slavery. Actually, Fitzhugh said much less about the South than he did about the North. Free society won't work: that was the heart of his defense of slavery. His polemic drew on a social psychology of considerable sophistication for its day, for all its roots in Aristotle and previous use by De Tocqueville. At a time when progress still seemed to consist in men's continuing liberation from old authority, Fitzhugh sensed that the loss of social tradition might cost much. "What disturbs and disarranges society, impairs the happiness and well-being of its members." To the "ultra-liberals" of the North, committed to "no private property, no church, no law, no government—to free love, free lands, free women, and free churches . . . ," he declaimed that a ". . . world of universal liberty was a world of universal selfishness, discord, competition, rivalry, and war of the wits." Where "individual sovereignty" took precedence, society could only crumble.[6]

Fitzhugh hoped to convert the "ultra-liberals." For they, apologists for total liberty, and he, defender of slavery, were agreed on one thing. He delighted in quoting them, page after page, as they attacked the "Manchester system," the "Adam Smith philosophy," the "value principle," which was to say, "individualistic," laissez-faire competitive capitalism. They were quite right, Fitzhugh applauded. Only their cure was wrong. Northern "free" economy was really a form of slavery in which the slave masters were excused from having to care for their "free" workers. Northern free economy was irresponsible.

Undefeated in mind by military defeat, Fitzhugh explained in 1867 that the grand task of the age was to "roll back the reformation on its political phases."[7] He had already insisted the Reformation had been wrong on its psychological side, "the right of private judgment." Protestantism meant simply anarchy in the first place, leading toward the repression of the weak by the strong. Fitzhugh knew well enough that the "Adam Smith" men, the "laissez-faire" industrialists, were not "universal liberty" men at all. He predicted that, facing the spreading disintegration of community and security, they would impose some kind of new feudalism of their own. All this, out of the original Protestant principle of the priesthood of all believers!

The hard-scrabble, poverty-bred Orestes Brownson was one of those very "ultras" with whom Fitzhugh had such fun. In his salad days Brownson threw himself into one romance of universal liberty after another. Determined to translate Protestantism into that total social freedom and democracy he knew it meant, he, too, came to launch attacks upon that Northern business economy Fitzhugh scorned. Finding true Protestantism in the spirit of the workers, Brownson went further, in meeting the issues Fitzhugh posed, than any other of the ultra reformers. He made it clear, for instance, that Emerson, in failing to appreciate what transcendentalism meant in social and economic terms, had gone only halfway with his principles.

Brownson never surrendered on his goal—a free society. But the realities of American political life seemed to teach the need for recalculating means. The election of 1840, for instance, showed, Brownson finally concluded, that democratic majorities were incompetent, in and of themselves. Not only could they not be expected to opt for general liberty; they could not even be expected to vote for their own; they could be fooled, as they had been fooled by the obfuscatory Whig campaign that elected General William Henry Harrison. Radical Protestant doctrines about the immanence of divinity in every individual failed of proof in the test. If governments were to be instructed by the people—and Brownson never ceased thinking they should—then the people in their turn needed better instruction than libertarian religion supplied. As Protestant, industrial society would careen into mass delusions. The correct religion for an industrial democracy such as America was Roman Catholicism.[8]

Naturally, their cures being bizarre, the diagnoses of these two men were destined for repression. At least once, Fitzhugh formulated his perspective—which was also his preference—in such a way as to foreclose Brownson's sufficiently outrageous prescription in favor of a still more terrifying one: "Popes and cardinals are not infallible, but society is."[9] Which was to say—given Fitzhugh's polemical purpose of defending the South—what so many Americans had suspected was indeed the truth: society was slavery. Fitzhugh, however, approved.

It is revealing that in one regard the right-wing Fitzhugh repeated a myth of the greatest of his left-wing libertarian opponents, Jefferson. Jefferson had simply finessed many of the hard questions of social organization and political responsibility by projecting a "thousand years" of agrarian expansion for the United States; and Fitzhugh, just possibly influenced by this agrarian fantasy, agreed that "many centuries" might elapse before the American economy became so crowded and pressed as to force the choice between slavery to capital and slavery to human beings.[10] Even the critics, that is, of nineteenth-century dreams of self-sufficiency and universal freedom recoiled from finally insisting that the hard questions they raised were really real, real for the here and now, or even "soon." Thus, when Jefferson's thousand years ended in 1890, Fitzhugh's "many centuries" by 1900, the tradition of social imagination was almost wholly that of evasion, of postponement, of simply "going on," of simple "growth." Nevertheless, the possibility had been voiced that the identity in which Americans saw themselves, in their concentration upon liberty, upon "individualism," upon "character," and upon the Protestant ethic, might not be sufficient for the mastering of social organization. The possibility had been voiced that economic and social crisis might signify religious crisis.

The crisis at its deepest could consist of inhibition against recognizing crisis at all. For the industrial master-builders themselves, this inhibition rooted in their own purpose—to order chaos into a new order. For them, the achievement by 1900 represented *telos*, indeed it represented *finis*. But alongside them, it is important to see, other men could still imagine "going on" in the old perseverant way. Actually, from the first it had been the farmer rather than the businessman who was logically adapted to incarnate the Protestant ethic without bringing it to contradiction. As Henry Nash Smith has described it,[11] according to the sociology of the nineteenth-century agrarian "myth of the garden," no real problems of social organization could arise with the expansion of agrarian America, for progress and expansion would consist just of the simple modular addition of more identical units along the westering fringe. Society's growth would consist simply of more and more of the same. But it always was questionable whether the American farmer, in his conspicuous reality, ever did embody the kind of inner quietude the myth of the stable family farm implied, rather than the dynamism of commercial ambitions. And at all events, by 1900 the American farmer had become what he was to remain, no longer a majority but an increasingly organized, self-conscious special-interest group on the peripheries of the issues of industrialized urban society. The crisis was not really his crisis.

The saints of money

More interesting were men defined not by their occupation or profession but by precisely their spirit, and more interesting just because of that—the speculators. Crucially, speculators enjoyed the use of a language of peculiarly religious relevance, a language capable of symbolizing infinities. This was the language of money.

When freed of every consideration of tradition, security, habit and similar inhibitions, money could serve as the basis for subverting every established order in favor of new dimensions of being, endlessly. In principle, money knew no limits. Though perhaps only sympathetic insight, not plain documents, can say so, there was religious ecstasy accessible in this transcendence. The speculator, wildcatter, plunger, gambler was the saint of money, a true mystic. The passion was evident in the eighteenth century; we can trace its roots much further back. In the post-Civil War decades its pure devotees sometimes seemed ubiquitous—the Drews and Fisks and Goulds, and a Wild West where they seemed destined. Curtis Jadwin in Frank Norris' semi-documentary novel of the Chicago wheat market, *The Pit* (1902), exemplified the man whose spirit flowered only in the game, as did the hearts of a generation of gamblers whose real-life exploits were muckraked by the speculator Thomas Lawson in his notorious *Frenzied Finance* (1905). The "frenzy" was more internal than external, a whirl of inner being before it led to public chaos. Norris' Jadwin quite literally did not know how to quit: he did not want to. He offered no cant about the "usefulness" of speculation in "trimming the market" nor did he have any cutoff point where he would cash in. He wanted the feeling of vertigo, the peculiar dizziness of freedom, when everything has become a matter of speculation.

The sign of the speculator in his pure image was that he cared nothing for any works. He produced nothing, organized nothing, distributed nothing. He lived alone, without the vision of community, for nothing but a state of the soul. In a way he constituted a final, wonderful purification and parody of a Protestant logic—a man for whom all authorities had vanished, and given to the limitless perpetuation of this vertiginous state. He had solved the eternal problem of Protestantism: how is God to be symbolized? How is idolatry to be avoided? How is the Will hidden behind all merely apparent laws and regularities to be experienced? Pascal likened the religious problem to a gamble; the speculator took the gamble not as a problem but as the religious reality. Money could symbolize everything—Being-in-general—therefore it allowed nothing to become idol. Its language, infinite in reach, was always good. Money freed the speculator from the restrictions of particular places, things, people. He belonged everywhere. He dealt with all men, impartially, equally. He was a perfect democrat. All men were money; he therefore need not shape them, reform them, affect them, lead them or obey them. The last remnant of the relation of sheep to shepherd, of laymen to priest, was purged. All was interchangeable. At all points one could feed on the ultimate: money was the One, the monistic All in which everything shared. Everything being one, there were no stages in life, no projects to draw a person on and out, no invasions from alien forces, no incitations to breakdown and rebirth. For the pure speculator, "waiting" was over: history had come to an end; he lived in the absolute.

Were only a heroic few capable of such ecstasy? In the concluding chapter of this section, we shall find humbler minds exalting such flights exactly. With money, the mystic flight became possible for everyone.

The speculator's parody extended to Luther's original insight, the spring of Protestantism. Luther came to see that the way to handle anxiety was to cease trying to repress it, for repression meant, secretly—and hopelessly—to be enslaved to efforts to kill anxiety. Instead, to open oneself to anxiety freely, living with it, in it and of it, was to be liberated. Luther did not argue that to do so would be to dispel anxiety, for the amount of consciously felt anxiety would increase. But the result would be freedom—the capacity to live out one's capacities for living. The great concept of God as sovereign Will had aimed at preserving this psychological acumen: God could not be known in terms of any order, which was to say, as a scheme of security. The speculator's passion parodied this logic—precisely as did any monistic philosophy, and any science devoted to one "method" alone. To reduce everything to one thing—to money or to mind (or matter)—to try to see everything in the same way—in mathematical terms or behavioral terms—all such efforts were in honest fact to commit oneself to a gamble, a risk, a thoroughly unsecured, un-underwritten bet, and, finally, one which could never be collected. There never came an end; the present was eternal.

But the industrial master-builders had not been speculators, mystics, fools of God. And they, not the mystics, were the ones who had changed the world. True, just as the farmer continued to press his special interests within the new economy, so did the speculative instinct press against it. But after all, in the final reckoning of mortal life, money was not infinite—except as the plaything of children, true play-money—and while the economy could be strained by ecstasy beyond its all-too-earthly limits, as it was by 1929, this amounted to retribution.

The crisis of 1900 was not that of a dizziness of freedom, it was that of a cage. "God gave me my money," said the senior Rocke-feller, and meant, contrary to those who mocked, that his money represented the actualization of a definite, manageable order out of the formlessness of pre-rationality, the early oil industry. Through him anxiety was ended. After him, presumably, all that was needed was administration.

If so, then the crisis was one of self-conception. The men of the new generation would have to be different sorts of men, and/or find different things they wanted to do. In the four chapters to follow, I intend to dip into the stream of identity, fishing for the various ideas and exhortations and ideologies swarming around a central agitation: if they were to avoid captivity in their fathers' creation, men would have to rethink themselves. As in preceding chapters, I shall be selective; I can hardly pretend to have caught every variety of imagination. Still, I hope to have sounded the crisis as one of psychological depth. And in again examining what people thought more than what they were or did, it is on the as-sumption that it was the problem of how to think about themselves that constituted the heart of the crisis for most men.

CHAPTER XII

LONGING FOR HARMONY

THE LAST YEARS of the nineteenth and the first years of the twentieth centuries were marked by debate over very large-scale alternatives for the use of the new industrial system. This fact showed that some men at least did realize they faced not only a private and personal but a public and social challenge to self-determination. If the iron cage was to be broken open, if clear styles of free personal life were to be linked with the new economy, more than individual heroics were called for. Rethinking the purpose of the entire system was necessary.

The most dramatic proposal for putting the economy to work projected a fascinating fusion of boldness and anxiety, nostalgia and innovation. This was the call for imperialism. None of the imperialists revealed the complexity of motivations better than their remarkable Protestant spokesman, the General Secretary of the Evangelical Alliance of the United States, the Reverend Josiah Strong.

In 1900 Strong announced in *Expansion* that the United States needed a new foreign policy. America, putting Washington's farewell advice firmly behind her, should set forth boldly as leader of a new world life. The key to this new world life was the Pacific, the "new Mediterranean." Would America—assisted by Britain, Canada, Australia and New Zealand—guarantee the Pacific as an Anglo-Saxon sea? If not, Strong warned, she would eventually be dominated by "the Slav," that is, the Russians. Let America go forth and she would find new peoples beyond number to be led—Japanese, Filipinos, East Indians, and of course, above all, those of the new China in birth.

Strong's mixture of race, religion and geopolitical mysticism—God had planted the Isthmus of Panama to guard the Pacific until the industrially inspired Anglo-Saxons could cut a canal for themselves—can hardly fail to inspire irony. But it is more important to see that Strong clearly grasped what, sixty-five years later, still remained confusing if not incomprehensible to the good middle-class Protestant folk of his faith. He knew that sense had to be made —religious sense—of such massive realities as the geography of continents and oceans, the disparities of industrial and military power, and the statistics of population. Anyone who wanted life and history to reveal meaning had to make sense of them. Even while echoing a Calvinistic piety at times, Strong resembled the rising pragmatists in economics, sociology, philosophy and law: let us not drift, imagining we are sheltered, protected, anchored. There are no final harbors. Let us be bold; let us draw up our charts and proceed in good courage.

This geopolitical ecstasy, alert to the material ponderables of gold, sea lanes, coaling stations, treaties, markets, demographic projections and firepower, was not unaffiliated with the expansive spirit of missions. The American churches had been sending missionaries out East for decades, and especially since the eighties. American China policy was directly affected by Protestant missionary leaders under President McKinley, and by the time of Theodore Roosevelt's administration the missions had become agencies for direct intervention in and—from American Protestant perspectives—reform of Chinese life. The association was to reverberate in American policy to the present day.

What has not been clearly recognized was the profoundly domestic tension in the churches from which missions at least in part derived, and, in parallel, the sharply domestic anxiety from which Strong's imperialism was an evasion.

The perils of change

Strong had won his national reputation with *Our Country*, his best-seller of 1885, which catapulted him from his local Cincinnati pulpit into his world cockpit. But *Our Country* had been no enthusiastic assessment of American resources, no kind of preliminary toting up of what it might take to move toward world horizons. It had been one long cry of alarm. In *Our Country*, Strong, pure product of the Puritan-rooted, mainstream Protestantism that had come to hold itself true exactly as it dominated the national culture, lamented, chapter by chapter, that the country was changing— for the worse. He was much bothered by immigration. He was much bothered by "Romanism," and of course the two perils were much the same. Structurally, he feared that the machine would "separate classes more widely," and, worse, make classes hereditary. The "money power" based on rising industry was proving itself irresponsible. Industry was spawning cities, and cities, as Protestant church statistics showed, were bad. Finally, Strong feared what he called socialism. Surprisingly, he blamed socialism not upon alien Europeans or native distempers, but upon individualism. Individualism, preoccupied with rights and possessions more than with duties and community, meant disintegration.

What was the answer? Just as later, so in 1885 Strong invoked the spirit of the Anglo-Saxons, but the real problem was to call the Anglo-Saxons back to their task. The answer to each of his perils was for the Anglo-Saxons simply to carry on, persevering in what they had already been doing. This would work because, in a markedly formularistic way, Strong had ended each chapter on a particular peril in the nation by declaring that that peril flourished most virulently beyond the Mississippi, in the West. Therefore, let the Puritan Protestant Anglo-Saxons press on as before to their final dominion. Clearly this answer saved Strong from asking any questions about the possibility of the Protestant Anglo-Saxons reconsidering their own selves. But clearly, it was a shallow answer.

By 1893 Strong had abandoned his preoccupation with the West (about the same time Frederick Jackson Turner was discovering quite another West altogether). Still obsessed with perils, Strong now identified the Nation, not just the West, as the field for action, and called upon the churches to get hold of a great deal more money and, taking a tip from industry, to eliminate their inefficiencies by consolidating, into what would amount to a kind of Church Militant, as preparation for the mission.

Strong then moved on to his call of 1900 for a mission to the world. Had he satisfied himself about the West and the nation? Had the nation become the Church Militant, fit and willing to master the world? On the contrary, it appeared that in at least one respect the world mission would not so much express American superiority as solve American problems. Strong quoted the chief of the National Bureau of Labor, Carroll D. Wright:

> It is incontrovertible that the present manufacturing and mechanical plant of the United States is greater—far greater—than is needed to supply the demand; yet it is constantly being enlarged, and there is no way of preventing the enlargement.[1]

Imperialism concealed an impulse of flight and evasion. What Strong could not accept was the prospect of an America, or better, of American character, drastically changed with industrialization. He himself, for instance, raised the prospect of "universal abundance" based on the machine. But the prospect bothered him. He was certain about the dangers of luxury. He was dubious about spending money on "art and beauty." At best, the beautiful should be useful, though, of course, "it is difficult to determine how useful the beautiful may be."[2] Imperial America would be ascetic America. Imperialism would help Americans remain what they were.

As geopolitics, Strong's program did not lack profundity. To imply that it would be better for America not to become an island of opulence in an ocean of poverty was hardly foolish. For Americans to associate their industrial resources with the Chinese, the Filipinos, the Tahitians—even the Russians—was a policy of prudence, not just of idealism. But Strong's anxiety about life in America under industrialization came first, and it is well to appreciate that here, too, his sensitivity ran deep.

> It is very true that within a century there has been a great multiplication of the comforts of life among the masses; but the question is *whether that increase has kept pace with the multiplication of wants.*[3]

Strong foresaw that abundance would by no means consist simply of an "answer" to the age-old problem of scarcity; he saw that it could easily be itself a source of unending discontent. Men could suffer the torment of wants, desires and needs that constantly surpassed the wants and desires of yesterday, that constantly compelled them to outrun themselves in obedience to stimuli over which they had lost control. These wants would not even be "theirs" at all but merely ratifications of what the productive system was geared to turn out. Men would no longer know themselves even in their appetites. This would be the most refined captivity to the cage. Imperialism would be escape from such loss of identity.

The American imperialism that did in fact transpire after 1900 lacked what was needed for Strong's purposes. It had nothing to do with asceticism. It sharpened, it did not reduce, the contrast between American wealth and world poverty. It had nothing to do with preventing alienation. Partly this was because the actual exercise of American power was disguised behind the narrow forms of dollar diplomacy. Dollar diplomacy was hardly suitable as bearer of those missions cultural, psychological, political and religious that Strong had envisioned. Elusive, technical, secretive, its ways were hardly subject to spiritualization and its motives were suspect. But even had Strong's evangelical imperialism won the day, it would have had to transform itself or else quickly founder. Neither the domestic perils nor the world opportunities he saw were to be met by sheer perseverance, by sheer "expansion" of what already was. Men of Strong's tradition were being challenged to self-reform before being called to reform. It was true, Strong agreed, that industrial expansion "is not the ultimate way out, of course, for it cannot continue always; there are limits to this earth of ours, and we shall not establish an interstellar commerce." But the habit of postponing hard questions to the indefinite future had not ceased to operate: ". . . The 'ultimate' is a long way off, and does not concern us in this discussion."[4]

Clergymen of an earlier day might have been discontent with so distant a confrontation with the ultimate. Evidently Strong had little feeling for what he was confessing: how finite, time-bound, ego-enslaved had become the Kingdom of God in America.

The failure of paternalism

Palpably, one of the springs of Strong's imperialism was his realization that he and his sort of people did not control the industrial system. In his eyes, the industrial leaders were new men, potentially dangerous to the sort of middle-class urban Protestant culture he imagined traditional and stable. With a rather higher, more aristocratic background, imperialists such as Theodore Roosevelt, Brooks Adams, John Hay felt the same way. They did not want the industrial leaders to be national leaders. It is not surprising then that many, perhaps most, of the industrial leaders were not attracted to imperialism, at least as more than dollar diplomacy.

At the same time, in answer to the question, what was the industrial system to be used for, many, perhaps most of the industrial and business leaders had nothing to say, probably because they had no thoughts on the matter at all. They kept on being busy, eyes never raised from affairs. Among those who did have ideas, though, one general answer dominated, echoing ancient religious teaching not yet lost in the spread of democracy. This was the answer of stewardship. No one was more talkative, if possibly not more thoughtful, about this ideal than the self-made man of all self-made men, the iron-and-steel master Andrew Carnegie.

Perhaps Carnegie's special sensitivity derived from his somewhat special guilt about making money. Other titans knew guilt, also, but few as keenly as Carnegie. As late as age thirty-three, by which time he was already making $50,000 a year, Carnegie still was agonizing over his appetite, regarding it as "degrading." He feared "idol worship." But apparently money had become entangled with his sense of his own nature by the time he was ten years old. That young, he had fancied his mother and father, both, broken, defeated, no longer real persons, because of their poverty. Whether this came from the young Carnegie's own unassisted imagination or from his parents' own teaching, we do not know. At all events, Carnegie, unlike Benjamin Franklin, was able to give up money-making only toward the very end, too late to indulge in that exploration and cultivation of his own potential which Franklin enjoyed.

If his retirement suggested that business life was not a whole life, certainly Carnegie showed no desire to use it for individualistic self-expression. Firmly recommending to men of wealth that they live without ostentation, he was far from imagining that the industrial system should support a new class of Medicean display and magnificence. The destiny of the rich industrialist was not to pioneer a new style of affluence but rather to socialize himself, giving himself over to the community, becoming its protector. Indeed, he should socialize his wealth, regarding all his "surplus" as funds in trust. Carnegie never clarified just what was and was not "surplus," but the principle was clear. Naturally the administrator of the trust funds would be the rich man himself. He would administer them "in the manner which, in his judgment, is best calculated to produce the most beneficial results for the community." He should serve his poorer brethren with "his superior wisdom, experience, and ability to administer, doing for them better than they would or could do for themselves."[5] Fitzhugh stood answered; capital would conceive of itself within community, it would be responsible.

Carnegie realized he was moving onto dangerous ground. Had not the old ground rules for success been that everyone should do for himself as he would and could? Carnegie felt constrained to offer reassurances:

> The laws of accumulation will be left free; the laws of distribution free. Individualism will continue, but the millionaire will be but a trustee for the poor; intrusted for a season with a great

part of the increased wealth of the community, but administering it for the community far better than it could or would have done for itself.[6]

This was sinuous, if sincere: individualism will continue, "but" the millionaire will be "but" a trustee "but" administering. . . . The plain implication in "doing for them" was that "they" could or would not have been successful in the first place. In order to save something of his Spencerian ideology of competitive testing, Carnegie specified just what it was the successful man should do for others. "The main consideration should be to help those who will help themselves." But this was curious too. Were these the ones who needed help? Carnegie hadn't needed it. And he himself added: "Those worthy of assistance, except in rare cases, seldom require assistance. The really valuable men of the race seldom do, except in cases of accident or sudden change."[7]

The fact was, Carnegie's philanthropic notions dissolved, willy-nilly, the coherence of his old Protestant ethic. Actually, Carnegie himself did not really vaunt himself as an individual. Sigmund Diamond, studying the reputation of businessmen from Stephen Girard to Henry Ford, has shown how the great success stories came to be read not so much as evidences of the personal traits of the hero as confirmations of America, as testimonials to what democratic society made possible.[8] Carnegie read his own story this way. He saw himself as a culture hero, and his ideas of stewardship were a logical extension of this image. Exercising his talents in administering better than the community could for itself, he would carry it to further self-realization. In this stylization, both of himself and his community, the psychological traits of the Protestant ethic fell away in favor of the capacities of a basically paternalistic administrator. And the goal of the administrator would be—administration. Which is to say, Carnegie's stewardship was its own end. Stewards would manage the community precisely in order that it be managed, as, presumably, it had not been before. And if this meant two styles of men, why, then, that was the natural upshot of the competitive testing.

Carnegie simply ignored politics and the state. His notions for trusteeship clustered around schools, libraries, museums and parks paid for directly by men of wealth. In complimenting Peter Cooper for having disbursed his money—"surplus," evidently—for Cooper Institute rather than in the form of higher wages, Carnegie never dreamed this might be regarded as a subject for political choice by the community. Tacitly assuming that community no longer lived by custom, tradition, unspoken, unbought and unrecognized treasures of order and value, he knew that a new ordering principle was needed, and, having proved himself as a master of new order, offered himself as that principle with no sense of pretension.

Other men, less personally involved, characterized the Carnegie-style future more sharply. Writing for *The Independent,* the writer-journalist W. J. Ghent prophesied, in 1902, that the next stage in American life would be a "benevolent feudalism."[9] Concentrated economic power would express itself as social power and, soon, Ghent argued, as political power as well. Quite without overt constitutional changes, the political system would simply "register" the will of the lords of industry. Since the "aspirations and conduct" of the people at large would be conditioned to support the new economic order, no "democratic opposition" would exist. Obviously, as Ghent implied, the psychology of the Protestant ethic would wither in such a society.

Contrasting with Ghent's poker-faced ironies were the more apocalyptically lurid predictions of men such as Ignatius Donnelly and Jack London, imaginative freebooters both as they lurked on the outskirts of power. In Donnelly's *Caesar's Column* and London's *The Iron Heel,* not feudalism but plain oligarchy ruled, and not as "benevolent" but as sinister, tyrannical, bloody and mad. Cool or hot, ironical or lurid, specters of enslavement had come to gibber in the turn-of-century air. Some years earlier Edward Bellamy had projected his vision of a cool, rational, managed middle-class Utopia; harsh realism suggested as more likely the rule of "superior" men.

But in retrospect it seems that there was not really much danger. Ghent, Donnelly and London really made a mistake. They assumed that the ominous new day would represent an extension of the immediate past, that it would register the continuing enforcement of the manifest and rather terrible will of the master-builders. What they did not see was that the master-builders had no will for anything further. The stage of building had had as its underlying aim its own completion, its own rest. As a group, or class, businessmen had few large ideas about what to do with the system once it was established. If the oft-cited statement of the railroad president George F. Baer, during the coal strike of 1902, was a peak of feudal pretension, then it was a crumbling peak:

> The rights and interests of the laboring man will be protected and cared for, not by labor agitators, but by the Christian men to whom God in His infinite wisdom, has given control of the property interests of the nation.[10]

Baer had nothing in mind with the words "protection and care." He had not the slightest program for the national community. Of politics and the state he asked only subsidies, and otherwise, that they stay quiet. All he really meant was that businessmen did not like unions.

Even assuming that some potentials for paternalistic stewardship still remained undissolved in Protestant culture, the businessmen were not prepared to realize them. In their own affairs the businessmen simply kept on going, turning insensibly from builders into administrators, pioneering a few uninteresting frontiers of consumption in their private lives, finding increasingly in their immense new machinery an increasingly routine fate. Soon they would become anonymous.

The first American sociologists

In proposing their new departures both Strong and Carnegie clearly hoped to conserve what to them was the heart of the past, and yet neither was truly nostalgic. Both realized that effective conservation would require genuinely new management. It is instructive to recall that in the debate over what to do with the industrial system, the party of nostalgia was also the party that fancied itself new—the party of science, of sociology; social science.

Of course, little is gained by noting the nostalgia in the iron father of American sociology, the tough-talking but melancholy-minded William Graham Sumner. Sumner was indeed critical of the corruptions of the present, pessimistic about the future, and attached to an essentially Jeffersonian model of life and work. But Sumner belongs in the slim ranks of American mystics, not among the mainstream of practical, pragmatic righteous humanists, testifying tirelessly as he did to the reality of a transhuman, unchangeable, universal process to which wise men would surrender themselves, against which only fools would rage. More tragic in his outlook (for he was no Christian) than his liberal critics commonly appreciated, Sumner fathered sociology in America only as he had rebel sons.

The first generation of American sociologists—for Sumner was alone—were Midwesterners saturated in the ethic of the Protestant town. If they had not become sociologists, they would have become pastors. Or better, becoming sociologists was their updating of the pastor's calling. Some, like Lester Ward, resembled Sumner in discarding Christian faith as though sociology in truth had become evangel. But most—Albion Small and Charles Ellwood and Franklin Giddings and W. I. Thomas and others—believed they were implementing not superceding the faith: ". . . Is it not wonderful that in the Gospels we find provided just the religion which is best suited to realize the sociologist ideal?"[11] In this delight of E. A. Ross one might measure the power of the method to transform itself into the end, somewhat as Strong had congratulated Christianity for its service to the Anglo-Saxons. But the sociologists' reversals were invitations to love, not struggle.

Good men had never had good methods in the past: that was the source of the enthusiasm. Sociology offered method. It was while buoyed on this enthusiasm that the immense fact-gathering of American—as contrasted with the more philosophical European—sociology began. The ultimate use of this knowledge was to be in education. Auguste Comte, at the beginning of European sociology earlier in the century, had argued that scientific sociologists must be free to manipulate society as an elite; anticipating the parallel arguments of Brownson and Fitzhugh, he had said that scientific sociology and Protestantism could not mix, since the Protestant principles of freedom would always mean the frustration of science by unscientific majorities. But the American sociologists refused to accept this dilemma, proposing in effect to convert Everyman to science. In this they only followed the lead of the great philosopher of social science (and education) himself, John Dewey.

This assumption that sociology could, as it were, steal upon the scene of modern society without raising serious questions about liberty and the distribution of power, nicely registered the central hope of the late nineteenth-century educated middle-class churches. Sociological knowledge would be somehow in and of itself moral knowledge applied by moral men. The sociologists manifested this spirit in their choice of topics. What fascinated them was the culture of the teeming cities, immigrants, crime, bosses, Catholics and Jews. They examined not their own but an alien world. Modern American sociology, in short, began very much as a study of "others," not of self, with its dominant goal very much the hope of selves and a culture without suspicion of a need to inspect their own hope.

The social gospel

This hope was the hope for harmony. In the sociologists' diligent collection of data, the facts they collected more than all others were those of other peoples' social and individual disorganization, and the rhetoric by which these were interpreted was the rhetoric of restoration. Conflict was the problem, conflict-reduction the answer; tension was bad, tension-reduction good. Paradoxically, sociology-minded pastors—the "social gospel" pastors—gave a more "sociological" rendition of the hope (and the anxiety) than did the sociologists themselves.[12] For the sociologists the common root of all perils was ultimately an intellectual, not a sociological, fact—ignorance of sociology itself, to be repaired by education. But the pastors dwelt steadily upon class schism, the struggle between capital and labor. The pastors regarded both as alien entities, and their conflicts appalling not because of the wounds they dealt each other, but because of the earthquake they threatened beneath the innocent third party caught between. What they sought was reconciliation of these powers through the dissolution of power. Capital and labor would be brought to accommodation not so much through compromise as through absorption. The class spectrum read: capital-"church"-labor. Innocent and moral, the party in the middle was in truth not to be thought of as a "power" at all. It was where spirit was. It was where love was. It was where unity was. It had no need for self-inspection. It had only to prevail.

This was the dream of nostalgia—that industry, and the ominous new populations it spawned, could be absorbed into the life of the beloved community, could be socialized by an applied science and piety, and, thus, almost, be as though it had never been. No one asked whether perhaps just those Protestant farms and towns had not secreted the energy that had been projected out into the new industrialism, whether the rude new cities, frightening to sociologists and pastors alike, were not just the Protestant ethic inflated, and exploding. No one asked whether the problem might not be that of alienated selves rather than of disorganized others.

By the twenties, salvationist sociology had withdrawn into hygienic objectivity; the eagerness for methods of change had been transformed into eagerness for methods of research. In a long drift sociology returned toward Sumner and the acceptance of what is, its myth the "structural-functional" analysis of the "social system," as though history had ended. Only after World War II, in the semi-popular sociological investigations of "alienation," did the science recover some religious resonance, and only then, under the biting criticism of C. Wright Mills, recall its association with the real life of power and politics. And it was this conspicuously non-Protestant sociology that showed that sociology meant something when it was engaged in self-reform more than in the reform of others.

As for the sociology-minded pastors, they, unable to fulfill themselves in research, found themselves inexorably drawn into painful debates over the use of power and withered by the fire of Reinhold Niebuhr insisting that the fairest visions of life must accommodate conflict. More tragic than their fate was the fact that Niebuhr's realism, while widely understood in post-World War II seminaries by a new breed of tough-minded Protestant young, was sidestepped in the suburban congregations as these inspired the proliferating ministrations of a new science, therapeutic psychology.

The Progressives

But sociology and the social gospel were after all esoteric—if not cultish, then surely unfamiliar to the broad majority of those whom they represented. The less scientific and evangelical but more conspicuous embodiment of the nostalgic dream of harmony appeared in politics. And, if only because it lacked the promise of science and the morale of mission, the political dream showed greater anxiety. Of those exposing the scandals and perils and evils of the time, the Progressive muckrakers—Ida Tarbell, Lincoln Steffens, Ray Stannard Baker and the rest—Judson Grenier has observed:

> These journalists came from families which were devoutly Protestant; they were well-schooled in the Christian ethic. Their writings are replete with Christian moral concepts and Christian symbols.[13]

Progressivism amounted to the last rising of the middle-class Protestant folk in our history, in anything like coherent and relevant fashion. Its failure was to be portentous for the future. That failure meant that the political democracy of the nation would not, as Jefferson and Jackson among others had thought it must, mean approximate economic democracy. Failure meant that the economy would continue to evolve into giant bureaucracies with all they implied for the "psychology" and "character" of the people manning them. It meant the spread of tactics of adjustment, attitudes of passivity, moods of indifference to questions of social power, punctuated by outbursts of regressive indignation. It meant the erosion of a reasonably coherent and reasonably wide culture in which to ground questions of power.

Progressives took up two distinct tasks, one of means, one of ends. They wanted to reform politics and to reform economics; they lost themselves in the politics.

The importance of Progressive concern for politics should never be slighted. It manifested revival of a long democratic and Protestant determination to check purely formal, organized, external authority in favor of private, inner, personal energy and authority—in favor of will. Progressives showed intellectual vitality in realizing that, for the first time in the experience of broad, mainstream, middle-class Protestantism, this tradition of self-possession and self-determination required not only jealous suspicion of the state but new, positive use of it, especially Washington. Inevitably this realization came to focus on the Presidency. As everyone knows, the great Progressive experience was the popular romance with Theodore Roosevelt.

Roosevelt ended the era anticipated as early as 1862 by Nathaniel Hawthorne predicting a succession of "bullet-headed generals" as Presidents, the era lamented by Whitman in *Democratic Vistas,* the era scorned by Henry Adams remembering his own ancestor-Presidents. Roosevelt eased anxieties that the nation had disintegrated into a mindless collection of monster powers, its unity as a community lost. In renewing politics and the Presidency, Roosevelt made it clear that the recovery of will for individuals was to be pursued through recovery of national purposes. That they realized this, Progressives showed in all those improvements and perfections of democratic political machinery which they carried through in state after state, and in Washington. With these political reforms, politics might be captured once again by the good people of the mainstream, who would use it to burst open the door of the economic cage.

It was never to be so simple. The discrepancy between the appearance and the reality of T.R.'s performance as hero-representative facing the monopoly dragon has often been noted, and in any case, T.R. reached his own mature views on effective policy only after he had left the Presidency. The tragedy in which he entangled the Republican party for the indefinite future, by depriving it of its most imaginative and adventurous minds after 1912, still counts as a major theme in the psychic history of twentieth-century Northern Protestants.

As for Woodrow Wilson—whom H. L. Mencken's piercing eye insisted upon caricaturing in his religious identity—while some Bull Moose Progressives might have feared from the Democrats an anarchic return to rural ideas of small, local economic life, Wilson himself knew perfectly well a new economic day had dawned, indeed, already approached noon. He, for one, explained it as the result of "natural" and "irresistible" evolutionary forces, dimly expressive of God. What Wilson wanted to do was to embrace the new economy firmly in the garb of law, hence he came to support regulatory commissions differing from those imagined by Roosevelt and his Progressive big-business advisers in 1912 hardly at all. No less than Roosevelt (and Strong) did Wilson encourage overseas expansion on the theory that consumption in America could not keep pace with production. Like Roosevelt, Wilson declared that "business underlies every part of our lives; the foundation of our lives, of our spiritual lives included, is economic."[14]

This is to say that neither Roosevelt nor Wilson, as political heroes, had a yardstick to bring to bear by which to measure economic life, unwarped by notions that the major structures and operations of big industry were "inevitable." Whether the purest of Progressive leaders, Senator La Follette, could have acted more freely one cannot know, though we do know that La Follette thought so.

But it is doubtful that the leadership of the two Presidents missed opportunities offered by any significant fraction of their political followers. What did the Progressive, Protestant, middle-class majorities really want? Haunted by thoughts of giant corporations above and of labor insurgency beneath, they wanted a sense of security they had lost. But what did this mean? For some it might mean simply the protection of local as against national monopoly. After all, small-town merchants, lawyers, doctors, bakers, shoemakers, smiths, crossroads bankers throughout American history had sought and enjoyed monopoly. Competition had never been welcomed with enthusiasm, especially when reaching in from outside the local community. On the other hand, security and opportunity might be imagined in terms of new rules for big business and giant bureaucracies, rules of relevance to middle-class ethics—not just for narrow economic security and opportunity but for the terms of employment, the styles of authority, the adjustment of civic and corporate and private interests, and, increasingly, for process and quality, that is, consumption.

Another sort of contrast also worked immanently among Progressives. From what perspective of age were Progressive desires conceived? For those in the fullness of life, at the season for fruition of their careers, the task of checking and even rolling back the new powers of organization could seem central. But for younger men, just starting out, the new order might appear to indeed be "given," "natural," and the task of reform simply that of seeing to it that the new order not be administered in stewardly benevolence by an exclusive few.

The missing allies

Above and beyond these inherent contrasts, the basic Progressive population might have benefited in thought and resolution from allies. Insofar as the industrial system they wished to reform had been built with energy sanctioned largely by their own culture and ideology, in attempting to reform it they had to reform themselves. They were called from nostalgia, called, in the relevant religious vocabulary, to be born again, and the difficult course of self-transcendence might have seemed more negotiable, if not with friends, at least in loyal company. But the company the Progressives kept was, unhappily, useless, and the useful company they might have kept they ignored or rejected.

The farmers were useless to them. Certainly alarm and anger at big business burned nowhere hotter than among the late nineteenth-century farmers of the West. But the farmers' desire and answer were at once too deep and too irrelevant for Progressives. The farmers were ready to insist upon what came to socialization of railroads, banks, communications—even, by implication, manufacturing. They visualized a two-sector economy—free private economy of family farms side-by-side with nationalized bigness. This did grasp the problem firmly, that industry had to be harnessed to an independent purpose, that it had to be understood as a utility, as good for something beyond itself, beyond simply "going on," automatically and self-sufficiently. But the answer served no ends beyond those of farmers. Indeed, it raised the specter of an economic system doubly closed by being made political as well. What might socialization guarantee to city people by way of opportunity? or by way of industrial democracy? or of local community? or of individual security? The purely expedient nature of the farmers' industrial tactic betrayed itself later as farm policy followed nothing more than the rise and fall of farm prices. The sterility of agrarian outlook was not costly primarily as a matter of voting strength; it was costly as an intellectual, cultural, imaginative decline, betraying as it did the disintegration of a precious tradition of individualism into merely defensive rigidity. Later years were to show farmers incapable of recognizing the revolution in their own order, as whole regions converted to industrialized crop production in eerie silence.

The allies and friends who remained ignored must be named culturally rather than functionally or economically, and this is the point. It was in the failure of the Progressives to engage in cultural self-questioning that their failures to master issues of economic and structural power were rooted. These potential allies were the immigrants, both from Europe and the South, outsiders, aliens, by ethnicity and religion, by class and by race. Collectively they could be lumped together, most of them, as "labor," and Progressives did so lump them in their symmetrical alarms at both "capital" *and* "labor." But it is essential to remember that, by and after 1900, "labor" in America looked to be overwhelmingly Catholic (as well as, in some enclaves, Jewish), plus, after 1917, Protestant, but— black Protestant. For Progressives, the vast mass process of proletarianization never seemed to affect "their own." In their exclusiveness, Progressives made a contribution to the fact that American labor came to see its interest in the fashion of the farmers—in the pursuit of narrow, "bread-and-butter" guarantees having little significance for the issues of character and culture, psychological style and individual freedom, raised by industrial organization and bureaucratic institutions in and of themselves. However unlikely one might judge the chance to have been, that leaders among the non-Protestant multitudes would have responded to an ecumenical Progressivism, the fact remains that strong ecumenical gestures were lacking. As from the beginning, old-stock Protestant Americans welcomed newcomers coldly. Indeed, Progressives allowed themselves to be drawn into a more or less overt culture-war: the laws against alcoholic beverages—which did not exempt the immigrants' culturally benign wine and beer—and the laws against more new immigrants were achievements of Progressives after World War I— not of Progressives alone, but nonetheless of Progressives.

As for Negroes, here some Progressives actually had a tradition of their own to renew had they chosen, that of abolitionism. It is not so important to adduce many reasons why the tradition had run into the sands, as to confront the naked fact: in this regard as well, Progressives were alone, choosing themselves, in their purity, narrowly.

If in the twenties, on both the religious and the racial frontiers, xenophobic and obscurantist Protestants took over the defense from Progressives, thereby exposing the very idea of enrichening culture through religious symbols and religious concerns to ridicule and disgust, this only testified to a vacuum. Naturally the primitive and repressive Protestant crusaders of the twenties, anticipating their descendants in the fifties, had no sense to make of industrial and organizational realities. It would become clear enough in the fifties, when even ignorant folks prospered, that what they wanted was to suck the sweets of industrial affluence without having to be responsible for anything. By that time, in a logical irony, they were twinned by their primitive and repressive Catholic counterparts, once snubbed, now in a position to repay the slight by claiming precedence in the status of conformity and self-righteousness. In wide circles, to be Catholic was to be exempted from the cancerous suspicions from which even Progressive Protestants had difficulty in disentangling themselves.

What might have been

What might Progressivism have been? It is not an empty question. In thinking about history, to raise hypothetical questions usually is an empty business if there was no one on the scene who also had imagined such possibilities at the time. But such men were on the Progressive scene. Charles Forcey, in *The Crossroads of Liberalism* (1961), has carefully studied the thinking of three of the most interesting—Herbert Croly, Walter Lippmann and Walter Weyl.[15] True to Progressivism generally, all three of these men spoke for intelligent control rather than laissez-faire, for "mastery" rather than "drift" in Lippmann's phrase. But for these men, distilling harmony out of conflict held no particular priority. They were more interested in development, in fresh possibilities, in new beginnings. The United States, they felt, deserved the high scientific, literary, artistic and social achievements its resources could easily support. The United States, they were convinced, had, in the deliberate application of its democratic politics, a tradition that could evolve quickly into a great and handsome new stage of culture and well-being. Forcey has narrated the gathering sense of frustration of their hopes under Roosevelt and Wilson and the world war. But again, the story cannot pivot on two political leaders. One can seriously wonder, for instance, whether the role of men such as Croly and Lippmann might not better have been that of tutoring political publics rather than political leaders, especially as Lippmann and Weyl, and Croly, too, were somewhat peripheral to the center party of mainstream Progressivism, and, therefore, did not so much represent as—they hoped—anticipate popular demands. But in any case, large visions had been in the air, and it was exactly large visions that Progressives did not pursue.

John Dewey's passing criticism of Progressives as men of "moral emotions" rather than of "the insight and policy of intelligence" has not been faulted since. Far from what it sometimes seemed to be, an impulse of men to explore their own minds for new and plastic forms of society, Progressivism clung to itself, trying only to seize in its embrace powers that had outgrown it. Progressivism was remarkably thin. No mysteries beguiled it. "The foundation . . . is economic." Numb to creative impulses beneath the crusts of late nineteenth-century culture, Progressives opted for the spreading materialism that came to provide the standards for security and welfare in the twentieth century. Wanting—like religious fundamentalism—only to be able to believe what it already wished to believe, it died readily enough once new terms for life and power were offered. A mass culture was being not so much created as manufactured. All that was necessary was to let the machines run, and consume. The community did not have to rise to self-consciousness or pioneer in self-exploration through politics. Nostalgia could be transmuted into the new harmonies of suburbia.

CHAPTER XIII

SPIRITUAL AUTOMATION, OLD STYLE

TRYING TO GRASP and master the system from "outside," so to speak —as through imperialism, paternalism, nostalgia—was one thing. Trying to sustain an old psychology without thinking about the system was another. The men I want to talk about next followed this line. They simply went on explaining how to be a success. My argument will be that they also began to talk about a different sort of man.

By 1900 the honest young man who wanted to succeed really needed a warning. Times were changing. Opportunity still abounded, but of a different sort. Whereas once a young man could count on certain psychological traits while picking up practical skills along the way, in the new scheme of things more was needed. A man should have precise professional knowledge, administrative training, technical know-how from the start. He needed skills even more than traits. So urged Albert Shaw, New York editor, lecturer, Ph. D. in political science, in his book of 1907 with the suggestive title *The Outlook for the Average Man.*[1] Speaking to college audiences, Shaw, well up on the latest developments in the business world of the East, plainly believed he spoke to the problems of a whole new generation.

His book was no best-seller. Perhaps the title was mischosen: how many young men wanted to think they were average? But by its nature, the sort of advice Shaw was offering had a future, not in traditional exhortatory best-sellers but in the rising schools of business. By its nature it fed cool pragmatics.

But the old, exhortatory, evangelical "gospel" of success did not vanish. In popular ideology it remained a distinct theme into the twenties, and then experienced a revival after 1945. It is well to see its adaptations, for it constituted a last stand of coherence for many uncool, unpragmatic minds, bizarre as that coherence sometimes may have been. I have not sought out the bizarre for its own sake. Drawing mostly on widely popular, best-selling tracts, I leave it to imagination to guess eccentricities too extreme to win attention at all. After 1900 the old gospel of success was a psychology and ideology *in extremis;* it is only justice to avoid its excessive excesses.

The "Power Book Library"

In the same year Shaw's book won its small renown, 1907, Frank Haddock, inspirational author of the "Power Book Library," including *Power for Success, Practical Psychology* and *Business Power,* published his *Power of Will.* Just that year, J. P. Morgan, mastering the nation's financial panic from his library on Fifth Avenue, showed the system to be so rationalized as to invite a one-man monopoly on will. Haddock's more democratic assumption that every man could still be a man of will ran closer to popular tastes. His book succeeded. A best-seller in England as well as America, revised for a second edition in 1915, it sold over 600,000 copies in fifteen years. It was another kind of climactic parody upon the Protestant ethic.

"Power": the monotonous repetition of the word was equaled only by the monotony of Haddock's prose. "Its literary deficiencies [may be] overlooked in view of its practical purpose."[2] Haddock knew what he was about. He was teaching a psychological drill, and literary style could only interfere. As unreadable as any mind-cure book, his, like them, was not meant to be read but "practiced." Haddock carefully allowed that his book had "nothing to do" with Christian Science or "mental science." He was not interested in theological puzzles about mind over matter. That was a false issue. "The Will is higher than the Mind," he announced, and handed over to Will the basic claims mind cure made for Mind. Without Will, he observed, Mind operates simply by reflex action; a person endowed only with Mind therefore could have no purpose. "It is the Will . . . who [sic] should now step forward to take the command. . . . We can make our own brains . . . if only we have Wills strong enough to take the trouble."[3]

Thus stripping nineteenth-century success psychology to its obsessional core, Haddock denuded it of religious cover too. The old evangel had assumed that will followed what mind grasped of the intentions of God; defining mind as purposeless, Haddock cut the cord of piety. Not that he argued atheism or even agnosticism in so much as a line. He was interested only in efficiency. Drills for the eye, the ear, taste, touch, smell, for the nerves, drills in attention, thinking, memory, imagination filled the book.

> (a) *Exercise No. 10.* Stand erect. Summon a sense of resolution. Throw Will into the act of standing. Absorbed in self, think calmly but with power these words: "I am standing erect. All is well! I am conscious of nothing but good!" Attaining the Mood indicated, walk slowly and deliberately about the room. Do not strut. Be natural, yet encourage a sense of forcefulness. Rest in a chair. Repeat, with rests, fifteen minutes.
>
> (b) Repeat every day indefinitely.[4]

Efficiency for what? For success, of course, as Haddock's other books endlessly repeated. But with the will superior to mind, was will to seek its destiny on its own account? Perhaps Haddock was preaching titanism, his endless rules, regimens, exercises, resolves and drills inflating Benjamin Franklin's simple code into a mania, the price of the pretension.

But this was hardly the case. Haddock was teaching spiritual automation. The hero of will did not find his center in himself. Walking, with an almost audible clank, "slowly and deliberately" about the room, his hero was converting himself into his own mechanical double: repeat each day . . . indefinitely. With the titanic master-builders already fading into mythical haze, the efficient managerial philosophers already spinning their organizational lore, Haddock sensed his times. Men must be programmed on the new master-tape, the business system itself, about ready to play the role of All-Good-Mind itself, a superconsciousness into which men should learn how to plug themselves.

In Haddock's version, will power lost the last of what it had meant in Protestant psychology short of obsession. Will had not been its own master. It had served the will of God, or of evolution (understood as the way God worked), or even of "democratic ideals" (understood as God's ideals), and of America (understood as God's country). But Haddock had no notion of anything the will was supposed to create. Not at all titanic, will became empty, its only possible task that of willing itself into becoming an automaton.

In one chapter, "The Control of Others," Haddock did stumble on what was to become a large problem in the process of self-automation. In order to influence people, one needed "personal magnetism," and Haddock taught this in fifty-four "suggestions." What lay hidden in these was the problem of sincerity. Franklin, when warned by friends that he was thought proud, frankly assumed an insincere humility and recommended it to others. But for the "average man" of the new twentieth-century gospel of success, such honest insincerity in frankly manipulating others contained perils. Calculated manipulation could induce reciprocal suspicion that one was meeting countermanipulation in turn, the suspicion that the mechanical double one used was influencing not people but their own mechanical doubles. Clearly this was a problem that would have to be resolved.

Techniques for cultivating will power were taught after Haddock, naturally. Through the twenties even middle-class magazines such as *American Magazine* went on featuring sketches of business leaders incarnating the triumph of sheer perserverance. Yet sheer will power became slightly comic, even vulgar, the promise of its secrets relegated to the advertising columns of pulp magazines alongside prospectuses for building body power. The popular hero of will became Charles Atlas. In circles alerted to the new depth psychology, will power came to seem simply an illusion of adolescents.

"Think success!"

If success was to go on serving as a useful ideology, the alarming drift away from its democratic base had to be checked, a drift obvious in the notions of an Andrew Carnegie, and hardly concealed in the views of an Albert Shaw. Even will power, as Haddock unconsciously made all too apparent, tended toward elitism, with its grueling apprenticeship—too many exercises, too many drills. The basic reform needed in the gospel of success was one which would again place success within reach of any man. This reform consisted of teaching success on the basis, not of character or will power, but of mind power. Insofar as every man could control his own thoughts, every man could succeed by thinking right.

Some of the new preachers of success went far in their exploration of mental mastery. Even while penning such success tracts as *The Secret of Success* (1908) and *The Psychology of Salesmanship* (1909), the Chicago businessman William Walker Atkinson was, as Yogi Ramacharaka, expounding subtler lore. But if one had to learn yoga for success, success had indeed moved beyond reach of the generality. Much more accessible was the pre-eminent mind-cure success writer, Orestes Swett Marden, New Hampshire Yankee, Boston Latin School graduate, Harvard Medical School graduate, vice-president of The Success Company, editor of *Success Magazine.* Marden understood the importance of saving success as a popular goal. *Every Man a King* rang as his most significant title. A master at weaving standard New England sources and various mind-cure writers—Trine, Ella Wheeler Wilcox, Charles Brodie Patterson, Helen Wilmans, Elbert Hubbard, along with Emerson—and, in fact, some bits of yoga, into neat worldly discourses, Marden always said the same thing: Never admit defeat. Always feel powerful. Think success. Echoing older teachings, he warned that mental automanipulation could be imperiled by "overculture and wider outlook." "The weakening of self-confidence, the development of timidity, is often an unfortunate result of a liberal education,"

Marden said. "[The] brain powers [of the ignorant man] have not been weakened by theories or by the knowledge of how much he does not know. He simply plunges ahead where a cultivated man would hesitate."[5] How much Harvard-man Marden was attempting to live down his own educational disadvantage, how much he was condescending, we do not know. But evidently, even more than an empty will was it helpful to have an empty mind.

Will power's decline in favor of mind power soon was advertised to wide audiences on a simple secular basis, and for purposes as large as life, when for a few months in 1922 the teachings of Dr. Emile Coué earned the stature of national fad. Deriving from the so-called Nancy school of French psychiatry, noted for its research on hypnotism, Coué, somewhat like Phineas Quimby, had converted hypnotism into techniques of mental suggestion, above all autosuggestion, summed in his famous motto, "Day by day, in every way, I am getting better and better." His orientation on the hierarchy of power was explicit: "Our actions spring not from our Will but from our Imagination." "Will must not be brought into play in practicing autosuggestion." "The unconscious self is the grand director of all our functions." "Every one of our thoughts, good or bad, becomes concrete, materializes, and becomes in short a reality."[6] A man of Roman Catholic training, Coué recommended that his followers, while repeating his slogan twenty times, ensure the mechanical, will-less quality essential by using a string with twenty knots in it. Couéism was not quite just one more fad in a faddist era. Enterprising publishers saw reason to issue his work once again in 1961.

Self-manipulative mind-cure techniques aimed at success itself drifted on further and further from anything like a discipline centered in character, will, or distinguishable ego, toward magical psycho-science. Napoleon Hill, author of *The Law of Success* and *How to Sell Your Way through Life,* drifted far. Evidently enjoying Hill's faithful echo of the amiable, traditional platitudes of optimism, diligence and self-help, successful men gave him testimonials: Frank Woolworth, Robert Dollar, John Wanamaker, George Eastman, William Wrigley, Jr., and Woodrow Wilson, William Howard Taft and Samuel Gompers, too. But Hill was probing much more exotic resources. In 1937 he published *Think and Grow Rich*. Somewhat mysteriously, Hill announced that he was at last ready to reveal to the public at large the "magic formula," the "secret" which Andrew Carnegie had revealed to him long before. It was not clear why Hill had had to wait. Nor, oddly, did he in the end reveal any "secret" after all, on the rather coy theory that "it seems to work more successfully when it is merely uncovered and left in sight" and not "directly named."[7] But what Hill did do was expound an interesting psycho-metaphysics.

Around and about all men, it appeared, was a kind of universal ether carrying vibrations—vibrations of fear, of poverty, misery, disease and failure, and vibrations of prosperity, health, wealth and happiness. From this ether a man attracted whatever harmonized with the vibrations in his own mind. The implication was obvious. The chief problem was to have faith in this metaphysics. How? "Repetition of affirmation of orders to your subconscious mind is the only known method of voluntary development of the emotion of faith."[8]

Hill's subconscious had a considerably more positive religious role to play than William James's.

> When faith is blended with thought, the subconscious mind instantly picks up the vibration, translates it into its spiritual equivalent, and transmits it to Infinite Intelligence, as in the case of prayer.

> The subconscious mind is the intermediary, which translates one's prayers into terms which Infinite Intelligence can recognize, presents the message, and brings back the answer in the form of a definite plan or idea for procuring the object of the prayer. . . . Mere words read from a prayer book cannot, and will never serve as an agency of communication between the mind of man and Infinite Intelligence.[9]

It was plain in any case that money was a term Infinite Intelligence had no trouble deciphering. In a book on getting rich, Hill logically counseled his readers to "hold your thoughts on . . . money by concentration, or fixation of attention, with your eyes closed, until you can actually see the physical appearance of the money. Do this at least once each day."

In addition to mind-cure techniques, Hill also recommended elements of the older teaching ("decision," "persistence") and of the new sophistication ("specialized knowledge," "organized planning," "power of the master mind"—by which he meant corporate committee-think), as well as a "mystery of sex transmutation" following from his explanation that too few men were successful before their forties because of too much sexual indulgence. But these traits and skills would materialize into success only in the matrix of the faith emotion. *Think and Grow Rich* ran through twenty-eight printings in twenty-one years. Then it was reprinted as a fifty-cent paperback in 1960 and 1961.

In *The Magic of Believing* (1948)—which quickly went through seventeen printings—another expert in psycho-success, Claude Bristol, mixed Eddington, Freud, psychosomatics, electroencephalography, telepathy, Emerson and a host of other sources into his explanation of all events whatsoever as functions of "mind stuff," hypnotism and suggestion. Bristol explained his own success accordingly: "I 'just knew' that I would have that fortune I had in mind."[10] In the early years of his career, he explained, he had filled every paper across his desk with a single doodle: "$ $ $ $ $ $ $ $ $." Though drawing on New Thought, Christian Science, Unity and religious science among others, Bristol proclaimed no particular religious view; the magic of believing was itself all that religion was. "One with the Divine," Marden had proclaimed in *The Miracle of Right Thinking* in 1910, for right thinking *was* the divine, and by the laws of the divine, "Success and Happiness Are for You."

With such as these we are quite outside that old circle in which individual success, individual character and respectable community joined, serving each other. Such disintegrated, eccentric and mostly magical notions—purveyed more widely than even these few popular examples suggest—testified to a matching audience—men on the fringe, men with some, but only precarious and hazy, schooling, men without special skills, men of the underworld of earnestly struggling underpaid unimportance, clerks, stockroom assistants, branch salesmen, business-college teachers, side-street professionals. In lonely isolation they undertook their own transmutative self-hypnosis. The role of the "subconscious" in these regimens was to vibrate with the mystic ether of money. To these audiences it would have been absurd to address exhortations to titanism, to heroic individualism, to self-sufficient consciousness, even to grim perseverance. The individual was weak, consciousness—because frail—dangerous. But in the subconscious a man could link his wishes with infinite power. A kind of white-collar proletariat, men suffered—as C. Wright Mills diagnosed—an almost total incapacity to generate or identify with any kind of coherent social myth or philosophy, or politics. They became sleepwalkers in the routines of modern organizational society.

The post-World War II lamentations

By contrast, where sophisticated tongues still spoke of success to presumably sophisticated minds, the old psychology faded in favor of naked pragmatics.

Not that the simple empirical insistence upon the chance to make good money on one's own lacked roots in anxieties about what was happening to character. Soon after World War II lamentations were to be heard over the loss of spirit among the young. Bright young men entering business, it seemed, no longer desired to dare. They asked about pensions, they wanted security, upper-middle-class salaries, and vice-presidencies just below the level of top and tough responsibility. They were content to be less than the men their (grand)fathers had been.

This anxiety differed from that expressed during the twenties and the depression. Then it was the working man who was said to be going soft, from high wages, then from relief. Now, here, were signs of decadence among the rising managers, among the Young Republicans themselves.

The most interesting of these lamentations appeared in *Fortune Magazine*, the evangelical voice of big business. *Fortune* had hailed American capitalism as a "permanent revolution." Obviously, this revolution depended on large-scale organization and sophisticated management. Yet, contemplating the business-school graduates, *Fortune's* editors decided that their preferences for security were somehow equivalent to a failure of nerve. Beginning in 1951, therefore, they ran "short stories of enterprise" in each issue of the magazine, some of which were collected in 1954 into a book, *100 Stories of Business Success*. This was reissued in 1957 as a thirty-five-cent paperback, the first of a series. *100 Stories* was an attempt to reenthuse men about their chances to go it alone.

"What these enterprising citizens do seem to share," the editors deduced, "are certain distinctive traits: abundant energy, considerable intuitive intelligence, and a frank desire to get rich as fast as possible." Their success, the editors said, was evidence that "there are plenty of opportunities, in good times and bad, for those who have the wit to see them."[11]

. Since none of the hundred successes had been gained during the "bad times" of the depression thirties, this detail of the editors' interpretation seemed dubious. But the stories did indeed go far to prove there were plenty of opportunities. Marked by their frank desire, a good many of the hundred were in truth getting rich, though some of them not very fast. At the same time, in at least a third of the cases, the enterprising citizen had certainly not got rich at all. He had gained, often, a delightful income—$15,000, $20,000, $25,000 per year, although in some cases less than $10,000. This was not getting rich in anything like the original sense of that term. It was entirely plausible that many of these men (and women) could have made much more money elsewhere, and just as fast. What they had all gained was not riches but a kind of independence. Raising and selling truffles, trout and chinchillas, making hand-painted table linen, running a country hotel or a small-town bank or a forty-four-mile railroad, managing parades, manufacturing back-yard pools, they were on their own. The spirit of a good many could evidently have been summed up in the "Zany Motto" of one of them, a successful inventor of zany mottoes: "This job is more fun than making money." Head of the Let's Have Better Mottoes Association, making $20,000 a year, this man might have shot for much more on Madison Avenue. But he hadn't done so.

The editors' collection was, in short, a confused one. Plainly equating "success" with getting rich fast, they allowed themselves to become fascinated by people whose jobs really were more fun than making money, but they never did highlight the desire for fun and independence. Any chance to probe the spirit of these anti-organization men went neglected.

More important, perhaps, in light of the larger purposes of *Fortune Magazine*, was the obscurity surrounding money itself. What did it mean to get rich? No hint of correlation between plentitude and piety appeared. Nor, considering the failure to exploit evidences of desire for independence, was money really correlated with character: it did not seem linked with that sense of inner power inherent in the old evangel. And it certainly did not seem to be the language of speculators' mysticism. What about power and status in the business world? Slinkers, Sno-Cats, Marsh Buggies, Zippo Lighters, Bug-Trap Wax, home massages, truffles, chinchillas and trout made money, but these fell far from the central institutions of the economy. Was it not, after all, the young man heading for the big corporation, the big bank, the big law firm, the big government agency, who was more likely someday to feel the levers of power under his hands? True, a successful truffle grower might use his profits to move on into more exalted realms, but the editors of *100 Stories* assumed not. Money meant, according to them, split-level houses, private airplanes, Cadillacs and race horses; it meant private indulgence. Oddly, these heroes evinced no particular urge, apparently, to become real capitalists.

Was it some free-floating nostalgia for a style of entrepreneur no longer dominant that inspired these stories? Or something more strategical? In deploring the ideal of mere security among the young, the prophets of permanent revolution might well have been bemused by the image of one total, over-all system, given, external, simply "there." Well might more and more men wish for assured places within the system. But were not such wishes dangerous for the system? How could they make for more than stagnation? The system had to be fed and impelled by something prior, something outside, by men not mere products of its routine but instigators of its innovations and expansion. In seizing on the motive "to get rich fast," the editors were celebrating a dynamic that might keep the system going. Though dubious psychology even for millionaires, it was a recoil from the prospect of the economy becoming sheer bureaucracy.

By identifying the meaning of money with sheer private affluence, however, the editors hardly met their problem. Private affluence could be got by bureaucratic belonging, too. Strangely, larger purposes were close at hand. On somewhat the same basis as Josiah Strong, John Hay, Theodore Roosevelt and Elihu Root before him, Henry Luce himself had long wanted to harness the American business system to the service of the American Century, a world-wide projection of the old American Protestant will. But the independence, will and energy of the one hundred stories had precious little to do with such a world-wide missionary enterprise.

Another popular thirty-five-cent tract in the fifties was *How I Made a Million*, compiled from their back files by the editors of *Stag Magazine*. Less philosophical than *Fortune's* editors, *Stag's* compilers betrayed some of the foregoing confusions more blatantly. Again, promises outran performance a bit: it was not at all clear that all the twenty-odd heroes had made a literal million. Still, none were of that humbler bracket conspicuous in *100 Stories*. All the more conspicuous, therefore, was the location of the fields where these modern Horatio Algers had scored: wigs for Hollywood, cut-rate phonograph records, cars for lease, "crowd engineering," storm windows, custard cups. Again, we contemplate successes on the periphery, in the chinks and crannies of the economy—satellite-effects, so to speak. In *How I Made a Million* the origins rather than the destinies of the heroes said more than anything else. Out of twenty-two, six were immigrants, six sons of immigrants. Sixteen were raised in cities, seven of the sixteen in New York City. The classic hero of the nineteenth-century tale, the boy from farm or village, Protestant, Anglo-Saxon, was transmuted into the East Side slum kid.

How I Made a Million suggested some of the problems these late-comers faced. For them, making their way had a much less

clear moral and sociological context, as their routes led through neglected byways and twisting interstices within the system. In this
embrace of new breeds, the characterological psychology of the old
gospel of success simply evaporated. The successful man did not
project his own nature. Success followed from imaginative perception of secondary and tertiary needs of others, too marginal to have
been gathered into bureaucratic bigness. And again, success did not
enroll a man in the ranks of power. *Stag's* editors never did indicate
what money might be used for; for them being a millionaire still
had in and of itself a self-confirming, mystic status.

The human computers

Tacitly, individualistic latter-day success depended upon recognition, then gratification of other people's immediate appetites, many
of them appetites not yet conscious or fully perceived by those to
be gratified. It followed that the chief talent of the successful man
would be such sensitivity, and, from the record of *100 Stories* and
How I Made a Million, it was at least an inference that his sensitivity flourished in identical immediate appetites of his own. So far
as fundamental wishes were concerned, the successful man was like
everybody else.

But what made for truly big-time success? Surely not the mere
drive for security luring the young men into the big corporations.
In a quite different book, *The Art of Success* (1956), the editors of
Fortune again presented a collection of exemplary sketches, this
time, however, of men exercising—in most, though not all, cases—
large executive power. The book had practically nothing to do with
the Horatio Alger tradition, for many of its cases were men who
had immense personal advantages of wealth and position to begin
with. The book dwelt little upon sheer money-drive. Nor did it
highlight any psychological urges toward independence. In his introduction, Donald K. David, dean of the Harvard Business School,
hazarded the view that the key quality manifested by these men
with big-time business power was a certain outlook he called "social
consciousness."[12] Dean David warned that he meant this in a technical sense. It did not mean moral feelings of one kind or another. It

did not mean stewardship. It certainly did not mean political interest. Rather, these men were marked by an acute sensitivity to the interdependence between their own particular business organization and the larger national, often international, society. They were marked by a large capacity for input, receiving messages of all sorts from all sorts of sources, and responding to them in global decisions.

More suggestive of military commanders than of independent entrepreneurs, these business leaders simply transcended the alternatives of personal "security" and personal "risk-taking." Neither the persevering ascetics of the early capitalism studied by Max Weber nor the creative captains of industry of the late nineteenth century nor the hedonists of *100 Stories* and *Stag*, in their business life they suppressed identity. Though—unlike military commanders —they expected vast monetary recognition as a matter of course, they were "selfless" in the technical sense true of military leaders. Their acts did not express personal character, desires or will. Their success turned on suspension of self, and upon the neutral exposure of every faculty to the teeming signals demanding interpretation and integration. One might ask whether the role required any "self" at all. Perhaps what the managers were, as men, was no more and no less than the bureaucratic rationality they allowed to be pressed upon them, sometimes into the heart. Human computers—still decisively superior to the manufactured kind—they testified to the reality of a "system" with its own immanent urge to be kept running. Plainly, religious imagination centered in concepts of character, personal existence and the whole man were unneeded here.

Neither pious magic nor supple opportunism nor selfless sensitivity were enough. All these gospels and secrets and tips were shallow. They did not tell a man what sort of man he should try to be. They told him how to exploit himself or others, how to suck power and money from the circumambient ether or the market for truffles or the buzz of the system. They did not protect him against losing himself.

CHAPTER XIV

SPIRITUAL AUTOMATION, NEW STYLE

OF COURSE, one solution to life in the system was simply to insist that all was well. Take up Emerson's dilemma and accept it: to abide in the house was to abide in the spirit. Of such sanctification of things-as-they-are in business life, it is easy to think the supreme case was the famous book of Bruce Barton, first published in the heydey of the twenties, *The Man Nobody Knows*. Domesticating Christianity to the Chamber of Commerce, enlisting Jesus Christ into the ranks of Madison Avenue, Barton, one of the new breed of scientific salesmen, it might appear, quenched all anxieties in idolatrous adoration.

But whatever Barton's popular reputation, his book contained—and perhaps half-concealed—more of interest than sublime idolatry. Barton did not write of what he took to be true; he wrote of what he hoped might come to pass. He was a critic before he was a champion.

The hero of *The Man Nobody Knows* was a liberal version of Jesus. That was clear throughout. Barton repeated constantly that Jesus Christ was best known as a person, that his significance consisted of his exemplification of the potentials of personal existence. Hardly new, yet this was the first time this image of Jesus had been linked with business. Insofar as such earlier success-preachers as Henry Ward Beecher and Russell Conwell had been "liberals" theologically speaking, their liberalism had been revolt against old doctrines of predestination, rather than exploration of personhood. Barton by contrast was part of the new—and old—humanism.

Jesus as a model executive

Even this is not saying quite enough. The virtues of the liberal evangelical Jesus—He of the social gospel as well as of individual piety—were basically moral: brotherhood, peace, love. Barton alluded to these, but he did more. Evidently reacting against images of the sentimental sacrificial Jesus common in his boyhood, Barton attributed to Jesus qualities unusual in much liberal faith, let alone orthodoxy. In Barton's Jesus we find a blithe spirit. Stretching things only a little, one might say that Barton's Jesus evinced touches of that antinomian heedlessness that made liberal moralists as well as the orthodox nervous. Certainly, in His advice respecting little children, the lilies of the field, and the fears of tomorrow He did not encourage the psychology of the Protestant ethic. Moreover, not only could He preach and exemplify personal wholeness, He could induce it in others. Love, not as "moral ideal" but as immediate power, shone forth. It was clearer in Barton than in, say, his liberal contemporary Harry Emerson Fosdick, how the orthodox view of Jesus could be discarded without forsaking a classic Christian sense of Jesus Christ as divine power. In some ways this power approached ideas of mind cure and New Thought. But Barton was not preaching mind cure. The power he praised was not that of impersonal Mind or of "the Christ" or of superconsciousness. It was the power of personal existence, which was to say, of individual creative energy and self-transformation.

In his book on the Bible, too, *The Book Nobody Knows*,[1] Barton again presented the fundamental categories of the faith as those of full personal outreach. Faith consisted of intimacy with a person, and out of that intimacy flowed the help, the methods, the secrets and the grace needed for personal unfolding. If at times the supreme Person seemed to be a kind of extroverted general practitioner who liked camping, still, Barton was pointing at life in terms of inner resources when they were at the flood. His lapses into parody—Jesus as "Outdoor Man," "Organizer and Executive," "Founder of Modern Business"—if painful, were not destructive of his theme. Insofar as Barton raised the prospect of inner abundance, there is some justice in regarding him as a significant figure in postwar Protestantism.

Barton's pre-emption of Jesus as First Great Executive, First Great Advertising Man, Founder of Modern Business made it easy to assume that he read into Jesus qualities he found in modern business, and not the reverse, and that he thus took business as the measure. On this interpretation, he was not calling Jesus in to save an ailing world, but calling Him in simply as business's supreme sanction. But this was not Barton's view. His whole polemic turned on his insistence that business was not all right. Business was ailing. Something had been lost—some sense of excitement and meaning work once had had when gathered under the religious concept of the "calling." All work is religious work, Barton cried. All business is our Father's business. Business as an autonomous realm, unmeasured from beyond itself, as a realm merely of efficiency, let alone merely of money-making, suffered from a spread of meaninglessness.

How, then, was the abundant and creative Jesus to be integrated with business life? What did His supreme heedlessness have to do with business practice? What did the spontaneous laughter which delighted Barton have to do with business manners? What part did outdoor vigor play? Unfortunately, Barton never explained. The one point of contact appeared to be a correlation between Jesus' personal magnetism and the purported qualities of business leadership. Perhaps such magnetism did have something to do with executive success. But what were the sources of such magnetism? And did the business system as it was really invite ·it or allow it or nourish it? Perhaps such magnetism was not compatible with any "system" at all, perhaps it was a revolutionary and innovative force rather than an administrative one. Barton did not say.

Again, it is only fair to appreciate how Barton differed from conventional apologetics. He was not trying to "protect" business. He had nothing to say about immutable economic laws. There was nothing of stewardly condescension in him. He wanted to justify and reintegrate business in terms of personality, personality not in the Puritan style of diligence, thrift, dogged perseverance, but along the "Jesus" dimensions of joy, radiance, wholeness. But he had no nerve for any hints as to what this might require. He never equated the "service" rendered by Jesus with the service of a service station or a store, he never ranked the human needs tended by Jesus with needs met by big steel, auto factories or the stock market. Rejecting Puritan asceticism, responsive to a life-style of psychological abundance, at the same time his ideal rose well above the materialistic abundance of commodities. And yet, he was unable to establish relevance. Himself one of the super-salesmen, he wanted selling itself to radiate wholeness. He wanted the system to fulfill personality in its own operations, not just in the products it ground out. But Barton never could express more than the pure wish, alone.

Dale Carnegie's ethic of cooperation

Implicitly, Barton's ideal signaled the need for changing the system. Was it not easier frankly to embark upon changing men to fit the system?

No image of the adapted, new-model man was presented as sharply as by Dale Carnegie in his latter-day success classic, *How to Win Friends and Influence People*, first out in 1936. If *The Man Nobody Knows* was unwitting parody, *How to Win Friends* was perhaps unwitting parody on unwitting parody, for what Carnegie offered resembled nothing so much as the means for achieving a self-automated caricature of Barton's personal-magnetism ideal. The book is one of those pulse points in modern American popular culture where the murmers and racing of hidden currents can be discerned.

Of the book's influence, one can say only that it no doubt confirmed as much as it stimulated broad feelings. We do know the book was no lucky accident. Carnegie had been refining his lore through the twenties, in instructions to businessmen about practical, effective human relations, and his manual *Public Speaking and Influencing Men in Business* had been itself a success among a specialized audience.[2] In any case, whether leading or following popular sentiments, Carnegie performed the task of scripturizing them. Thereby they came to constitute a "mind," with its own inherent logic—and problems.

In his advice to young men, Albert Shaw had been hazy about the characterological style the average young man should nourish —or affect. The closest he came to enjoining any particular trait was in his recommendation of "cooperation." In the old ethic, the value of "cooperation" had been ambiguous. Naturally, Alger-style heroes had had sufficient interpersonal competence to impress rich benefactors, and certainly in the Protestant praise of "trade" from the time of Daniel Defoe, a psyche able, even willing, to please, stood posited. Yet "cooperation" hardly could count as more than an ornament, as the subtle dialectic of a master competitor and aggressor, such as Franklin, who never disguised the fact that the cooperation he commended was manipulation. Cooperation in the old ethic, in short, attested the strength of the old character structure to accommodate a deal of duplicity, insincerity, hypocrisy.

It was Dale Carnegie's business to transform the ornament into the keystone, to bring the occasion of insincerity into the heart— and make it sincere.

The first hero-bureaucrat

His favorite hero was a man of the transition, Charles Schwab, rising in the age of creation, arriving in the age of administration. Schwab, as was reiterated time out of mind on the luncheon circuits, was a man who knew how to handle men. He was an expert in human relations. He knew how to get men to want to do what he wanted them to do. Schwab's enormous ideological reputation was symptomatic. He had not, after all, been the "original" hero of his own tale. That had been Andrew Carnegie, who had picked Schwab to run his, Carnegie's, creations. Schwab was the most famous early success in a new sort of job—executive management. Neither building steel companies in ambitious passion nor juggling them in financial empires, he was their immanent genius, the first hero-bureaucrat. Over the long run it would be seen that bureaucrats need not, and should not, be heroes, except to themselves. But Schwab's reputation facilitated the new role-identification.

A man chosen by another man: one could take this as the crux of the new gospels of success. In Horatio Alger's tales young lads were chosen by older men upon their display of courage, pluck or industry, though of course it is well to note how much luck had to do with these decisive choices: what if the girl one rescued was not a merchant's daughter? Still, these displays presumably revealed total character: one was chosen for what one really was. Schwab's secret, according to Dale Carnegie, was a prodigiously winning smile—a smile "worth a million dollars." Was this the revelation of Schwab as a man? Interestingly, the favorite anecdotes about Schwab portrayed his capacity for charming workers in the mill rather than in more usual executive scenes. If the smile revealed character, evidently there were some power-interests at stake as well. Smiles might defeat unions. Anyway, had Andrew Carnegie chosen Schwab because he, Carnegie, had found Schwab's smile irresistible? It seemed unlikely; but perhaps Carnegie knew workers found it so. Schwab's symbolic status was not due to the specter of labor problems, however. It was due to the need, understood by Bruce Barton, for believing in personal significance among the successful.

Dale Carnegie's book was full of salesmen, many identified by name. It was suggestive that none had real stature as culture heroes. Not even Barton had that. Nevertheless, though incapable of producing culture heroes, salesmanship had become a critical phase of the economy. Salesmen sold things to people. Frank Haddock's warning not to sell people things they did not really want evinced an old spirit about to be engulfed in a new dilemma. Could the economy safely rely upon "natural" demands alone? As long as

130 years before, Joel Barlow, the Jeffersonian advocate of un-Jeffersonian economic expansion, had urged the deliberate cultivation of "artificial" wants as necessary stimulus to progress and prosperity. But, heir of the fabled Yankee trader, the modern salesman might still find himself, among people still inhibited by ascetic thrift and frugality, regarded as the Yankee had been, a man who could make you buy despite yourself, who could get inside you somehow, manipulate you, get the "better" of you by seducing the worst in you. In this ultimate salesmanship between retailer and consumer there assuredly lurked a nest of questions about sincerity, curling and uncurling about each other. But this was not the salesmanship discussed by Carnegie at all.

One section of his book—Part Five, "Letters That Produced Miraculous Results"—defined his focus. The two letters Carnegie discussed were both written by a man named Ken R. Dyke, sales-promotion manager of the Johns-Manville Company. What were the miraculous results? Dyke's letters went out, not to customers, but to dealers in Johns-Manville products, asking them simply to tell him whether the sales campaign being carried on by the company was doing any good. Miraculously, 42.5 per cent of the dealers actually did reply to tell him. The ordinary return on such requests ran, apparently, from 5 to 8 per cent. The second letter went to architects, inquiring whether the company's catalogue was any good. Dyke got back a little less than 50 per cent returns, as against ordinary returns of 2 to 5 per cent.

What Dyke's letters overcame—temporarily, of course—was a kind of organizational noise, or friction, or better still, automatism. With the establishment of national bureaucratic organizations, naturally the problem of communications became immense. Dyke himself had no product to sell, no sales resistance to overcome. He was trying to help dealers and architects to sell. But ordinarily not even self-interest overcame the routine and security of the system. Letters by the thousands vanished into the void, moths beating for attention against the screens of standard operating procedure. Relationships had become distant, mechanical, abstract.

Making man feel important enough to smile

The job of the manager was to repersonalize, rehumanize, reanimate this world of increasing rote. This was Dyke's talent. Of course, the point at which the salesman had to do this most specifically was the point of contact with the ultimate consumer, by linking commodities with symbols—of status, of success, of character, of power, of belonging, of morality, of patriotism, of potency. But the salesmanship taught by Carnegie was salesmanship within the system itself, the salesmanship of the system selling itself to itself. And in this regard, the book was witness to the collapse of older theories of economic behavior, theories assuming that economic self-interest is rational and decides. Why did more than half the dealers fail to respond even to Ken R. Dyke's seductive appeal to their self-interest?

What did decide? Feelings, and more precisely, a certain feeling. The deepest urge in human nature is the "desire to be important," Carnegie said, and this explained the success of Charles Schwab and Ken R. Dyke. They made men feel important. (Though he might as well have credited any number of sages over the centuries, Carnegie attributed this insight to John Dewey.) What in Frank Haddock had been only a peripheral intimation now became the center: organization is people and people want to feel they count. One plain implication of Carnegie's book was that the system had not been making people feel they did count. Something was needed. Carnegie's prescription was simple. Smile. Be like Charles Schwab.

It hardly took modern psychology to explain the cogency of smiles in improving human relations, or of some of Carnegie's other recommendations: extend "lavish praise"; offer "hearty approbation"; talk about what people are interested in; let them think new ideas are their ideas; be interested in them. All this helps them feel important. This in turn, in some way, helps you.

But just how does it help you?

Carnegie's rules were clear and commonsensical with respect to the object, the man smiled at, the man whose name is remembered, the man allowed to imagine the idea is his. What was not so clear was the position of the subject, the man who smiles.

Why does a person smile? Because, perhaps, he is happy. Perhaps he already feels important and therefore can smile. But Carnegie was not writing his book for people who already were smiling. He wrote it for people who evidently were not smiling and needed to be told to do so. What reasons would they have? As in the psychological sequence pointed out by William James, that wondrous technique of acting "as if" which attracted the mind-cure writers, it was possible to smile in order to feel happy. The idea attracted Carnegie as well, who, like the mind-cure leaders, quoted James frequently. But this was not Carnegie's main lesson. By that logic a person could make himself feel important and have an end with it. Carnegie's emphasis fell upon people's need to be smiled at by other people.

A man might smile at other people because he was glad to see them, was interested in them, did find them important. Here was Carnegie's chance to propose the soft liberal Protestant answer to all problems of human relations. Really love other people. Everyone is sacred. The richest field of experience is the community of others, of brotherhood, teamwork, the group. Really be a member of the family of man. But this was not Carnegie's strategy. Far from displaying any hint of the liberal faith that in their deepest selves people *are* loving, Carnegie worked instead from a harsh principle. "People are not interested in you. They are not interested in me. They are interested in themselves—morning, noon, and after dinner."[3]

A Hobbesian view that people are universally self-centered and selfish logically implied the Hobbesian predicament, the war of all against all. Quite consistently with his original premise, Hobbes escaped it by invoking the action of rational self-interest which would lead people to see that in self-protection they must accept authority and order. Rejecting the evangelical liberal Protestant effort to break the premise by winning people from selfishness to love, and the humanist liberal denial of the premise, Carnegie's answer was to substitute smiles for Hobbes's political authority.

This, too, was consistent, presumably. To feel important, one must be smiled at. Therefore one smiles in order to elicit smiles.

But instantly, this raised a problem Hobbes had not had to face. "No! No! No! I am not suggesting flattery," Carnegie admonished. "An insincere grin? No. That doesn't fool anybody. We know it is mechanical and we resent it. I am talking about a real smile, a heart-warming smile, a smile that comes from within. . . ." "Make the other person feel important—and do it sincerely."[4]

The troublesome sincerity

Hobbesians had a perfectly rational basis for sincerely committing their safety to the autocrat. Unfortunately, one thing missing in *How to Win Friends and Influence People* was instruction in how sincerely to like people, sincerely to be interested in them, and sincerely to find them important.

Naturally, Carnegie could not help vitiating his exhortations to sincerity a bit. What was a "real" smile? One that was "heart-warming," yes—though that did not prove it came from a warm heart; one that "came from within," yes—though "within" was not necessarily always sincere; but then also, in a transition to which Carnegie himself was obviously insensible: "the kind of smile that will bring a good price in the market place." There was nothing subtle about the trouble here. Heart-warming smiles worth good prices which nevertheless did not come from warm hearts were easily imaginable. Such were learned routinely by professional actors, for instance, for whom, according to some schools of dramatic science (though denied by others), to have to feel the emotion one believably projects is an interference. Carnegie's real—though hidden, since he could not face the issue—point was not that the smiles of non-professionals would be so crude as not to work, for there were many talented amateurs. It was rather that the man who used smiles must believe in his smiles in order to believe in the smiles directed at him. His sincere smile was his allegiance to the system of smiles.

In Carnegie's world, people did not seek importance by seeking some power. They did not seek importance by doing something important. They did not seek importance by giving themselves to some important process. Where sincerity became an issue was where people lacked these sorts of importance. Sincerity was a problem for the weak. In accord with Carnegie's Hobbesian assumptions, the purpose of the smile was to disarm others, to remove from them their reality as power, and this could be done only if one believed in one's own smiles, only if one believed that one really did like the other, that is, that the other was truly smiling, likable, and therefore as innocent as oneself. What one achieved by smiling was not power but the neutralization of power, so long as one smiled sincerely.

In the long run this was a self-consuming logic. It was not the potential hypocrisy and cynicism that vitiated the method. It was rather that trying to solve the problem of sincerity by self-manipulation involved one in an infinite regression, an endless effort to disarm oneself as well as others. The idea that liking people would serve the purpose of influencing people ran onto the reef that the purpose for having influence was disintegrated. What happened when likable people met? They could only seek to resemble each other, concealing their ulterior purpose of exerting influence not only from each other but from themselves. Of such a situation it would not be enough to say that character had become "personality" in the sense feared in early mind cure—a mask, a pose—because the fact that the mask was a mask was forgotten. The one purpose that seemed to remain clear was, of course, to make money. But money, an impersonal symbol, now symbolized precisely the impersonality of personality, that is, the dependent reflection in everyone of everyone else. Implicitly, Carnegie here did have the medium which buoyed up his logic. Money, he clearly assumed, did not have to be in short supply; smiles could earn it, and everyone could smile —even more easily than everyone could have right thoughts. The indefinite regression of smiling disarmament could proceed so long as the money lasted.

Still, likability was victimized, not just by the suspicion that there were those playing the game insincerely, but by the stress of being likable. To be a mirror in which others might find themselves important, to commit oneself sincerely to what one appeared to be, to consist primarily of behavior, talk and smiles that others liked was to become still more vulnerable, exposed still more to what lay outside, when it was precisely to disarm outside power that one smiled. It was to engage in the disintegration of one's own awareness of reality, one's own ego-consciousness, one's own integration as a self.

As for winning friends, one of the peculiarities of the famous book was that it had practically nothing to say of friendship.

It may be wondered whether Carnegie's book was primarily about gaining success after all. To be sure, for men of an older, work-oriented, tool-oriented temper, it could come as a revelation to be told that smiles were helpful. If such men could learn the lesson, they might well smile their way higher up some one or another ladder than their technical competence might have carried them. But Carnegie never realistically asked just where and to what extent in the business world smiles did count. Were there no gruff or impersonal or strictly analytical or even sour-tempered successes left? There were, and it was not at all clear that some of them were not still the men of real power. The business of smiling did correspond to a shift in the nature of the business world, but it was also very much a betrayal of uncertainty and sometimes schism in the sense men had of themselves and their worth. Perhaps men still sure of themselves, men who already felt important, were the ones who, even in the personalized bureaucracy, smiled most influentially because they smiled only when they really did mean it.

The new world of industrial psychology

Since it was self-consuming, Carnegie's teaching could hardly support a new character style. Something more was needed, relieving the individual of having to rely on his own sincere consciousness. Ego already suffered only too easily from a sense of unimportance and thus only that much more readily detected what really was threatening in the system of other men. In the end, absorption of consciousness, ego and self altogether into the harmonic operations of a larger order would be preferable, whereby it would be the system itself that smiled. This was the upshot of the great new mystique of mid-century business life—human relations in management. With human relations, the corporation became not just a house but a home, and if a cage, full of peace.

That management would have to progress from the intuitive methods of the early founders—who hardly thought of themselves as "managers" at all—to more formal methods, to science, had been widely understood early in the century. But what kind of science? Thorstein Veblen, for one, had believed that scientific management would follow from the influence of the machine and its visible, mechanical, cause-effect operations.[5] This to Veblen suggested the triumph of the engineer, the mechanic and the rational-minded sociologist, an idea surviving into Technocracy and popping up now and then in social-gospel calls for "spiritualized technicians." But the managerial science of the future was not destined to derive from engineering. Management would rest on psychology.

It was precisely the engineering-oriented time-motion studies of Frederick J. Taylor that opened the door. Every job could be analyzed into a succession of elementary motions, and Taylor took it for granted that workers could and should be trained in those motions. This training itself implied a psycho-physical, not just physical, adaptation. Taylor's work, promoting individual adaptation to physical work processes, anticipated the larger practice of analyzing work into its psycho-social constituents and manipulating these as an organizational as well as a mechanical system. And there was no reason in principle to inhibit the same careful analysis of the work done by the managers themselves.

The larger role of the manager as psycho-social organizational symphonist gained its stature and theoretical justification in the work of Elton Mayo and his colleagues from the late twenties. Mayo was an Australian who came to the United States in his forties, where, perhaps, it was his freshness of eye that allowed him to see with explicit awareness what to Americans themselves had remained immanent in business process. As professor of industrial research at the Harvard School of Business Administration, he became the prophet of sophisticated, big-business managerial philosophy.

Mayo had directed the famous study of the telephone girls at the Hawthorne plant of Western Electric in Chicago, where, after many mysteries, the researchers were led to the startling conclusion that the prime influence upon the girls' efficiency had been, not color of walls or sounds of music or coffee breaks or personality of supervisor but—the study itself. They had been made to feel important. The conclusion also opened the Pandora's box Carnegie had so anxiously sought to shut. It invited insincerity.

From the Hawthorne study Mayo proceeded on far into the wonderful new world of industrial psychology, scientific human relations and managerial self-consciousness, the gist of which was: managers should be a race apart. Industrial psychology had discovered that motives which, from the standpoint of sheer formal and planned efficiency, were non-rational lurked behind and determined on-the-job behavior. Managers should act accordingly. Mayo explicitly encouraged a managerial elite exercising psychological techniques known to itself alone for the good of the organization. Let the managers be logical in their management of men who were not. Still again, Franklin had anticipated science long before.[6]

After World War II the business of human-relations-in-business boomed, spawning a host of personnel men, expert psychologists, consultants, new business-school courses and divisions and institutes, testing organizations and so on. "Making management human" as an exciting new goal reflected oddly on the reputation of previous management, while proposing, it seemed, a spacious new purpose. Yet this vast display of self-consciousness almost never lost a certain cloudiness at its center and dim mistiness at the outpost.

What did it have to do with the management of labor, for instance? In much of big industry, unions spoke, after all, on the issues clustering on the assembly line. In at least one earnest human-relations symposium, the lone trade-union participant argued sharply that, if they really meant their human-relations approach sincerely, managers would prove it by helping strengthen unions;

so long as they did not, union leaders would not be charmed.[7] As for the growing ranks of white-collar workers, usually not unionized, the human-relations approach seemed to carry little force. And confusion still ruled on the more general issue of the humanization of work itself. So distinguished a business spokesman as Clarence Randall, head of Inland Steel, in effect surrendered here, concluding that the route toward more meaningful life lay through shortening the hours of work for a larger leisure. But a Standard Oil executive, O. A. Ohmann, disagreed: "No, I am afraid the job *is* the life. *This* is what must be made meaningful."[8] It was an old issue, long agitated by intellectuals, radicals and conservatives, but human-relations management did not seem to advance matters any.

The fact was that, in dialectical reversal of Mayo's original intent, the human relations manipulated by human-relations programs were most of all the human relations of the managers themselves.

The basic mood promoted by human relations was "participation" or "sharing." Technically speaking, the primary problem in the new large-scale corporations, as in all large-scale organizations, was that of communications. A huge amount of the psychology taught to the scientific managers clustered here: how to set up systems of efficient two-way flow. This included knowing how to overcome blocks to effective communication located deep in individual psyches. Just what was to be communicated? Hard data, of course, along with orders, inquiries, confirmations, etc. But evidently the communication of hard data also required communication of complaints, sympathies, emotional discharges and "honest" responses. Men should communicate as men, not just as machines, and this "whole" communication was thought to advance efficiency as much as narrow factuality did. As men truly "shared" in the processes of the system, feeling their own identity in its identity, they would cease to constitute problems for communication and become instead the open channels for the processes of the system.

There was an assumption, more or less explicit, enabling such open communication. This was the assumption that it was safe to be open. To be emotionally clear and unrepressed and unguarded and frank was of course to be vulnerable, and to be so a man had to feel secure. Obviously then, one of the tasks of the new-model executive was to reconstitute himself so that he did seem safe as the recipient of whole, honest, frank communications, and, in precise analogy to Dale Carnegie's logic of smiles, to do this he had to give himself honestly and frankly to the process, to be sincere. How? That would be hard, unless he in his turn could trust that the power which gave order and meaning to the process of honest communication was not that of manipulating managers but that of the organization itself, with its intrinsic integrity.

The personality tests

Bartonian hopes for ripened business personality could mount to rapture. A John Hancock Insurance Company executive, Abram Collier, urged upon managers the vision of "co-operation, together-ness, and sharing the great adventure," the vision of exploring "a changing, growing, and infinitely exciting world." Since "creative-ness" was at once ideal fruit of the business environment and divine attribute, Collier urged that "business is also religion."[9] But if we do not know how many business leaders shared the great adventure, we do know something of the drift in techniques of executive re-cruitment, and it does not seem Mr. Collier could have been satis-fied.

By 1950 methods of standard testing, measurement and evalua-tion had been put to use on up beyond the clerical staff (unions resisted testing vigorously) into the executive suites, to the very threshold of the office of the chief himself, and in some cases even past that door. The culmination of this process came with the proliferation of personality testing in the mid- and late fifties.[10]

Certainly, quite apart from their validity, personality tests could have been intended to identify any of a number of dominant in-terests of a man: did he like working with slide rules? or with people? or with words? or with materials? But in the clear, if not even overwhelming, majority of cases, one aim came first in using personality tests for executive recruitment: find the man whose personality already fits that of the corporation. In order to succeed in such an effort, the corporation had to be thought to have a personality, so companies—that is, top managers and recruiters—self-consciously composed them. Then they could look for men who matched. The significance of this was not only its goal of getting the right man for the right post, which was ordinary enough within limits. What the tests expressed more deeply was the wish to englobe the whole man on the job. Then, in finding the right man, all problems of sharing and participation vanished, for, by definition—his personality profile—the new man was a psychological fit from the start.

By another odd dialectic, Taylorism, management's early attempt at physical fixation of the worker, had turned back on itself in management's attempt at psychological fixation of itself. Taylor's meticulous job descriptions for men on the assembly line were repeated in the meticulous listing of psychological traits required of the man in the oak-paneled office. And at least it had made no difference what the worker was like off-hours; the new executive, however, was expected to fit in his reading, in his tastes in art and politics, in his sports, was expected to manifest the blend that blended, everywhere, always. That testing sometimes tested his wife was only logical. The anxiety was circular, self-accelerating, without logical cutoff point. Consciousness-centered integration was to yield to the superconsciousness, the individual was to take cage for cosmos. "Business was business" after all.

That the personality tests were commonly held by academic psychologists to be unreliable, unvalidated, superficial, antiquated and often fallacious by their very nature, only suggested the strength of the wish. The tests were what managers who needed to be sincere in managing themselves needed.

The mystique of human relations simply added another layer of imposed socialization upon consciousnesses already severly burdened. Naturally, where the extrinsic rewards were great, men might very well adopt the credo of "belonging" more or less cheerfully as cheap enough a psychic bargain in return for the stock options and juicy bonuses. Other men might adopt it simply to ease the strain, for after all the corporation's way of life was better than some. But still others, knowing perfectly well that in the non-democratic, authoritarian, leader-oriented hierarchies of the modern corporation, free, frank and open communication was in fact not safe, would treat the mystique as a game to be played. In an endless recession, sincerity escaped capture. The most interesting by-products of the personality tests were precise instructions on just how to cheat.

Dale Carnegie would have been startled, at least; Bruce Barton would have been dismayed.

CHAPTER XV

THE DIVINE ECONOMY

ONCE UPON a time a kind of man, a kind of economy and a kind of religion had, the three of them, resonated with each other, linked in a closed circuitry of mutually impelling energy. The man of the Protestant ethic, an economy of individual enterprise, a God of Will comprised a trinity of standard male existence. Whatever a spectator from outside might have found by way of narrowness or precariousness or callousness or obsession, from inside this style of existence felt compelling, more than sufficient, indeed impelled toward a fusion—psychology, economy, theology becoming each other—which spelled its own end. To the economist and presidential adviser Walt Whitman Rostow we owe the concept of "take-off" in the historical development of an economy. The man of the Protestant ethic supplied power on the runway. Once in flight the economy moved ahead not on character but on technique. Hence if at the center of nineteenth-century social imagination there had stood a man, in the twentieth he was replaced by the vision of a system.

Some of the failures to spiritualize the system by harnessing it for purposes from outside we have seen—imperialism, paternalism, harmonic absorption. What it meant to try to save the central individual we have seen—psychological automation, self-disintegrating self-manipulation, ego-abandonment.

But there was one more alternative for sanctifying the system without doing anything about it, another way of thinking to make everything come out right. This was to regard the economy in a traditional religious fashion, as an object of worship rather than for imitation, an occasion for dependency rather than belonging. Men know the hidden God, the God of Will, only in His works, not in His nature. In a downward spiral, men could return by way of dialectic to the position of early Protestants, between whom and God there opened an abyss, to be bridged not by insight, by knowledge, by intelligence, by courage, by politics, by tradition, but by faith alone. Awesome, inscrutable, self-impelling, the system invited adoration.

The spell of Henry Ford

Abstraction lives in detail. Ralph Waldo Trine went to Dearborn, Michigan, in 1928, for an "intimate talk on life" with Henry Ford, and one realizes after a bit that this was a modern pilgrimage.

Even among mind-cure writers, notable for their collective discard of old assumptions of scarcity in favor of new assumptions of abundance, Trine had been exceptional for his sense of bounty and overflow. Twenty-nine years after publishing *In Tune with the Infinite,* he was as a man for whom the word had in truth been made flesh. Ford, of course, appeared regularly in articles and stories and sketches perpetuating the old gospel of success; untainted by the turn-of-century anxieties about monopoly, hailed for a purportedly enlightened labor policy, rising uncultured from appropriate rural circumstances, he far surpassed all peers in suitability for myth. But Trine saw him from another and much more interesting perspective, undoubtedly the perspective of most other people as well despite the old-fashioned myth. Trine saw Ford as Supply.

The transcript of their conversation—published as *The Power That Wins*—was as interesting a revelation of the mind of Henry Ford as of Trine. Ford's theory of man:

Each is a world in himself—and at the same time a part of all there is; and all—the All—is here now. To his center—himself —he is continually attracting *little entities*—invisible lives—that are building him up. . . .[1]

Ford on his own success:

Perhaps I ought to explain that I believe we are reincarnated. You, I, we reincarnate over and over. We live many lives, and store up much experience. Some are older souls than others and so they know more. It seems to be an intuitive "gift." It is really hard-won experience.[2]

Ford on his early life:

I was never more discouraged than I am at this minute—*not a particle*. I have never been discouraged. . . . I didn't think that there was any chance of failure. Anybody can do anything he imagines.[3]

Ford's recommendations for life:

. . . Food specialists should try to find some food or combination of foods that will help to develop strong will-power. . . . Why should there not . . . be a possibility of feeding a man so so that he may be built up against mental or moral sickness?[4]

And it was gratifying to hear from Ford that *In Tune with the Infinite*—along with Trine's other books—had sustained him greatly in his struggles to organize the Ford Motor Company before the war.

Ford's presence seemed to exert some sort of spell over Trine, at once exciting and confounding. As proven Power and Success, Ford qualified as Judge of every conceivable solution for every conceivable problem of mankind. Trine tried out some of his food fads—"The avocado has very wonderful food qualities, if we are able to get it"—and Ford obliged with nostrums of his own: ". . . Salt is one of the best things for the teeth. And also for the hair. . . . Yes, I am a great believer in salt."[5] But he refused to get programmatic. When Trine, protesting that people ought to live longer, suggested that Ford sponsor an institute for research and education in longevity, Ford weaved away: "Well, letting that go—if it is to be done it will be done—."[6]

Ford exploded Trine's old pastoral idyl of cottage individualism with a casual sweep: "Agriculture will be handled on a very large scale. There won't be much more small farming. The fences will come down, and farm operations will be planned on a large scale."[7] Trine could hardly protest, having come for wisdom to the genius of the assembly line. Later he got another bit of economic wisdom. Evidently the "plenty" of the twenties had made Trine somewhat uneasy, and he asked Ford if people should not be saving more, ". . . as an aid against the days of no work, or a greatly altered income or wage." It was Ford who brought Trine back to basic mind-cure economics. Having suffered from sticking too long with the Model-T, he had begun to appreciate the consumers' economy:

> One day some one brought to us a slogan which read: "Buy a Ford and Save the Difference." I crossed out the "save" and inserted "spend"—"Buy a Ford and Spend the Difference." It is the wiser thing to do. Society lives by circulation, and not by congestion.[8]

But if congruent with Trine's sense of plenty, this hardly helped him understand Henry Ford, the power who provided. Trine's notions had been very simple. "Wealth beyond a certain amount cannot be used, and when it cannot be used then becomes a hindrance rather than an aid, a curse rather than a blessing." He had warned against accumulating "enormous wealth" on the spiritual ground that it took time and thought from "the real things of life." But in 1928 he sat facing a (reputed) billionaire. His notions of abundance did not begin to comprehend capital. His orientation was that of the consumer quite uncomprehending of the sources of his supply. Ford—Supply—was inexplicable, like God. So was the Ford Motor Company.

The possibility seemed plain: Trine did not really want to understand Ford. He came to worship. Ford was not traditional hero-representative of thousands of imitative would-be Fords but hero-provider. It was enough, altogether sufficient, to be in tune with this supply. Not will or character or purpose or politics or reform mattered, but correct thinking, for the simple fact was, there was plenty for everybody.

The lyric of plenty

This had been the mind-cure faith early, as it was to be late. In *Practical Methods for Self-Development*, Elizabeth Towne, New Thought editor of *The Nautilus* in Springfield, Massachusetts, had rather wonderfully sung the mood in 1904, not without some special flavor of yoga:

> The only thing that keeps us from taking plenty of either money or air is fear. . . . We take in breath or money by expanding. We force out air or money by contracting. The trouble with us is that we are afraid to expand. . . . We are afraid to expect more than a couple of dollars or so a day. . . . Wake up. Expand. Take deep, full breaths of air, and your mind and purse expand in sympathy with your lungs. . . . Money is *really* as free as air. Take it in by knowing that it is yours. The world is catching an inkling of this truth. Prices are going up. The miner is learning that he has just as good a right to big pay as the mine boss has. . . . Edward Bellamy was no visionary; he, too, was a prophet, a sure one. The wildest dreams of socialism are prophecy. The miner who digs out coal is exactly as valuable to this world as J. Pierpont Morgan is, or Andrew Carnegie; he has use. What is more, he is coming into his right. . . . Wake up and stretch yourself. Yawn. Take long, full breaths of air and money and glory. All you desire is YOURS NOW. Take it in mentally and work it out physically.[9]

So lyric was the mood that sometimes it could bypass money to strike directly for abundance all literal. From 1912 to 1922 Herbert W. Eustace of San Jose, California, was a member of the board of trustees of the Christian Science Publishing Society, as well as an esteemed practitioner. Along with his fellow trustees he waged a prolonged legal struggle with the five-man board of directors, to, as he said, "free Christian Science from the materiality of organization and loose it for its higher destiny of pure metaphysics."[10] When the directors won in 1922 and froze the church under authoritarian leadership, Eustace went on to teach Christian Science on his own, loyal, by his lights, to Mrs. Eddy. He did not fail to avail himself of his freedom to soar:

> . . . Suppose you found yourself stalled in the desert, apparently without gasoline? Must you necessarily wait until someone brings you gasoline or tows you to the nearest filling station? Suppose no one comes along? Do you think that Christian Science would leave you helpless? . . . What is the truth about gasoline? . . . Gasoline is as omnipresent as Mind. There is no place where it is not available. . . . The question is, are you finding gasoline as a state of Mind, or of matter?[11]

Mr. Eustace had already analyzed another highway problem—bad brakes. What would you do?

> You would turn to Principle, to Christian Science, as your Mind and there find the truth about what was being presented to you —the truth about inoperative brakes. . . . "Brakes" is merely the truth upon which the lie is built, that lie whereby malicious suggestion operates to induce an acceptance of a belief of imperfect brakes. . . . It is not imperfect brakes, but the hypnotic suggestion of a *belief* of imperfect brakes, that is the trouble.[12]

Don't think about hard times

The most thorough of all mind-cure tracts on economic well-being was *Prosperity*, by Charles Fillmore of Unity. First published in 1936, Fillmore's little book has continued to be printed and sold ever since. First impressions would suggest that Fillmore had just rewritten Russell Conwell with his famous complaint that "it is all wrong to be poor anyhow." "We cannot be very happy if we are poor," Fillmore said, "and nobody needs to be poor. It is a sin to be poor."[13] Poor clothes were also a sin. And like Conwell and his peers, Fillmore emphasized that opportunity was never lacking, a dogma more pointed in 1936 than ordinarily, during the "so-called depression." Fillmore taught the value of industry and effort also, though not, as we shall see, with entire consistency. But *Prosperity* was not just another success tract, and Fillmore's more important ideas were not echoes of the old ethic.

First, Fillmore was eager to get his philosophy of money understood. Money was not power, but purely a convenience. What counted were correct thoughts. It was no good even being rich without also holding the proper thoughts. Perhaps recalling his own experience of sudden riches and sudden loss in the Kansas City real-estate bubble of 1889, Fillmore warned: "People who come into riches suddenly without building up a consciousness of prosperity soon part from their money."[14] A further conclusion Fillmore drew was still more serious:

> Those who are born and bred to riches usually have plenty all their life even though they never make the effort to earn a dollar for themselves. This is because the ideas of plenty are so interwoven into their thought atmosphere that they are a very part of themselves.[15]

This was hardly the old gospel of success. Moreover, strangely enough, money here did seem to exercise a power of its own. The inference was not unfair to the spreading ethos of the new economics. If riches were to become universal, there would be no need for special teaching of how to get rich. The system would be closed at last, as prosperity became its own church.

At all events, the "metaphysical" character of money served as ground for Fillmore's polemic against possession, accumulation, hoarding. These betrayed fear of lack in the future, which in turn amounted to a mistake about God. "There is no lack of [Supply] in infinite Mind. Regardless of how much God gives, there is always an abundance left."[16] Such misunderstanding provided Fillmore his explanation of the depression—in its way a variation upon President Hoover's complaints about lack of "confidence."

> Insulate your mind from the destructive thoughts of all those who labor under the belief in hard times. If your associates talk about the financial stringency, affirm all the more persistently your dependence upon the abundance of God. . . . We have thought that there is only about so much. . . . We have

thought that we must be careful how we spend it and put some of it away for a time when there won't be any more. . . . We begin to pinch in our mind, and then our money becomes pinched. . . . Then comes depression, hard times, shortage. . . .[17]

"Don't talk about [hard times]," Fillmore advised, for talking is thought and thoughts are things.

Fillmore's admonitions meshed better with New Deal Keynesianism than with the old laissez-faire. And when he pushed on beyond unpleasant analysis of lack to the more congenial evocation of possibilities, the political economy of the old gospel of success simply faded away:

There is need for reform in economics more than in any other department of everyday life. Money has been manipulated by greed until greed itself is sick and secretly asks for a panacea. . . . Far-seeing Christians look forward to an early resumption of the economic system inaugurated by the early followers of Jesus Christ. They had all things in common and no man lacked anything. . . . The divine law holds that the earth is the Lord's and the fullness thereof. If this truth were thoroughly understood, men would begin at once to make all property public, available for the use and enjoyment of all the people.[18]

Here was a "social" gospel indeed.

Wasting no praise upon competition, casting serious—if confused—doubts about the value of the frugality exalted in the old teaching, Fillmore went on to break with the heart-of-hearts of the classic Protestant ethic:

The time is coming when we shall not have to work for things. . . . Labor has ceased for him who has found this inner kingdom. Divine supply is brought forth without laborious struggle: to desire is to have fulfillment. . . . Some physical scientists are telling us that the time is near when men will manufacture from the ether, right at hand, everything that they need or desire. Man will not have to wait for seedtime and harvest when he learns to use the power of his mind.[19]

And could there not be automotive engineers to promise wear-ever brakes and fuel-less cars just as there were psychosomatic doctors to confirm the intuitions of an afflicted lady?

The situation of faith in the religion of Supply was analogous to the situation of a woman out shopping. Supplied with money by her husband (God), offered the inexhaustible wares of the American industrial bazaar, she need know nothing and be responsible for nothing of the sources of either money or goods. The world, as Fillmore had observed of Yellowstone, was tame, abounding and friendly. Everyone smiled. True it was that men were not in that world yet, because they had not learned to think correctly yet. But Fillmore plotted only a feminine, that is, non-political, route of passage. Men (and women) would advance utopia by coming to Understanding one by one. "'A little leaven leaventh the whole lump,' and even one life that bears witness to the truth of the prosperity law will quicken the consciousness of the whole community."[20]

Not that there were not dangers:

> . . . Before we can have a truly Christian community . . . we must be educated. . . . If we should all get together and divide all our possessions, it would be but a short time until those who have the prevailing financial ideas would manipulate our finances, and plethora on the one hand and lack on the other would again be established.[21]

Were these the "malefactors of great wealth" indicted by the New Deal President, in echo of old Populist and Progressive suspicions? If so, Fillmore had no proposals to offer. On the contrary, he made it hard to see that there was anything to be done about them:

> Do not envy the rich. Never condemn those who have money merely because they have it and you do not. Do not question how they got their money and wonder whether or not they are honest. All that is none of your business. Your business is to get what belongs to you.[22]

Others too, such as Thomas Jefferson, placing their faith in the general education of mankind, had warned about an irreducible minority—one in fourteen or so, Jefferson had estimated—of what he called "rogues," and Jefferson had assumed that decent men naturally would have to protect themselves politically. But Fillmore wanted thoughts about only one's own thoughts, one's own mind.

Yet, however incoherent as a tract for depression years, Fillmore's *Prosperity* concealed a deeper coherence. In effect urging people simply to wait, to hold on, he met the situation of people without the resources of tradition to do more. Incapable of either robust political protest or dogged political resistance, at the same time far too identified with the economy to escape in religious transcendencies, they had no role but to survive until prosperity returned—why, they would not know. Once prosperity had returned, for whatever reason, the waiting in faith would be justified. The idea that personal response, personal intelligence, personal action made a difference Fillmore deprecated: ". . . We so often think that increase is the result of our personal efforts. Increase comes by the operation of a universal law, and our part is to keep that law."[23] And, deep down, the faith had a specific nationalistic coloration; depression-thoughts were not only un-divine, but un-American:

> Fortunately, there are many in this country who have the prosperity consciousness. If we were all in a poverty consciousness famines would be as common here as they are in India or China.[24]

It might have been imagined that the new center of character in the willing consumer would be his (her) desires and needs. But this was not so.

> Do not center your thought upon yourself [Fillmore warned], your interests, your gains or losses, but realize the universal nature of substance. . . . Do not reason too much. . . . Do not give too close study to yourself or your present condition.[25]

In short, do not think about anything, neither the rich nor the system nor your own being. "Your business is to get what belongs to you," but there was no basis for knowing what this was, except for the answer that was obvious: the system decided.

The unselfish consumer

Selfish only impersonally, the willing consumer, to be adequately integrated into the economy, was also to be the passive consumer—weaned from saving and hoarding so that he might spend, weaned from piling up possessions in order to expedite planned obsolescence, weaned from ascetic discipline that he might respond to every innovation, weaned from work-identities that he might have the time for consumption. Actually still an ascetic, since he denied himself what the system did not supply him, the perfect consumer did not know he denied himself. The man of prosperity-faith was the man whose very desires had been automated.

With postwar prosperity rising and spreading to new levels and new people, the yearning, religious, consumer's communism of Trine, Mrs. Towne and Fillmore could be let fade in the fluorescent glow of overflowing shopping centers and showrooms. Fantasies of supply were freed for banality.

In 1955 Joseph Murphy of the Church and College of Divine Science and Psychology in Los Angeles explained, in *How to Attract Money*, the more esoteric art of beating the stock market.

> If you are seeking wisdom regarding investments, or if you are worried about your stocks and bonds, quietly claim, "Infinite Intelligence governs and watches over all my financial transactions, and whatever I do shall prosper." Do this frequently . . . you will be prompted to sell your securities or holdings before any loss accrues to you.[26]

Happily this technique had as its support the great postwar bull market in which nobody ought to have sold at all.

Murphy also undertook to reconcile the modern young man to his new situation:

> If you are working in a large corporation, and you are silently thinking and resenting the fact that you are underpaid, that you are not appreciated . . . you are unconsciously severing

your ties with the organization. You are setting a law in motion; then the superintendent or manager says to you, "We have to let you go." You have dismissed yourself.[27]

Clearly, human relations might have averted this subconscious self-defeat by honest, open communications.

Elsewhere Murphy analyzed the case of a young lady embittered at the bankruptcy of her "very beautiful hair salon" because of embezzling assistants. Her mistake, Murphy said, was to believe her problems lay in the material world rather than in her own mind. Properly instructed by Murphy, she "became rich mentally." So long as she was about it, she extended her "constructive imagery" to include early marriage as well as solvency. Nothing happened for three weeks. She persevered. Then, "in less than a month this young girl got married. . . . Her husband gave her a check for $24,000 as a wedding present, as well as a trip around the world."[28]

A California school teacher yearning for an $8000 ermine coat had to wait three months before anything happened to her, but she too persevered.

One Sunday morning after our lecture, a man accidentally stepped on her toe, apologized profusely, asked her where she lived, and offered to drive her home. Shortly after he proposed marriage; gave her a beautiful diamond ring, and said to her, "I saw the most wonderful coat; you would look simply radiant wearing it."[29]

There was no doubt which coat it was.

At this stage of things, wish became invulnerable:

The student of the laws of mind . . . believes and knows absolutely that regardless of the economic situation, stock market fluctuation, depression, strikes, war, other conditions, or circumstances, he will always be amply supplied regardless of what form money may take.[30]

There was something uncanny about such a situation, an eeriness which theological deduction did not hesitate to express:

. . . Creation is finished. When you know God does not have to learn, grow, expand, or unfold, you begin gradually to awaken from the dream of limitation, and become alive in God.[31]

You, too, do not have to learn, grow, expand, unfold. You need only wish, and consume the supplies that are provided. You, too, are finished.

Cultivated ignorance of the economy as a whole was not the most drastic characteristic of mind cure. Mind cure's ultimate passivity was its cultivated ignorance of personal existence, of desires, impulses, reasoned hopes expressing some power of personal imagination. Not only did the mind-cured individual have no political thoughts, he (she) had no personal economic desires and appetites. He (she) could not be in tension with the system. It was possible to be politically indifferent, yet a free and independent soul, but mind cure systematically expelled the irreducible minimum for independence—the capacity to wish wishes of one's own. The wish for plenty was not the wish to have one's wishes fulfilled; it was the wish not to have to wish wishes of one's own at all.

Was this not piety in truth?

PART THREE

Peace in Peace: Psychology as Psychology

CHAPTER XVI

THE EMPTY ADVENTURE

In this final section I aim to examine therapeutic psychology as a spreading theme of religion. Assuming from Part Two the frustration of new vitality in thinking about business life, I devote the first four chapters here to sketching still further frustrations between the wars. The failure of the hopes of a Barton for business did not have to mean the failures of the hopes of a Harry Emerson Fosdick for the culture, but the failure seems evident. Again, I intend no panorama; at most I can only allude to some vital, contrasting stories. But I believe the story I sketch does justice to a broad element in the culture—middle-class, white, mostly Northern Protestants in cities and the suburbs. I assume this same audience for the post-World War II psychology I go on to discuss in the remaining chapters.[1]

Harry Emerson Fosdick's liberalism

The eleven years between Armistice and the Crash posed unusual possibilities for liberal religion. In the general ferment of culture, liberal religion had a chance to identify itself positively as much more than escape from orthodoxy, and as more than a code for social reform. More widely than at any time in the nineteenth century, more widely than in Emerson's time, for instance, it had a chance at cultural experimentation, it had a chance at shaping cultural style. It had a chance to live up to the title of one of the books of the first-ranking liberal preacher of the time—*Adventurous Religion,* by Harry Emerson Fosdick.

Fosdick won his national reputation for his leadership in the struggle against fundamentalists. Skillfully he blocked the fundamentalists off from isolating liberal religion in the narrow camp of intellectual "modernism" and instead helped force on them the stigma of sustaining an arid, rationalistic, impersonal formalism. He mediated to more people than ever the liberal way of reading the Bible, practiced by Washington Gladden, Horace Bushnell, Emerson and, indeed, Thomas Jefferson long before him. Fosdick refused technical theological disputation; basically, he wanted theology itself played down, insisting, with William James, that the life of religion lay in action, not logic.

Fosdick's avowed indebtedness to James ran deep, and his echo of one of James's warnings had special significance as, over the years, he confirmed it in a longtime association with a leading New York psychiatrist.[2] In his most popular book, *On Being a Real Person,* published in 1943, Fosdick counseled against the willed, rigid, radically rationalized character that James had found so common among his Puritan-derived audiences. "Moral ideals, stiff, rigid and promiscuously applied," were psychologically dangerous.[3] Among his cautionary examples he narrated the sad case of the boy who broke down under the weight of great self-expectations—a kind of Alger tale in reverse and one steadily more common in the popular literature of psychological advice. Previous to his psychiatric studies, Fosdick had already threaded a polemic against "conscience" through many of his sermons, criticizing it as an illusory guide for life and an inadequate basis for self-integration, as illusory and inadequate as the tyrannical superego criticized by psychoanalysts, and in fact the same thing. As with James, so with Fosdick: a capacity for getting beyond one's willed self, a readiness for new things, a capacity to avoid being characterologically locked up counted for much in being a real person. What was more explicit in Fosdick than in James, though, was the point that this freedom from petrifaction was actually to serve the ends of richer purposefulness and integration, a larger strength of self. No one could ever have doubted this point in James, but for Fosdick it had to be made clearer. He had worried about it. "Multitudes of people are living not bad but frittered lives," he said in *Twelve Tests of Character*, "split, scattered, uncoordinated."[4] For the Puritan these would have been bad, not just frittered lives, but in any case Fosdick recognized a problem.

Reinhold Niebuhr's challenge

A basic question appeared, then. If liberal religion aimed at a richer psychology than that of orthodoxy, where would it show itself? What coordinations and integrations and purposes would it display? What adventures would it pursue? It was precisely at this point that Fosdick found his most pointed critic, not a fundamentalist but a fellow-liberal, Reinhold Niebuhr. Niebuhr declared, in sum, that Fosdick, like his typical parishioners, comfortable people of the middle and upper-middle classes, failed to discern the real challenges to purposefulness in the modern world. These were social, political, economic, rooted in the injustices and imbalances of industrial society. The trouble with Fosdick, Niehuhr said, was that in urging adventurous religion he was not adventurous enough. The adventures he proposed always fell within the framework of the existing social and economic order, were always conservative, never entailed, to use James's word, risk. They were tailored to the leisure and privileges of a complacent class. This criticism expressed Niebuhr as he was about to execute his famous double-leap—into neo-orthodox theology and radical politics at once, in protest against both the religious and the social illusions of liberalism.

Was this fair? The peculiar impasse at which liberal Protestantism had arrived can be further appreciated by refining Niebuhr's criticism of Fosdick at this point. Fosdick was not an empty preacher. In his autobiography, looking back over seventy years, he recalled his concern for Sacco and Vanzetti, for Tom Mooney, for the Scottsboro boys, for planned parenthood, for municipal reform, for Alcoholics Anonymous, against racial discrimination. He looked back with favor upon the fundamental aims of Woodrow Wilson and Franklin Roosevelt. He disparaged laissez-faire. At the same time it was quite true that Fosdick never identified with the adventures of the social gospel, either in the doldrums of the twenties or the crisis of the thirties. Like most liberal Protestant pastors he had only a sketchy sense of modern industry, and like most of them responded nervously to new, more obvious, less accustomed organizations of power. Thus, in the twenties, with no sense whatever that the unionization of industrial labor had barely begun, operating on the assumption that labor-union power had already risen to approximate some kind of balance with the power of capital, he worried more about how labor was using the power it did have than about the basic problem of the social gospel as Niebuhr soon defined it so no one could miss—how labor was to gain equal power in the first place.

Yet Fosdick was not quite what Niebuhr's criticism implied. Raised in the warmly evangelical atmosphere of an upstate New York culture that never had gone to the city with the Alger heroes, that never had lost its sense of being an intact community, Fosdick was in fact the heir to one of the many sectors of nineteenth-century Protestant life that never had surrendered to the harshly atomistic individualism of the gospel of success and Social Darwinism. If, in emitting such rounded phrases as "constructive statesmanship for the kingdom," and "progressive welfare for society" as Christian imperatives, Fosdick failed in the task of translating such standard good intentions into the tougher terms of tactics, strategy and real politics, still, when he spoke of the economy as "the basic social service of the people," he was expressing an indigenous outlook quite without strain, far removed from that Protestant ethic and gospel of success which Niebuhr combatted in its laissez-faire form. The economy, as Fosdick saw it, was something to be superintended essentially in terms of over-all social needs, utilities and expediencies. It was not an arena for sacred competition, a proving-ground for ultimate character. This was true all the way to the point that Fosdick could not be found preaching the old work ethic or celebrating the conventional virtues of the Protestant ethic.[5]

If, then, the major area for purpose, will, risk and adventure in nineteenth-century Protestantism had been the economy, with its prodigious opportunities and challenges, its tremendous sanctions for personal "hard" integration aimed at definite goals, its support for potent myths of rugged self-made individualism, Fosdick found himself at the center of a vacuum. Was his purpose—like that of so many gently idealistic Protestants of the century past—to expand the culture of upstate small-town New York to embrace the industrial nation? He did not say so and never tried to suggest that it could be so. Indeed, to the extent that comfort led some people to the assumption that twentieth-century America constituted acceptable community already, Fosdick tended to bristle. Periodically he let fly with attacks upon "American faith" taking American life as somehow the embodiment of right order and religious meaning. His attacks lacked focus; he did not name names, judge power, convict specific evils; and from concrete proposals he fled usually to the transcending level of warning that no "real" gains were made except as heart and soul, not just externals, were changed. Yet it was plain he suspected complacency; not the failure of the system but its successes triggered his doubts. "The most comfortable religion on earth . . ." he observed of a common middle-class faith, and despised it.

But how was he to combat it, short of becoming a straight-out social-gospel man? Fosdick was perhaps the first of the great liberal preachers to be confronted in its full force by the fact that for millions of persons it seemed reasonable to expect a comfortable world, that for millions a comfortable religion and healthy-mindedness seemed the most plausible reflection of reality. He could hardly help himself from contributing to this sense of things so far as America was concerned, for Fosdick, along with all else, was one of those who suffered most severely from the trauma of America's first involvement in the great whole world. Recoiling violently and guiltily from his own contribution to wartime crusade psychology, he became one of the best-known exponents of an American quasi-pacifism over the next twenty years, contributing to a hope that America might indeed escape harsh realities. No more than any other pacifist minister, less than some, did Fosdick succeed in untangling the terrible moral as well as geopolitical contradictions in this liberal pacifism, but the movement itself registered the depth of an undisciplined, diffuse, "ungathered" nostalgia in vast sectors of the churches and the population that only Korea, perhaps, was to shake.

Personal counseling and pastoral psychology

Had he remained merely the defender of liberal religion, Fosdick would have remained hung up on this reef throughout his career. But in fact Fosdick had another mission. "I am commonly thought of as a preacher, but I should not put preaching central in my ministry. Personal counseling has been central."[6]

Fosdick's interest in personal counseling began in New York City in the early twenties in the simplest fashion. Although expected only to preach at his church, he announced himself available for individual consultations. Pastors over the centuries had counseled, naturally, but Fosdick, unsystematically but acutely aware of the rising modern depth psychologies, instantly recognized that he was in over his head. He couldn't help. He himself, he later recalled, had had no training for pastoral counseling whatever; the seminaries of his youth had not provided it. Seminaries began to provide it only in the twenties. Fosdick turned for help to Dr. Thomas W. Salmon, medical director of the National Committee for Mental Hygiene, formerly chief psychiatric consultant to the armed forces overseas. From then on Fosdick's interest grew, issuing eventually in *On Being a Real Person*.

This involvement in psychiatric wisdom represented no conversion in Fosdick's imagination, but rather a fulfillment. It was plain to see what sort of persons had always struck Fosdick as the exemplars of true religious energy. Year after year, book after book, he invoked the names of people who had been stopped, blocked, wounded and defeated—and then gone on to triumph: Edison,

Steinmetz, Florence Nightingale, Helen Keller, Beethoven, together with such less grand persons as John Callender, the Massachusetts officer guilty of cowardice at Bunker Hill who redeemed himself at the battle of Long Island, and John B. Gough, the alcoholic who became one of the leading prohibitionists of the eighteen-forties. The most exemplary of all these figures loomed behind this Victorian and Puritan sense of life as struggle—John Bunyan, as meaningful for Fosdick as for generations of determined Puritan types. Fosdick's rendition of the theme was essentially Jamesian: religion means vitality, religion means more life. The business of religion was to unlock inner resources. "Religion's central and unique property is power to release faith and courage for living, to produce spiritual vitality and fruitfulness; and by that it ultimately stands or falls."[7] Like James, Fosdick saw this power of religion in two ways. It was a power of support in moments of breakdown; it was itself a stimulus to high endeavors. For Fosdick, as for James, this raised the issue whether religion testified not just to inner resources but also to outer resources, the issue whether religion was purely psychology or also philosophy. And like James—indeed, quoting James as his best evidence—Fosdick resolved this issue purely into pragmatic psychology itself, declaring that faith in outer resources, in a "MORE," ". . . literally and objectively true . . ." was justified precisely because such faith did unlock inner resources. The life of struggle was based on a faith that it meshed into larger meanings.

For the rest, *On Being a Real Person* was pure therapeutic psychology, a layman's guide, written with perfectly reasonable lay sophistication, to the sorts of psychological problems in depth from which people suffered without knowing what was wrong. Their way out was to come to know—to recognize conscience's tyranny, locate pervasive anxiety's origin, comprehend the displacement of instinct. As a criticism of the old Puritan, Victorian and fundamentalist habit of meeting psychological woes with legalistic, impersonal, moralistic prescriptions, *On Being a Real Person* was a liberating book indeed.

At the same time, Fosdick was left in a peculiar position. Was psychological sickness the key to religious vitality for the major

portion of his liberal congregations? What about those who were
not sick? What would incite comfortable people, people supplied
with the abundancies of American civilization, to real adventure?
The answer to the problem in Fosdick's case could well have been
that he left the question of what to do with healthy energy to the
democratic discretion of individuals. He would not presume, as,
say, Calvin had, to tell men what to do. He would try only to
tell them how to do. And this seems likely. True, it could have
been that the more a counselor counseled the more sickness he
discovered. It could have been that a counselor might feel that the
problem of what to do with health and abundance was a false
problem because what people really needed was to realize they
were not healthy but sick.

But we have no particular evidence that Fosdick even contemplated these possibilities. He never wrestled with the problem
of why comfortable people, if they really were comfortable, should
ever wish to live life according to the pattern of heroic overcoming. Nor did he ever, in trying to dispel "the most comfortable
religion on earth," follow the tack of diagnosing comfortable people as being, really, sick people. Hints were not entirely lacking
that Fosdick sensed some of the drastic quality of the issues he
touched. Thus, at least once, in contemplating just how Christianity
might be put into action, he suggested a tactic that composed
poorly with democratic liberal psychology and with leaving things
to democratic discretion. "Quantitatively small, vitally active leaven
—that is a true simile of the method of Christianity's transformation of the world,"[8] he said, and actually supplied a figure for the
minority upon which "history has depended": 2 per cent. This was
not very many. We may infer also that this vanguard 2 per cent
would not have needed to read *On Being a Real Person*. But
Fosdick never pursued the implications of tactical and strategical
thinking with that intensity which in circles of the social gospel led
to the emergence of neo-orthodoxy.

What was at stake was theological after all. Fosdick's turn to the
problem of "sickness" saved his liberalism. Unlike Fosdick, the
leading critic of comfortable people and comfortable religion did

follow precisely the tack of declaring that such people were not what they seemed, even to themselves. On the contrary, argued Niebuhr and the neo-orthodox. Such people were sinners. And sin and sickness were not the same. But the plausibility in Niebuhr's argument that sin was to be found in all human action was lacking in any argument that psychological sickness was similarly universal. Fosdick's message seemed to come to rest simply in the assurance that sick people could get well by a technique and that religious faith would climax their cure. He thereby lost much of his chance to inspire the heroism he admired. Hence, the final refinement upon Niebuhr's criticism that Fosdick's adventurousness was not adventurous enough was that Fosdick defined no adventures at all —except on the definition that getting well was an adventure.

None of this qualified Fosdick in the least for the ranks of mind cure. That should be clear. While giving a somewhat more positive assurance than did James that objective spiritual power did exist, he like James was repelled by any wish that this objective power take care of everything. This could be seen in the quality of the inner lives of the great souls he celebrated, as he himself described them. Torn, racked, tormented, driven; in conflict, turbulence, struggle, tension, his heroes found little if any of that "peace," that healthy-mindedness, that cheerful serenity, that assurance of supply advertised by mind cure as evidence of its Truth. No Infinite Intelligence, no All-Mind-God constituted a One of which men were but individualizations. In the Jamesian fashion the life of Fosdick's heroes was real struggle because there was real struggle in the universe.

What Fosdick could not do, however, or did not do, was to face just what some of these real struggles were, and he could not, or did not, because he was diverted to the problem of psychological sickness. Almost certainly without knowing it, he had demonstrated that theology could be converted into psychology only by concentrating on the psychology of sickness and that to concentrate on the psychology of sickness was to risk neglecting adventure.

CHAPTER XVII

THE TWENTIES: ADVENTURES IGNORED

THE UNADVENTUROUSNESS of liberal religion was not the fault of the twenties. There were plenty of adventures about.

One obvious spectacular theme of the decade was the "revolution in manners and morals," at the center of which stood Woman. The basic myths of the Age of Enterprise had not recognized the existence of women. They had been safely and bodily frozen out of the "real" world of masculine energy. The early mind-cure cults were, among all else, early protests against this meaninglessness, and they were well adapted to women because, as we have observed, they assumed what was true, that women were in a weak position. Mind cure was a philosophy that could work for a woman without the help of a man.

What was new in the twenties was that women had gained many allies. From the nineties, the revolution in manners and morals proved attractive to growing numbers of both women and men. So long as the myths of the Protestant ethic prevailed, so long would men live for busyness in business; stated baldly, so long would they live for themselves. Nothing in the gospel of success or the Protestant ethic assigned value to intimacy. To value intimacy would have been to surrender the idea of being self-made, of being totally organized; it would have been to give up the addiction of obsession. With the disintegration of the myth, men were freed to become interested in beings unlike themselves.

The chance for liberal religion to fill some of its concepts and symbols with the substance of real life in the domain of manners and morals was great. Reinhold Niebuhr's implication that "realism" was the realm of politics and economics, neither he nor anyone else ever justified. The social gospel always suffered, even in its own circles, from a severe dilution in the felt, experienced, immediate quality of its religious ideas. The holy phrases—"Fatherhood of God," "Brotherhood of Man," "the Kingdom," and above all "Love"—seemed more to becloud than penetrate the realities of steel strikes, assembly lines, labor unions and political parties. But in the realm of manners and morals, religious ideas might have found an intensification of drama.

The leading response of the liberal churches when confronted by moral ferment was, however, silence. The twenties saw the last concerted effort by the old Protestantism to save its moralistic authority over individuals, notably in the prohibition experiment supported most heavily in evangelical circles of Midwestern Methodism, and, although Harry Emerson Fosdick, for one, thought prohibition a tragic mistake, the liberal churches felt themselves entangled in this furor. Yet, in general, liberal Protestantism showed no stomach for a defense of the Victorian past. It simply let things happen. In the most sensitive and potentially fruitful realm, certainly liberal Protestants did not protest birth-control literature, clinics and practice. Some churchwomen supported them under secular auspices. Rising divorce rates did not inspire alarmed demands in liberal quarters for tightened laws. These were matters of too much concern in the perfecting of middle-class life. But they could not yet be grasped in fresh religious terms.

Similarly, writers of the day, expressing a new range of personal and sensuous feeling in explicit contrast to the poverty of the past, some of them "serious," some of them not, suffered no such dismissal as had overtaken Whitman. Chances for rendering themes of richer life, including sexual life, had expanded rapidly, but neither with the support nor against the opposition of liberal religion. Its silent observation marked a barrier.

That there was reason for plenty of anxiety promoting this silence it is easy to see. Liberal religion was nothing organized and distinct. Its spokesmen felt a host of involvements and investments with a still living past where popular, often primitive evangelical and orthodox experience still ruled. Their feeling about their position within the churches was one of loyalty. Liberal leaders saw themselves as climax and fulfillment, not as a break. Lacking any divisive impulses whatever, they were hardly likely to embrace adventures that would exacerbate the tensions within Protestantism as a whole, already stretched tight by the fundamentalists.

Revolution in manners and morals

But just as plainly this "diplomatic" inhibition disguised deeper inhibitions. The revolution in manners and morals was threatening in itself. The deep psychological question raised by revolt from any code was the question of one's capacity to make use of the new freedom. As early mind cure reflected, Victorian morality had induced a profound doubt, not at all of one's capacity to control oneself but of one's capacity for a greater range and depth of experience. The revolution in manners and morals provoked this doubt still more sharply, and now among men as well as women. The unadventurousness of liberal religion expressed this doubt, a doubt owed to the failure to conceive decisively of spirit as capacity for more life, not as obedience to rules for life.

Of course, the image of moral revolution in the twenties was nothing organized and distinct either. It frayed off into excesses, absurdities and scandals, and, both at its most serious and most frivolous, challenged items in the religious ethic dating back far behind the nineteenth century or even Calvin, to Paul and Old Testament law. Not remotely could one think that the ferment called for less than critical dialogue and debate. But my intention is to highlight the simple fact—liberal Protestantism's practically universal silence, that is, the absence of voices proposing explicitly religious dialogue and debate. Journalists, doctors, publicists and judges as well as literary men had been steadily more voluble since the eighteen-nineties, speaking often with honest secular directness; the voices of liberal religion floated on abstractness, or else, as through the Federal Council of Churches of Christ in America, sank in bureaucratic heaviness, and, when occasionally heard, rang empty of experience.

The collapse of the Victorian sexual code into religious silence only deepened the fatal flaw of gentility. The Victorian sexual ethic had not really been an ethic at all, for an ethic had to presume alternatives. Denying that sex was in the realm of spirit, its code was a form of hygiene. Perpetuation of this incapacity to embrace sexual life in terms of spirit, or freedom, marked the post-Victorian era deeply. Aside from various obvious and minimum standards for public decorum, the realm of sex was left isolated, free of the merely repressive morality of the past but also exposed to the perils besetting any human enterprise left insufficiently linked—by tradition, criticism, reason—with all the other permanent enterprises of the race. As a realm alone, sex was fated to become an obsession, oddly inheriting the marks of the obsession with work. It was no longer crudely repressed, yet its freedom would be baffled by the erratic blindness of isolated individuals, turning, in the poverty of their isolated fantasies, to the mass fantasies inevitably generated by any widespread obsession. This was one of the many avenues to mass culture. By the time new sexual ethics were beginning to be discussed imaginatively in Protestant circles—in the late forties—a generation of religiously unmediated experience had accrued.

Sex and family

I have already indicated the gist of mind-cure teaching in this area. In its origins a therapy for the woes of mature Victorian women, mind cure preserved, in fact sharpened, an anti-sexual animus in perfect consistency with its drive toward less, not more intimate human relations. In the twenties and thereafter this protection would remain appealing. The more sex emerged from hiding the more dangerous it could be. But the attraction of mind cure would not depend simply on its tactic of denial. In its larger future it would meet the danger by including sex within its circle of perfect harmony, allowing it a natural existence—as Mrs. Eddy and Charles Fillmore had not—but depriving it of meaning as an expression of personality, neutralizing its promise as a frontier for human self-exploration and consciousness.

Confusion in a sexual ethic accompanied confusion in a family ethic. Much of the effective thought of historic Protestantism had drawn on the figure of the father, who had often mingled the hard qualities of material provider, judge, disciplinarian and guardian in the wilderness with the softer qualities of educator and personal exemplar. On the noblest levels of nineteenth-century evangelical and liberal religion emphasis had shifted from the structure of the family to its atmosphere, from its order to its love, a shift given theoretical ground by Horace Bushnell in his *Christian Nurture,* and nowhere practiced more successfully than in the family sensationally fathered by Henry James, Sr. But this transformation of the structure of the family into love could hardly have been trickier, for it raised the problem of saving the position of father. The Victorian scheme did not solve it. At best it continued to incarnate a paterfamilias large with authority, but authority somehow arbitrary. At worst it fell to the dominion of mother's gentility and sentimentality, with father a kind of power-political intrusion.

The revolution in manners and morals proposed, implicitly, a new pattern altogether. It was not an attack upon father in favor of mother. It was rather an attack upon father and mother in favor of the husband-wife team. The shift carried large implications about relations between parents and children, and about the role of children (and adolescents) in the culture at large. Great perils and great liberations alike impended. Here were decisive opportunities for adventurous religion indeed. Countless books, surveys, educational and above all countless private experiments were devoted to exploration. But the record shows no crystallization or even persisting ferment in liberal religious imagination polarized by this experience. The essential problem was that of authority, of knowing how to speak, when, and to whom, the same problem Fosdick had faced in preaching, and which he had resolved by choosing the sick.

In respectable popular culture the hard Victorian paterfamilias gradually faded into the sentimental shades of Father Remembered, a despot whose rule was amusing because so safely past. In the real present he was succeeded by the soft father of family love, his indulgences earning him a role as the object of endless comic slanders. In less respectable—and symbolically more potent —culture, the culture especially of raw and familially disrupted immigrant stock, father as object of revenge and even contempt was not disguised in countless movies. In the face of this disintegration what was needed was abundant and realistic imagination for the family in its modern settings. With its stress upon love as the supreme religious category, liberal religion was prepared for this in a general way. But more than the ideal of love was needed. In order to be translated into action the ideal had to be equipped with a sophistication about the outside world that the older family had not had to have. Less often knit into local units of local community, the family was thrown more often upon itself, but at the same time it was opened up to contact with larger and more various centers of communication. Movies, radio, popular literature, consumer's goods, the images of national entertainers and performers invaded its life in ways for which the old order had had to have no preparation. Leisure and new measures of education of children rose to major issues in family politics. Child-processing services competing with (and liberating) parents proliferated.

There was no necessary harmony between these pervading new forces and the interests of family love. Politically sentimental, liberal religion was unequipped to see the problems. It could not think badly enough of the larger world to act strongly enough to defend the smaller world of the family. No matter how keenly new ideals of more intimate emotions, interest in the varieties of personality, concern for permissiveness and the release of inner potentials might be felt, until these were felt in such a way as to lend strength for criticizing, not just consuming, commercial abundance, they were weak.[1]

One point at which Protestant adventuresomeness did take some definite form was religious education, yet the adventuring betrayed the fatality. Sunday schools in liberal churches had been converting from old methods of Bible drill and catechism from well before the war. The new progressive methods had been anticipated long before by Bronson Alcott in Boston before the Civil War, but in the twenties they were pressed by men indebted primarily to John Dewey, the influence of whose theories loomed large in the progressive Religious Education Association. But a major aim of progressive education was to link the classroom with the world outside, and the liberal Sunday schools lacked coherent links. Like many public and private schools the progressive Sunday schools tended to celebrate a method only. As expounded by men such as George Coe, the method stressed a process of "socialization" of the individual, wherein group-thinking and group consensus served as the context of values and in fact the route to values. This did not make the student sophisticated in the ways of the world; it only adapted him to accommodate himself to them. These schools, too, like the progressive family and the liberal church, faced the problem of authority. Dismantling the patterns of authority of the nineteenth century, they assumed that they constituted a new authority of their own. Yet, no Sunday school, any more than a family or a church, incorporated in itself the dangers and opportunities, the range and the risks contained in the macrocosm of the nation— let alone of the power-political world. The liberalized small group —Sunday school, family, church—bent upon "democratizing" authority, treating all issues in terms of personality and love, was more likely to be preparing its members for a reflexive, passive role beyond the boundaries of the group than for criticism, resistance, independence and action.[2]

Mind cure at least used a finesse. Moving directly into unity with the All-God of Mind and Supply, it bypassed all these issues clustering around the cultivation of personality and love. There were no tensions between small groups and life at large. The family was not a focus for heightened intimacy, variety, and psychological abundance; it remained simply an order of nature, the main business of which was to reflect the order of the All-God, which was, according to mind cure, impersonal. The impersonality of Father-Mother was not, as I have suggested, contradictory. It correlated perfectly with mind cure's sense of change in the economy, from a realm for competitive self-assertion to a source of provisions. Supply presupposed neither self-assertion nor criticism; it required no adventures. It required only identification on the part of the consumer-child, to whom it would provide all for the asking. In this symbolism, mind cure, not liberalism, was correct, for the economy, the system at large, was indeed not personal, any more than the rain or the wind or the sun.

The loss of Protestant creativity

In the foregoing I have tried to hold to matters close to the aims and interests of religious liberals themselves. Even assuming that their indifference to the economic and social reforms of the social gospel was inevitable, their essential incapacity for action—their unadventurousness—was notable on its own terms. To expand the point, and to belabor its implications for the culture at large, would be to belabor the obvious. But the obvious needs belaboring, since it was a striking fact in Protestantism itself that it ignored the obvious. As an example, this was true of its relation to the spread of mass communications and its corollary, a new commercial mass culture.

The twenties made conspicuous what had been visible enough through most of the nineteenth century—that Protestantism, including its liberal vanguards, had lost creative contact with the arts. As the high art of professionals in many fields—poetry, architecture, painting, sculpture, music—moved decisively beyond nineteenth-century forms, separation gave way to uncomprehending alienation. It would be almost impossible to locate an instance of significance, apart from a few churches designed by Sullivan, Wright and Maybeck, where Protestantism fed on modern energy, and theirs was that special energy of Emerson, Thoreau, Whitman and the heretical transcendentalists. What novelists, in the constellation of excitement from the twenties, owed their character to specifically Protestant culture? Lewis—who made his fame by skewering the shriveled heart of the commercialized Protestant small town; Faulkner—who envisioned a Christ crucified by tribal Southern fundamentalism in *Light in August;* Hemingway—whose classically Victorian Oak Park mother incited endless fantasies of death and who assigned to his Protestant heroes religious longings of a Catholic stamp. None were recognized. In its architecture, music, rhetoric, liturgy, hymnology, in the literature consumed by religious people, liberal churches no less than others abode in traditions already sterile by 1870. Not until after World War II would this grotesque anachronism begin to be repaired.

At the same time religious liberals lost touch with whatever genuine folk culture Protestantism had ever fed upon in the United States. Not since Jacksonian times at the latest had middle-class white Protestantism flourished in terms of a spontaneous popular vitality, and the Jacksonian furor had soon given way to the basic Jacksonian drive for commercial success, fortified by the Protestant ethic. Only in one branch of the theological community did Protestantism still enjoy such creative energy on a popular scale—among Negroes—and of course between liberal and Negro Protestantism there was nothing but bureaucratic communication.

On both levels, in short, that of professional, self-conscious "high" culture and that of folk culture, a sense for religion's cultural dimensions had withered. Like sex, the arts were not felt as a part of the realm of spirit.

The impact of commercial mass culture

The major consequence was that liberal religion was helplessly unprepared for any kind of vital response to the rise of commercial mass culture. Some of the basic patterns of modern mass culture had been laid down, first by newspapers and then by magazines, in the nineteenth century, but through the Progressive era, approximately, these agencies—with the exception of a few newspapers—had not taken on that autonomy they were to gain later, and remained distinctly flavored with the morality, taste and inhibitions of the Protestant middle classes. It took the explosion of industrial technology in movies, automobiles and radio, along with the perfection of publishing and distribution methods, to expand these patterns to a national scale and lend them a penetrating power sufficient to dominate the imagination of otherwise local millions. None of these patterns followed from traditional religious communities. All, without exception, were threats to inherited spiritual coherence, all required leadership if they were to be incorporated in a new coherence. Except as some church groups succeeded in imposing various moralistic "codes" on the movies, and mounted sporadic attacks on "immoral" literature, contact between Protestantism and mass culture hardly existed—except as child and teen-age Protestants consumed it widely, along with parents oblivious to the unconscious impact of what they saw, read and heard. The failure of religion was not its failure to fasten inherited moral standards on the mass media. Its real failure was its incapacity to realize that mass media had to be judged by their service to the cause of consciousness at all.

Aesthetic and intellectual considerations apart, the crucial feature of mass culture was its psychological impact, its impact upon wishes, its presentation of models of meaning. Had it been morally as pure as the angels, mass culture still would have simply overwhelmed the sociology of the religious tradition. The "upstate" moral community, the family ethos, the rugged individualism of the gospel of success—the coherence of each alike dissolved in the flood of mass imagination. In the world of mass culture Protestantism was simply parochial. As William McLoughlin has observed, Protestant evangelists from Dwight Moody to Billy Sunday were themselves among the pioneers of American mass culture.[3] It was all the more ironical, therefore, that even Protestant evangelists failed to make effective use of the new techniques, at least before 1950 and the rise of Billy Graham. The liberal church could do little more than compete with golf on Sunday mornings.

At the center of mass culture writhed the gospel of consumption, with its accompanying myth of supply. The rise of mass culture registered the transfer of spiritual authority to the system. The good life consisted of consuming the good things provided—from above, from beyond, from distant, dimly comprehended processes and sources like a transcending God who could nevertheless be known in His true character by His works, by His products, and who therefore also was an immanent God by being consumed, and who, of course, existed simply in terms of the desires that He satisfied.

Naturally, none of this is to say that liberal Protestantism was peculiarly distinguished or different by being badly prepared for mass culture, or for the organizational world which mass culture spread. By comparison, fundamentalists were capable of nothing more than occasional narrowly frantic crusades. For the most part they contracted religion into the tense securities of dogma and legalistic morality—usually racist—decreasingly relevant to the affairs of anything but their own security. So primitive was fundamentalism as to constitute one seedbed for the hysteria of post-World War II "anti-Communist" isolationism whereby America was to go on serving as cradle—nuclear-powered. Other large Protestant communities always had been and remained parochial—most of the Lutherans, along with the centrifugal sects such as the Mormons and Jehovah's Witnesses, plus the Negro folk Protestants. Like most of these, orthodox Judaism deliberately sought isolation. Otherwise Jews duplicated, with special intensity, the spectrum of Protestant and secular life. The basic pattern of Catholicism was to expand its own parochial culture within the nation, quite unburdened with creative contact with things outside itself. Radically unlike Protestantism in construing its American religious mission in the first place defensively and therefore narrowly, excluding its laymen from responsibility for that mission, American Catholic leaders learned to speak to more than their sectarian flocks only as these came to constitute local majorities. As a result, they spoke without inner sensitivity to American themes.

Therefore, it was not as though liberal passivity bespoke the success of any others. It was rather that, above and beyond the authority of any of these others, another authority was being defined, the realm of the system itself, which these others might resist indeed in selected times and in selected places, in selected ways, but which they could not escape. Still, the failure of liberal Protestants was greater. Why? Because liberal Protestants had made the greatest investment in the economy and culture; they had expected the most of the nation. But they had expected more than they had prepared themselves to guarantee, by way of security, progress, moral growth, personal fulfillment. Therefore their failure to play a creative role in any significant ferment of the twenties was most significant. Liberal Protestantism's failure to share in shaping the norms of a system capable of claiming autonomy for itself was more dangerous if only because there was no other real alternative for making great expectations come true.

Some open questions

Is it quite fair to "judge" the religious liberalism of the twenties (and thirties) in this way? Is it not inevitable and natural that there should be some considerable lag between the challenge of new problems and clear recognition of them, let alone between the challenge and clear answers? And is not the inevitability of lag doubly assured when one speaks of large populations, whole cultural communities, and not just of a few exceptional leaders? All this is so. No story of sentiments and emotions should fail to convey some atmosphere of fate. But my aim is to establish a fact, the fact of liberal Protestant inhibition, its unadventurousness. The failure of liberal Protestantism to recognize its impasse was part of its fatality.

There is another question as well, more concrete, more historical. When one speaks of "Protestantism," of what does one speak? In speaking of "Catholicism," one knows that, according to the canons of the Catholic church itself, one must place special emphasis upon the clergy, since in Catholicism the clergy bears explicit canonical responsibility for most—if not all—that merits the label "Catholic." But was not the point of Protestantism, partly, its promotion of lay, democratic status, religiously? And in that case, is it not necessary, when speaking of "Protestant" responsibility, to inquire into the doings of the Protestant population at large, laymen as well as clergy? Especially in modern times, in America, where, for over a century, the authority of the clergy had been dissolved to a point where the pastor's plain duty was, like any politician or salesman, simply to service the desires of his clients? And was not, by the nineteen-twenties—if not much earlier—the true bearer of Protestantism the layman, his behavior the index of belief, his adventures the measure of faith?

I have already indicated some of the ideology generated by laymen in the business world. Beyond these there were, assuredly, the adventures of countless persons, men and women, whose achievements remain known to those who knew them best. Still, assuming no matter how many private adventures untold, it remains that no religious ideology emerged from them. For all the pioneering of judges, doctors, critics, teachers, housewives and artists, none came to a focus providing guidance and assurance. Whether such a focus had to renew some notion of "church" as the supreme concentration of cultural imagination remained a question acutely embarrassing to sophisticated Protestant leaders, since, in the best of neo-orthodox thought, "church" was even more vulnerable to prideful sin than state or class, and no alternative had been located. Only primitive Protestants, exploited by such sinister specialists as the Reverend Billy James Hargis and Dr. Fred Schwarz and layman Robert Welch, indulged in fanatic idolizations. In any event, cultural analysis of Protestant energy, sensitive to laymen as well as clergy, reveals no community imagination shaken free from the insidious trait here sketched—passivity.

CHAPTER XVIII

THE DEPRESSION: CONFUSION OF SOULS

THERE WERE many reasons why, with the depression and the New Deal, any lingering coherence of a traditional Protestant ethos should have crumbled finally. Not that massive inevitability was at work. "Accidents," not just predestinations by character or social interest or history, were in play, too. Thus, from our standpoint, it was accidental that just four years before the crisis-election of 1932 the Democratic party should have been so dramatically revealed as a vehicle for the new millions of recent immigrant origin—and should not have won. From the perspective of long party history, that is, it was accidental that the Republican party, so long the party of the Protestant middle, rather than the Democratic party, was not called upon in 1932 to face the crisis. There were indubitably more resources available within the Republican party than President Hoover utilized. Old Progressives and new "enlightened" businessmen might have summoned nerve for a bold Hamiltonian Keynesianism. Had the Republicans been called to take over from a Democratic administration in 1932, some of those resources might have been tapped.

Partly because of such an accident, one potential association between the New Deal and Protestantism was blocked—that indicated by the social gospel.[1] Suffocated and ignored in the twenties, the vanguard social reformers might have been in position to offer both their flocks and the nation a plausible—and possibly even a powerful—rationale for a vigorous recovery of national self-direction. As it was, the New Deal legislated many social-gospel demands, only to earn the distrust of widespread respectable congregations. Liberal social-gospel pastors themselves commonly preferred to safeguard their perfectionism rather than their practical hopes by supporting the Socialist party of the ex-Presbyterian preacher Norman Thomas. A brave handful of pastors and laymen —often youths—identified with the labor movement, to become education directors, political-action secretaries, and even organizers, but even their example hardly lasted out World War II. Reinhold Niebuhr's effort to introduce some old Protestant iron of realism into the perfectionist softness of the social gospel did not markedly reduce the confusion, if only because Niebuhr found it necessary through the thirties to reject the New Deal, not to support or even adequately to interpret it, as proof of his own realism.

The major exception to this picture was the Protestant South— traditionally Democratic in politics, largely fundamentalist in its Protestantism. Pathetically, Protestant culture found its link with liberal politics only where Protestantism itself was most petrified in social imagination and most seriously compromised in its local culture. Niebuhr and others hopefully watched for the emergence of a genuine "proletarian" Protestantism in the South, but they were never really looking at the American South, rather at a figment of enthusiastic theory.

Whatever the chances might have been along any of these lines, and whether one wishes to think of the results as accidental or not, deeper reasons did obtain for the confusion wrought in the old ethos by the crisis of the thirties. The first was the fact and the nature of the depression itself. The business cycle never had been decently integrated into the logic of the Protestant ethic and its corollary, the gospel of success. What did such massive dislocation have to do with individual character after all? At most, depressions could be construed as "tests," winnowing winds sent by the Lord or the nature of things to separate the strong from the weak. Bunyan's Christian, in his Progress, persevered through storm as well as sun. But surely the winnowing did not seem morally selective. Nor could practical men be satisfied any longer with piety. In the past, it had been acceptable to blame depressions on factors outside moral logic, such as piratical speculators, misbegotten monetary policies and the like, and their immediate impact could be absorbed by general confidence in long-range expansion. The great depression of the thirties did not yield to such finesses. The crash of a speculation-mad Wall Street symbolized the Fall, yet all the blame could not be shifted onto some image of unscrupulous, conniving gamblers. Nor could blame be localized, as the President tried to localize it, in some purely extrinsic or technical flaws, such as the collapse of the German banks. Both government and private business leaders had staked their claims to legitimate power on the permanence of prosperity, on the system. Every one of the respectable institutions of the economy was entangled. Almost all the respectable administrators of the economy were entangled.

After the crash, while leaders of the economy from the President on down pursued the mind-cure policy of insisting that the system was fundamentally sound and only men's thoughts impeded recovery, something became apparent. The system actually had no leaders. Its spokesmen had small power over it; they had power only within it, and when it broke down they were at a loss. The rugged individualism, the business-as-service, and the individual freedom by which the system presumably was justified, were found irrelevant. The extent, depth and duration of the depression made it less and less possible to go on relying simply on transcending hope. American society was being severely shaken, and with it, the assumptions of that society nourished by nearly three centuries of Protestant morale.

Protestant morale in crisis

The New Deal answer to the depression shook them still more. Again, one can imagine less severe a test. It was not "inevitable" that, by 1936, Republican-party opposition to the New Deal should have fallen into the hands of the least sophisticated sectors of the business community. The Liberty League and the National Association of Manufacturers preached an ideology reactionary not only measured against the Progressives but even against the trade associations of the twenties blessed by Secretary of Commerce Hoover himself. This regression served to disguise the facts of modern corporate capitalism still more thoroughly, and thus further to inhibit the perfectly plausible possibility of a Protestant imagination, drawing perhaps on old Progressive morale, geared to mastering an organizational society. Of course, the "accidental" element here could be overstressed. The captivity of the Republican party to primitive thinking followed from the free choice of Republican businessmen and politicians alike, and their audience of millions. Yet the early New Deal had drawn business leaders into its national program, and it was not until their palpable reluctance to think in terms of a national community jeopardized the program that the New Deal turned into a coalition of non-business interests.

From this point on the New Deal simply transcended the Protestant ethos, leaving it without national political relevance. As a national and governmental program the New Deal decisively revealed that the self-made man did not guarantee the good order of the economy, and that the harmonic local community was not the model for the national community. Self-help failed to help a multitude of selves. Help even on the cooperative level of the corporation or association of corporations had not helped. Ascetic self-denial, perseverance, the power of will—none availed. What could alone avail, evidently, was some plan for the community at large, implemented by its supreme agency, the federal government, and the connection between such planning and personal moral traits was highly obscure.

This was only the beginning. In the old ethic, charity supplemented self-help. Those who were successful were not to be divided from their fellows in pride, but to spiritualize further their good fortune and merited fruits by administering them for others. Drawing from Gospel texts, the relationship between the charitable and the needy appeared as personal and local, clearly defining differences in character. Naturally, the point of view in this ethic was that of those who gave, not those who received; the philanthropy praised in the gospel of success was praised most freely by the philanthropists. The New Deal in its program both for relief and for recovery seemed to convert millions into recipients with no clear rationale of character as guide. The personal and local sanctions for philanthropic relief were shaken. Where local good fortune made it hard to comprehend mill and mining and factory and slum communities where all were afflicted, where none were left to be charitable, the old ethic saw the new charity as boondoggling, as bureaucracy, as centralization of raw power, as taking from the provident for the lazy.

Collapse of Protestant sociology

Collapse in the ethic of self-help and philanthropy shared in the larger collapse of over-all nineteenth-century Protestant sociology. The government was taking over Reform. Voluntary private action and organization was being overtaken by official public action. What were to be the chances, the status and the real significance of the locally based, popularly generated and democratically led private associations typical of the century past? Over them all now loomed the apparatus of the state. Given such apparatus, how could society be imagined as projection of moral character, the moral man writ large? Of course this problem had already been posed, as symbolized in Standard Oil or United States Steel. But as "private enterprise," these bureaucratic giants had enjoyed at least the thin fiction that they did merely extend the qualities of their hero-creators and that they were, as the Supreme Court had said, "persons."

Progressives, breaking the fiction, had been able to feel that the state was not an inherently alien thing; democratically based, the state, too, could be a projection of character, a kind of "incorporation" of the whole society. But the Progressives had visualized a regulatory and mediating state, reconciling private conflicts brought to its adjudication, defining standards for private power to observe. Despite the hopes of men like Croly and Lippmann, the Progressive state had not been aimed to enter the economy and society as an energizing and creative force itself. It was hard to think of the New Deal so confined. From 1935 New Deal policies appeared to be intended to change basic power relationships, adding the resources and energy of the state to some groups against others. The New Deal appeared vital with all-too-many projects of its own. The fact that both the old laissez-faire state and the Progressive state, too, had in actuality been allied with particular groups to the disfavor of others could be ignored, since this alliance had been traditional. Not the alliance but the partners to the alliance made the New Deal shocking. This made it difficult to comprehend the New Deal in terms of moral character; or else, often enough, it made it tempting to construe the New Deal as projection of the wrong kind of character. At the same time, the New Deal's intervention in the economy appeared much more direct, persistent and far-ranging than anything contemplated by Progressivism. At times the government seemed to be going into business on its own, in the TVA, FHA, PWA, WPA. Even when men remembered that much of the work of these agencies always had been accepted within the public rather than the private economy, it was still possible to feel alarm at the subordination of local government and its local democracy. As a "class" state, therefore, and as a "positive" state, the New Deal violated even Progressive imagination, let alone the imagination of those still dreaming in terms either of unreconstructed laissez-faire or of the local harmonic community. It was no easement of confusion that many of those dismayed were nevertheless forced to accept Washington's help.

More deeply challenging was the longer-run heritage of the New Deal as the symbol of a welfare economy. The welfare state, as it emerged in the late thirties, and then decisively after the Second World War, had roots as old as the Republic, and continued to draw on those roots. It had limited aims. It did not presume to make society the ward of the state; it did not presume to make individuals wards of the state. It aimed rather to extend the sort of minimum police standards the state had always provided, but into new fields and for everyone. Minimum wages and maximum hours, guaranteed prices on farm produce, reasonable protection of savings, reasonable loans for housing, some beginnings on old-age security, renewed attention to community amenities and utilities, on all of which the private economy had failed, were taken up by the New Deal on the national scale, matching the scale of failure, as later local concern for such areas as health and education was to be supplemented by national attention. It was the limited character of this program that the old ethos could not appreciate. Opposition argued as though guaranteed minimums sapped ambition for maximums. Refusing to comprehend that the modern American welfare state derived finally not from moral and humanitarian idealism but from incipient chaos, opposition read into its pragmatism a moral softness.

But both moral opposition to and pragmatic economic justification of the welfare state missed its most compelling implication. The idea that every person should be assured a certain minimum welfare implied the idea that every individual ought to have a certain minimum freedom in his choice of life-style. This was not true of competitive laissez-faire, where, logically, every individual was totally responsible for all the conditions of his life. This had a simple, drastic effect: work-ethic and work-ethic alone held priority over every other style. True for men directly, it was true for both men and women indirectly insofar as there was reared upon its basis a scheme of self-measurement according to economic status values. Guaranteed welfare, denying the primitive assumption of the work-ethic, that sheer survival techniques must define the basic alternatives of life, offered people the chance to liberate their imagination about themselves. The welfare state might have been comprehended as at last a turn from scarcity psychology to abundance psychology.

It is easy to see one reason why the New Deal should not have been appreciated this way. Though sometimes inclined to ascribe depression scarcity dialectically to boomtime overabundance, the New Deal leaders were faced by the immediate problem of what to do about scarcity, not of how to allocate abundance. Yet this suggests the deeper issue. It was only in a society previously dominated by an economic ethic that the chances for a personal, psychological ethic, an ethic based on imaginative abundance, would seem to depend upon large margins of economic abundance. It was not a fact of nature—or of human nature—that a culture on fixed and spare economic rations had to be dominated by economic ethic. Neither anthropology nor psychology nor sociology said so; history did not say so. Only an "economics" already out of date seemed to say so. At all events, welfare implied the chance to judge and shape economic institutions according to their usefulness to personal abundance, and the chance to deny that personal abundance varied according to economic abundance. This was in effect the chance that liberal Protestantism had missed in the twenties. After the moral confusions induced by the depression and the New Deal, liberal religion was still less prepared, even as the chances grew, to seize them.

Under the stress of the circumstances, it was the personal religious liberalism of the sort preached by Harry Emerson Fosdick, widely diffused to congregations across the land, that suffered most. Passive and content in the twenties, in the thirties it was passive and confused. New mind-cure preachers such as Emmett Fox appeared. Peculiar mixtures of old individualism and new psychology were offered, as by Henry C. Link in his best-selling *The Return to Religion*. The best-selling religious novels of the decade were those of Lloyd Douglas about healing. In 1937 Norman Vincent Peale started his clinic for the harassed of Manhattan. And while the political and religious tough-mindedness of Reinhold Niebuhr's neo-orthodoxy met incomprehension, elite suburbs here and there stirred with that strange substitute for realism, Moral Rearmament.

As context for religious vitality, the depression was not sterile. Pentecostal holiness sects grew sharply among people hopelessly uprooted amid rural poverty mostly in the South and the border states, for whom it was natural to find nothing in history and everything in that premillennial anticipation of what would follow the end of history which had always lurked around the edges of nineteenth-century Protestantism. Never having identified religion with a prosperity they had never had to lose, these people still had a religious imagination to use. Much more sensational was the mission of

George Baker, Father Divine, who, rivaling in the brilliance of both his religious and his administrative gifts the talents of Mary Baker Eddy and of the team of Joseph Smith and Brigham Young, rallied still another audience of the dispossessed. Baker's movement, like Mormonism, powerfully demonstrated the vitality to be unleashed in fusing religious with community revival, a vitality hidden in an individualistic society. As it had not among Protestants since the Mormons, religion among the followers of Father Divine meant an economy and a culture, a way to work, a way to eat, a way to play, a way to love, and not only a way to "believe." The movement aimed at complete repossession of life for spirit, even if at the cost of savage repression. The strong attraction of the movement for Negro women displayed Baker's intuitive comprehension of the deepest disaster among his followers, the chaos of the family, heritage of slavery, perpetuated by segregation, in Northern slums even more than in the South. (In liberal Protestant communities, meanwhile, the family, which had been left exposed during the twenties to the manifold attritions, invasions and fresh opportunities of abundance playing upon it like the weather, tightened up somewhat during the depression.) At the same time, in Detroit, the male obverse of Father Divine's movement was taking first root, the Black Muslims, a sinister mirror held up in the sinister face of American racism. For the first time in its history, American Christianity, viewed over the vast variety of all its resources, was being challenged, not as "religion," but as "a" religion, a religion that had failed, and by people who had known it. The Black Muslims were saying that another religion was better.

In contrast, the National Preaching Mission of 1935 and 1936, set afoot by the respectable offices of the denominations, promoted on what one might feel the somewhat opportunistic, if not quite cynical, theory that economic depressions prepared spiritual harvests, and pitched in somewhat old-fashioned evangelical accents, failed badly.

It seemed entirely possible that, while the liberal and liberal-evangelical leaders were talking more and more of ecumenical togetherness and, after the war, began to translate talk into several denominational marriages, nevertheless Protestant culture taken as a whole was losing all coherence even in its church life. It seemed entirely possible that the great center itself was adrift.

CHAPTER XIX

MORE DEPRESSION: A RELIGION PRESCRIBED

IF THE National Preaching Mission's evangelism meant little to those disoriented not only by the depression but also by the New Deal, perhaps more individualized, specialized help was needed. Certainly some might, like Charles Fillmore, subsist in fantasy, "not thinking about it" on the principle that the troubles of the time resulted from too much and faulty thinking. Others might assert their self-reliance and fortitude as the sufficient response. But for still others, that was precisely the problem: self-reliance was not sufficient.

By all odds one of the strangest efforts to reconstitute morale and redefine characterological efficacy during the depression anticipated what was to become after the war the bright new alliance of religious promise. Once, in the days of the Progressives, sociology had been the science of hope. In the days of postwar drift and abundance it was to be psychology.

The fact that the marriage failed of real consummation during the depression suggested some of the postwar incompatibilities. Even so, Henry Link's best-selling *The Return to Religion*, of 1936, prefigured one of the major terms of the partnership, far more than did Fosdick's *On Being a Real Person* of 1943 with its implicit call for heroism. Religion and psychology would join, to promote not ego strength but surrender.

Link's book went through thirty-four printings in five years, into a dollar edition in 1941, then into Pocket Books in 1943, fading thereafter, its bizarre blend of several old reliables in popular economics, psychology and religion proving unpalatable to postwar taste.

The "personality quotient"

Link was not pointing to some general revival of religion. That would not occur until after the war. He was announcing his own return to religion, and not as a result of personal conversion, but of his psychologist's scientific observation. Having been raised in Methodist evangelical piety during childhood and youth, Link had experienced the entirely standard conversion to agnosticism as a Phi Beta Kappa student at Yale. There he entered applied psychology, earning a Ph.D. in 1916. From early in the twentieth century certain groups of American psychologists had begun to concentrate on tests and measurements, the most famous being tests of intelligence, first widely applied to draftees in World War I. From this early interest the ideal of psychology as a "mathematical and quantitative" science spread rapidly. It was, of course, not the sort of psychology represented by James, or that of Freud or of any psychology concerned primarily with the dynamics of personality. This test-and-measurement psychology also found the experimental "rat psychology" of the universities too slow. It was eager for practical application, and Link was one of the appliers. After Yale he went into private industry, where he administered tests. In 1931 he joined the Psychological Corporation, founded ten years before by the eminent James M. Cattell, to the end of making scientific psychology available to individuals and institutions "on a business-like basis." Link was director of social and market research. Here he devised a "Psychological Barometer," an instrument for polling consumer behavior and public opinion. He also directed vocational, educational and personality testing.

Link's special pride was his invention of a "Personality Quotient," or PQ, test. Despite the popularity of various IQ tests, many psychologists had realized there were still some severe difficulties in knowing just what intelligence was, let alone in measuring it. Reservations with respect to measuring personalities quantitatively were even sharper. But Link was not troubled. Psychology was already quite scientific enough to justify PQ tests.

Evidently it was also scientific enough to justify religion.

Link did not return to religion because of any individual experience of his own. Presumably this would not have been scientific. He found his evidence in other people. For one thing, as a counselor— still an agnostic—he had found himself recommending church and religion to many of his clients. More telling was one of the findings drawn from his tests. During 1933 and 1934, 15,231 people in New York City had been processed, and it was learned that "individuals who believed in religion or attended a church had significantly better personalities than those who did not."[1] What was Link's measure of personality? It was "the extent to which the individual has developed habits and skills which interest and serve other people."[2] Introversion, self-centeredness, selfishness were the curses of humanity; extroversion, sociability, unselfishness were salvation. Except for his addition of the modern "introvert" and "extrovert" to the traditional words, this sounded truistical and traditional enough. Link meant the label "extrovert" with a special vengeance, however. After all, the question was how to become unself-centered.

"The whole trend of modern, scientific psychology," he said, "is toward the emphasis on work, on doing things, as the road to happiness, and away from the emphasis on thinking, self-analysis, or talking oneself out of a difficulty."[3] This meant quite literally that psychology was to discourage self-awareness. "Behave yourself" rather than "Know thyself," Link quoted approvingly.[4] Obviously Link had no patience with concepts of the subconscious or the unconscious. What this meant for counseling he narrated in several cases. To a young man who could not hold a job he prescribed: get a job and hold it. To a young woman who had difficulty making friends he prescribed: make friends every chance you get. While here Link the behaviorist intersected with James, in telling people to act "as if," Link never allowed that the crucial problem was precisely an incapacity to "let go" so as to be able to act "as if."

It was not as though Link was revivifying old Protestant reliance upon the will. Rather he was invoking Annie Payson Call's principle of keeping busy, with a particular insistence that this busyness be with other people. Link recommended dancing, playing cards and joining church groups and clubs. Not to be busy all the time left surplus energy available for introspection and introversion. This advice carried all the way to doubts about education. PQ tests revealed that formal education beyond grade school did little or nothing to improve personality. "Indeed, there is some good evidence that the contrary often occurs, and that the prolongation of formal education results in a deterioration of personality."[5] Marden and Smiles had thought so before. Employers, Link thought, were no longer so anxious to get college graduates; when they were, they were more interested in extra-curricular activities than in academic achievement.

In correlating religion with good personality, Link was obviously judging religious discipline by its contribution to sociability, and one might therefore discern in his portraits of the extrovert the "other-directed" style of man, dependent on others as well as serving others, without purposes or even a mind of his own. But Link's most obvious polemic contradicted this image of other-direction. Repeatedly, with vehemence, he deplored the decay of character in the United States. He assailed consumer-orientation and praised the producer. He felt the thirties especially betrayed widespread psychological weakness. Not only did he attack Dr. Francis Townsend's plan for old-age pensions and Father Charles Coughlin's scheme for redistribution of the wealth. He attacked the New Deal and all ideas of social planning. Naturally he despised the social gospel as "the exponent of class hatred."[6] As his scientific basis for this gloom, he quoted a poll of 1933–35 showing that people had come more and more to think that the federal government should take care of unemployment relief. "We see here a national tendency toward introversion . . . a nation of people . . . dodging the realities of life, avoiding personal contacts with suffering . . . which lead to extroversion, competence, and an abundant life, for themselves as well as the unemployed."[7] In line with this Link recommended that every young man, rich or poor, spend a year in the Civilian Conservation Corps, observing that a poor boy has a tremendous advantage in life so long as his parents don't teach him the world owes him a living.

The debris of laissez-faire

This was the debris of late nineteenth-century laissez-faire. That it was debris, Link's further wrestling with education neatly showed. Despite his suspicions of formal education, he lamented the abandonment by progressive educators of the old tough curriculum—which, after all, had stressed not personality but intellect. Then he complained that psychologists, having developed good eight-to-ten-hour batteries of aptitude tests prescribing the right education for everyone, were frustrated by educators who would not use them—but presumably not by the progressive educators, who did use them. This incoherence reflected Link's over-all difficulties. His image of human nature was still indebted to "hard" nineteenth-century male Protestant individualism, that of Social Darwinism, the gospel of success and competition. He was therefore vastly offended by the assumptions of the New Deal. Yet a revivification of the old individualism could hardly be pursued on the basis of "personality" conceived as sociable extroversion. And at the same time he could not challenge the welfare policies of the New Deal by an appeal to greater self-awareness, more purposeful, conscious desires. As a psychologist, his kind of psychologist, he was confronted by the fact that the psychology which urged a greater self-awareness, pre-eminently that of Freud, seemed also to invite people to make demands upon their society they had not made before. Hence Freudian psychology spelled self-indulgence. Though sensing plainly enough that the tendency of the nation away from old-fashioned individualism was partly the fruit of growing self-awareness and conscious experience on the part of some new groups, Link could not do justice to such new experience and awareness.

When recommending extroversion and being of interest and service to others, Link failed to ask what the "others" wanted. This followed, since the only logical model he could use was the being-together of extroverts, lacking introspection and self-awareness. In recommendations to the girl fond of reading good books that she substitute the *Reader's Digest*, the Y.W.C.A. and the church, the "content" of this emptiness was specific.

Why religion?

What help was religion in producing extroversion? It provided the values by which people might live outside themselves. Why religion? Because logic, reason, science could never provide them. Easily the most intriguing theme in Link, this argument left him at a far remove from mind cure and, in fact, affiliated with ancient piety. Religion was non-rational, indeed "irrational," faith—trust which no logic, reason or science could justify. "Religion has been called the refuge of weak minds. Psychologically, the weakness lies rather in the failure of minds to recognize the weakness of all minds." God as mystery was once again invoked. In specifying the rewards of faith, Link was perfectly logical and perfectly explicit in rejecting mind-cure notions. He spoke of those lacking religion as "fools" of "every faith which promises the abundant life *as he, at that moment, desires it.*"[8] Again: "Your religion does not promise you a perfect life on earth, nor freedom from suffering; it does guarantee you the strength to bear suffering." The "basic values of life and character . . . are religious, often unreasonable, and in the last analysis beyond reason."[9]

Yet, despite these noble echoes, religion was, after all, the super-ego superconsciousness of mindless extroversion in Link. No existential hero staring courageously into the dazzle of irrational mystery assumed his stage, but rather the child grown into man, still abiding by obsessions induced in childhood. Discussing the difficulty parents faced in raising children, Link deplored the conflicting authorities in modern society—schools, neighbors, shows. Religion provided the only unity and ever-present force, and "the strategic time to teach children to subordinate their impulses to higher values is when they are too young to understand, but not too young to accept."[10] Link made no recommendations for helping the child to develop understanding later.

If scientific psychology could do so much to prove that it could do so little, if extroverted unawareness promised so little gratification, if religious faith amounted to faith in so little, it was likely another psychology would be more attractive, linked to a more promising religious optimism. Still, if depth psychology was to replace Link's behaviorism, this did not mean the goal had to be changed—the self's management of itself toward automatic harmonic uncritical adjustment.

CHAPTER XX

PSYCHOLOGY IN THE AIR

"Psychology is in the atmosphere. Christians are being exposed to it through lectures, reading material, radio, television, and even sermons."[1]

Psychology was indeed in the air. The man who said so was a doctor, L. Gilbert Little of Topeka, Kansas, in 1956, and he did not like it a bit. He found it bad psychology and a menace to religion. As we shall see in later chapters, he was not alone in finding a "crisis" in both psychology and religion by the late fifties. But the crisis had deep roots in a prolonged serious scientific venture.

The first, and famous, venture in adding modern scientific psychology to the armamentarium of Protestant pastors had begun in the early home of mind cure—Boston. In 1905 Elwood Worcester and Samuel McComb of the Episcopal Emmanuel Church organized a tuberculosis clinic under the medical direction of Dr. Joseph E. Pratt. Basically a medical mission to the slums, this was no different in kind from older medical missions anywhere. But in 1906 Worcester and McComb expanded their work in a Class for the Treatment of Mental Disorders, with the help of more doctors, notably a psychiatrist, Dr. Isador H. Coriat.[2]

The Emmanuel Mission arose explicitly in response to Christian Science. Somewhere along the line, Worcester and McComb agreed, the church had lost its therapeutic power. Mind-cure groups, they agreed, had been right in trying to recover it. Worcester and his fellows were bothered most by mind cure's medical primitivism or obscurantism, less by its theology. Yet this involved them in questions of, at least, philosophy. Operating with the then standard distinction between functional and organic diseases, they rejected mind cure's monism totally. Each case of strictly "organic" affliction rested entirely in the hands of doctors. This at least was clear: pastors should not act as M.D.'s. Troublesome questions still lurked, however. What if mind cure had been basically right in rejecting hard-and-fast mind-body dualism? And then, suppose there *were* purely "functional" disorders: should pastors act as psychologists?

Here and there brother Episcopalians imitated the Emmanuel enterprise. At St. Paul's in Chicago, Samuel Fallowes spread the word in books such as his *Health and Happiness, or Religious Therapeutics and Right Living*, in 1908. Bishop Nichols in San Francisco started a center at St. Luke's hospital where divinity students might learn religious psychotherapy. Worcester carried on the Emmanuel Mission itself into the twenties before resigning to concentrate on training young clergymen and pursue private counseling on his own. With his death in 1941 the direct line of the Emmanuel venture ended, but the Episcopal church, from the thirties and especially after World War II, spawned new groups and healing centers. By then so had many other denominations.

The fascination with psychology led to the tactic of equipping pastors with psychiatric and psychological training systematically. More than any other one man, the Reverend Anton Boisen, chaplain of the state hospital in Worcester, Massachusetts, set things going with a clinical training course for divinity students in 1925. Doctors helped and Richard Cabot himself initiated another program at the great Massachusetts General Hospital in 1933. Previously, in 1930, following some years of careful pilot work, a Council for Clinical Training of Theological Students had been formally organized, with a notable pioneer in psychosomatic medicine, Dr. Helen Flanders Dunbar, serving as its director, and with Boisen as its leading pastor-sponsor. Modern "pastoral counseling" in American Protestantism dates from this period.

What Fosdick was assaying as an amateur was being professionalized. Within ten years a large cluster of important books, theoretical and practical, was available. Men such as Russell Dicks, Carroll Wise, John S. Bonnell, Seward Hiltner and many others appeared as specialists. Seminaries began to install regular, and sometimes required, courses. After 1945 the process snowballed. At a 1948 conference on religion and psychiatry, there were representatives from the Council for Clinical Training, the Institute of Pastoral Care, the Federal Council of Churches' Committee on Religion and Health, and from the National Committee for Mental Hygiene. An interested pastor could have kept pace by following the older journal *Pastoral Psychology* or the new *Religion and Health* or the *Journal of Pastoral Care*. In 1954 an Academy of Religion and Mental Health was founded to stimulate training of young clergymen further.

Healing by spirit

How far did the infusion of psychology spread? A survey by Professor Samuel Blizzard of Princeton yielded the raw figure of 175,000,000 man hours per year spent by pastors in pastoral counseling. The total was absurd; cut by 90 per cent it remained impressive. Not all proceeded by the canons of one or another brand of modern therapeutic psychology. Still, no one doubted it was an age of psychology for the churches.

Why was it so? The psychology was therapeutic psychology, directed at sickness; the goal was health. Evidence of a tide of postwar preoccupation with health abounded. Were more people getting sick? Perhaps it was just that, say, by comparison with depression times people had more chance to seek treatment. Perhaps, in an economy devoted with unprecedented prodigality to "fulfilling needs," health really did constitute the most vulnerable and most precious arc in the magic circle of supply. Certainly in this existential vulnerability of everyone to sickness and death, the social glamour of modern medical doctors seemed to have struck deep roots. Having begun at last seemingly to wreak miracles, doctors had won first place in every sociological study of status-prestige, ahead of engineers, of ministers, far ahead of lawyers, far ahead of businessmen, even ahead of atomic scientists. In that common denominator of middle-class literacy the *Reader's Digest*, unforgettable old country doctors were memorialized alongside breathless prospectuses on the latest wonder-drugs, in a fusion of past and present and with an elusive but evident "American" overtone. On radio, in popular magazines, on television, doctors emerged as supremely suitable for romantic identification, equipped for moral decisions and with incredible skills, purged of any last lingering associations with blood, butchery, and, among women, profaned modesty.

But if the doctor's hero-status was comprehensible, why should the doctors' goal have also attracted pastors? Why, with the decline of one of the reasons for the early antagonism between mind cure and medicine, should mind cure's preoccupation actually have spread? The answer is not the obvious one—that doctors and pastors had different jurisdictions, the one laboring for one kind of health, the other another.

For one thing, a great many pastors had become occupied with "spiritual" healing. In an admittedly small sample taken by the National Council of Churches in the early fifties, nearly a third of the pastors replying had attempted spiritual healings; over one third knew of what they regarded as such healings.[3] These were men of the National Council denominations—Episcopalians, Methodists, Lutherans showing most interest, with Baptists not far behind. Spiritual healing was not healing of spirit, but healing by spirit, and the healing might well enter upon the jurisdiction of standard medicine. At the same time, it was not psychological healing. What underlay the interest in spiritual healing was more specialized than the general interest in health, or the general interest in psychological therapy. It may well have been eagerness for a "sign," evidence that religion and church life did in truth

have to do with an entirely autonomous power, an eagerness traditionally associated with the healing pentecostal sects and now,
perhaps, related to those trends toward re-emphasis upon liturgy
and sacraments especially evident in postwar Episcopalianism and
Lutheranism, less so in the denominations of historic Puritan descent, the Congregationalists, Presbyterians and their relatives.[4]

But jurisdictional haziness on the part of religion was more than
matched on the part of medicine. Not that a "pure," "materialistic"
medicine did not persist, move from triumph to triumph, and comprise for probably the large majority of doctors the sum of practice.
Nonetheless, the currents of change discernible at the beginning of
the century had swept on. One major movement was toward larger
appreciation of the unity of the body. Though the search for
"specifics" continued—one specific agent aimed at a specific affliction, such as the Salk vaccine—this was not the highest road of advance. Clearer and more detailed understanding of the body's "in-
terior environment" became a prime goal of research, helping the
body help itself in treatment. Though no less "materialistic," the
processes discovered by microbiology, for instance, richly illuminated "natural healing," that which Walter Cannon had called "the
wisdom of the body." Associations with the old tradition of natural
theology were possible, identifying *vis medicatrix naturae* with
vis medicatrix dei. Even more radically, *God Works through Medicine,* as V. E. Lukens entitled his book of 1935.[5]

However, this particular medical reform did not open many
doors to religion. If a new contemplative piety was implied, glimpsing God in processes of homeostasis, new pastoral practice was
not so clearly indicated. As Worcester and McComb had insisted,
pastors were not to be doctors. Even natural healing implied doctoring, as it implied the new non-specific antibiotics and stimulant
and tranquillizing drugs.

But medicine was also deepening its appreciation of mind-body
unity, blurring the old hard line between functional and organic
afflictions, adding to the afflictions which intuitive insight had long
assigned to minds and moods—ulcers, heart attacks, strokes—a growing list, with whatever degree of caution, speculation, surmise—

asthma, allergies, diabetes, tuberculosis, miscarriages—reaching out to touch even the most terrifying. If the jurisdiction was often obvious—the hemorrhaging patient required a doctor whether or not his ulcer was psychogenic—yet perhaps the zone of overlap was greater than common sense suggested, in preventive measures, recuperative measures, and so on. Doctors themselves were quoted as to the varying, but usually high, proportion of their patients whom they diagnosed as suffering for psychological causes.

In short, health in its medical sense was by no means monopolized by medicine. In fact, as medical theory and research more and more associated the health of organs and body with the "health" of person, more and more doctors fell further short of fulfilling theory in practice, as their purely "materialistic," "physicalistic" practice grew ever more specialized—and as the training of doctors lagged. One result of this situation was that the practice of construing psychological—and spiritual—health by analogy with medical health, given the intermingling of sicknesses, continued uncriticized except on subtle frontiers of analysis.

Indeed, the opening and expanding frontiers of medicine were one of the reasons the mind-cure cults themselves did not expand. Of course, they survived. Unlike third parties in politics, "third-party" religions rarely die even when their "issues" are taken over by the major denominations, and indeed, as I have indicated, the output of straight mind-cure books in the fifties came close to duplicating that of the years 1900 to 1910. Alongside the practitioners of Unity, Christian Science, New Thought and the others, new leaders appeared—an Ernest Holmes from the twenties, and Erwin Seale, the vastly popular Emmett Fox from the thirties in New York, drawing the direct competition of Norman Vincent Peale and John S. Bonnell. Having been dealt with sharply by Gaius Glenn Atkins in his survey of the church scene in 1923, then with neutral scholarship by Charles Braden and Elmer Clark in their surveys, the cults won the uncritical sympathy of Marcus Bach, to whom any devisements of technique were religiously reputable provided they "worked," for somebody. In William Oursler's special survey, *The Healing Power of Faith* (1957), they won places of honor along with a variety of other techniques.[6] But the mind-cure groups no longer had competitive advantages. Where they insisted most firmly on their spiritual methods, now they faced spiritual healing in the churches. Where their methods were plainly psychological, they faced the assimilation into the churches of more systematic, sophisticated psychotherapies. They faced a more flexible medicine itself. As for their embrace of wealth along with health, it was true that the raptures of the most explicit mystic monism were likely to occur where mind-cure atmosphere remained sectarian. Thus, the sensation of the International New Thought Alliance convention in Washington, D.C., in 1956 was a pamphlet with the all-resolving, all-dissolving title "Money Is God in Action."[7] But prosperity-thoughts had ceased to be their monopoly. Even Oral Roberts, an Oklahoma healer on the ancient pentecostal model, had insensibly expanded his evangel, in obvious symbiosis with his prospering fundamentalist congregations, to include "God's Formula for Success and Prosperity." Some of the strangest mental complexes in American religious history would evolve in the Southwest as simple holiness folk grew rich and anxious.

Old antagonisms softened

What mind cure had practiced without naming or confessing it, the pastors now could. If psychosomatic theory was cogent, then approaches from the psychic as well as the somatic side were cogent. And then, beyond the goal of narrow medical health, there was "mental health," for years the goal of psychologists independent of, as well as along with, doctors. If it was reasonably clear that pastors ought not try to be doctors, still they might practice psychology.

But was this so certain? In an early survey of the preoccupation with health, Charles Reynolds Brown of Yale, a Congregationalist, had stressed one feature of the Emmanuel experiment: "Dr. Worcester and Dr. McComb are exceptional men and they have had exceptional training in psychology."[8] Although it would not appear that either man really had competence in a true clinical psychology, Worcester had indeed studied under Wilhelm Wundt at Leipzig and taught psychology at Lehigh, while McComb had studied it at Oxford. Out of his training and practice, Worcester eventually became a full-time private practitioner. But, if it was the route of the pastor to become psychologist, what was his significance as pastor? Worcester and McComb did not say; neither did Harry Emerson Fosdick later. In a more recent, enthusiastic overview of the therapeutic scene, *God and Freud* (1959), Leonard Gross roundly cheered on the pastors training in psychology. "Good religion and good psychiatry are identical."[9] The comment posed a puzzle: if so, why did religion need psychiatry? On the other hand, in their more theoretical examination, *Psychiatry and Religious Experience* (1958), Dr. Louis Linn and Leo W. Schwarz carefully sought to clarify a distinction. In words of as much implicit challenge to religion as of invitation, they observed: "Of course, the religion that is centered in personal psychological needs is still the undeveloped religion of childhood."[10] Although they were basically sympathetic to the outreach of both religion and psychology to each other, the authors' categorical point was that the task of the religious leader was not that of the therapist.

Still, in a new atmosphere old antagonisms softened. Pastors worked with doctors and psychologists. Doctors worked with psychologists and pastors. Psychologists worked with pastors and doctors. Terminologies blurred. Therapies overlapped. Was the primitive fusion of all three being restored in sophistication? If so, was it possible that, as in most amalgamations, one or another party was in danger of losing identity? It seemed unlikely the danger could be met simply by definition. In one of the most sophisticated symposia on the whole field, *Religion and Health*, published in 1958, Cyril Richardson of the Union Theological Seminary, agreeing that the church had in truth lost much of its understanding of the power of spiritual healing—which was neither medical nor psychological—approved efforts to "set the stage, as it were, through which the Spirit of God *may* operate. It is God and not we who does the healing; but without our prayers and sacraments, the channels of His grace may be wanting." In the midst of this discussion, however, Richardson insisted upon something more:

". . . In the experience of the Church, [spiritual healing] is *extremely rare*."[11] Dr. Gotthard Booth, psychiatric adviser to both General and Union Theological Seminaries, echoed the point. While "psychologic methods" had come to be scientifically recognized, Booth said, "'spiritual healing' cannot be expected to be recognized on the same basis: it does not occur often enough to satisfy the statisticians and it cannot be produced deliberately. . . ."[12]

For more than prayerful and sacramental "waiting," then, religion had to turn to psychology if it was to find in its devotion to health a new mission and new means for vitalizing men.[13] But was it in their sickness that men revealed their problems as men, the potentials they had not expressed, the persons they might seek to become?

That the practice of trained pastoral counseling on the basis of one or another school of therapeutic psychology was of benefit to countless persons could hardly be doubted, with what incidence of success no one tested. I do not intend to probe this practice, but rather to look at the ideology of character as it appeared in the most famous case of the marriage of psychology and religion, that of Norman Vincent Peale. Without at all representing the labors of a host of pastor-counselors, Peale's phenomenal popularity represented a culture in impasse. The psychology which for this culture was also religion culminated the treatment of weakness by weakness.

CHAPTER XXI

POSITIVE DIVINE PSYCHOLOGY

Like Harry Emerson Fosdick, though ten years or so later, Norman Vincent Peale, too, as a young minister in New Jersey, had found himself unequipped for counseling. The psychology he had been taught had been "too academic and theoretical." And as Fosdick had done, Peale sought out an expert, in his case Dr. Smiley Blanton, a psychoanalyst trained by the master himself in Vienna. Blanton eagerly agreed to be a consultant on difficult cases. Evidently he had long felt psychiatry and religion could be harnessed together. Who would do what? What was the division of labor? This did not have to be decided; let things progress on an *ad hoc* basis.

Progress they did. Within twenty years of this original rather casual two-man collaboration, a vastly busy clinic mixing the labors of ministers, psychoanalysts, psychologists, doctors and social workers—more than twenty of them—had come to take up more and more of Blanton's time, he serving as executive director of the renowned American Foundation of Religion and Psychiatry, with a budget, in 1956, of $170,000. It took up much time from Norman Vincent Peale, too; he raised the money. The religio-psychiatric clinic of Peale's Marble Collegiate Church on Fifth Avenue in New

York City was one of few vivid success stories in Protestantism over the period.[1]

But Peale's deep attraction was not to personal counseling. It was to mass counseling. He deliberately sought best-selling audiences, traveled perpetually to speak everywhere, processed his message into forms suitable for magazines, newspapers, radio, television. In 1954 he was named one of the "Twelve Best U. S. Salesmen."

Peale's negative beginnings

This personal success did not come without perseverance. In fact, Peale did not try his hand at the printed word until, after training at Boston University Seminary, he had served a church in Brooklyn, several years at the University Methodist Church in Syracuse, and then Marble Collegiate. His first books, before World War II, disappointed him; they did not sell. Although written in a popular manner—anecdotal, inspirational, with that unerring avoidance of fresh language at which so many liberal Protestant pastors were adept—there was no particular reason why *The Art of Living* should have sold. It was hardly distinguishable from a host of other books. Peale did announce his permanent theme: ". . . applied Christianity helps people to tap [the] reservoir of power within themselves."[2] Inevitably he quoted William James on "The Energies of Men." But the book was not a program for power, strength, effectiveness, mastery. In fact, in contrast to masterful Christianity, Peale proffered a Christianity of escape. The world is too much for us, he lamented. "It is obvious that people are breaking in their minds under the stress and strain of modern life."[3] Among their riches, position, power and friends men yearn for a little cottage by the sea, for old grape arbors, "green meadows with golden cowslips." Peale—a small-town Ohio boy—declared that religion is that cottage, that meadow, that peace. From time to time —again, in a fashion common to the liberal pulpit—he sorrowed that the poets, "the abiding seers of the race," were ignored in an age of practical men; he recalled the supreme spiritual value of "things like music, art, literature"; and, of course, of religion.[4]

This religion of the gentler, finer things was to evaporate in the later, successful Peale. A Christianity which preferred meadows to Manhattan was not really "applied." Not that Peale's nostalgia ever lured him into suggesting that, if modern life was strained and stressful, something should be done about it. His sociology was strictly atomistic. Individuals were on their own. No "fumbling with materialistic processes" would help. Already the common man had too often had his self-respect drained off by government relief. (This was a book of 1937.) "Our problems are too great for any one mind or any group of minds."[5] Let God work in individual lives, and the collective will take care of itself.

The first book was too complicated; it was too negative; it was evasive about practical applications; it had too few techniques.

Peale did better in his second, *You Can Win*. He simplified more cleanly, hewing more faithfully to one line: "The Art of Self-Mastery"; "God and You Are Unconquerable"; "You Have It in You to Succeed"; "Overcoming the Tension of Modern Life." This was Peale's struggle book, the plainest revelation of his inherited Social Darwinist instincts.

But Peale's sense of struggle also was a bit peculiar. He still reacted to the image of harshness with flight rather than competitive fight. "No man, however resourceful or pugnacious, is a match for so great an adversary as a hostile world. He is at best a puny and impotent creature quite at the mercy of the cosmic and social forces in the midst of which he dwells."[6] Orthodox response to a hostile world had been the dualistic supernatural God, and so was Peale's. Man's only hope, he said, was "to attach himself to some force superior to and more powerful than the world of things." At the same time—and, implicitly, "therefore"—God was also an "inner spiritual power" that man had only to tap to be unconquerable, all-conquering. As in many other popular preachments, this scheme, of a hostile nature squeezed between a transcendent and immanent God, led by an underground logic to the notion that perhaps the world was not so hostile after all: "This world is somehow built on moral foundations. This . . . is the one lesson history teaches. . . . The good never loses."[7] The theology was hazy, the metaphysics tenuous, but of course this did not interdict popularity.

So far as popularity was concerned, the trouble with *You Can Win* was that Peale still did not get very far in explaining how to go about applying his ideas to make them work. Technique was still missing. He offered some clues. If, he instructed, you saturate your unconscious mind in good, clean and noble thoughts, "by and by" your unconscious will send up good and clean and noble thoughts to rule you. Generally, though, all he could advise was "to believe." How? "Simply accept faith. Believe you have it and you will have it. That, you see, is itself faith."[8] An exhortation that would have charmed James, as a perverse echo of Luther and Wesley, it could not have escaped James's criticism that such "belief" was contingent upon psychological "letting go," giving up one's self-centered anxiety. Luther had explained that faith itself—having faith, believing—was a gift of grace, God's free act.

Peale's ascent to sensational prominence began after World War II. In 1946 the circulation of his printed sermons began to climb, reaching 17,000 by 1948. In that year he had his first best-seller, *A Guide to Confident Living*. His speaking engagements multiplied. His publishing venture, *Guideposts*, began to get off the ground, reaching 800,000 circulation in the late fifties. *The Power of Positive Thinking*, first published in 1952, rose to the top of the best-seller lists and stayed there, week after week, month after month, for two years. Under the auspices of the National Council of Churches, he appeared on radio and television on Sundays, and on Mondays, Tuesdays, Wednesdays, Thursdays and Fridays as well. In *Look Magazine* he joined the ranks of weekly counselors on matters of morals, manners, ethics and life.

The secret of Peale's success

Did Norman Vincent Peale simply ride the postwar (especially the post-Korean War) "revival of religion" to its crest? Or had he been in part responsible for its surge? Peale's own position would be plain: he had at least met people's needs. Still the question has its interest, since no simple resolution will do. As Peale found his immense audiences, so too had others—Billy Graham conspicuously. Were both men simply riders of the wave? Obviously, in any completely satisfying history discrimination between the two would be called for. But short of that, another resolution is possible. Whatever his responsibility, it was Peale who rode the wave (as it was Graham who rode his) and not someone else. This was recognized. His omnipresence earned, by 1955, widespread anxiety in Protestant leadership.

Actually, one can think that Peale began to get the hang of his real message. in the book on which he collaborated with his psychoanalyst colleague, Smiley Blanton, in 1940, *Faith Is the Answer*. This book, too, disappointed expectations in the bookstores, but it exhibited Peale as a man devoted to expounding techniques, not ideas. *A Guide to Confident Living*, a satisfactory best-seller at last, was also above all a "how to" book: "How to Get Rid of Your Inferiority Complex"; "How to Think Your Way to Success"; "How to Achieve a Calm Center for Your Life." Expositions of philosophy, theology and indeed of psychology were minimal. It was a book totally immanent in the culture: no question was ever raised about any ends, as though all men needed only to learn the means. It was not so much that philosophy and theology were absent; they were assumed and swallowed into technique, dissolving silently.

Rapidly capitalizing on this success, Peale as expositor of pure technique revealed himself distilled and concentrated in *Inspiring Messages for Daily Living*, first out in 1950 and reprinted year by year. In Section One of this mentally salubrious manual, forty "health-producing, life-changing, power-creating Thought Conditioners" were supplied. Part Four offered assorted "spirit lifters" and Part Six provided ten "how" cards. Peale wanted any given section of his manual read through first, then one thought—a spirit lifter, for instance—was to be read each day. It was to be repeated as often as possible, the patient "savoring its meaning and feeling it drive deep within your nature." At night, before sleep, the booster words were to be repeated: "The Spirit Lifter that I read and committed today lies deeply inbedded in my mind. It is now sending off throughout my thoughts its healing, refreshing effects."[9]

Peale had "discovered" the power of suggestion over the human mind, and, therewith, had caught up with Henry Wood, Charles Fillmore and Emmett Fox, sixty, forty and twenty years before him. He was teaching Mental Photography all over again. Thoughts were things. The magic of words in the philosophy that thoughts were things depended, as James had seen, not on the words but on the minds using the words, and for minds prepared to find words magical the same techniques of automanipulation were inevitable. *The Power of Positive Thinking*, catching its audiences full in the throes of post-Korean, McCarthyite anxiety, running up a sale of over two million copies in the Eisenhower years, simply wove status and success into a smooth identification with the mind-cure techniques of Inspiring Messages, thus becoming the Bible of American autohypnotism.

The nuances of Peale's instruction should not be washed out. The theme of "power" rang as relentlessly through his pages as through Frank Haddock, but there was a difference. "Faith is stronger than will," Peale had said, in *You Can Win*, and in true mind-cure fashion, power—the Higher Power—was never human, as Haddock thought, but always divine. And what was this power for? "You can win," certainly. Peale promised everything. The Higher Power can "blast out all defeat and lift a person above all difficult situations." But Peale hardly imagined himself addressing people afflicted with Promethean urges, Faustian drives, people with limitless desires. It is simple to think that the "winning" to which he referred was simply success—success in the simple meaning of more money and higher status, the "material" rewards that good and persevering men deserved. As in the gospel of success and mind cure, Peale's gospel of positive thinking did indeed embrace this equation. "There was a time," Peale said, repeating Fillmore and the preachers of success, "when I acquiesced in the silly idea that there is no relationship between faith and prosperity."[10] Eager toastmaster at Horatio Alger awards dinners, popular speaker before countless businessmen's booster groups, Peale was unmistakably an heir of the old gospel of success. In *You Can Win* and thereafter, he indulged in its ritualistic negative thoughts about the decay of self-reliance, the decline of rugged individualism, and the lack of desire for risk in the younger generation—to conclude with the standard positive affirmation of America as still the land of opportunity as always. Testimonials to the power of faith in business success were regular features of his books and especially of the inspirational *Guideposts,* exactly duplicating the testimonials filling Unity's *Good Business, Prayer in the Market Place,* and a score of other mass outlets. But just as Charles Fillmore was more than a reincarnation of Alger, Conwell, Thayer and even Marden, so, too, was Peale. And in Peale there was something going beyond even Fillmore.

Even in his depression-decade books, when the effort to restore morale for pursuing success might have dominated, Peale responded to another woe. Success did not seem to be paying off. People might be successful, and yet be "still the unhappy victims of fear and anxiety, harassed by feelings of inadequacy . . . haunted by the specter of a possible failure. . . . In my interview work I find on the whole more personality disorganization among the favored class than among the common run of folk."[11] In *The Art of Real Happiness,* in 1950, the joint authors Peale-Blanton began: "Successful living hinges on the capacity to believe." Did this refer to the power of belief in bringing prosperity and higher status? Not at all. The authors had found their audiences suffering from a different sort of need.

No age has a monopoly on misery, although our own can claim more than its full share, and, at that, misery of a most particular kind. For in the midst of economic plenty we starve spiritually. Surrounded by unmatched potentialities for the good life, we are overwhelmed by the deadly fear that all is lost.[12]

Published in the full flood of mid-century prosperity, the title of Peale's sequel to *Positive Thinking* defined the deadly fear: *Stay Alive All Your Life.* American nervousness—the incapacity for abundance—still abounded. George Beard would have understood.

Controlling the unconscious

Peale's psychology repeated early mind cure, now blessed with some modern confusions. "In the personality of every individual is a great reservoir of unused power."[13] This was his primal insight, stated in his first book. Later, in *Stay Alive All Your Life,* he explained it more precisely: "There is resident in you an immense reservoir of force; the power of the subconscious mind. Faith releases this power."[14] As in mind cure, this did not mean quite what it said. In Peale's case the confusion was greater because he had come in contact with Freud in his collaboration with Dr. Smiley Blanton. Peale evidently imagined that he marched with Blanton in their joint labors in the Religio-Psychiatric Institute and in their books. This was not exactly so.

In their first collaboration, *Faith Is the Answer,* Peale and Blanton each discussed various topics separately—"The Power of Faith," "Conscience and the Sense of Guilt," "Love and Marriage," and so on. In "The Hidden Energies of the Mind," Blanton offered a drastically simplified but not intolerably distorted psychoanalytic discussion of how the unconscious could harbor hidden drives with the power to twist, misdirect and deplete a man's conscious life. In his own section, on the other hand, Peale—beginning with the usual quotation from James about untapped powers—began immediately to talk as though the unconscious was in itself the source of successful living. At one point, he identified the unconscious with biblical references to the "heart": "As he thinketh in his heart, so is he." "The ideas or thoughts which finally determine our actions and character are not those which we receive and examine in the conscious mind," he said. "It is not 'as a man thinketh in his conscious mind' that constitutes his personality."[15] Peale later identified the unconscious with the "soul." The inference was simple, evidently. Be sure the unconscious is full only of good thoughts. "Religion teaches us to allow only good and beautiful thoughts to enter the unconscious because of the obvious fact often demonstrated that the unconscious can only send back what was first sent down."[16]

This was peculiar. In this case how could the unconscious be the ruling center after all? As Peale himself put it in his contradictory way: "A man is in the last analysis what he has been predominantly sending into his controlling thought center." The controlling thought center—the unconscious—was itself controlled. By what? Peale's explanations suffered from ambiguity. "A thought enters the mind," he said, "is weighed," and accepted or rejected. Where did the thought come from? It came from Inspiring Messages for Daily Living, from the Power of Positive Thinking, or, more generally, "religion." It did not come from the mind itself. Like the unconscious, the mind in general was basically empty and passive, "only a reception station," Peale said, where thoughts were passed on.[17] This was the mind-cure psychology, the sub- (and now the un-) conscious and the conscious alike absorbed into "thoughts," and these in their turn into a trans-mind, trans- (and super-) consciousness, to wit, simply "religion" itself.

Obviously, Peale and Blanton were at odds on the significance of sheer thoughts and wishes. One of Blanton's points accorded closely enough with common psychoanalytic theory and therapy: "'When you have wished to do a thing, then you have done it,' says the unconscious mind."[18] That is, guilt in particular derives as much from having had forbidden wishes as for having committed forbidden deeds. Peale, on the other hand, echoing early nineteenth-century Protestant debates about sin, said that a thought does not count "unless and until the mind acting as judge admits it with a welcome. . . . A thought that enters the mind, is weighed and rejected, and is passed, condemned from the mind, leaves no stain of guilt but instead greatly increases spiritual power." "That which is received and accepted by the conscious mind determines ultimately the automatic reaction of the unconscious and in effect may be summed up as character."[19] Peale, in short, aborted the whole point of Blanton's Freudian discussion of the unconscious— that it could exercise a hidden power, made up of forces prior to character and impervious to indoctrination. He saw the unconscious as in itself passive, empty, waiting to be filled and activated by spirit lifters.

Then why did Peale make use of a concept of the unconscious at all? Why did he not preach simply the rule of obedience to right thoughts in the fashion standard to moralistic Protestantism? For one thing, coming, like Fosdick, to recognize increasing problems of counseling which did not yield to the old impersonal moralism, endeavoring to devise an "applied Christianity" in response, he inevitably came in touch with the only modern therapeutic psychology—that is, "depth" psychology. It should not be forgotten that Peale's clinic with Blanton was a pioneering venture, and in its way a daring, an adventuresome one. But his idea of the unconscious allowed something more important. Peale's aim in preaching positive thinking was not that of inducing contemplative states of Oneness nor of advancing self-insight nor of strengthening conscious will, let alone sensitizing people to their world. The clue here lay in Peale's reiterated concern that the operation of his positive thoughts and thought conditioners should become "automatic," that the individual truly become "conditioned." As the determining power, the unconscious by definition directed behavior without intervention of consciousness or will.

This automatic functioning on the basis of "inner power" was the heart of Peale's applied Christianity. Naturally, like mind cure he designated this power as divine. "In the subconscious God presides with His illimitable power. If you are allowing yourself to be defeated, practice thinking confidently and focus your thoughts on God. This inward power, this power of God within you, is so tremendous that under stress and in crises people can perform the most incredible feats."[20] The purpose of the Religio-Psychiatric Clinic was to clear the way for the operation of this divine power. For all the incoherence of his idea of the unconscious, Peale was ready to see that thought conditioners and spirit lifters could be inhibited by emotional patterns deep within a person and that these blocks had to be cleared away. But was the automatized power of positive thinking liberty or just one more form of mind-cure hypnotism? Was this new power really health or simply further weakness disguised?

CHAPTER XXII

POSITIVE PSYCHOLOGY—NEGATIVE PEOPLE

AFTER TWICE collaborating with Peale, in *Faith Is the Answer* and *The Art of Real Happiness*, Dr. Smiley Blanton published his own reasonably popular *Love or Perish* in 1956. Together with Rabbi Joshua Loth Liebman's best-selling *Peace of Mind* (1946), *Love or Perish* was one of the best postwar popularizations of Freudian psychology. It was one of the best because it preserved some of the quality of Freud's dramatic vision of life as a matter of dynamic tensions, interpenetrations and remarkable conversions of energy from one form to another, one purpose to another. It was not a book of technique.

Despite his misleading title, Blanton did not indulge in the universal promise to which Peale—like all mind cure—was addicted. It was a major error, he said, to imagine that "love will banish strife and frustration forever from our lives." This was true on two counts. There was no final inward harmony to be found. There was no outward harmony to be expected. "The world is indeed a dangerous place! But then it always has been and probably always will be. It is our fate and glory to face this danger and bring order out of chaos, love out of hatred."[1] This sentiment was not equivalent to Peale's early sense of the "hostility" of the world, for that hostility had provoked only the reflex of feelings of weakness, to be compensated by turning to the guaranteed triumph of the higher power. Peale had had to neutralize hostility utterly, and thus to neutralize any dialectic between danger and courage. Blanton preserved some of the Freudian fortitude.

His discussion of the emotional experiences of infancy and childhood, and the resonance of these in adult years, need not have unduly offended standard Freudians. Like the neo-Freudians Karen Horney and Erich Fromm, Blanton did argue that love in a rather more social than biological sense was the basic need of man, but he did not, as both Horney and Fromm at times seemed to do, and as liberal Protestants revising Freud persistently did, move from this into notions that love was the natural, normal manifestation of human nature properly reared. On the contrary, Blanton declared, the need for love guaranteed that hate, fear and anxiety would inevitably be generated in the infant, since he could not possibly escape deprivation of love once he left the womb. Blanton could say: "In every child's unconscious mind lie the crawling beasts of selfish aggression, of murderous hate, and of powerful sexual drives that will run rampant if not controlled."[2] This was hardly that empty passive receptacle waiting to be filled by the inner power of higher thoughts celebrated by mind cure and by Peale.

Conceivably, it was true, the phrase "if not controlled" in Blanton's description might have pointed to the magic of words and positive thinking, evicting bad contents with good. *Love or Perish,* however, advertised no mental photographs or thought conditioners whatever. True to psychoanalytic theory, Blanton strove for cultivation of insight. Consistently, his stress fell upon transmuting unconscious drives into consciousness through re-experience and rational comprehension. To the power of the unconscious he gave strong witness but he never leaped to the idea that this power amounted to those famous unexploited "energies of men" adduced by James.

Further, in the spirit of Freud, Blanton discerned a real conflict between the individual and society. Talents are unequal, he said, but what blocks most men is not their lack of talents but their failure to use those they have. For this failure civilized life bore major responsibility. Society placed primary emphasis upon order and regularity, thus demanded the sacrifice of natural impulses, and these sacrifices meant trouble. This tragedy—or even simply this tension—it had been part of the business of mind cure to deny, as it was of Peale. Blanton did not try to deprecate it. One of the problems in the interpretation of Freud was whether Freud conceived this conflict as eternal or as a feature of only some societies. What was clear was that Freud did lament some of the repressions demanded by the society he knew. Blanton, in partial accord with neo-Freudians, evidently believed the conflict not inevitable and eternal. This, however, only led him into still more excoriating attacks upon modern society, modern American society included, as "needlessly" inhibitory. "We are increasingly disturbed by the thought that society's passion for obedience and conformity may have overreached itself, causing us to lose in individual happiness perhaps as much as we have gained in group security."[3] Still more specially, like Horney and Fromm, Blanton attacked modern American business life. Work, he said, should satisfy desires for creativity and love, not just efficiency.

> Modern industry commits a basic psychological error when it fails to provide these conditions for the individual worker. . . . Our contemporary industrial society, far from encouraging the fusion of love with aggression, tends to place a premium upon their separation.[4]

Blanton was led to criticize precisely the behavior encouraged by Dale Carnegie. Why were salesmen periodically subject to the "dry spell" of personal depression? "Because business practice usually places emphasis upon the sale rather than the thing sold, salesmen tend to view their work primarily as an act of aggression in which they rob and injure their customers."[5] The Hobbesian war of smiles was one of self-inflicted wounds.

In his culminating pages Blanton felt called to plead that people openly voice a humanity censored by a culture turned into a system:

> Men and women are not content to hear their inner aspirations voiced merely in the maudlin accents of mass-entertainment media, for these offer only fantasies which do nothing to alter the essential burden of their lives. They wish to have their needs fulfilled in the world of action—in business, in politics, in everyday human contact. . . . By our acquiescence in this tacit contempt for human beings, we have imperiled the stability of society and, in the midst of material abundance, reaped an emotional harvest of disillusion, frustration and anxiety.[6]

Mind cure, from Quimby through Trine, Mrs. Eddy, Holmes, Fox and Peale, conspired with silence, in autohypnotic persuasion that in silence metaphysical harmony might be heard. Certainly Blanton had no politics, not even a social gospel, to suggest. At one point he observed that "businessmen of imagination" were beginning to see the problems, and one may wonder if he might have been susceptible to Elton Mayo-like philosophies of managerial manipulation, if not to the behaviorism of a Henry Link. Yet his mere exposure of society as a source of infection was at a far remove from mind cure, a worthy echo of Dr. Beard.

Predictably, Blanton encouraged the liberation of sex as a realm of human expression, adventure, spirit—long repressed by mind cure. And here Norman Vincent Peale, too, improved upon his mind-cure ancestors to the extent of including chapters on marriage in his books, but he—the creature of his audiences and his origins—hardly passed through the door he opened, into what was at long last emerging in some small circles of Protestantism—liberal and neo-orthodox alike—a comprehension of the body not just as vehicle of death but as substance of the life of spirit and human meaning. This was only one focus of a larger reorientation. Blanton included a chapter on the "glory of the senses," dispelling the darkness of liberal and mind-cure Protestantism alike in celebrating the senses as channels of communication and the media, therefore, for knowledge, rational consciousness, communion and religious experience itself. Mrs. Eddy's deprecation of "sensory experience," like that of moralistic Protestantism with its derivative and thin aesthetics, repeated by Peale, had been a form of "transcendence by denial," rejecting what the senses told of one's own flesh, but also of the tender flesh of others, of their moving voices, and of their gesturing creations, of real community and in fact of natural Being.

A healthy life, as it seemed in Blanton, did not enjoy freedom from stress or frustration. It did not enjoy decisions made automatically by a higher inner power. It did not even enjoy religious certitude. Blanton quoted Aquinas: "Every mind must face the rebuff of mystery," a sentiment repeated by Puritans who, like Aquinas, had not thought that God and even the highest of human lives were necessarily in harmony. Though, as we shall see, Blanton, too, was sucked back into the cradle of mind-cure religiosity (if only because of his collaboration with Peale), still in his one major independent exposition of his psychological insight he portrayed life in a realistic mode, not as a tissue of solipsistic wishes but a permanently dynamic interplay between inner and outer forces, both at struggle within and between themselves, the most crucial element of which was vital and realistic consciousness.

The ego as a middleman

How could it happen that Blanton's own book contrasted so distinctly at so many points with Peale's evangel and with the Peale-Blanton collaborations? How, that is, could Norman Vincent Peale have learned so little from the psychology he supposedly wished to exploit for his applied Christianity?

There was one reason that had to do with a soft spot in Freudian psychology itself. In the first, and prolonged, period of Freud's work, the dramatic—and tragic—struggle he portrayed was that between libido and superego, the most basic, primitive impulses of the organism and the demands of society at its fullest and most authoritative, the one clamoring for unmixed gratification, the other insistent upon obedience and conformity. In this drama what was the role of the ego? It was easy for the ego to be construed as a mere middleman, a "poor servant," at most the rider on libidinal horseback with no important energy of its own. It was easy to imagine its job as that of devising some kind of harmony between the two more active agencies, at least an armed truce, or as that of guiding the charger down the roads marked out by superego. It was easy to imagine that, under the stress of this precarious duty, ego itself was mostly unconscious. (And hence, in the popular literary Freudianism of the bohemian twenties, it was easy to imagine that "liberation" consisted, not of promoting ego to some higher assignment, but of granting libido precisely the gratifications superego had denied it.) Peale's notion of the "mind" which transmitted higher thoughts into the unconscious as a "reception station," a mere telephone switchboard, parodied this early Freudian ego-theory. Blanton was not a sophisticated analyst; he evidently knew nothing of the later Freud, or of the "ego-psychology" which had already begun to be developed in the twenties, and the psychology Peale learned from him was therefore unsophisticated. In fact, when—as he did—Peale avowed himself a disciple of Emerson and James, he showed himself using a psychology which Blanton's popular Freudianism simply supplemented as often as it contradicted—a psychology postulating some innate depth in tune, by its inherent nature, with the infinite, without need of reason or will, a debt, of course, shared by Peale to popular mind cure.

But a much more important reason for the difference between the two collaborators had to do with Peale's mass audience. Blanton, in standard Freudian fashion, was concerned with repression, the tyranny over id of superego. Blanton thought of men whose purposes were confounded by their inner conflicts, persons of will with perfectly clear conscious aims made miserable by conflicting unconscious aims. As Joshua Loth Liebman's famous book ten years before had made clear, there were still immense numbers of people suffering from such inner contradiction. Yet from the eighteen-nineties, and pervasively from the twenties, multitudes were being released at least in varying degrees from this classically Freudian malady by the revolution in manners and morals, by a permissiveness that, certainly, had not existed in Freud's Vienna when he was making his original discoveries. Moreover, even the problem of neurosis due to repression itself had its sociological correlates. Those who enjoyed strength due to their unquestioned status and usefulness in society possessed means to discharge their inner conflicts in ways that averted ego-sickness sometimes altogether. Thus, schematically, one could say that men in the late nineteenth century were as repressed as women—but suffered less. In that case, the crucial symptom was not repression but uselessness. As I have indicated, this was the symptom to which early mind cure addressed itself, that state of social existence portrayed some time later by Lord Keynes:

> To use the language of today [1930]—must we not expect a general "nervous breakdown"? We already have a little experience of what I mean—a nervous breakdown of the sort which is already common enough in England and the United States amongst the wives of the well-to-do classes, unfortunate women, many of them, who have been deprived by their wealth of their traditional tasks and occupations . . . yet are quite unable to find anything more amusing.[7]

The identity seekers

It was quite clear that Peale had not addressed himself to people suffering from conflicts, as had, for instance, Rabbi Liebman in *Peace of Mind*. He had sensed as his audience, his mass audience, people marked not so much by unconscious repressed forces as by perfectly conscious feelings of incapacity, not so much by a struggle against impulses as by feelings of diffusion and even loss of impulses. He warned his readers that of course the Higher Power would be of no help if they had no notion what they wanted help for.

> Naturally in this process of achieving the best it is important to know where you want to go in life. . . . Spiritual and emotional planlessness is a definite reason for the failure of many people. . . . Your expectation must have a clearly defined objective. Lots of people . . . have no clear-cut, precisely defined purpose.[8]

Likewise, Peale's audiences were not those of Billy Graham, pouring by the trainload into big cities to hear their simple Bible-identity reaffirmed. Peale treated the original malady of mind cure, that loss of nerve force noted by Dr. Beard, that objectively abundant life of successful middle-class people who felt themselves subjectively poor. He treated not defeat but disappointment, not disintegration but disorientation, not guilt but anxiety.

Others were bringing the problem into more formal focus. In 1958 a San Francisco psychoanalyst, Allen Wheelis, published his reflections on what he found to have changed in the typical clientele for contemporary therapy. The older orthodox Freudianism had dealt with "symptom disorder," he noted—disruptions of the well-defined patterns of the patient's life. With growing frequency, however, Wheelis declared, therapists were confronted by "characterological disorder," or, better, the disorder of, in effect, having no real order at all. Vague, uncertain, elusive in their sense of self, people came on the "quest for identity," as he entitled his book. Wheelis then tried to confront the obvious question: what to do? Traditional psychoanalysis was of little help. It assumed that, once liberated from his self-defeating conflicts, the patient would be about his business. Healthy, he would achieve whatever his talents and desires led him to achieve. But these new patients evidently needed to become persons with purposes to pursue in the first place. And it could not possibly be right, Wheelis felt, for the therapist to tell them what to do, to act as surrogate ego—or super-ego. The therapist could not preach.

Despite his more traditional outlook, Smiley Blanton himself was sucked into the vortex of the new-model malady, the malady against which mind cure had pioneered eighty years before. And it conditioned his final prescription of God. Only on the last two pages of his book did Blanton turn to faith, but then with a statement unconsciously revealing the pathos of a religious ideology cut off from roots and strength in human warmth, community and vitality: "Of all human emotions, perhaps the most devastating is the feeling that one is alone in the world."[9] Faith in God was the way to overcome this loneliness, as we feel ourselves "part of the great design that controls the universe." Of course, Blanton offered no justification for such faith beyond the nakedly psycho-pragmatic plaint that men needed it. Nor, as I have mentioned, had he been fertile of suggestions as to how men might go about moderating some of the chill of a lonely society.

Earlier, in one of his collaborations with Peale, Blanton had perpetrated one of his rare corruptions of his master, to a more extreme effect. He described God in simplified Freudian terms as the product of the transference of the child's yearnings for perfect, all-powerful parents, an expression of man's "natural craving for a perfect friend," and then, far from questioning the perpetuation of such transference and projection into adulthood, encouraged it. When appropriate, as he reported in the case of a highly dependent ulcerous young engineer, he urged a man to think of God as a great mother capable of sating those desires his own mother had not met. (Nor was this the only instance of mind-cure Mother-God in Blanton, Blanton-Peale, or Peale.) His position was ambiguous, for Blanton had warned against overwhelming parental love. Was it possible that a God projected on the model of such parents might also be overwhelming? William James had thought so. As a further complexity, what Blanton feared was not so much that a child would become excessively dependent, as that he would become "afraid of being dominated by anyone, either human or divine." If it seemed odd that Blanton should have worried about this, it was only because he, too, had noticed people whose identity was little more than that of childish resentment, who needed a new, better superego, and whom it was awkward for him to help. When it came to religion, and his collaboration with Peale, he found himself assuming an ego-weakness which original Freudianism had not had in view.

As for Peale, religion hardly had to be ego-oriented at all, any more than the dosages administered by doctors. The analogy was his: the minister, drawing on the New Testament—"his. textbook of laws: spiritual laws as specific as the laws of physics or chemistry, compiled by the most subtle and skilled students of behavior"— prescribed the texts to be ingested daily. "Gradually, almost like a powerful drug dissipating a center of pain, the religious 'prescription' dissolved" the patient's trouble.[10] In advice of some interest in light of the new managerial theories, Peale urged executives to learn the technique of "spiritual sub-conscious decision-making."[11]

In speculating on the origins of the malady of his new-style patients, Dr. Wheelis utilized standard Freudian topography—id, ego, superego—plus neo-Freudian emphasis upon changing social experience. The spreading quest for identity, he thought, followed from decline in the authority of the superego, decline in the authority of schools, of intimate stable communities, of the church, and of parents as these mediated for society. The superego had been fragmented, diffused, depersonalized, its major center resting more and more simply in the "group" where the abiding imperative was not to be alone. In this situation the task of repression of impulses was handed over to the conscious ego. In standard Freudian theory, and in theories of social psychology, the superego's work of repression was for the most part unconscious, the conscious authority of "conscience" representing only a small fraction of the work. When the task of repression was handed over to conscious ego, this alone was enough to conduce to ego-disintegration, for the ego engaged in repression had to hide from itself what it was doing, since what it was doing was to deprive itself of power.

Theology of non-politics

In Freudian terms, Peale's mind cure could be described as a technique whereby a precarious ego repressed recognition of its own precariousness. The obvious way to do this was for the ego to conceal itself from itself, and the basic tactic for doing this was for the ego to reconstitute a superego. It was at this juncture that mind cure's social passivity, apolitical quiescence and fear of reform illuminated itself. Fleeing recognition of the chances in "modern civilization" for greater conscious experience, fleeing realization of the disintegration of old authority and of both the terror and opportunity this entailed, mind cure substituted the vision of Perfection, One and All, a total self-sufficiency, metaphysical, divine, and above all absolutely reliable as Supply.

That a superego reconstituted by an ego should be an image of perfection followed in the nature of the case, for in reconstituting superego the ego displayed its desire *not* to be ego, will, purposefulness or self at all. It displayed itself as consciousness engaged in trying *not* to be conscious—since as conscious ego it was weak. And the wish here was in no way a hidden desire to yield to the impulses of libido, in no way that "sluttish antinomianism" which George Orwell rightly observed follows only from resentment against strong superego. True freedom to indulge basic impulses was the privilege of egos powerful enough to make choices. For the weak, impulses constituted threats more than promise, challenging tests of capacity provoking fears of failure. In fact, whereas in classical Freudianism the danger from the id consisted of its power to invade and disrupt lawful ego and superego alike, when both superego and ego had lost form and power, the danger from the id could become something totally different—its specifications vague, its insistence weak, its pleasures flaccid. The sense of being a center of vitality could fade. It might become necessary for ego to invest desires themselves in the new superego, locating wishes themselves around and about and external to the heart. Abundance might have to be defined mechanically, demand in terms of supply.

Peale rendered just this scheme into religious terms—in words that just could have been thought to approximate sentiments of Luther and Augustine. God will give you anything you want, he said; but he did not mean quite that. "When you put your trust in God, He guides your mind so that you do not want things that are not good for you or that are inharmonious with God's will."[12] "Love God and do as you wish," Augustine had said, and Luther after him, but it was not clear that they thought it easy to love God, or that doing what you wished was inevitably good for you or divinely harmonious; they thought God had grace for you anyway. Most pertinent, they did not think man's mind mirrored God's mind; they thought men had minds and wishes of their own.

But Peale's ideas about God were minimal. If his psychology was that of mind cure, a superego super-consciousness inducing automatic behavior through the medium of an autohypnotized sub- or unconscious, the superambient realm of authority, beyond criticism and even comment, had more definite social and economic than divine features. The extrapolation of his psychology was less into a theology than into a politics, or better, a non-politics.

CHAPTER XXIII

SOCIAL ANESTHESIA

PEALE BETRAYED no real ideas why so much "personality disorganization" afflicted the "favored classes" he met in his work. The
notions that occurred to him he owed to traditional Protestant morality of the late nineteenth-century decadence. Greater leisure allowed "more time to think about oneself." Perhaps there was too
much "participation in the loose and pagan morality of our time."
Perhaps the "heavier responsibilities" borne by the favored classes
had something to do with it. These he suggested in 1937.[1] In his
later work he hardly even tried to explain.

As exemplary instances of the power of positive thinking, Peale
drew freely on top-level executives and a few military heroes in
the fashion of the gospel of success. But his primary world of discourse was not that of ceremonial top society, but that of small-
business, professional men, struggling executives and of course the
middle-class ladies supporting him on the best-seller lists. With respect to the males among his clientele there was no sign Peale had
the remotest appreciation of organizational economy. The would-be
independent entrepreneur trying to succeed on his own guts and
resources in accord with standard laissez-faire morale might well
have felt haunted in the managed markets of a newer economy.

Junior executives gnawed by dreams of promotion, roots withering with every transfer, might well have suffered some fear and anxiety. But Peale conceded nothing to these institutional and social environments.

What possible help could he have been then in providing some sense of purpose? What identity were thought conditioners to serve? Obviously, the old one: success—only now a success proving not the power of will, character and purpose in the individual but the power of the Higher Power, deep in the subconscious.

Peale's social anesthesia entailed its specific political symptom. Aside from a few oblique references in his early books, Peale left his politics implicit in his writing, especially after he hit the best-seller lists. But his position was clear. In 1937 he joined the Committee for Constitutional Government, an organization inspired by the far right-wing New York State publisher Frank Gannett, and lent his name to its efforts over succeeding years. During the war Peale personally endorsed the sale of a book suggesting that Franklin Roosevelt, too, was a dictator. He served on the advisory committee of James Fifield, Jr.'s, Spiritual Mobilization, a movement headquartered in Fifield's Los Angeles First Congregational Church teaching that true religion meant radical laissez-faire and opposition to taxes, minimum wages, maximum hours, pensions, unions and all other devices sapping individualism. Peale served on the board of directors of the Christian Freedom Foundation, an Eastern group also dedicated to radical laissez-faire. There was nothing sophisticated in any of this, or, certainly, in Peale's case, sinister. In fact, in his choice for the Presidency in 1948 he betrayed that vaporization of the old rugged spirit of the late nineteenth century into the wish that all problems be gathered up into the One of complete assurance and safety. He announced for General Douglas MacArthur.[2]

In that year, however—according to his eulogistic biographer—Peale was offered some pointed advice. His political views, a presumably friendly newspaperman warned him, were not appreciated in all their spirituality. Certain persons otherwise susceptible to his psychological instructions might find their association with the Republican Right confusing. Peale considered. Perhaps partisan activity might alienate part of his mass audience, perhaps he might thereby be reducing his own spiritual efficacy. His first best-seller was just then proving itself; was not his duty toward the largest and widest clientele he could reach? Yes. Political resonance would have to be stilled; Peale, for the next twelve years, censored himself.

Did this rather awkward, semi-suppressed relationship then suggest that mind cure was after all simply the miasma of a dying laissez-faire, and Peale simply Orestes Swett Marden reborn? On the contrary, Peale's reluctant depoliticalization of himself suggested that mind cure's dreams derived precisely from the flight from rugged individualism. If those dreams only occasionally reached the pinnacles of a Trine or Mrs. Towne or Charles Fillmore, they were fixed in their expectation of a certain repletion, a certainty of Supply guaranteed by the perfection of the circumambient Higher Power. And if this Higher Power in Peale's case remained that of pre-New Deal business economics, the certitude he offered was no less than that of Charles Murphy and the shop girl's fur coat.

The fate of efforts to link mind cure, however tenuously, with out-and-out right-wing laissez-faire was plainly displayed by James Fifield, Jr., in Los Angeles. In his own gesture at winning mass audiences in the religious revival, Fifield brewed together a stew of the old-fashioned gospel of success ("If you can take the view that life is full of conflict and that God put us here in a world of conflict, then you can love conflict . . ."[3]), Dale Carnegie ("Have you ever noticed how friendly the top men in a business organization are? Did it ever occur to you that this friendliness emanated from a deep sense of Christian love toward their fellowmen? And that at the same time this profound good-fellowship was the best possible political weapon for getting to the top?"), and mind-cure applications of psychiatry and psychology.[4] But Fifield's effort miscarried. The hard core of First Congregational in Los Angeles—a maverick in Congregationalism nationally—was its laissez-faire right wing, leading it eventually into the sectarian isolation of Mr. Robert Welch and John Birchism. Prophets might speculate whether in some longer run Fifield's audiences, willing to petrify a nation in their hysteria to petrify their own narrow affluence, might not prefigure the largest audiences of all, but meanwhile there were vaster numbers still trying to make sense of the struggle for affluence in the first place.

Peale's contribution in this regard was simple. Think exclusively about yourself—that is, concentrate exclusively upon saturating your sub- (un-) conscious with the automatic power of positive thoughts. The world in which the subsequent automatic behavior took place need not be thought of, since it was already defined. The proper analogy here was—again, in echo of ancient business jargon—that of the "game," and once again Peale's prodigious mass-instruction service spelled it out, in one of several inspirational anthologies turned out by *Guideposts*. This was *Faith Made Them Champions*. The image of the game amounted to Peale's final resolution of the problem of the "hostility" of the world. It was not truly hostile since it was constructed according to fixed ground rules, and to find yourself in life, to be an identity, to stay alive all your life was simply to give yourself to the rules. The rules were no part of your action; none of your power was directed toward the invention of the game or any games; you had no imagination you must call upon in conceiving your actions; you need only perfect yourself in those "habits" that will define the degree of your identity.

The genteel picture of success

By a not very subtle paradox, this concentration upon oneself in one's faith in victory in the game amounted to a deliberate rejection of self-knowledge. At issue here was the famous fun poked by George Santayana at those enthusiastic evocations of "hidden energies" by William James upon which the publicists of mind cure drew persistently. "Assurance," Santayana had said, "is contemptible and fatal unless it is self-knowledge." Santayana failed to credit James with an interest, absent from mind cure, in how people do come to have self-knowledge, but his failure to close fully on James did not vitiate his general point. In effect, the best justification a man might have for having faith that he would "win" was to be in very good condition. In fact, as Santayana suggested, the source of such faith was precisely being in good condition. Faith was a sign of self-knowledge. Lack of faith could also be a sign of self-knowledge—knowledge that your system was out of gear or that your opponent could run faster. Faith that you could defeat an opponent who could run faster than you would be contemptible since it could only mean that you expected God to lend you power He refused to lend your opponent or that you hoped your opponent lacked self-knowledge, lacked faith and hence failed to use his real powers. Such faith could be fatal if it led you into competitions it would be fatal to lose. As for those competitions where luck or accident or providence might decide, certainly that faith which looked to luck or accident or providence would be contemptible, and also possibly fatal.

But perhaps one had faith simply that the Higher Power would help one "do one's best." In that case, faith might make for second place, or even last place, for failure, for poverty, for death.

It is in line with these general reflections that the picture of sports found in *Guideposts' Faith Made Them Champions* should have omitted some details—the sweaty hands, the cottony mouth, the pre-race vomit, the headaches, the convulsive gasping, just as tales of business success from Samuel Smiles through Dale Carnegie had omitted the dyspepsia, the taut nerves, the ulcer, the coronary and the angina. It was, of course, a matter of values whether vomiting and ulcers be regarded as signs of weakness and evil or not. Were there to be championships without contusions? Were no heart attacks ever worth the strain and cause of them, for the victim or for his fellows? The *Guideposts'* picture of success was genteel—it was highly likely the editors knew as little of those more aggressive and gripping emotions inciting athletes to effort as did the cautionary preachers of the Protestant ethic of the resounding, religiously undomesticated passions of nineteenth-century business. One saw the champion only as he testified, neat and smiling, at a meeting of Youth for Christ. For all the marks he bore of the real world, this champion might as well have appeared at one of the mind-cure afternoons on Beacon Street in Boston in the eighteen-eighties.

Standing at the end of a succession of preachers of popular appeal to Protestant middle-class audiences, Norman Vincent Peale, with the pervading motif in his career his claim to mass succor, registered in the incoherence of his own psychology and the suppression of his own politics the impasse of millions. He left his patients in a trap. Peale was not really prescribing techniques for success. Like Dr. Beard he was prescribing for those still unhappy in their success. He could not tell them about abundance and abandon and adventure. I have observed that Harry Emerson Fosdick's adventurous religion made no contact with economic abundance. Aside from his rejection of the "silly" idea there was no connection between faith and prosperity, Peale also was silent. Indeed, he reiterated the immemorial rhetoric not only of liberal pastors but of sages through history: "Material things fail; riches tarnish; sensory responses become satiated and jaded."[5] (His eulogistic biographer tells us that Peale defiantly—and delightedly—bought Cadillacs; which may have been more a function of taste than of materialism.) But this was a sign of vacancy of imagination, not of lingering asceticism. What was "winning" worth? The life Peale's most immediate patients led was that of the city, which meant more specifically Manhattan. Peale commonly evoked the New York scene as one of traffic, noise, tension, trial, conflict, the status panic. Was it the business of religion to mold this stupendous energy into community? As defense against the urban confusion Peale recommended the ten-minute nap, the ten-mile drive into the countryside, the ten-minute prayer-break. The city was not a world of culture. Never was the addict of positive thinking pictured wandering a museum, entering a concert hall, strolling a street, discussing a movie, gathering with friends at parties in walk-ups in the city. He suffered the city because that was where the game was, but basically it was something to endure. Abundance did not mean culture. It meant instead the nightly and weekend retreat into the isolated familial sanctuary of private consumer's goods. Peale knew this was not enough. But, the religious apothecary, all he could do was brew his ever more potent spirit lifters and psychic energizers on the one hand, and, on the other, his drugs to minimize the pain.

Peale and other Protestants

Peale's position within Protestantism grew progressively more curious after 1955. Rebounding after the concerted attacks from his critics, he resumed his mass-production operations in the defiant spirit that, after all, he had helped millions. They said so. But among a new generation of Protestant leaders, engaged in the gravest sort of re-examination of the health and role of the faith in the nation, he was out of touch. One of the subjects of this re-examination was the necessity for "dialogue" between Protestant and Catholic. Another was the necessity for overcoming Protestant disunity. Both were hinged to the fear that "religion" in the United States was rapidly becoming mere "culture religion," imaginatively empty, socially inert, its role nothing more than that of therapy for individuals, the labels "Protestant" and "Catholic" (and "Jew") mere emblems of clan or caste or class. Peale did not understand.

In the midst of the campaign of 1960, when the vast majority of liberal and neo-orthodox Protestant leaders were determined to avoid a repetition of the scandal of the campaign of 1928, Peale associated himself with a group invidiously self-designated as the National Conference of Citizens for Religious Freedom, opposing John F. Kennedy's election on religious grounds. Hundreds of other Protestant pastors and thousands of Protestant laymen also opposed a Catholic candidate, for good reasons and bad, but Peale's unique prominence and special position had deprived him of the chance to offer social guidance. Positive thinking had nothing to do with public issues. Therapeutic religion had nothing to do with commonweal. Furor abounded, and, as twelve years before, Peale found it expedient to surrender his social voice. Explaining that he had "never been too bright anyhow," he withdrew from the citizens' conference.[6] Though some agreed, the self-judgment was harsh. Peale had simply trapped himself.

Two years later, utilizing in the *Reader's Digest* the aptest possible organ for his own audiences, Peale himself raised the grave question his critics had opened years before: "Can Protestantism Be Saved?" In his worry, Peale wondered if perhaps he hadn't made a mistake or two himself. For instance, "We have made it too easy to join the church. I have been guilty of this myself. . . ." On the other hand, Peale wondered if the revival of theology in the seminaries wasn't a bit mistaken. "It's all very well for our divinity students to stretch their minds wrestling with the concepts of our tremendous theologians. But too often, in the process, they lose what Kipling called the common touch." And then there was the state of the nation, and "the church's apathy in the face of the challenge posed by the decaying society that surrounds it." It seemed that the "great postwar return to religion" was ebbing because people had not found what they were looking for, which was personal salvation. "Instead, they found preachers offering intellectualized sermons on social problems. They found pastors who condemned corruption in politics or government, but ignored corruption in the lives of their listeners."[7]

Had Norman Vincent Peale suddenly become a preacher of sin? If so, he was thirty years late. It had been the greatest of all "political" preachers, Reinhold Niebuhr, who had castigated the liberal churches for their neglect of the classic doctrine of original sin. Unfortunately, it had not been Niebuhr who rode the "great postwar return to religion." It had been the priest of positive thinking. What the multitudes had heard during the revival was precisely not political sermons. And if that "return" was now ebbing, who was really being stranded?

But the most intriguing among the whole scatter of Peale's laments and complaints was one that set him squarely against a mainstream in all non-fundamentalist Protestantism. He deplored the "amalgamation of denominations, the whole ecumenical movement. . . ." Utterly without denominational color of his own, this was strange from Peale. The ecumenical movement of over forty years had been aimed to recover what had been lost in fragmented parochial defensiveness, what had been lost to religious caste and clannishness, what had been lost in courage to suburban congregational withdrawal, what had been lost to the nation in the idea that religion was what a person shopped for as good citizen and for private gratifications. The movement had aimed at recovery of the idea of religion as a challenge to culture. Himself complaining that there were not enough ministers unafraid "to challenge their congregations," Peale neglected to narrate any challenges he had ever made. His opposition to the ecumenical movement, otherwise regarded as one of the key routes to the recovery of Protestant strength, rather nicely fixed his conception of religion and of the place of religion in the world. Not "challenges" but "needs" defined religion. Religion was doctoring. Like the doctor-patient relation, it was a "private" affair. Except that in religion the doctor could be a mass therapist.

CHAPTER XXIV

THE BIBLE VERSUS PSYCHOLOGY

THE ATTACKS on Peale were aimed at his political and economic obscurantism. They were aimed at the tenuousness of his theology. They were aimed at his promise of what the German pastor-martyr Dietrich von Bonhoeffer had called "cheap grace." What Peale had done, above all, was to shrink religion itself to a vanishing point. This was apparent in the theory behind the practice of the Peale-Blanton clinic. The clinic never advertised itself as a quick, cheap alternative to deep analysis. Blanton agreed that persons with truly deep-seated psychological troubles should be referred elsewhere. Implicitly, then, the clinic dealt only with mild cases, "the countless cases of persons who worry and fret and feel inadequate to the fulfillment of their desires." The psychiatric staff treated these, then turned them over to ministers. But then it appeared there was a third category of cases, those that "yield quite rapidly to religious guidance alone." Evidently religion was fitted for only the most superficial cases of all. Were psychoanalysis and psychiatry for the depths, religion the surface? This would be a humiliating sort of alliance indeed. Was there more to religion than this? Peale did not explain.

The compatibility of religion and psychology came to be ques-

tioned from several quarters, on several motives. One harsh, un-
subtle attack was simply to insist that real Christians had no need
for psychology or psychosomatic medicine at all. So said Dr. L.
Gilbert Little, member of the American Psychiatric Association and
the American Medical Association, practicing, as of 1956, in Wich-
ita, Kansas. The Back to the Bible Publishers of Lincoln, Nebraska,
brought out his little book, *Nervous Christians,* in 60,000 copies in
that year. Using words incited explicitly by the mind-cure atmosphere of the churches, betraying explicitly the confusion into
which the pursuit of health had led, Dr. Little is worth quoting at a
little greater length than any logic or evidence of his own might
merit.

> Satan is battling for the minds of men through his gigantic
> psychological propaganda, denying that man has a soul and
> placing therapeutic emphasis on the mind as the seat of fear,
> anxiety, worry, maladjustment, and nervousness. . . . Even the
> few who express a desire to find God are channelled into a
> bloodless religion, where psychology of the mind continues to
> hold sway.[1]

> Psychology is in the atmosphere. Christians are being exposed
> to it through lectures, reading material, radio, television, and
> even sermons. . . . Some ministers reluctantly give their ser-
> mons a psychological flavor because they feel that is what their
> audience desires; others freely substitute the reasonings of man
> for the scriptural truths. Many Christians are searching the
> Scriptures, hoping to find Biblical passages to substantiate
> their psychological views. Jesus Christ and the apostles did not
> spend time expounding psychological theories of man; they
> preached the Gospel. Psychology appeals to the mind. The
> Gospel appeals to the heart.[2]

After recounting the case of an ulcer victim, Dr. Little concluded:

> When he turned to his early Christian training, he gradually
> forsook the conventional religious reading "stuff" which seems
> to gravitate to these tormented souls. It seems that these peo-
> ple, once led astray by mind-appealing religious literature,
> need to be tutored in Bible-reading in order to get rid of the

psychological interpretations that they want to place on God's word.[3]

A long-drawn-out course of analyzing subconscious layers of thought is not necessary for the Christian. . . . The Christian cannot get by with transposing his cares, worries and anxieties, and guilt and fear from the heart to the unconscious mind, or to a mysterious subconscious, so that he can resort to mind treatments of forgetting and covering up. These thoughts and feelings are more than mind deep. SO-CALLED NERVOUS BREAKDOWN IS A MISNOMER FOR EMOTIONAL CHAOS IN THE SOUL OF MAN.[4]

Here was defense of religion that was a defense, yielding neither depth nor clientele. Of course, the defense was actually a flight, simply abandoning the tough problems clustering around the delusive dualism of mind-body in favor of a safe, old, rhetorical "heart" or "soul." But was this just fundamentalism speaking? Dr. Little's inherited fundamentalist upbringing could hardly be missed, yet he was a doctor, a psychiatrist, and something more could be felt. He had a suspicion about sickness itself. "Does the Christian in bondage to self, in bondage to his nervousness, show forth love? No! He is all taken up with self. . . ."[5] Was sickness self-centeredness? Dr. Little had some interesting things to say about schizophrenics in this regard. In short, was there, in true therapy, some main line to theology? Was it possible that the mission of all therapy at its highest was to dissolve itself in . . . what? that forgetfulness of self impossible to the sick? possible to the healthy and well?[6]

Dr. Little breathed no hint of politics, economics or social reform at all, yet his criticism approached arguing that mental health amounted to moral health, and that it would be gained not without moral, even psychological, pain and stress. He did not say what chaplain Anton Boisen had argued, that schizophrenia itself was, while a gross and serious sickness, also a massive effort at curing the real sickness, which was social, moral, existential.[7] As for psychiatry, let it return to its purity, its physicalistic concern with real somatic damage.

Psychiatry of the Bible

Another kind of fundamentalism could promise health without psychology simply by claiming that the Bible was God's psychiatry, as did the Reverend Charles Allen of Atlanta and Houston in a paperback of 1953. Allen did not fail to bow to Peale, but he also did not omit chiding wishes for peace of mind, winning friends, and forgetting fears with the pain of God's purging.[8]

The discovery of psychiatric sufficiency in the Bible could be prompted by prior appreciation of its economic wisdom also. *God, Gold and Government,* by a businessman, Howard E. Kershner, first worked up as a series of lectures at the conservative Fuller Theological Seminary in 1955, then taking an essay prize of the Freedom Foundation, was a late manifesto for unreconstructed laissez-faire, replete with references to the asceticism and solitude of the Protestant ethic. Expatiating upon the nation's good fortune in having its "one-hundred corporate giants," then a few pages later avowing that people who "do not own the means of producing food, clothing, housing, tools . . . cease to be independent," and having already worried about the individual's subordination to the group, Kershner's apology for the Jacksonian era averted incoherence no more than others of its kind. What attracts us here was his inclusion of therapeutic in addition to economic wisdom in the Bible. "The Bible is the greatest book ever written on health, childcare and psychiatry. It contains more psychiatrical wisdom than all other books on that subject."[9] Heart trouble, arthritis, ulcers—these need not afflict those reconciled to God. One can infer that, for Kershner, his conviction that "the Bible is the greatest book on business ever written" conditioned his discovery of its psychiatrical lore. Comparison with Norman Vincent Peale is instructive. More interested in gold and government than people, Kershner suppressed psychology; more interested in people than laissez-faire, Peale suppressed his politics. It was Peale who was in the mainstream—and the question remained: did religion really have a job of its own to do?

One plain answer had been offered by Rollo May, a pioneer in counseling, years before the storm over Peale. "Psychotherapy needs theology." Here was a switch. If countless religious leaders were finding they needed therapeutic psychology, what about the reverse? Why did psychotherapy need theology? In steering to this conclusion, May offered a diagnosis of and therapy for sickness that ran directly against both mind cure and liberal Protestant imagination:

> In man's particular situation all is not right; there is disharmony within himself and there is disharmony in this diseased world. Psychologically and religiously, illness follows from any attempt to escape this disharmony.[10]

Disharmony as reality; illness as flight from reality—the contradiction was complete.

What did this have to do with theology? May went on to invoke a purely psychological argument for belief. "The individual must have some belief in purpose in his life, however fragmentary, if he is to achieve personality health."[11] This was not yet theology, though. A tough-minded person's belief in his own purposes was belief. So, May moved on:

> Personality health also requires that the individual believe in some purpose in the total life-process as well as in his own life. For one cannot live on an island of meaning surrounded by an ocean of meaninglessness. If the universe is crazy, the parts of it must be too.[12]

As for what sort of faith this nakedly pragmatic sanction allowed, May commended the attitude of Job: "Though He slay me, yet will I trust Him." The healthy individual could endure insecurity and "affirm" truth and goodness even though "truth is on the scaffold and goodness is never perfectly achieved." Yet, tough-minded as this was, it did not fully avert the admonition that had inevitably been generated by the psychological justification of religion. As James B. Pratt had put it years before:

> If the subjective value of prayer be all the value it has, we wise psychologists of religion had best keep the fact to our-

selves; otherwise the game will soon be up, and we shall have no religion left to psychologize about.[13]

Mind cure had claimed "objective" results: health and wealth. Others were claimed. *Pray Your Weight Away*, the Reverend G. W. Shedd of Texas urged. The Reverend Franklin Loehr explained *The Power of Prayer over Plants*. But of course in this demonstrated power the believers found reason for content, serenity, peace, perfection. Pratt's warning was not met by objective tests, but by the subjectivity of a certain sort of man. May only hinted at this in his description of personality health in the state of faith:

> . . . The more one receives the grace of God, the more one realizes one's guilt, and therefore the more one needs God's grace. The paradox is understandable that the man who is most sensitive to God's grace should, in fact *must*, call himself the "chief of sinners."[14]

Prefigured here was the existential therapy of which May would become the leading American exponent after the war, and in it, at last, health would no longer be defined in terms of the absence of sickness.

But the very real difficulties in extricating a concept of man's health from the undertow of concepts of psychological sickness were perhaps best revealed by a psychologist rather than a theologian, as, in his efforts at rescue, he climaxed the captivity.

CHAPTER XXV

THE PROBLEM OF GUILT

Has evangelical religion sold its birthright for a mess of psychological pottage? In attempting to rectify their disastrous early neglect of psychopathology, have the churches and seminaries assimilated a viewpoint and value system more destructive and deadly than the evil they were attempting to eliminate?[1]

THE MAN who asked these drastic questions in 1961 was Dr. O. Hobart Mowrer, eminent Research Professor of Psychology at the University of Illinois. He did not hedge his answer: "As a psychologist and churchman, I believe the answer to these questions is in the affirmative."

Mowrer had more or less boxed the psychological compass over thirty years—following the strict experimental canons of learning theory, examining philosophical social psychology, studying and evidently practicing clinical psychology, and logging time as patient and champion of psychoanalysis. As a churchman, he was a "liberal," explicitly insisting upon the need for sharp modernization of theology and symbols. By the late fifties he had moved strongly toward harsh criticism of the churches' embrace of Freud.

Protestantism itself, Mowrer argued, had opened the door to psychoanalysis. Holding men responsible for their sins, it had then insisted men were helpless to effect their salvation; only God could save them. Thus Protestantism had failed to deal with guilt. Psychoanalysis had met the issue by holding that men were not responsible for their sins either.

One may wonder if this did not oversimplify a complex story, and Mowrer himself took pains to cover his flanks: ". . . I have chosen to deal with both Freudianism and Calvinism as they are *popularly* understood. . . ."[2] Unfortunately, Mowrer did not offer a useful description of popular understanding either. But the bite of his work was not historical or sociological; it was conceptual.

The heart of Mowrer's evangel consisted of the argument that psychological sickness did not derive from frustration, from intra-psychic conflict, from repressed impulses. It derived instead from guilty consciences, from repression of the superego. Sick people were sick because they were guilty people repressing their real guilt. Sicknesses were in fact not sicknesses at all, but forms of irresponsibility, of wrongdoing. Mowrer found it natural to revive an old label: sin. His spirit was therapeutic, not vengeful:

> "Sickness" . . . is a concept which generates pervasive pessimism and confusion in the domain of psychopathology, whereas sin, for all its harshness, carries an implication of promise and hope, a vision of new potentialities.[3]

And, obviously, where sin and guilt held the stage, religion could expect a richer role.

In his attack upon traditional psychoanalysis Mowrer was by no means alone. Aside from various studies seeming to demonstrate a disappointing rate of "cure" in Freudian therapy, many psychologists and psychiatrists had been occupied for years in building on beyond Freud himself into newer methods and concepts. Nor was Mowrer alone in arguing that the concept of "sickness" confused the ultimate issues of psychology and religion. He quoted one of these peers, Dr. Thomas Szasz:

> . . . The notion of mental illness has outlived whatever usefulness it might have had and . . . now functions merely as a convenient myth . . . mental illness is a myth, whose function it is to disguise and thus render more palatable the bitter pill of moral conflicts in human relations.[4]

"Real" guilt had appeared in the new existential therapies imported from Europe after the war by Rollo May. And Reinhold Niebuhr had been rehabilitating a concept of sin in political life for nearly thirty years.

Yardsticks for sin

But just exactly how did it help to call sickness sin? Just what did converting a medical problem into a moral problem entail? Actually Mowrer was talking about two sorts or phases or stages of sin. The first consisted of wrongful acts, all the mean, vicious, petty things done by (perhaps all) individuals all their lives. But: ". . . are all sinful, guilty persons neurotic or psychotic? Manifestly the latter is not true."[5] It was not true because some persons recognized their guilt, repented of it, made restitution for it and were relieved. The second sort of sin, thus, consisted of denying guilt. It was this denial, or repression, that produced neurosis. Thus sickness was not so much itself sin, or even the wages of sin, but the wages of sin unconfessed.

This was to assume that the yardsticks for sin were reasonably clear, and part of the time Mowrer seemed to assume so: ". . . The superego (or conscience), more commonly than we might wish to believe, is a reflection of enduring social realities. . . ."[6]

> Our society . . . is still pretty well consolidated . . . with respect to a lot of things; and it is in the areas in which virtually everyone is at least overtly agreed that personal sin, secrecy, and psychopathology follow in that order.[7]

Given this situation, the recourse was obvious. Abandon psychoanalysis, with its presumption that guilt was "merely" neurotic, a product of inner conflict rather than outward acts. Let the churches reform their ministrations. Reinstitute the confessional. Equip churches to see people through their periods of acute disturbance (mental hospitals were useless). Let some ministers equip themselves to accept referrals from other ministers (as Russell Dicks was doing in Florida). Revive the tradition of good works through charity and philanthropy as routes open for guilty people coming back into community.

Yet this hardly represented the major animus of Mowrer's criticism. If sin did not necessarily produce sickness, it was not only because some sinners avowed their sin. Others simply did not feel it at all. In aggrieved exasperation, Mowrer returned again and again to:

> . . . that class of persons who engage in thoroughly evil, antisocial behavior but who simply do not have the character—or, as one may say, the "common decency"—to go crazy. It takes a fairly adequate personality to be seriously "disturbed"; in fact, the very *power* of neurotic and psychotic affects attests to their strength of character.[8]

What obsessed Mowrer was the conviction that such persons were growing in numbers, that modern society was bringing them up that way systematically. Thus, in contrast to his assumption of superego stability, he engaged in repeated lamentations over social decline:

> There is, in our time, no social, moral, and ethical solidarity and confidence. . . . There is, in our time, a widespread distrust of moral injunctions and values. . . . We . . .[9] bring [children] up *without character*.[10]

There was no real way to weave consistency between laments about disintegrated superego and confidence in intact superego. The contradiction was needless, for Mowrer might have dealt in degrees. But it could only have been with astonishment that, on the rare occasions when he got down to cases, his readers found Mowrer preoccupied with the personal sin of—incest. Freudians talked about incest fantasies as a source of guilt; Mowrer countered with an instance of a patient actually victimized by her father as a girl. Obviously, real incest should not have been dealt with as a delusion, and obviously superego incest-taboos were as strong as ever. Did Mowrer believe that actual incest was a pervasive problem? Did he think psychoanalysis tried to weaken incest taboos? Also, people still knew that murder, rape, stealing and the like were evil, but it would have been hard to believe that the epidemic mental sickness bothering Mowrer derived from an epidemic of concealed murders, rapes, thefts, etc. It appeared that Mowrer was bothered by what he saw as a decline in the superego standards for sexual behavior, but he never troubled to explain just how and why modern as against Victorian standards conduced to guilt and sickness. It appeared also that he regarded "the doctrine of an 'expanding economy'" as an evil, but he explicitly designated this as a "corporate," not a personal evil, and therefore not a cause of repressed guilt and sickness.

The possibility remained that the people he called upon to confess had no such sins as he imagined. Clearly a man still shaped by an older, "pre-Freudian," late Puritan sense of the virtues of self-discipline by self-denial, he found what he took to be the drift in psychology, church and society toward a life of comfortable, purposeless impulse-gratification, repellant. But this did not mean such lives were being led in violation of superego. At the same time, when, following Anton Boisen, the pioneer psychologist-chaplain at Worcester State Hospital, Mowrer emphasized isolation, estrangement and aloneness as elements of sickness, this did not point unambiguously at repressed sin and guilt. Such lives and such symptoms might have been faithful emanations of modern community itself. Terms more and more commonly in use by postwar psychologists describing their patients—"lack of affect," "reduced feeling-tone," "depersonalization," "lack of identity," all signs of isolation and estrangement—might have been evidences not of guilty withdrawal but of the constricting limits of ordinary community opportunity.

Liberation from conflict

What underlay the unresolved contradictory diagnoses offered by Mowrer was his desire to afford the same thing he took it that popular Freudianism and popular religious therapy wanted to provide: freedom from conflict. He was sure the important conflicts were moral, interpersonal, social, not psychological, inward, private. As to this, sophisticated psychoanalysis concurred more than he would recognize, but in seeking to overcome conflict as in itself the way to health, Mowrer only advanced the malady of personal weakness. Resolutely "scientific" in his psychology, and morally oppressed by soft hedonic life, his recall of superego to the center of the self followed. It was true that psychoanalysis had come to "recognize the ego as much more important than formerly," but, he quoted a colleague, "they know next to nothing about the conditions for modifying or strengthening it."[11] Learning-theory psychology was the answer, according to which the individual's behavior was monopolized by a set of social stimuli.

Mowrer's solution turned on more than questions of technical science, however; there was the ideal of a normative healthy life in which there need be no sickness at all because the very mechanisms allowing sickness might be absorbed into a larger harmony. Will power might be absorbed. So might consciousness.

> . . . Some of the banks in Chicago regularly give their employees lie detection tests. . . . I . . . realized that the purpose of this procedure is not so much to detect anyone who has already done something wrong; rather it is to create a feeling that if anyone *begins* a dishonest practice, it will soon be known. This amounts, in effect, to periodic "confession." And if one knows that whatever he does is going to be *known,* one usually finds that he has the "will power" not to do it.[12]

> We are likely to think of strength of character and so-called will power as something we have or exercise deep down inside us. . . . Instead, is it not basically a *social* phenomenon?[13]

> . . . The normal individual has actually a "larger" unconscious than does a disturbed person; and support, direct admonition, and counsel may be one of the best means, in the latter case, to get conscience to relax and again become "unconscious."[14]

Here society, as lie-detector God, absorbed the religious substance of the God in Whose eyes it once was grace to be "completely known and all forgiven." Here small urgency was felt for fortifying the individual as a self-conscious center. In endeavoring to rescue Protestantism, Mowrer came ironically and strikingly to resemble Brownson and Fitzhugh with their polemic against the irresponsibilities of free society. Like Fitzhugh, though lacking Fitzhugh's skepticism, Mowrer was intrigued by Mormonism as a solidaristic therapeutic reaction against individualism, and like Brownson, though with sharp criticisms of Catholic dogma, he manifested a warm regard for Catholic moral discipline. As with Fitzhugh, for whom "society rules," as with Brownson "the Church," so with Mowrer superego was to control. Sickness being estrangement, individualism appeared once again as the sin against the holy ghost. At the same time, this absolute socialization of the individual liberated no energy for doing anything about society, for politics, for reform. Indeed, it pressed the individual all the more to see that any problems he might have of a serious psychological sort were really just his own, never to be blamed on society, never to be solved by action. Whereas Fitzhugh had wanted to "roll back the Reformation on its political side," Mowrer wanted the Reformation to "go on," but not toward further evolution of the priesthood of all believers and of justification by faith.

In this therapy, preferring obedience to judgment, unconscious socialization to conscious conflicts, Mowrer had brought mind cure to another climax, explicitly revealing its fatal meaning. To center religion in curing sick selves led to dissolving the selves. Then there was nothing to get sick.

His almost totally irreconcilable assessments of the state of the superego (by which Mowrer did mean the norms of the society at large) oddly echoed the peculiarities in Henry C. Link and Norman Vincent Peale, and the unresolved yearnings that had fed mind cure. On the one hand, both Link and Peale criticized the deliberate, consciously planned, welfare aspects of the economies of their day —New Deal and Fair Deal, perpetuated under President Eisenhower. On the other hand, both urged their clients into "extroversion," uncritical acceptance of the rules and stimuli of the system, self-induced submission to the superego. It was as though, when shaped by intelligence and purpose, by ego and decision, the environment or the system lost its spirituality, its magic, its divinity. It was as though the fruits of abundance must appear automatically; as though to transmute corporations and society and organizations into expressions of choice and will provoked an intolerable dizziness of freedom. It was as though it were better to dream dreams of a garden, an Eden, a tame Yellowstone, a realized eschatology where wishes and obsessions prevailed. Deep down perhaps was a wish that real challenges be over, real work ended, real manhood dispelled. As the religious psychology of both Link and Blanton-Peale explicitly avowed, there was a hope to live in the house of the fathers, to be children, to be childish, not to become men.

In Mowrer's case, his identification of "conscience" with "super-ego," that is, society, along with his lament for those who were psychologically lonely, hidden, secretive and isolated, revealed perhaps the deeper, most repressed impulse that at once impelled him to try to get beyond the immaturity and weakness of mind cure, and tempted him into an untenable position: the impulse of an ideologically individualistic but bureaucratically constricted people toward *real* "human relations," toward warmth, toward love. This impulse had been schooled into the suspicion, shrewd enough, that "human relations" could be trusted only when freed from systematic manipulation. But it was *self*-manipulation, inducing auto-hypnotic faith in a mythic automatically harmonic society that consistently blighted warmth, human relations and love, not the purposefulness joining men when they had the pleasures of real sociability and community in view.

For the pleasures of reality were not those of wishes gratified, needs fulfilled, and demands supplied, but the surprise of fresh experience, unprevisioned insight, unsuspected capacities for expression and response. Neither subconsciousnesses saturated with superconsciousnesses, nor addictive stimulant texts, nor impulses checked by superegos could promote intimacy, but rather the fully functioning ego, with its appetites for truth and expansion and association and intimacy and its readiness to carry the responsibilities these entailed.

The psychological sickness that underlay mind cure was a protest against emotional starvation; curing it by feeding it techniques for superconscious, superego identity was to feed it the poison of which it was dying. A better psychology would know better what nourished men.

CHAPTER XXVI

PSYCHOLOGY VERSUS PEACE OF MIND

THE SOPHISTICATED postwar psychologies that escaped the morass of mind cure had no such immediate relevance to the churches as did Mowrer. Where Protestants—and Catholics, for that matter, along with Jews—saw themselves simply as accredited constituent elements of a postwar affluent society, they needed only Peale, not Mowrer. In those sectors where either residual resistance or new disturbance led Protestants—and Catholics and Jews—to see themselves still—or again—as defenders of a faith, defenders of a threatened morality, wherever the faithful accepted themselves as parochial and defensive, wherever their energies continued to be monopolized by tending the holy institution, then Mowrer's addition of superego guilt to Peale's positive thinking could be useful.

Wherever, on the other hand, the call was felt to break loose from defensive positions and out of suburban passivities, into encounter with a rapidly and radically changing metropolis, other psychologies were needed, but until such a call was felt, such psychologies would remain esoteric, difficult, dangerous. All this chapter presumes is to sketch them in their largest outline and most general thrust, for they carry this story far beyond its narration of popular ideologies.

Above all, the postwar psychologies emphasized "real" responsibility, "real" guilt, "real" problems, "real" decisions. In this they were not "disavowing" Freud, or even "going beyond" Freud, so much as localizing the phenomena that had dominated Freud's attention, while developing problems Freud himself had sometimes opened, sometimes not anticipated at all. From Anna Freud, through Heinz Hartmann, Ernst Kris, David Rappaport, to Eric Erikson, a sustained inquiry of several decades came to enough collective coherence to earn the label "ego psychology." From the perspectives of ego psychology many of the classic phenomena described and explained by Freud were understood to derive from infantile experience and to possess all the potentially coercive influence he found in it. Without dismantling these basic insights, ego psychology studied the continually emerging powers of selfhood on into adult life, notably with Erikson. It has in fact probed deeply into "the conditions for modifying and strengthening" the ego, and, in the process, made contact with sociology, and the chances for politics and social reform. In ego psychology there has been an acutely tuned revival of themes of freedom and grace, responsibility and rebirth, long neglected in the drift into culture religion and personal therapy. Ego psychology has inspired two major feats of religious imagination: Erikson's *Young Man Luther* and Norman O. Brown's *Life against Death*. Both remain esoteric, absorbed only into a few student and lay circles and a few seminaries.

The same thrust far beyond psychologies preoccupied with "instincts," "impulses," "drives," and "needs" has marked a variety of other explorations in addition to that of ego psychology. The psychologist A. H. Maslow, for instance, well before Mowrer, asked whether psychology was to dissolve the guilt people felt over such behavior as "dishonesty, duplicity, lying and concealing," or to help sharpen the guilt.[1] The neurologist-psychiatrist Kurt Goldstein had asked whether it was true after all that the normal pattern of life was simply that of the unrepressed discharge of tensions as and when they arose. Surely not, Goldstein insisted: any healthy organism knows how to discipline impulses and sustain tension.[2] Without claiming the label, Maslow and Goldstein—among many others—meshed in closely with the postwar existential therapy imported from Switzerland and Germany by Rollo May. In existential psychology, attention to guilt went quite beyond that of Mowrer altogether. May and his teachers insisted that guilt was an inherent feature, not of some human lives but of all. Men felt guilt—rightfully—at their failure to fulfill the potentials of their personal resources of impulse and reason, body and spirit. They felt guilt—rightly—at their failure to know and experience the lives of other people, in society and history. They felt guilt—rightly—at their failure to experience the unbounded resources of nature. Guilt, that is, was a function of restricted life, a function of living by habit, in safety, by closed and completed achievements, for harmony, satiety, peace.

Maslow and the existential psychologists were able to make a distinction clearing Mowrer's cloudy air. In not excusing dishonesty, lying, etc., Maslow referred the guilt these provoked to what he termed the "intrinsic superego." He found no reason to discard the "Freudian superego," recognizing that it had reference to an irrationally punitive, vindictive and destructive source of fear—irrational and destructive because it was what Freud had said it was, a deposit of uncomprehended, pre-rational experiences of infancy.[3] Similarly, the existential psychologists distinguished "neurotic" from "normal" or "ontological" guilt and found no reason to disparage standard psychoanalytic efforts to release people from neurotic guilt.

The emphasis on selfhood

Whatever the empirical or logical foundations for such distinctions, they were fruits of the larger theme of postwar psychology. This was to insist upon the concept of "self" as the heart of an adequate psychology and an adequate therapy. The "self" here emphasized was meant explicitly in opposition to the whole range of academic and therapeutic psychologies that had dominated the twentieth-century scene. It was a rejection of psychologies construing people in terms either of given drives or given needs, of psychologies construing people in terms of stimulus-response arcs, learning theory and conditioning, of psychologies construing people in terms of their social roles. Drives, needs, learning, conditioning, and roles all shaped and impelled life, obviously, but in no combination whatever did they add up to the reality of personal existence. The self was indeed a "product," not an inexplicable miraculous implant, but while a product of experience it constituted a power irreducible to anything else. No research tracing its performance to internal or external stimuli "explained" it. Nor did this mean that it was unamenable to research, only that the final research could be done only by the person himself. As in Carl Rogers' "client-centered" therapy, so in the new existential therapy the primary task of the therapist was to help the patient grasp his own existence as a self, and clarify to himself his responsibility for deciding what he wanted to do and become and achieve.

One of the reasons why William James was coming to be recognized as an American existentialist was just his emphasis upon these traits of selfhood:

> The deepest thing in our nature is this *Binnenleben* (as a German doctor has called it), this dumb region of the heart in which we dwell alone with our willingnesses and unwillingnesses, our faiths and fears. . . . In these crepuscular depths of personality the sources of all our outer deeds and decisions take their rise.[4]

> The truth is that we are doomed, by the fact that we are practical beings with very limited tasks to attend to, and special ideals to look after, to be absolutely blind and insensible to the inner feelings, and to the whole inner significance of lives that are different from our own.[5]

> I for my part cannot but consider the talk of the contemporary sociological school about averages and general laws and predetermined tendencies, with its obligatory undervaluing of the importance of individual differences, as the most pernicious and immoral of fatalisms. Suppose there is a social equilibrium fated to be, whose is it be,—that of your preference, or mine?[6]

In these "post-Freudian" psychologies, people were not blamed for getting sick, as Mowrer blamed them. At the same time these psychologies took the clue Mowrer had taken, only to misread it. People got sick for a purpose. The only purpose Mowrer could discern was something like shame, in the ordinary sense of the word—a fear of what other people would think. But if it took "common decency" and "character" to feel shame, this meant— oddly enough in view of Mowrer's own argument—that sickness was owed to one's dependence on other people. In the post-Freudian psychologies the purpose that earned more attention was generated by the self itself, not in estranged isolation but certainly autonomously. The purpose of sickness from the standpoint of self-psychology was the rejection of false health. Sickness manifested the justified guilt of people wronging themselves by failing to realize themselves.

From this perspective more or less drastic implications followed, as formulated by A. H. Maslow:

> I am deliberately rejecting our present easy distinction between sickness and health, at least as far as symptoms are concerned. Does sickness mean having symptoms? I maintain now that sickness might consist of *not* having symptoms when you should. Does health mean being symptom-free? I deny it. . . . It seems quite clear that personality problems may sometimes be loud protests against the crushing of one's psychological bones, of one's true inner nature. What is sick then is *not* to protest. . . . Most people do not protest. . . . They . . . pay years later, in neurotic and psychosomatic symptoms of various kinds, or perhaps in some cases never become aware that they are sick, that they have missed true happiness. . . .[7]

The difficulty in defining health

It was not so much the difficulty in defining sickness that prompted A. H. Maslow here, as the difficulty in defining health. It could remain that "sickness" meant, one way or another, "malfunctioning" or "non-functioning." But if, then, health meant "functioning," what was the "functioning" of the self? The point of the post-Freudian psychologies was to insist upon what they took to be a clinically observable fact—confirmed in literature and life at large as well—that the functioning of the self included what had often been categorized under sickness: anxiety, guilt, conflict, despair, "nervousness," psychosomatic afflictions and so on. The functioning self was not to be construed on the model of the functioning liver or stomach or machine—self-contained, harmonic, homeostatic. Evidences of the functioning self were not to be found in peace of mind, peace of soul, social adjustment, peace with God, positive thoughts. Health was not the absence of sickness but the power to cope, withstand, use, transmute. Health was not the polar opposite of sickness.

It was from such a perspective that the population that inevitably eluded Mowrer's moralism could be grasped: good people not suffering from deficient "sociality" or guilty secrecy but all too socialized. Suppose they were people who had learned from Dale Carnegie, been knit into human-relations organization-families, avoided introversion and scored high in extroversion on Henry Link's PQ test, saturated their subconsciousnesses in the medicine of positive thinking? Suppose theirs were the churches of the suburban captivity, offering the precious boon of status in the gathering anonymity of classless abundance? A sense of thinness, "lack of affect," "identity diffusion," emptiness, nervousness, even anxiety would hardly be surprising; it would be nothing more than honest response to the "false affect" taught by Carnegie and human relations, the sacrifice of inwardness by Link, the repression of awareness with Peale. Treatment could not consist of confessing such feelings and then "returning" to community, because the patient had never been away. Treatment could consist only of regarding the "sickness" as evidence that the autohypnotism of social mind cure had not, in the end, completely taken, evidence that forces of resistance and protest were at work. Such sickness did not call for "cure" or "healing." It called for strength to understand it, then endure it, until more strength was available to attack its roots.

And in the psychology of the churches, in business sociology, in the popular ideology of abundance, the first need was self-recognition, recognition of selfhood. In a 1957 study addressed to our subject, *Nervous Disorders and Religion*,[8] the English psychologist John G. McKenzie emphasized the inherent dynamism of the self, or, as he preferred, "original human nature." That dynamism was the drive to unify all experience, unify it both morally and rationally, unify objective facts and feelings, unify conscience with behavior. In her recent analytic survey of modern psychologies, *Shame and the Sense of Identity*,[9] Helen Merrill Lynd concluded that the sea-change under way in theories of self and human nature was carrying from psychologies of "scarcity" to psychologies of "abundance." People have a surplus of existential energy, far more than enough needed simply to respond, cope, adjust, compensate, maintain inner harmony. This surplus propels—or can propel—people into an active quest for experience, a self-driven search for engagement and knowledge and intimacy.

In part, the new post-scarcity psychologies derived from a probably irreducible minimum of philosophical assumption, which is to say, "faith." But partly they derived from evidence, and one crucial shift in evidence was in the understanding of "sickness." The maladies of nervousness, of neurosis, even of psychoses, and also psychogenic somatic afflictions, were not necessarily evidence of mental malfunction, personality malfunction, spiritual malfunction. (When due to physical damage they could be.) It was in the nature of the case that self-dynamism, "self-realization," "questing" should generate recurring stress, for they demanded constantly renewed exposure. Every self-system had to remain open to reformation, revolution, new integration. Nothing guaranteed that the self could always be prepared to negotiate advance serenely, smoothly, painlessly. The capacity to live with anxiety, stress, dissonance and conflict measured health. Health had no definition except as measured by threat. Identity was power before it was order. Healing the sickness of disorder without inducing strength to bear even greater disorder was to impair selfhood.

Such new-model psychology and therapy carried a reasonably clear theological implication. Given man's brain as an organ thrusting inherently toward new experience and new, larger integrations, there was no known limit to his experience of himself. His pursuit of self-knowledge was in principle without end. In psychology, a quest without end, theology had its model as a quest without end. Science, in the one, piety, in the other, would be known, as both gave first priority to reality, not wishes. And in both this objectivity would be manifested to the degree that they realized that the source of the reality continually bursting in to scatter fantasies was man himself.

A CONCLUSION

Mind cure in the first place registered a protest. It was a protest against an inadequate science of medicine. It was a protest against a theology no longer nourishing. It was a feminine protest against a society careless in meeting the need of many of its members for worthy roles. It struck for a more effective science, a more relevant faith, a richer world. In its insistence upon the practical test of psychological fruits, it brought to bear a standard too long repressed in crude apologies for mere authority. In its evocation of abundance, it struck at disabling assumptions of scarcity still dominant in the thoughts of theology, philosophy, psychology, medicine, sociology, economics, politics in the more respectable world. As a popular stream, mind cure rather impressively evinced the vitality of democratic imagination in the United States, welling up as it did through crusts of convention and anticipating in its wishes what later sophistication often found reasonable.

But in striking out, mind cure struck too far. No medicine would ever heal "sickness"; learning to cure old diseases it would uncover "new" deeper ones, harder even to diagnose, let alone treat. No theology would ever finally satisfy; every scheme of words would become a cage. In no society would people find enough roles and roles rich enough not to imagine more and richer. To try to strike beyond this inherent lag was to repress its source, the vitality of human imagination.

So long as it impelled men to deeds of building and creating, the nineteenth-century model of male psychology was viable, like any story implying a beginning, middle and end. But when the end came, to attempt to save the old model was to enter the fantasy of a departed past. To realize new models were needed was a source of vitality. But to derive a new model from the new institutions was to deny psychology in favor of mechanics, of automated living. To discern psychological potentials in the material potentials of the new machinery was imaginative mastery. But to assume the new potentials were defined by the machinery was to abandon psychology in favor of biology, the science of consumption and digestion.

Acceptance of psychological maladies as legitimate was a twentieth-century advance. People might indeed feel tense and nervous in automated life. They could very well feel something lacking in an abundance pouring forth smoothly without pattern, without beginning, middle and end. People geared to the operations of institutions calculated to keep the institutions running rather than the people running could easily find it hard to feel like real persons and to be alive all their lives. But to treat them with a therapeutic psychology practiced under the auspices of religion was to force a final surrender. Telling legitimately discontented people to find the source of their discontent in themselves was to tell them to shrink further from testing their powers in the society around them.

Mind cure was compromised in its origins. Its dreams were the dreams of people who lacked the tools of imagination and of tradition for translating dreams into action. In the first place, this was a lack characteristic of good middle-class ladies and of the genteel gentlemen so common in early mind cure.

But such weakness had another, deeper source, common to far more people. This was the tradition of popular Protestant culture itself. Steadily, popular Protestantism had dissolved social authority, showing itself jealously suspicious of centralized agencies both of the church and of the state. From time to time this liberating process proved so threatening to stability that it inspired countermovements, such as the Mormons with their new, hard and total hierarchical order or the Jehovah's Witnesses with their visionary escape from the present. But in the middle, Protestants held to this life and moved toward "the ultimate unit," the freedom of the irreducible individual. What they relied on for stability was just the moral psychology of the individual, as prefigured by a Franklin, as preached by an Emerson, as inculcated according to the precepts of the Protestant ethic. Essentially, in popular Protestantism there was to be no middle term between psychology and theology. The sociology of Protestant culture was to be essentially the psychology of Protestant individuals.

Thus, when in fact—partly as a consequence of the energy of such individuals—the immense new system of the industrial economy arose, Protestants had no real bearings. They were unequipped to realize that industrial economy required a middle term—politics. Industrial economy was insusceptible to the Protestant strategy of dissolving rather than directing concentrated power. Protestant psychology was drawn into swamps, dissolving its own final authority, the individual. Concurrently, Protestant theology was drawn into sanctifying a set of new coercions far surpassing those of earlier centralized churches and states. Where tradition has ceased to guide, all community must collapse into system unless psychology and theology are linked by the middle term, politics. Without politics, man and God dissolve into each other, leaving neither a standard of psychological well-being nor an image of divine incitement by which to measure and criticize the powers of the world. "Health" was a fatal ideal, for ultimately discontent is divine, discontent with the inherently limited "supply" offered by any given science and society. To invent psychologies of content was to repress the divine.

WILLIAM JAMES AS THE AUTHORITY

FROM Trine to Peale (Mrs. Eddy excepted, of course), William James counted as a chief authority for mind cure. His discussion of "The Energies of Men," his reference to "wider selves" of which men remained unaware, his fascination with the "subconscious," his overt and sympathetic interest in early mind cure itself, above all that general philosophy seeming to justify any philosophy "that worked," all qualified him as a hero in the loose pragmatism of the movement. It is of some use therefore to grasp James's analysis of religion, sickness and health in its precise bearing.

James discussed mind cure in the two lectures in *The Varieties of Religious Experience* which he entitled "The Religion of Healthy-Mindedness." These were followed by two more lectures entitled "The Sick Soul." In this contrast between "healthy-mindedness" and "sick souls" we have one of the most crucial of James's discussions of human fulfillment.

In all James's writing, references to a robust, cheerful, vigorous style of life leap out as one to be celebrated, as against middle-class Chautauqua, flatness and flabby peace. One has the impression of some hearty, manly, beer-drinking, meat-eating—even, in one footnote, "cannibalistic"—extrovert, whom one might think could safely be counted healthy-minded. This robust type strongly suggested the flavor of two other famous styles of temper: the tough-minded and the "once-born." But it was not this robust, tough-minded, once-born sort who dominated the chapters on the religion of healthy-mindedness. First off James called forth an exemplary roll: St. Francis and Rousseau, Diderot and St. Pierre, Emerson, Thoreau, Parker, Whitman. Which of these could be cleared for membership among the once-born and tough-minded? One might argue over one or another, but for most the answer was plain. James himself saw and appreciated the forced, deliberate, conscious, systematic elements in Whitman's vast affirmations, elements removing him far from the status of being, "by nature," a positive-minded man. But on the whole James's discussion of these cases was unsatisfactory by being no discussion at all, and it is fair to think he was simply indulging his taste for casual illustration too easily, an impression strengthened by his inclusion of Augustine and Luther. What was at stake came out more clearly in his detailed analysis of case histories of more obscure healthy-minded persons.

Many of his cases were women, and women of a certain sort. In three consecutive accounts, the following sentences appeared: ". . . My earlier life bears a record of many, many years of bed-ridden invalidism, with spine and lower limbs paralyzed. . . ."[1] "Life seemed difficult to me at one time. I was always breaking down, and had several attacks of what is called nervous prostration, with terrible insomnia, being on the verge of insanity. . . ."[2] "I had been a sufferer from my childhood till my fortieth year."[3] After this, it was not surprising to find—and we are still in the lectures on healthy-mindedness—the name of Mary Baker Eddy, leader of "the most radical branch" of mind cure.

Intermittently, James recalled what he was really dealing with: mind *cure*. Once, comparing the followers of mind cure with Lutherans and the early Wesleyans, he made the point: "*Things are wrong with them.*"[4] But on this point James never closed. What he was discussing was not healthy minds but healthy sentiments. The question—and the confusion—was: from what sort of minds do mind-cure ideas flow? What sort of people need them? And James, speculating on the future of the new teaching, even though he fastened unerringly on the label mind *cure,* inconsistently answered that one condition for its success ". . . is the apparent existence in large numbers, of minds who united healthy-mindedness with readiness for regeneration by letting go."[5] Not for the only time, James, in violation of his usual pragmatic mode of analysis, was reading back from the mere form into the function and origin. Verbal sunshine expressed, he found himself saying, psychological sunshine.

Just what was this healthy-mindedness then, really? James never did define it except by inference from his discussion of sick souls. The sick soul, instead of minimizing evil, maximized it. In some cases this could be debilitating, to the point of panic fear. But the burden of James's description did not rest here. The gist of his analysis was as follows: Evil is an actual and normal fact of human experience. Sick souls are those who know this. Sick souls are those who, knowing it, incorporate it in their religion. It is the religion of sick souls, therefore, not the religion of healthy-mindedness, that is the strongest and most complete. The distinction that James was really making then was between minds that knew less and minds that knew more of reality. As usual, he had already betrayed the whole issue neatly in his own words, speaking of the healthy-minded. Sometimes they were "quasi-pathological," he observed, and went on: "The capacity for even a transient sadness or a momentary humility seems cut off from them by a kind of congenital anesthesia."[6]

Could health possibly mean anesthesia? Could it be healthy to be partially numb? James did not mean anything like that. He clearly admired and commended his sick souls. Thus, after a previous appearance among the healthy-minded, Luther turned up again among the sick souls—with considerably better credentials. Goethe appeared. And so, as is well known, did William James himself, in the guise of a "French sufferer," sufferer in fact of the panic extreme, that is, James's prolonged depression in his late twenties. These three alone made the point: their achievements were not separate from their "maximization" of evil, had not depended on "denying" evil. They had fed on it.

A few years after publishing the *Varieties*, James covered this ground once again, in *Pragmatism*, and some of the obscurity in the *Varieties* was cleared away. In *Pragmatism* apparent paradoxes vanished. The man ready for risk, danger and adventure was healthy, and his health was identical with his capacity, not to deny evil but to face it. In fact, he demanded it, sought it out. He rejected the "achieved" good. Health was energy, vitality, power, but these abounded as they rebounded, rebounded as they were inspirited by danger.

It is pleasant to know that these ideas about varieties of religious experience flowed from a man capable of religious experiences himself, and a variety of them. The best known was James's prolonged depression. One fascinating aspect of this episode was that it hardly fitted James's theories about the role of the subconscious as vestibule for religious appearance. The first step in his recovery was to conceptualize it, to give it form, and thus, in other words, to "master" it in consciousness, will, and ego. His problem, he concluded, was that of determinism. There was no real freedom, therefore no real "meaning" in life. His recovery consisted of his highly conscious, highly intellectual determination: logic, philosophic and empirical, could not really "prove" determinism, therefore one was free not to believe in it. One had a "right" to believe otherwise. Thereupon, James chose to "will to believe" in free will. This had precious little resemblance to that "letting go" into the subconscious of which he later spoke.

But during another, more mature, more vivid experience, James did evince that letting go which he exalted as the style of real religious freedom.

Early in July 1898 on the slopes of Mount Marcy in the high Adirondacks, fifty-six years old, James spent a night in the open. The moon had risen before midnight, flooding the woods; no wind stirred. The sky was cloudless. From a fire in the cabin close by where his companions slept, smoke rose straight. Within this luminosity James himself was in ferment, caught up, as he said, in a "regular Walpurgisnacht."

Walpurgisnacht is no Christian occasion, and it is worth noting that James never troubled to find orthodox labels for his insights. His own instinct to reach for a pagan tag pointed dead ahead to the depths of his famous book: beneath all the forms and styles of established faiths and, indeed, beneath the forms of standard non-faith too, there was a level or substrate or ground or reservoir of human experience which no forms could ever finally catch, to which no forms could do justice.

What was the content of his night on Mount Marcy? A breakdown of habitual associations came first, and then new, "free" associations. Things "whirled" together, all sorts of things—wife, children, brother, woods, moonlight, lectures, stars, America, memories, anticipations, sharp particulars and terrific abstractions. James underwent, in short, his "letting go," mind, imagination and senses "abandoned," no longer in control by concept, reason, character and will.

There should be no doubt about this side of the experience. It was a kind of disorganization, therefore threatening as well as potentially liberating, the last sort of occasion acceptable to the self-system dependent upon fixed forms, routines, habits and good order, the sort of experience, that is, which, to be acceptable, required courage, ego-strength.

"Whirling," then, was the condition for illumination. What illumination? For one thing, whirling did not subsequently pattern out into a new harmony. Instead, a sense of "immense complexity" remained, an immense complexity in which, James said, poets might make some provisional tracks although he himself, lacking poets' talents, could not. Moreover, not only did the experience not generate a monistic rapture, it actually divided the body of the divine:

. . . It seemed as if the Gods of all the nature-mythologies were holding an indescribable meeting in my breast with the moral Gods of the inner life. The two kinds of Gods have nothing in common—the Edinburgh lectures made quite a hitch ahead.[7]

Nor did intimacy with either sort of God come to dominate. "Intense inhuman remoteness" came through more strongly, along with the sense of trackless immensity. Here, in experience, not only in logic, concepts of hiddenness, inscrutability and indefinite transcendence took on emotion. The illumination did not lead to identification, or to a state of harmony with something or into submergence in something. The ultimate fruit was not any confirmation of "beliefs" to be carried back down the mountainside with dawn. What was the fruit then? Just this, that in the whole experience James felt "intense significance of some sort," for which he could find no word but which was powerful nonetheless. The state of abandonment induced a heightened alertness. The illumination was essentially an enhancement of reality.

In its structure this mountainside experience resembled certain episodes of insanity. Anton Boisen was later to observe the similarities between some schizophrenic attacks and certain episodes of religious insight—which sometimes were not only similar but identical. The point of their similarity, Boisen argued, was that the schizophrenic episodes were best understood as attempts of the self, convulsive, tremendous, terrifying, to break out of its true sickness into a new unity.[8] The mark of the sanity of James's illumination was not its content, but its rich and relatively easy assimilation into his regular life, its easy continuity with past and future: "The Edinburgh lectures made quite a hitch ahead." James had had the experience because of his access to his sub (or pre-) conscious, but he had it also because of the purposes of his conscious self. If he had not had the Edinburgh lectures to write he would have had a different experience. The experience was in part an action of his whole self, a transaction between conscious and subconscious in which the "higher powers" were clearly those of his purposefulness.

This in turn testified to the strength of his consciousness and ego and self, a strength lacking in the schizophrenic whose access to the unconscious was wildly out of control. Whirling, and the trackless immensity, along with the inhuman have all been associated with fear, and one of the main drives of liberal religion had been, and remained in James's day, to purge religious experience and theology of fear, as humanly debilitating. James made no less an assertion of human values than did liberalism, but he registered the decisive point in so doing: if human values were to count for anything, they had to endure fear with strength for experiencing the non-human and inhuman, subconscious depths and unmeasured transcendencies. Human values could not be based on the wish that only wishes define truth.

James's orientation was remarkably similar to Nietzsche's conception of health as the capacity to withstand disease. It was related to Dostoevsky's portrait of the saint as one with the most profound awareness of evil. It echoed Kierkegaard's analysis of faith as sprung from awareness of the abyss and the absurd. With these critics of European middle-class culture James had in common the choice against anesthetic, sedative death-in-life. Most of all he resembled Freud. Like Freud's, James's imagination teemed with visions of psychological abundance, great appetites and copious release of inner potentials. Like Freud, he repeated that health was expression and involvement. Neither James nor Freud thought to guarantee that the world and society and people would provide immediate gratification, but both rejected the alternative of rejecting them. The sure sign of sickness was denial—of disease, evil, conflict, disharmony, of trying out new life. Both saw the crucial problem in the individual's attitude toward himself. Obviously, for a self lacking a sense of its own resilience and resources, communications with reality would have to be guarded, narrow, distorted and even altogether cut off.

The religion of healthy-mindedness, in brief, was itself a form of sickness.

James's discussion of the origins of healthy-mindedness and sick souls was unsatisfactory, for he took them to be simply expressions of temperamental differences, just as he did tough- and tender-mindedness in *Pragmatism*. This was unsatisfactory not only because it was not true, but because it obscured James's real point.

These differences were not fixed; they could be worked on. The question of whether any given person denied or faced the dangerousness of reality was one to be dealt with in light of the most honest philosophy possible, that is, in light of the highest degree of consciousness and self-consciousness. James's position was at once descriptive and normative, mingling ideas of what is with ideas of what ought to be. Man is a purposive animal, James said as psychologist, and, as philosopher, he said man ought to be. Once a man began to live purposefully out of himself, any temperamental bias toward evasion of reality would begin to dissolve. His purposes would undermine his evasions and fortify his confrontations. The explicit rendition of this view appeared in James's arguments for a pluralistic philosophy. Pluralism was a third way, going beyond both tough- and tender-mindedness, going beyond merely "temperamental" differences. Pluralism celebrated human nature aware of itself as self-created, its own purpose, in an environment sympathetic to such self-creation. But it was not the environment that created selves.

In crediting the religion of sick souls with greater realism, James was speaking for "objectivity," taking this to mean attention to things outside in contrast to "subjectivity." Presumably the sick soul might never have become sick had he been able or willing to anesthetize himself. In this regard James commented upon the goal uppermost in those in whom subjectivity reigned. "Happiness," he said, "like every other emotional state, has blindness and insensibility to opposing facts given it as its instinctive weapon for self-protection against disturbance."[9] Were this true, happiness itself would be, if not a sickness, a vulnerability to sickness so long as it counted as the first of priorities.

Here, too, James could be compared fruitfully with Freud. Many of Freud's interpretations turned on the concept of homeostasis, or, more simply, tension-reduction. One ate to eliminate hunger. One drank to reduce thirst. This tension-reduction lay behind the idea of such processes as repression and sublimation. On the basis of this analysis, it was possible to argue that Freud defined ". . . the central nervous system as a mechanism of which the function is to reduce stimulation to its lowest possible level."[10] This view was fortified by Freud's contrast of the pleasure-principle with the reality-principle, by which the reality-principle was presented as a matter of disturbance and pain. But Freud did not identify the central nervous system with the self. In fact, since the pleasure-principle did not consist just of tension-reduction but of both heightened stimulus *and* reduction, it was not true that Freud saw pleasure just in discharge and release. Even so, the pleasure-principle did drive, blindly and insensibly, toward rest, and the plain inference was that, for Freud as for James, happiness and pleasure were not goals inherent to human nature. Neither deplored happiness and pleasure but neither imagined they were the goals that drew out the resources of humankind. Happiness and pleasure were side-products. What their reactions would have been to the subjective serenity of the Christian Scientists observed by Mark Twain one can only conjecture. James might have been more interested in its doubtful realism, Freud more interested in its dubious reality.

The alternative to an absorption in peace of mind was not a return to orthodox Christian and Puritan notions that human desires were to be submerged and forgotten in favor of God's, nor did it follow that there were no rational approaches to happiness, as though, like the sun, the sustenance of life, it blinded those who peered at it. One of the most interesting treatises inspired by modern wishes, Bertrand Russell's *The Conquest of Happiness*, first published in 1930 and then reprinted as a Signet paperback in 1951, displayed just such a rational regard. Russell nicely caught the pathos of the "ordinary day-to-day unhappiness from which most people in civilized countries suffer": it was "all the more unbearable because, having no obvious external cause, it appears inescapable."[11] The weight of Russell's advice fell on the side of action, not on adjusting thoughts: expand your interests, let them range beyond duty and the superego, in work let the primary reward be in the process itself. Whether or not this was as Utopian as any other advice, it did turn on the sense that energy flowed from engagement, that reality would reward interest. The answer to subjectivity was objectivity. With honest involvement in things outside, zest would follow. "External interests, it is true," he warned, "bring each its own possibility of pain," but pains of this sort "do not destroy the essential quality of life, as do those that spring from disgust with self."[12] Happiness was not equivalent to flight from pain, or from sickness, disharmony, poverty or death. "I cannot advocate any happiness based upon what seem to me to be false beliefs."[13] James agreed:

I quite agree that what mankind at large most lacks is criticism and caution, not faith. Its cardinal weakness is to let belief follow recklessly upon lively conception, especially when the conception has instinctive liking at its back. . . . Were I addressing the Salvation Army or a miscellaneous popular crowd it would be a misuse of opportunity to preach the liberty of believing. . . . What such audiences most need is that their faiths should be broken up and ventilated, that the northwest wind of science should get into them and blow their sickliness and barbarism away.[14]

MIND CURE AMONG CATHOLICS AND JEWS

THE DISINTEGRATION of a major style of Protestant character revealed in mind cure represented a crisis for American culture as well as for Protestantism, insofar as the mutual interpenetrations of American life and Protestantism were profound through the nineteenth century and into the early twentieth.

Among Jews and Catholics the spread of a mind-cure style of consciousness grew in significance as Judaism and Catholicism grew in significance in the emergent twentieth-century pluralism.

For obvious reasons mind cure among Catholics could not express itself as it did among Protestants in the form of new churches. A separate Catholic-derived mind-cure cult would simply not be Catholic. To leave Catholicism for a mind-cure group would have involved a more rending pain than that upon leaving a Methodist or a Congregational or a Unitarian pew. The dislocation would have been compounded by other, religiously extraneous factors: ethnic identities strange to Protestantism, and social antagonisms. I have no way of telling how many Catholics may in fact have left. There is no evidence their numbers were significant. At the same time, I have no way of telling how many Catholics availed themselves of mind-cure literature, listened to Emmett Fox or studied

Norman Vincent Peale, let alone lent themselves to the mind-cure psychologies and sociologies of the business mystique. There is no evidence their numbers were not great. But outright Catholic mind cure was impossible.

The Jewish Science Movement

The same was not true for Judaism. Jewish religion was, of course, close to the "congregational" model, allowing for varieties and innovations still within a tradition defined by memory, teaching and self-choice. In Judaism mind cure generated one organization of its own at least, Rabbi Morris Lichtenstein's Jewish Science Movement in New York, with its own publishing company. Lichtenstein's first book was *Jewish Science and Health*, exactly a half century after Mrs. Eddy's first edition.

Lichtenstein was able to locate all necessary biblical authority in the Old Testament without the New, and did not equate the power of the universal Divine Mind with the "Christ." The Old Testament prophets had been able to heal, just as had Jesus. The Talmud, too, enjoined positive thinking. Like Mrs. Eddy, Dresser and Fillmore, Lichtenstein insisted the operations of Divine Mind were not simply those of mental suggestion. Like Mrs. Eddy, Fillmore, Peale, etc., he explained procedures relevant to lungs, liver, heart and so on. He did not follow Mrs. Eddy on the non-existence of matter, preferring the more moderate mind-cure logic.

Lichtenstein explained that he had been inspired to Jewish Science by Christian Science and other competition: "We are in need of Jewish Science because, in this land in particular, Christian Science is lurking to grasp every Jewish soul it can lay hold on."[1] Evidences of Christian Science or other mind-cure missions to the Jews (or Catholics) are not available. What Lichtenstein no doubt had observed among some Jews were the same maladies and needs to which mind-cure groups had responded. Just what the Judaism was that he wanted to save Lichtenstein construed generously. Orthodoxy, Zionism, Jewish medieval philosophy, Jewish ethics, liberal Reform—all were worth saving, and if mind cure could be woven in, it should be.

This spaciousness in definition of Judaism was perhaps a reflection of the rapid and deep Jewish involvement in American life, and indeed Lichtenstein, like Dr. Beard, avowed that it was American conditions that made this addition to the Jewish treasures necessary, for Jews, too, were being made "exhausted and nervous and ailing." The stress in this American Judaism was upon techniques for mood-manipulation, as with the rest of mind cure:

> It has to do particularly with that phase of religion which deals with man's daily inner experiences; it dwells on that part of religion which influences man's mood, which determines his outlook upon life, which affects his happiness.[2]

The great issues were those of fear, worry, envy, inner attitudes blocking joy, anxiety, fret. Jewish Science like its Christian counterpart was wrought to the scale of subjectivity.

Rabbi Joshua Loth Liebman

As in Protestantism, though, the larger life of mind cure among Jews was likely to be within the standard congregations. In the post-World War II period Jewish rabbis competed not with Mrs. Eddy but with Peale. Louis Binstock of Temple Shalom in Chicago, for instance, mapped *The Road to Successful Living* in 1955 following his *The Power of Faith* three years before. Israel Chodos of Los Angeles' Conservative Sinai Temple published *Count Your Blessings* in 1958. But before Peale's first success, it was a rabbi, Joshua Loth Liebman of Temple Israel in Boston, who wrote the book first heralding the whole flood of postwar religious bestsellers, *Peace of Mind*, in 1946, reprinted thirty times reissued in thirty-five-cent paperback in 1955.

Still, while "inspirational," these books did not truly qualify in the mind-cure evangel, for mind cure was not just inspiration.

It is not easy to know just why Liebman chose the title he did. It was not new. One of Rabbi Lichtenstein's books had been called *Peace of Mind*, too, and in it Lichtenstein expounded the mind-cure implications of the title. But the chief fact about Liebman's book was its debt to Freud, and the phrase "peace of mind" hardly did justice to Freud's meaning. Moreover, in his theological sections, Liebman set forth ideas in the neighborhood of William James. In attacking—in line with Freud—old ideas of God, Liebman was attacking approximately the God prescribed at the Religio-Psychiatric Clinic by Smiley Blanton and Norman Vincent Peale. The "new idea of God," Liebman said—drawing on Whitehead and Arthur Compton as well—should be that of a "power who needs our collaboration." "Men will not only *say*, but will *feel*, that they are indispensable to God." They will grow aware of "His eternal yearning for our collaboration." James had said the same.

It is of some interest that Liebman's views at this point distinguished American experience. "A New God for America," he headed his theological suggestions, but it was not on the basis of America as the Father-Mother-Supply of automated happiness. America is "a civilization that has little of the father complex in it," he wrote, a culture that will "find it increasingly difficult to submit to the idea of a dominant Father." His description repeated standard contrasts of American experience with the "helpless, poverty-stricken, powerless motifs" of old Europe.

No more than James, though, did this social optimism lead Liebman to gild the drama of individual life with external gold:

> Basically all men and women in one degree or another feel guilty, dread pain, suffer loneliness, seek reassurance. It is merely the conspiracy of silence about our deepest inner feelings, our habit of hiding behind the masks of convention, which prevents us from recognizing the universal brotherhood of anxiety which binds the whole human race together.[3]

Liebman accused Christianity of teaching the disastrous technique of repression, of advising men "to choke down every evil thought" as though desire equaled truth.

In short, Liebman's book was only unfairly lumped into the postwar spate of books teaching "faith-in-faith"; he preached neither simple "inspiration" nor inspiration-and-repression, nor mind-cure techniques for the latter.

Inspiration did suffuse the other books of popular Judaism, however. Chodos' *Count Your Blessings* exemplified a type. Countering what he felt was an exaggerated pessimism in various quarters, he heaped up evidence of progress in the modern world (that is, the United States): better medicine, longer life, higher wages, greater opportunities for women, better psychiatry and education, fuller social justice. Yet facts, not the autohypnotic techniques of mind cure dominated, and if the facts were "inspiring," the inspiration was not bought at the price of anesthesia. Such facts were hardly the therapy for those suffering from "modern civilization," for they were well aware of those facts, but at least the therapy could not do harm.

Binstock's *The Power of Faith* did repeat mind-cure themes, on their inspirational side. "You, like everyone else, have access to a great storehouse of dynamic power on which you can draw. . . . That storehouse is *Faith*. Not religion. Not your immortal soul. Not the House of Worship. Not God. But—FAITH."[4] Will Herberg, seizing on this quotation, reasonably included Binstock—along with Liebman—in the "cult of reassurance," of "faith in faith."[5] But in Binstock's distinctions—"not religion, not soul, not God"—the "faith in faith" implied a kind of heroic psychological pulling-oneself-up-by-the-bootstraps operation that was far from mind cure, for in mind cure the *belief* that the power of faith was in fact the power of divine Supply was aimed precisely to dispute any notion of the adequacy of pure psychological heroics. Not altogether surprisingly, in his later *Road to Successful Living,* Binstock tried to present religion in tension with immediate needs. He attacked success ideals; he suggested that much the business middle classes allowed themselves to live for was self-destructive. Though rarely approaching Liebman's neo-Freudian suggestions for social reform, his ideas disguised none of that alienated individualism curdling Peale's positive thinking. Often blurring over hard questions, lapsing easily into sentimental "rules" for living, Binstock's second book did convey some sense of religion as a demand upon men and not as supply for their wishes. Most striking was his explicit attack upon Peale and the cult of reassurance. Hardly less so was his declaration that, as the neo-orthodox insisted Christianity was a "religion of failure," so too was Judaism.

I cannot intend these brief comments on popular Jewish writers to be more than suggestive. Widespread Jewish involvement in American middle-class business, professional and suburban life exposed Jews to the same problems faced by Protestants. Perhaps what needs explanation is why mind-cure techniques did not infiltrate Judaism more deeply than they did. Some hypotheses occur. It is doubtful that the pool of female clientele was as large in Jewish culture. Victorian sentimentality and sexual ethic; profound displacements in the emotional significance of the family; the highly ambivalent hopes of feminism—these were not to bite as deeply into Jewish life at least before World War II, and there is no clear evidence they have done so since. As for the myths of modern business, Jews have had less reason to imagine the economy a realm of "human relations" in which it is safe to give one's whole self. Indeed, Jewish business and professional men have been largely excluded from the chief centers of bureaucratic togetherness. At the same time, if concentrated more largely in the still individualistically competitive spheres of enterprise, Jewish male psychology remained allied one way or another to feelings for the first priority of community, hence less vulnerable to that psychic impotence befalling the atomistic individualists sucked into bureaucratic establishments—Peale's standard male clients. And if only out of their sense of minority status, Jews were drawn to watchfulness of society at large, drawn to politics. They knew, from bitter recent history, that anesthesia toward social reality could be deadly.

Perhaps it was for these reasons, as well as others, that the considerable involvement of American Jews with psychoanalysis and clinical psychology did not entail to the same degree the conflicts, confusions and mistaken identities featuring liberal Protestantism's complex affair with these therapies.

Fulton Sheen

Among middle-class Catholics, rising from the laboring-class majority of the nineteenth and early twentieth centuries, individualism, emphasis upon the classic secondary virtues of the Protestant ethic, and expectations of success, harmonic happiness and surburban abundance did not fail to appear. Nor did the maladies of "American nervousness." But this culture still carried over its original, obsessive problem: how to be wholeheartedly American while wholeheartedly Catholic. As many studies have indicated, Catholic Americanization did not dilute Catholic identity but intensified it. This was not promising ground for mind cure, which flourished among people who either did not feel gross status problems on class or religious dimensions or could easily repress them.

I want to glance at two styles of popular Catholic ideology aimed at "holding" Catholic identity. Bishop Fulton J. Sheen spoke to more than Catholic audiences in his flood of books and on his radio and television shows, just as Mrs. Eddy, Trine, Fillmore, Fox and Peale spoke to more than Protestants, but his message was obviously calculated to fortify Catholic self-conceptions. In commenting on his most popular book, *Peace of Soul*, I want, not to abstract from it hints and scraps of mind cure, but to assess his primary concerns in light of mind-cure issues.

Sheen began with a concession. It would be best, he insisted, if modern men *could* be "brought back to God and happiness" by the philosophy of St. Thomas Aquinas, for Thomism was sound and normal. But modern men were "too confused" to grasp it, and one must begin with men as they were.

> Not the order in the cosmos, but the disorder in himself; not the visible things of the world, but the invisible frustrations, complexes and anxieties of his own personality—these are modern man's starting point when he turns questioningly toward religion.[6]

If the more "rational" and "normal" way to God was through natural philosophy, how was it that men had become too confused? Sheen denied that the confusion was due to world conditions, political, social or economic. Such external conditions merely reflected prior internal confusions.

> World wars are only projections of the conflicts waged inside the souls of modern men, for nothing happens in the external world that has not first happened within a soul.

> The tormented minds of today are not the effects of our tormented world; it is our upset minds that have upset the world.[7]

Sheen's book therefore was aimed at correcting faulty ideas. Referring to "errant theologians about four hundred years ago," he attacked certain Protestant concepts. He attacked "the Liberals of the last few centuries." He attacked Marx. But *Peace of Soul* was above all an attack on Freud and psychoanalysis. Without attacking Liebman by name, at several points Sheen pointedly contrasted "peace of soul" with "peace of mind." Peace of mind obtained only on the "second floor" of reason, peace of soul on the floor above, of supernatural order; peace of mind resulted from *any* ordering principle, peace of soul from the order of God; peace of mind came from sublimations, efforts of men, peace of soul from grace; peace of mind sometimes visited those "indifferent to right and wrong," peace of soul never; peace of mind provided adjustment to the world, peace of soul asked whether we ought to adjust.

It is beside our point to probe Sheen's attack on Freud; like Mowrer, by "Freud" he meant not Freud but popular clichés; and like Mowrer, he was inclined to argue that Catholicism already contained everything good in psychoanalysis without the bad. More interesting was the fact that Sheen remained loyal to his original surrender of true rational argument. Facing "confused" minds, he devised no pedagogy for dispelling confusion. Instead he offered psychological promises. In his concluding chapter, "The Effects of Conversion," he said that one gained personal unity, one was freed of sinful habits and excesses, one's conscience was swallowed in love, one's moral life was no longer "austere or arduous," certitude filled one's being. "The only real pain the convert now has is his inability to do more for the love of God."[8]

The relevant comparison was with James's contrast between healthy-*mind*edness and sick *souls,* whereby entrance into the realm of soul had the function precisely *not* of transcending mind's questionable order but of dispelling mind's illusory order.

To whom was Sheen speaking? Inevitably he had a missionary motive, he wished to convert. But what did his evangel mean for Catholics? Possibly some of them were intellectually confused too, but, confused or not, Catholics could take from his evangel a plain message: it is enough, and everything, to be Catholic. In the peace of soul of being Catholic it was unnecessary to ask any questions, experience any doubt, suffer any moral arduousness.

The further implication of this was that the Catholic could act strictly to project his Catholicism. Sheen's historical logic indeed restricted action to such projection:

> The crisis today is so deep in its causes that all social and political attempts to deal with it are bound to be as ineffective as talcum powder in curing jaundice. It is man who has to be remade *first;* then society will be remade by the restored new man.[9]

Were Catholics restored new men?

Reinforcing this sense of superior identity, Sheen specified one result of conversion that was "less pleasant." "One becomes the target of opposition and hate." Why?

> This is because the [convert's] friends intuitively know that he no longer shares the spirit of the world, that he is now governed by Spirit, is lifted into a truly supernatural order, is united with Divinity in a special way, which is a challenge and reproach to those who would make the best of two worlds.[10]

His Protestant friends? His Jewish friends? His secular, agnostic, atheistic friends? Sheen did not say. The touch of paranoia was not intended to be sociological.

Father Keller

The fulfillment of this defensive identity, and its implication of a peculiar interpretation of the state of American culture, was spelled out in the writings of Father James Keller, Maryknoll missionary and founder of the Christophers, a loose allegiance of Catholics devoted, essentially, to Catholic self-affirmation. Keller dated the beginning of modern decline somewhat later than Sheen, specifying a "de-spiritualizing process which has taken place during the last seventy-five years,"[11] a chronology helping make plain what Sheen left implicit, that he was preoccupied with the status problems of American Catholics. Though not of "the full Christian heritage,"[12] the Puritans and the Founding Fathers had not been de-spiritualizers. Who were these then? Keller was unclear until he reached the present day: they were "materialistic atheists."[13] But had these been multiplying? It was hard to think so, because "it seems safe to say that less than *one percent* of the American people are set on the destruction of our country."[14]

One has the odd impression that, emanating from paranoid fantasies generally, as the enemies grew fewer and fewer the danger grew greater and greater. Keller had arguments why:

> You will invariably find, once you investigate, that practically all of this minority are in key spots where they pass on their hatred, not to a few, but to the mass of the people. This is so because those who have an active hatred of God are *missionaries* at heart and are never content to keep that hatred to themselves. They strive unceasingly to pass it into the bloodstream of our national life, defiling the minds and hearts of everyone they can reach with their foul ideas. Ever on the job, they use every possible medium—education, government, labor, press, radio, movies, comic strips, magazines, books, and countless other channels to further their purpose.[15]

As against these masters of deceit, Keller found what he estimated to be 100,000,000 Americans "living off the benefits of Christianity"[16] but "less and less conscious of the great fundamentals which make all their freedoms possible." "Confused and with little idea of true values, they are like immature children who fall for the 'come-on' of the kidnapper."[17]

From this evocation of doves defenseless against serpents, Keller could generate the basic alternative to the mind-cure response to the maladies of weakness. Those who were anxious, frustrated, baffled, sick, "for no obvious external reason," as Russell observed, could release their rage against practically any targets—schools, movies, books, big government, "liberals." It was a temptation especially strong in middle-class Catholic circles, for it remained true that, while Catholics had indeed been thoroughly domesticated as Americans, they knew that their identity had still to be maintained in tension with, in some cases in opposition to, most of the major institutions of communication and culture in modern American society. Protestants had not to be so defensive, if only from different illusions, and Jews realized such chauvinism for them was absurd. Of course, Keller's paranoia was attractive beyond Catholic circles, imitated as it was among the renascent Protestant fundamentalism of the fifties.

Perhaps among Catholics the Presidency of John Kennedy and the Papacy of John XXIII and of Paul VI would soothe agitated souls. Perhaps among Jews further assimilation might seem compatible with stable identity. Perhaps among Protestants, the emergence of a postwar generation of tough-minded young theologians and intellectuals and urban-oriented pastors, plus the racial challenge to integrity, might mean reawakening.

A RECKONING FOR 1980

EVANGELICALISM: THE OLD-TIME POSITIVE RELIGION?

Evangelicalism as politics

If the true faith of Americans was a "civic religion," a "religion of America," Bicentennial Year 1976 challenged the ingenuity of orators, politicians, philosophers, historians, and, certainly, preachers. Watergate and the forced resignation of a President had left the "bully pulpit" empty, for despite agreement on the amiable honesty of the caretaker in the White House, he was not sensed as a voice for the nation. The national stage was unusually empty of ordained spokesmen. No prophet had succeeded Reinhold Niebuhr. Norman Vincent Peale, Fulton Sheen, and such as Joshua Roth Liebman no longer sold their millions of manuals. Billy Graham, the one major survivor from the fifties, still touring endlessly, had wounded himself, probably mortally. From the start, Graham had divided his word. "Awake, for the End is near," he had proclaimed, as had countless premillenialists before him, but at the same time he had always promised fruits in the here-and-now from being born-again. The here-and-now had nearly smothered the prophecy in his association with Richard Nixon, and Nixon's fall exposed the narrowness of Graham's social imagination. In

Minneapolis and Wheaton, his mighty ecclesiastical machinery continued to turn over but increasingly with the effect of something automatic, on momentum. Of course, the one great prophet prepared by the sixties, free of all tired echoes from the fifties, Martin Luther King, who would have been only fifty-five, in his prime, at Bicentennial, had been stolen.

No confident declarations of secular identity were heard. No one could plausibly claim a happy birthday for rational Jeffersonian America. During the sixties, several liberal optimists, both in and outside the church, had discerned salvationary vitalities at work in the very "counter-cultures" then conspicuous, among environmentalists, ecologists, commune experimentalists, at Woodstock or at Haight-Ashbury, in black ghettos or in the anti-Vietnam movement. The year 1968 could seem a dawn, its confrontations holding the promise of liberating debate. Harvey Cox, the most notable religious interpreter of these secular phenomena, nicely held in suspension the "religious" question whether these vitalities testified to the "immanence" of God "in" American history or to the "grace" of a "transcendent" God still willing to re-visit American history despite its lapses. Liberal religion's determined search for reasons to hope had itself been stimulating, but by 1976 few if any of its signs any longer seemed convincing.

Perhaps this void was "sacred," however, in Paul Tillich's sense, a moment ready to be filled just because it had been so emptied, a moment for re-birth. Perhaps Bicentennial Year could be celebrated as "the Year of the Evangelical." Evangelicalism's leading magazine, *Christianity Today*, celebrating its own twentieth birthday, agreed, in a lead article by its senior editor, "The Year of the Evangelical '76." The National Association of Evangelicals, another post–World War II institution, held its annual convention in the Capitol, there addressed by the President and observed, questioned, analyzed, and reported by more journalists than had ever before attended upon evangelical affairs. Two acute observers, both Catholic, and therefore somewhat "outside," Garry Wills and Michael Novak, both opined that evangelical Christians had become the largest single element in American religious life. Media collaborated, *Time,*

Newsweek, and *The New York Times* each devoting major stories to something labeled the evangelical surge. Notable personalities were available for journalistic focus: Charles Colson, born-again in the ashes of Watergate; Eldridge Cleaver, saved from race hate; numerous athletes; the sister of the Democratic party's nominee for President, a proven divine healer; Marabel Morgan, converting anti-feminism into positive womanhood; and, of course, the Democratic nominee himself, soon President-elect. Statistics were available for the credulous. A bicentennial Gallup Poll indicated 50 million adult Americans—one-third the total—self-professed as born-again (one among them George Gallup, Jr., himself).[1]

Such evidences could be—and were—taken to prove a crisis in old middle-class mainline Protestantism. All the old denominations appeared to be struggling, losing members, money, seminary candidates, in the same vortex, evidently, that was draining Roman Catholicism. No longer were Methodists, their once popular, democratic flair long cooled into respectability, the largest church. Twelve million strong, the Southern Baptists had taken a huge lead. Most sensational seemed the growth of churches long regarded as a kind of fringe on the Joseph's coat of American Protestantism, holiness, and pentecostal groups of various origins, white and black.[2] One holiness-pentecostal healing preacher, Oral Roberts, had risen, out of the obscurity that had surrounded the dozens of itinerant charismatic preachers for decades, into national visibility. The irrelevance and decadence of mainline Protestantism, so often proclaimed in the sixties by men like Cox and Episcopal Bishop James Pike, appeared confirmed, if not exactly in the way they had anticipated.

No doubt, ingredients of myth were mixed in all this. *Christianity Today's* editors, for instance, displaying professional skepticism, took pains to publish studies showing that at least 4 million of the 12 million Southern Baptists didn't seem to be living where the church rolls said they should be.[3] And Gallup's 50 million: Why was it Americans still reported rates of religious attachment more like those of third- and fourth-world people than of other developed modern nations? Did polls somehow miss some important measure of meaningfulness in those multitudinous protestations of piety and faith and regeneration? As for being a "largest element," evangelicals still seemed adept at the infighting they had always displayed; the mighty Missouri Synod Lutherans, for instance, were slowly tearing themselves to pieces in remarkably reminiscent arguments over Bible "inerrancy." So at the very least evangelicals were not a united cohort, nor as numerous, probably, as some hoped. Yet altogether the signs did testify to a reality of some shape and of considerable dimensions that made worthwhile the efforts of observers to guess what it meant. But by far the most interesting efforts to figure out what it meant were those of the self-conscious leaders of evangelical apologetics themselves. If they could not be sure, who could?

The first "evangelical" explanation was essentially a temptation rather than a real reading of the times. Evangelism's temptation in shapeless America had always been to heighten anxiety as a cause for faith. Instead of trying to figure out the patterns of hope, evangelism won quicker results from proclaiming "the end is near." In the strictest sense, such premillenial evangelists—including Billy Graham—did not have to think badly of the world in order to insist upon the imminence of its end, but if only to preserve simplicity in the message they usually sought, as "signs" of the end, evidences of decadence, breakdown, and wickedness. Evangelicals had no particular difficulty in finding such signs in 1976. For many of them, the signs of hope made out by liberals in the sixties had already seemed signs of imminence, and the seventies brought confirmation. Some of these remained general. Technology and pollution were prompting "disillusionment about science and technology." Others were more specific: "Watergate helped us understand why humanism is on the verge of bankruptcy."[4] Most signs contained awkward implications. Careful polls showed, for instance, that Richard Nixon owed his victories in 1968 and 1972 not to "humanists" and "secular rationalists" but to good evangelical conservative Protestants, urged on by Graham.[5] Similarly, the leaders of movements against pollution and technological single-mindedness were more likely to be "liberals" and "experimentals" than born-again evangelicals. Besides, if the end was near, it mattered little who had elected Mr. Nixon; on the other hand, should his election have induced a new conscience in the nation, perhaps the end was not near. In short, premillenialism in its old, "William Miller" purity had no meaningful bearing. Certainly Billy Graham, following his embarrassment, was in no place to revive it.

The reading of the signs, then, evinced a large pragmatism: "Human beings now experience staggering insecurity about all those structures of thought and value and community upon which we heretofore counted.... Despair is the pervasive reality, and any theology which does not have in it an immense amount of faith in the loving and empowering grace of God is not going to be able to cope with that reality."[6] Here, no one was asked to become anxious because the end was nigh; rather, they were urged to consider an alternative to the anxiety and despair they already felt. For intellectual evangelicals, this was temptation indeed: it put them in the marketplace with competitive goods. The hazards, however, were great. For one thing, this competitive offer did not necessarily clarify the real roots of despair. For another, it had no leverage on those who simply denied feeling anxiety and despair in the first place. Most of all, it committed the evangelical alternative to producing results; and a few evangelicals, taking despair for granted, protected themselves by invoking the case of St. Augustine, whose offer to the faithful in the staggering insecurities of falling Rome was simply that of not letting mere history undermine them. Rome might fall, but they would be saved. It was just as impressive that there were any such "Augustinians" in 1976 as that they were few.[7]

The part of their past the evangelicals of 1976 most usually invoked was "fundamentalism," that embattled, rigid, humiliated struggle against "modernity" within Protestantism in the 1920s. The new evangelicals, still critics of modernity and modernism, still committed to "inerrant" Scripture, still certain that only baptism by the Holy Spirit promised salvation, at the same time agreed that fundamentalism had failed for its own weaknesses. Its apology had been needlessly defensive, intellectually unsophisticated, even emotionally immature. Now and then research was directed to repristinate the image and reputation of the fundamental fathers—and grandfathers—but in essence the evangelicals of 1976 saw themselves as having shaken off the handicaps under which fundamentalists had labored.[8] Their scholars were more resourceful, deeper, bolder. Their preachers were less crude. They had learned to use media better than the liberals did. And the modernity of the seventies enjoyed little of that glamour peculiar to the twenties, when it had seemed that all old restraints might be let go. In this, of course, the evangelicals of 1976 ascribed their new status to themselves, and not only were not proclaiming an "end" to be nigh but implicitly were interpreting American history itself as a medium for divine revelation. Just what did this heritage imply for evangelicals in 1976? So long as the model of the fundamentalists proved instructive, something very like triumphalism seemed at work, a determination that come what may evangelical forces prevail. Yet American history did not in truth yield so simple a guide. In *Discovering Our Evangelical Heritage*, the scholar Donald Dayton offered not the embattled faithful but such urgent reformers as the abolitionists Charles Grandison Finney and Sarah and Angelina Grimke as models for modern evangelicals, persons who had found American society deformed and in need of saving, rather than itself a saving history. This, of course, strongly suggested that reasons for the evangelical surge were less meaningful than what evangelicals did with their power.[9]

The most straightforward explanation of evangelical success drew less on history than on a kind of sociology. In *Why Conservative Churches Are Growing*, Dean M. Kelley had already concluded that the old mainline denominations were in decline because they had abandoned discipline, zeal, identity, orthodoxy, had ceased being what they were supposed to be: true churches. They had pursued reform, therapy, politics, culture. By contrast, the "conservative," that is, evangelical, churches were growing precisely because they had remained true, reliable, responsible churches. Therefore, let evangelicals simply go on doing what they had been doing.[10] This was not a wholly finished argument. For one thing, no evidence showed that the gains to evangelicalism were being won at the expense of the mainline churches. For another, the losses in mainline churches might well have been attributed to the success of those churches in fitting their members for some greater freedom beyond church boundaries. The argument, that is, betrayed a plain "church-centered" self-interest not necessarily wholly consistent with evangelism's old insistence upon the heart. Yet Kelley's approach probably best suited a consensus strategy: persist.

The end of everything; the end of liberal culture; the triumph of evangelical culture; the fulfillment of American history: these could not all have been true, but any one and some combinations might have been. Yet, the historian's eye for the sheerly accidental, "existential," and irreducible tells him that the story of evangelical rising would have lacked a dramatic and organizing focus without Jimmy Carter, who could be "explained" by none of these. With Carter, evangelicals faced certain questions they might otherwise have preferred to evade. Without him, they might not have appreciated what those questions were. Surely Carter represented a great opportunity for his brethren, the Southern Baptists, and for evangelical Protestants generally.[11] All presidential candidates testified routinely to the nation's reliance on religion, morality, values, faith, etc., etc., but Carter's testimony obviously differed. It was more personal. But what difference would that make to politics? The first puzzle was presented by his very openness. To reporters he candidly described the debt he owed his sister, Ruth Stapleton. To her he had turned in a season of doubt after defeats in Georgia, and through her he had experienced the kind of re-awakening that evangelicals took as a sign of their identity. Was this to say then that Carter could be counted on never to get discouraged whatever the frustrations of office? It might have been hard to detect the difference between this and that more familiar preservative of politicians' stamina—ambition. To interviewers from *Playboy* magazine, Carter attested his sins of the mind, specifically, lust for women other than his wife. Was this to assure citizens they need not fear arrogance in office? For non-evangelicals, the lesson might have been confusing: if being born-again did not cleanse sin from inner life, what did it do? Evangelicals were more likely to understand; it promoted humility. But was humility what Carter intended to project?

Carter's larger theme, that he would seek to make the government in Washington as "good and honest and compassionate and as filled with love" as were the American people held more complex puzzles.[12] Did Carter really believe the American people were good and compassionate and loving? To the editors of *Christianity Today,* a black evangelical, Jesse Jackson, pointed out bluntly that white evangelicals had no Jesse Jackson because of "racism."[13] In nothing did Carter win a more impressive success than in winning credibility with black voters and receiving 90 percent of their votes. He did not mount an open attack on racism. Rather, having already in years past, as an elder in the affairs of his church in Plains, shown that he did not share the racial views of his evangelical Southern Baptist white brothers, he relied on this record to lend credence to his addresses to blacks themselves. When confronted with difficult situations in the church, during the campaign, he avoided crusade-like rhetoric but sought, in quiet negotiations, compromises that satisfied no one eager for victory but that testified clearly both to his will to change and his skill in diplomacy. His behavior—as distinguished from his words—appeared to exemplify the theories of Reinhold Niebuhr, who had insisted that in politics love—and compassion, etc.—were unavailing in face of a general human tendency to selfishness. Justice, not love, provided the measure in politics, and politicians seeking justice did well to negotiate using the coinage of bargaining and self-interest. Report had it that Carter had in fact read, absorbed, and agreed with Niebuhr; if so, was there reason why here, as distinguished from the candor with which he exposed his personal religion, he dissimulated? And where had he got the idea the American people—or any people—were "good and honest and compassionate..." etc.? Surely not from evangelical orthodoxy, certainly not from Billy Graham, who knew mankind to be sinful. Fair-minded observers would agree, naturally, that no political leader in mid-twentieth-century American democracy had much to hope from discourses upon voters' sinfulness, but Carter's rhetoric seemed to go further than necessary. Had he concluded that Vietnam, Watergate, and the panoply of disorders sapping public morale justified some positive thinking? Any one of these possibilities might have been legitimate by one or another canon of political responsibility, but Carter had made a point of himself as something other than simply a superior politician. But what? His campaign left his understanding of his relationship to the American people mysterious.

Had Carter wished advice from his own people, "the Church that Produced a President," he could have read contributions sent in to *Christianity Today* in response to its editors' hypothesis, "If I Were President."[14] Combat "secularism, egoism, luxury, and hubris," advised one contributor. Another spoke for "justice," and still another, noting "the poor, the unemployed, the aged... the minorities," linked their claim to the need for Americans to restrain themselves "from their increasingly affluent and often wasteful use of funds and resources, so that these can be conserved and shared with those... in need..." This echoed, no doubt deliberately, the noteworthy conclusion to the 1974 world evangelical meeting in Lausanne: "Those of us who live in affluent circumstances accept our duty to develop a simple lifestyle in order to contribute more generously to both relief and evangelism." The year before that, in Chicago, a small number of American evangelicals had organized "Evangelicals for Social Action." Their leading spokesman, Ronald J. Sider, would eventually publish *Rich Christians in an Age of Hunger*, repeating the theme struck at Lausanne.[15] Was Jimmy Carter an Evangelical for Social Action? If so, he could only have known that ESA hardly proved to be a flourishing group, compounding the paucity of its numbers with the intensity of its own schisms. Would he attempt to promote economic justice by the same means he evidently meant to promote racial justice, quietly, by diplomacy, without rhetoric, knowing very well that not only "people" but his own people, the evangelicals, were hostile to "welfare" and "taxes" and all practical means to justice? Another of *Christianity Today's* respondents voiced the more representative line: "cut the budget, reduce the... federal government." Replacing "pragmatism with idealism, cynicism with honesty" might have been taken as a reverberation from Watergate, whereas selecting the right kind of persons for office, "including, where practical, evangelical Christians," appeared one point on which Carter could not have been expected to waste any thought.

The contribution of the editors themselves best illuminated Carter's relationship to his own evangelical people. During the presidential campaign, no speculations outnumbered those devoted to how Catholics would respond to Carter, on the assumption that Catholics would remember that the tribal anti-Catholicism that had swamped Al Smith and imperiled John F. Kennedy belonged precisely to those southern evangelicals to whom Jimmy Carter belonged.[16] Most Catholics were Democrats; how many might vote Ford out of fear of evangelical prejudice? On the other hand, most "evangelical conservative Protestants" were Republicans; could Carter win enough of them to over-balance his Catholic losses? The editors of *Christianity Today* were not in time with their suggestion, but the idea they presented on the eve of his inauguration had been in the air: "We urge that the incoming administration focus attention on the abortion issue." Here was the "issue" that offered Carter a chance to woo evangelical and Catholic votes together. His failure to seize it, in favor of carefully distinguishing between personal preferences and public policy, and thus easing the issue out of debate, suggested the familiar prudence of a middle-of-the-road politician who needed no born-again or any other kind of religious inner life to justify his prudence.

As it happened, Carter won enough ordinarily Republican "evangelical conservative Protestant" voters to compensate for his Catholic (and Jewish) losses.[17] But the mass of his victory remained that of any Democratic winner—Catholic and Jewish Democrats, plus black Protestant Democrats—while he lost the majority of not just Protestants but of evangelical Protestants. Could evangelicals feel implicated in his victory? expect anything from him as a consequence of his religion?

By mid-1979, following Iran, the energy crisis, and the withdrawal to Camp David, Carter dropped his invocations of popular goodness in favor of the notion that a spiritual and moral crisis underlay all more specific issues. This could not have been a belated avowal of Niebuhrian principles, since, for Niebuhr, the seasons and cycles of history turned on issues of justice, with spiritual and moral conditions running along pretty much on the same level. Had Carter decided to avow the Lausanne ethic of Evangelicals for Social Action? As his energy policy and his inflation policy both seemed ineffectual, the Lausanne call for self-denial would appear to have been well-suited to the times. Let people buy less gas and spend less money, and some progress on the two most harassing problems of his administration might have been made. If Carter believed such a policy was not so much morally and spiritually justified but a necessity for long-term national survival, would he nonetheless prefer to urge its spiritual rather than its pragmatic merits? The peculiar sense gathering by late 1979 that what divided Carter from his challenger for the Democratic nomination, Edward Kennedy, was not so much matters of policy as a matter of "leadership," implied that indeed Carter had not explained himself. His Midwest campaign manager during the election, James Wall, had already anxiously tried confronting this problem. Wall, the editor of *Christian Century Magazine,* the long-time voice of ecumenical "liberal" Protestantism, had resigned his post for the campaign. Now, early in 1979, he feared something going wrong. Nominally, his target was Arthur Schlesinger, Jr.'s, much earlier attack on Carter's prescription of a government of compassion and love, but many others since had argued that Carter's personal faith and evangelical heritage provided no political guidance whatever, with the barely hidden implication they in fact made for bad politics. Wall suffered a generalized suspicion that "there are some among us who resent all things religious, especially the heart-oriented brand espoused by our current president."[18]

But merely falling back among the evangelicals was not going to help a liberal Protestant show relevance. Wall could not demonstrate it on any terms and finally had to occupy an unusual position: "The president's homilies...present the simple faith of a complex public man, but they provide no magical connection between a specific political decision and the president's personal faith....It is frustrating not to have more specifics on how the president relates [his] faith to his public decisions." In his frustration, Wall at times seemed to entertain the thought that the faith and the politics were not linked at all: "The nature of his task requires that he avoid the connection between his public action and his private faith." What Wall finally concluded, however, was that Carter simply couldn't talk about it: "The connection is there, but he will not make it public so long as he holds office."

Evangelicalism as culture

By 1976 the atmosphere of evangelical centers was that of a general flourishing, of a whole people coming into its inheritance. This inheritance was very much economic. The evangelical press published relatively few manuals of the "how to get rich" variety.[19] Preaching the gospel of success was hardly necessary. Such aides as appeared seemed calculated more to advise people how to manage their money than how to get it. The ancient poverty of the evangelical urban fringes and rural heartlands, from the piney woods of the South to California's Central Valley and desert suburbs, but especially in the old Southwest, in Oklahoma and Texas, in Muskogee, Dallas, and Waco, at last was losing its grip. The Christian rest homes, Christian hospitals, summer institutes in California, conferences and conventions and congresses in Brazil, Africa, and Switzerland, took money, as did funding the newly flourishing seminaries and theology schools and institutes. Money was assumed in the manufacture of the cassettes and the movies of Christian meaning, and in the stream of books from evangelical publishers. This was not the kind of money that had built Catholic churches in the immigrant quarters in the nineteenth century, but rather sun-belt money, so to speak, the fruit of a spreading affluence.

The expenditure of this money might have been thought to express the Lausanne ethic, of spending not on self but on relief and evangelicalism. Statistics on giving showed that the faithful in the smaller evangelical churches gave far more than did mainline church members.[20] Yet the single most massive fact was the expenditure of this money to upgrade and strengthen the separate world of evangelical culture itself. We have no evidence that affluent evangelicals distinguished themselves from their contemporaries as to "relief." And the evangelism this money subsidized appeared to have a narrow focus. First bemused, then proud of "growth," evangelicals soon turned to a systematic social-science study of growth, led by the influential findings of The Fuller Theological Seminary in Pasadena, one of evangelicalism's new elite intellectual centers.[21] Church growth, studies at Fuller showed, happened where people of a kind congregated together; on the other hand, where diverse kinds of people—singles and families, say, or old and young, white and black—congregated, growth quickly proved limited. Church growth ought to exploit "homogeneous unity," then, assuming that such growth was wanted. The objectivity of the sociological finding here could be distinguished from the nature of the impulse that welcomed it. The newly prospering evangelicals were enhancing their own world, not evangelizing the world. Only the Salvation Army still remained to testify to the Lausanne ethic's roots, and still remained quite unlike any other evangelical body. At the same time, it was reasonably evident that in this evangelizing of themselves, evangelicals showed themselves aware of the need to make sure their old purity had not consisted simply of their old poverty. They used money to defend themselves against worldliness. Conspicuous in evangelical publishing lists were manuals for parents; what had once been a simple "traditional" practice of child-rearing was becoming a matter for self-consciousness, and the reason was not that of old liberal culture, to allow a new freedom to the young in the name of self-realization, but to protect the young against just those temptations money itself intensified.[22]

The one domain in which evangelical culture appeared to have assimilated a new freedom was sex. "Intended for pleasure," as the title of one manual had it, sex by 1976 had come to be affirmed as a realm for positive experience, no longer primarily as one of danger.[23] So much was this so that evangelicals were encouraged to learn "technique" of purely biological provenance, to supplement all spiritual, moral, psychological, and symbolic dimensions. Naturally this positive appreciation of sex applied only within marriage. Evangelicals did not succumb to those symposia among liberal churchmen common in the sixties painfully picking out new "situational" ethics for "premarital" relations. Yet, so secure was this new appropriation of sexuality as part of life's blessing that the new lines of prohibition occupied by evangelical police were not dug against premarital sexuality among the young, or even against divorce and its concomitants, "extramarital" and adulterous sexuality, but against abortion and homosexuality.[24] Neither, on the basis of any evidence, appeared a practice troubling evangelical culture; both, however, offered opportunities for symbolic display in repudiating the old stereotype of Christian purity as mere repression. Evangelicalism was not conceding to the standards of the world but rather fulfilling biblical promises. And the Bible clearly excluded abortion and homosexuality from those promises.

But the anxiety that the new sexuality be justified by the Bible, not by the "situations" of modern experience, left the evangelicals in the position of having brought a live bomb into their own camp, since they continued to reject most of the ways of exploring sexuality generated by modern culture. Thus, the adoption of "technique" itself had aspects of unnegotiated surrender to the world.

Rather clear expression of the ambivalence with which evangelical spokesmen sought to escape fundamentalism's rigid rejections appeared in their tentative engagements with modern art. No temporizing with plain decadence would be justified by mere reputation: thus, regarding movies of Fellini and Werner Herzog, "Artistically sensitive Christians need to respond forcefully to the nihilistic anarchism filling their screens." Yet *Christianity Today* could allow a painter to observe, in "Painting as Propaganda," that as propaganda Communist and Christian art bore close resemblance: both were bad. Reviewers took note of spiritual dimensions in the work of Saul Bellow, of Andrew Wyeth, of the science fiction writer D. Keith Mano, of Bob Dylan, almost as though to find in their popularity signs that in the world too large numbers were coming to evangelical awareness, with the promise that evangelicalism's own inheritance would include expression in persuasive art.[25] But the roots of all this in the history of American evangelical Protestantism itself were not clear; to an outside view it looked remarkably as though the new evangelicals were following behind their liberal predecessors in opening themselves to a cosmopolitan consumption of art and, like the liberals, would find no real basis for rejecting any particular art, whatever its origins.

No direct demand upon politics, and upon an evangelical politician in particular, followed from any of these commitments. No doubt a general preference for low taxes and little government fit in with the impulse to fund and improve evangelical culture itself as an autonomous world, and Carter's own campaign spoke to such feelings. On two other fronts, however, the evangelical inheritance did intersect with matters of public moment, that is, roles for women and the practice of healing. It was within the ultimate reaches of both these that the evangelicals' traditional debate with "the world," with science, "secularism," and "individualism" overflowed old prepared positions and threatened to become fusion after all. Since by 1976 the problem of healing had been given one powerful resolution, whereas the problem of women was still generating potential, I shall discuss them in that order.

The status of divine healing—at once crucial and ambiguous—was given national prominence by the President-elect's sister. Ruth Carter Stapleton's successful practice as a healer was no embarrassment to evangelicals anxious to shake the stereotypes of primitivism.[26] Stapleton's practice derived from deep personal struggles in her own life. She had no argument with "modern" medicine. "Miracles" were not her stock-in-trade. Persons sophisticated in modern theories of psychosomatic medicine and psychological healing could interpret her two books and reports of her practice in rational ways. At the same time, Stapleton's practice fit into the tradition of healing familiar for over eighty years in American holiness and pentecostal circles.[27] The healing power of itinerant evangelists manifested "charisma," that is, the living power in the here-and-now of the Holy Spirit. Another such power, also attested in the Bible, was speaking in tongues—"glossolalia." No doubt the patrons of healing evangelists, usually poor, often isolated on farms and in villages, had their share of medical need, perhaps a larger share of dietary origin. Yet, imputing to them a higher degree of credulity, in consequence of poor schooling, would be merely invidious, and to suggest they found spiritual healing attractive as within their economic means as orthodox doctoring would not have been requires some such imputation. Healing met the need that the group itself feel itself justified and fortified; healing itinerants provided unshakable identity to people lacking many of the other sources of identity. Almost by definition, fraud and scandal accompanied the practice of divine healing, so much so that some of the greatest itinerant preachers of the living power of the Lord, such as Billy Graham, almost conspicuously abstained from charismatic displays. But just as did "modern" medicine, politics, and other professions inherently open to fraud and scandal, divine healing survived its corruptions. In the most famous example between the world wars, that of Aimée Semple MacPherson, it remains impossible to tell whether the scandal in which she concluded her ministry implied fraud in her practice or whether the success of an honest practice led to temptation. Mac-Pherson's case did help compromise the evangel through the Depression, but healers would not vanish and re-emerged in large numbers after World War II. The instructive parallel with MacPherson was Kathryn Kuhlman, who for twenty years was the leader of an independent ministry of healing in Pittsburgh.[28] Not only did Kuhlman's ministry benefit from the greater wisdom of modern medicine itself; but as the daughter of Methodist and Baptist parents, Kuhlman herself represented the emergence of healing within the mainline denominations. Practitioners and beneficiaries of healing were no longer drawn to leave an old church home for a new. The most famous of these "neo-pentecostals" was, of course, Ruth Carter Stapleton, loyal Southern Baptist.

Yet the significance of Stapleton for evangelicalism was ambiguous, as had been Kathryn Kuhlman's, and in fact, that of very many healers, increasingly so the more "neo-pentecostalism" spread into a variety of churches. Stapleton testified unwaveringly that the healing she facilitated in its turn testified to the power of the Holy Spirit. Her power was only a "blessing." She was an orthodox "charismatic," and eventually affirmed and practiced speaking in tongues. Nevertheless, Stapleton resisted locating these charismas exclusively within the frame of orthodox evangelical theology; nor would she "use" her powers to induce doctrinal beliefs. Her interpretation of her own experience left open the possibility that the divine power could express itself through many channels. Stapleton, in short, left doors open to pluralism, syncretism, historicism. There was no "religion of humanity" here, no "humanism," for her acknowledgment of a power that was transcendent and supernatural was unshaded. Yet it was not limited only to Southern-Baptist American evangelical supernatural transcendence. This had been a danger with Kuhlman, as it had been, too, if on less subtle, more "anarchic" grounds, with MacPherson. Stapleton herself radiated stability, responsibility, predictability; the real problem was that the "uncontrollable," anarchic potential lay in divine healing itself, whoever practiced it. Whoever practiced it, it might very well undermine the foundations of a stable evangelical culture.

An answer to this problem had already been brought nearly to completion, however, by 1976, in Tulsa, Oklahoma.

Granville Oral Roberts entered upon itinerant ministry when he was seventeen years old, in 1935, serving holiness and pentecostal churches across small-town, Depression-girt Oklahoma.[29] Although he felt that he had been cured of tuberculosis, by a healer, he did not practice healing himself until he was nearly thirty, in 1947. Unlike many of the itinerant healers, orphaned or fatherless, both Roberts's father, a poor farmer and part-time pentecostal-holiness preacher himself, and his mother were comparatively stable folk, who allow us the inference that Roberts's ambition to rise and his ability to organize owed something to them. The beginning of Roberts's success was not 1947, when he commenced healing, but 1948, when he commenced publishing his magazine, *Healing Waters,* and formed his organization. Roberts continued to itinerate, using specially made super-size tents, but his base was now fixed. From Tulsa headquarters, books, magazines, letters, and "anointed handkerchiefs" went out by the thousands in response to growing thousands of requests. Roberts put together a radio network; soon he began televising. Theorists of the congregational community were made anxious by the new electronic evangelism; its mass audiences seemed dispersed in individual self-centeredness, without neighbors to do unto. But Roberts's ties were not only electronic. In the fifties he established ties with wealthy Midwestern businessmen, starting the Full Gospel Businessman's Fellowship. Roberts's rise won him wide notice, but well into the sixties the national press continued to present him as essentially a pentecostal primitive somehow become faddish and sleek, presumably all-too-typical of nouveau riche Oklahoma.

In 1962 Roberts began work on a university. Since it was to have his name, it was easily presumed to have purely missionary, evangelical purposes, but by 1965 Roberts was engaged in planning for a full liberal-arts program. In 1971 Oral Roberts University won accreditation from the North Central Association of Colleges, and in a few more years had won respect at first denied. Its direction appeared to be more that of James Duke University and Leland Stanford University than of, say, Bob Jones University. When Oral Roberts University came to include a medical school, it was a medical school like other medical schools, committed to modern scientific medicine. By 1977 Roberts set about to build a huge modern hospital. No more than his medical school was this to rationalize, promote, or otherwise underwrite divine healing. Interviewed on national television, Roberts had already explained that divine healing, as he knew it, utilized the understandings of modern, scientific psychosomatic medicine. Between divine healing and modern medicine there was no conflict, really. In effect, both divine healing and psychosomatic medicine testified to religious power. What more remarkable miracles could there be than modern hospitals themselves? Where but in Tulsa's whole new complex of university, medical school, and hospital might the power of Jesus Christ be seen more clearly? Embracing these, embracing Oral Roberts himself, blessed son of a stalwart poverty, Tulsa, Oklahoma, the whole Southwest, could know themselves blessed, and the condescensions of Eastern media confounded.

Roberts's most dramatic testimony had been personal, however.

In 1968, son of a pentecostal minister, servant of pentecostal and holiness congregations in their dustbowl poverty, integrity, and stubbornness, Roberts joined the Methodist Church, specifically the Boston Avenue Church in Tulsa.[30] His act caused pain; old pentecostal faithfuls, proud of him as one of theirs, grateful for his success rooted in their obscurity, felt betrayed. Yet Roberts's apostasy made sense. From 1948 he had been careful to evade any situation in which any body of church authorities might judge or control his work. The Assemblies of God, an old holiness church, were imposing discipline upon their ministers, for instance. Roberts meant to preserve his own freedom, and, ironically, protected it precisely in joining the Methodists, who, not only in their own historic intellectual permissiveness but in their new mainline liberalism nourished their ministers' individualism. Roberts himself justified his move in a brilliant simplification: without ceasing to love his father's church, he said, without ceasing to serve Jesus, he had long felt his calling was "to deal with individuals, not the denomination."

The motivation for this enterprise remained an appetite for signs, for witness, for proof of God's power, as Roberts's fight for his hospital suggests.[31] By any prior reckoning, Tulsa had not needed a hospital. It had the largest general hospital in the state, and five private hospitals in all. It had nearly 3000 beds; almost 1000 of these ordinarily went unused. The hospital Roberts wanted left all calculations behind, entering into perhaps mystic numerology. Its 777 beds were to be paid for by contributions solicited in sums of $7, $77, $777, $7,777, $77,777, and of course, hopefully so on. Oklahoma's medical advisory board (mandated by federal legislation aimed at controlling medical costs) told Roberts "no." But Roberts had political clout. His organization, business connections, and multitude of followers were instructed to deluge Oklahoma City with letters, calls, visitations. A visitation was made to Health, Education and Welfare in Washington. Roberts's spokesman pointed out that no less than 100,000 of the 400,000 letters received at Roberts's Tulsa headquarters each month were petitions of clear medical import. What if even a modest fraction of these availed themselves of the new facilities at the City of Faith? Not only would Oral Roberts Hospital be filled, so would all the other facilities in Tulsa, and then some. Oklahoma City could not resist; neither could Washington. Roberts got only 294 beds, but that was more than a start; and he got an option for the other 483 (making the original 777), to be exercised should the need be demonstrated.

The political power evidenced here was but the means of divine power. In turn, the need being serviced was not that of old, pre-Oral Roberts Tulsa; it was that of Tulsa evangelized, Tulsa awakened to the dimensions of its real needs that provided the foundation for Oral Roberts Hospital. Awakened Tulsa and Oklahoma and the whole Southwest consisted of all those individuals who would now realize what was available to them. Their old identity, as members of divinely blessed holiness and pentecostal, and even Southern Baptist, churches and denominations, would yield to their deeper identity as individuals, with individuals' needs.

This pilgrim's progress, so remarkable in its details, at the same time conformed to a deeply conservative anxiety in evangelical culture. The rock upon which Southern, Southwestern, and Southern California popular Protestantism had always rested had been its claim to charisma, to those signs that it hosted God. The very intensity of its own folk congregational life constituted the key such sign. This intensity generated in its turn the charisma of intransigent scholars, Book-bound and embattled against "secularism" and "modernity," and of the itinerant revivalists on the other side, bringing healing, tongues, and even more emphatic evidence. So long as this folkish life knew no deep temptations from within, so long as its poverty surrounded it, it could perpetuate itself without loss. But once tempted by an affluence that had been ever-envied and, so long as it was elusive, ever-scorned, evangelical people could see their dilemma. To allow themselves to succumb to affluence, comfort, middle-class hypocrisy, to "the world," would be to lose the signs, their proof of status in the eyes of Jesus Christ, the Lord. Yet, to cling to the signs, in all their inexplicable anarchistic power, to insist upon tongues speaking no language understood by the world, to rely upon healing inexplicable in any up-to-date research laboratory, would be to remain isolated in William Jennings Bryanish dusty, out-of-date, more than slightly comical prairie backwardness. To resist this was not a matter of mere pride. Evangelicals had to remember their evangelical duty: they must convey their word, in the best, most persuasive language possible. What language could be more powerful and persuasive than that of science itself? of modern science? specifically, the language that spoke to the final unit of evangelical reckoning, the existential, real, concrete, individual himself, the evangelizable human person existent as such in his mortal, physical, biological, medically definable body? And what other language was this than that of modern medical science? Evangelical duty, it was, then, that justified Roberts's domestication of divine healing to a "materialistic" hospital. What could be more convincing—more "convicting," in an old Puritan evangelists' word—to the individual than his realization that it was only in his bodily identity that he would experience decisions for eternity? Hospitals, underwritten by evangelism, could contain much of the immense energy resident in every individual awakened to himself, made aware that no poverty, no culture, no "denomination," as Roberts said, no "world," as all evangelicals said, limited him. How to promote this awakening, on the one hand, and prevent it from creating anarchy, on the other, found an answer in universities and hospitals.

Whether or not the evangelized Tulsa of 1977 would prove a model for larger triumphs in 1980, 1984, or even 1999, its provincial limits were more obvious by the summer of that year. In July, some 40,000 charismatic Christians—*Time* magazine said 45,000—gathered from all corners of the United States for three days and four nights in Kansas City, Missouri, in the largest convention Kansas City, at least, had yet seen.[32] Daytimes, these thousands fellowshipped all over town in workshops, conferences, and seminars. Nights, they rallied in the Chief's up-to-date new Arrowhead Stadium. Preachers declaimed, priests celebrated, and the giant electronic scoreboard's computer-controllers rendered visions of love-doves, spirit-flames, exhortations—"Praise the Lord"—and Jesus' own face, twenty times life-size, in primary colors. Again, as in the bicentennial year, national media, impressed by numbers, paid attention. But again, and even more so, numbers were not what mattered.

Some of the charismatics in Kansas City belonged to the old holiness and pentecostal churches, accustomed to tongues and healing. They, like the numerous Southern Baptists present, found the appearance of "independent Bible teachers" who "travelled widely," such as "Bob" Munford of Cupertino, California, quite unsurprising. Others, though, Catholics, found the presence of Leon Joseph Cardinal Suenens, primate of Belgium, while flattering, not at all exotic. The largest single group of Protestants was Lutheran. Others from mainline denominations, each already provided with their own denominational charismatic fellowship, included Methodists, Episcopalians, and Presbyterians. A number of United Church of Christ members, attending "unaffiliated," found each other and organized a fellowship on the spot. So did some Nazarenes, accustomed to seeing Nazarene preachers professing charismatic blessing disfranchised by Nazarene headquarters. The sheer variety of churches represented at this celebration showed that charisma no longer belonged to pentecostals and holiness people or to old-line evangelicals, to domesticate as they wished. In fact, the spirit of Kansas City was much more lyric, anarchic, and ecstatic than that of a tradition coming to assured maturity in organization and affluence. The planners of the meeting were a group of Catholics; for charismatic Catholics, charisma constituted a shaking of the church, a joyful sign that despite itself the old structure could be filled with immediate divine energy. Some churchmen were emphatic about the stakes; an Episcopalian at Kansas City predicted that soon only two kinds of Episcopal churches would remain: charismatic or dead. Practically all the mainline Protestants saw themselves escaping the sterility and stagnation that had overtaken their own church traditions, and could only hope charismatics might mean their own churches' rebirth. In Ruth Carter Stapleton, the celebrants heard a charismatic whose roots were not in mainline liberalism but old evangelicalism. Yet Southern Baptists were not without suspicion of the Word in charismatic forms, as Stapleton's evangel evinced the powerful attraction exerted by individual needs, individual cases, individual talent, the temptation to devise individual methods. Had not Graham built the Southern Baptists into Number

One by steady labor, without tongues, without healing? Was the inheritance now to be undermined by grateful patienthood and heedless rapture?

As Oral Roberts's Tulsa apotheosis suggested, classically biblical forms of divine healing were susceptible to assimilation within the forms of modern organization, modern science, modern technology, into "the magic of modern medicine." Modern medicine itself had become far more aware, on scientific grounds alone, of the unity of the person than it had been in Mary Baker Eddy's time, was far more "holistic" and "psychosomatic," proceeded in a more "person-oriented" way. The problem was to infuse the charisma of healing into the whole institution of healing, so that instead of seeming the gift of essentially unpredictable itinerants, it was obtainable as a predictable and rational expectation. Roberts's "City of Faith" in Tulsa was an inspired gesture of such institutionalization, but it was evident that the risk was too great. If "church" was allowed to become university and hospital, it would be exposed far more than the church in its usual guise to the dominance of reason, science, organization, and rationalization. The signs of divine power, diffused into the operations of the whole system, would once again seem to fade. Was there not a way that the church itself could enjoy charisma in its own operations, keep it from breaking out into schisms, yet shelter it against acculturation, institutionalization, "liberalism," and thus preserve its meaning as an evangel, as testimony that healing, revival, renewal, regeneration, rebirth, were the fundamental qualities of God?

Evangelicalism as religion

Along with such false philosophies of modernity as liberalism, humanism, rationalism, secularism, neo-orthodoxy, and science, evangelicals were very much inclined to include another, modern feminism. Systematic opposition to the Equal Rights Amendment flowed from evangelical sources. The counter-philosophy of positive womanhood offered sharp attacks on feminist leaders.[33] As evangelical preoccupation with abortion and homosexuality grew, it easily linked feminism to its targets, rarely trying to distinguish one kind of feminist from another. The basic reason for the generalized caution and suspicion seemed evident. Billy Graham did not indulge in anti-feminist stereotyping; in fact, he made clear his approval of all efforts to get justice for women in equal pay, and he never questioned the equality of young women so far as higher education was concerned. Yet Graham (and his wife) opposed ERA; ERA, they feared, would overreach justice and distort those relationships in which men were expected to take the lead, bear responsibility, and provide shelter for life; relationships in which women found true leadership and felt secure fulfilling their true roles. As a culture coming into its inheritance, evangelicalism gave high priority to its own stability. Everything was connected to everything else. The parents being urged to attend to their duties were connected to the churches, both parents and churches connected to the farms and the businesses and professions underwriting them. Not at all unlike manuals of liberal and secular origin, evangelical manuals stressed the importance of fathers being fathers. The legitimate joy to be found in sex in marriage was a shared joy, in no way intended to weaken parenthood or fatherhood. Feminism threatened all this, threatened connections, threatened stability. An odd sort of double standard appeared even among those sympathetic to the "evangelical feminists" emerging in the early seventies and organizing their Evangelical Women's Caucus by 1975. Naturally, they, like the anti-feminists, made their case by citing—and interpreting—Bible texts. Was it not true, though, it was asked, that the evangelical feminists had been influenced by "feminism" first, and then went to the texts to make their case?[34] If not disingenuous, this was unfair, for there was no evidence the anti-feminists had gone to their texts before becoming anti-feminists. In general, it was hard for evangelicals to interpret feminism sympathetically. They might often grant the "religious" origins of "humanism," of Marxism, and perhaps even plan to exploit that origin in their own effort to convert liberals, humanists, and Marxists back to faith. But feminism somehow was only secular, and no evangel adapted to feminism seemed prepared. One reason for this, evidently, was that the disturbance threatened by feminism bore, finally with most significance, not just against family order and even economic and social order but against religious order and the church. Feminism could only mean women as ministers. For most evangelicals, the ministry still carried its paternal, patriarchal, patristic charge; God was still Father and Fatherhood. Evangelical culture's attachment to the Word, Scripture, Law, still echoed of the Old Testament, of tribalism and of the tribe's patriarchs. None of this would be supportable with full enjoyment of the American inheritance, full settlement into affluence. The prospect of women ministers would threaten a culture crisis, but evangelicalism's own determination to master modern culture would render tricky all efforts to cope with the crisis by regression back into paternalism.

By 1976 some 10,000 women were ordained as ministers in American Protestantism.[35] As only about 5 percent of the ranks of their profession, women ministers were hardly of more consequence than women lawyers, accountants, engineers, or full professors in liberal-arts faculties. Still, the proportion was growing and it seemed certain to go on growing. Something like a revolution was happening in some seminaries from the early seventies: here and there entering classes enrolled more than 50 percent women. Of course, bitter struggles were still taking place, like those of the sixties, and of the more than two hundred Protestant denominations, from the handful with millions to the scores with handfuls, hardly a third had any ordained women at all. But there seemed little doubt which way things were tending. Whether women would do as ministers, in significant numbers, would almost certainly be tested before the century was over.

By no means were these 10,000 women the fruits of feminism. Fully one-quarter were Salvation Army women. Here, women had found equality, in that supposedly most masculine of institutions, an "army," prepared, in accord with an army's reason for being, to sacrifice their own lives for others. At least another quarter were ministers in small pentecostal and holiness churches, a strong fraction of these being black. The impulse here, less that of the army's begging pennies on Main Street to succor despair on skidrow than of offering stability and reassurance midst the ghetto's terrors and the impoverished prairie's hysterias, simply reflected an equality built into the culture women helped hold together. Ironically, as pentecostal people began to thrive, the incidence of women in their ministry would begin to decline. Where women ministers were on the rise was in the mainline liberal denominations, aside from the Episcopalians, whose debate presumably reflected some higher ingredient of sacramental meanings in their ministry, which more nearly approached that of priest than the ministry of Methodists, erstwhile Congregationalists, Presbyterians, etc. Of course, one wing of Christian opposition remained intransigent; obviously for Roman Catholicism to ordain women would be more revolutionary than for Unitarians or Methodists. The variety among the 10,000, then, testified clearly that there were several sources for women in the ministry; by the same token, there were several meanings, and there could be more.

The tension within evangelical culture over feminism may have been temporary. As the older leaders sensed a belated and unexpected triumph, they brought with them their memories of the old humiliation and their attachment to old styles. As Billy Graham's ministry wove toward its end, it did not suggest the need for a successor. Elsewhere, in such pulpits as W.A. Criswell's in Dallas, men of thirty, thirty-five, even forty years' service in one pulpit were recapitulating an old Puritan style of patriarchalism that had faded elsewhere a century earlier. These mighty pulpits, facing congregations of 10,000, 15,000, even 20,000, were unimaginable inhabited by a woman. Nor did they seem to fit new counsels in evangelical circles. Evangelical feminists met most welcome at the newest evangelical seminary, where the youngest new leaders were at work, at Fuller in Pasadena. There, one of the key programs was its School of Psychology, started in 1965, offering the Ph.D. in clinical psychology, fully certified by the American Psychological Association, obviously to the end of training a ministry skilled in counseling, counseling "individuals," plainly enough, in Oral Roberts's sense, not denominations. Billy Grahams and W.A. Criswells were unlikely to be generated by Fuller. But was it conceivable that Fuller was behind the times? that it was taking up "psychology" and "counseling" just as psychology and counseling may have begun to fade in the liberal denominations?

"Most clergymen who are honest with themselves would confess that pastoral counseling is too often a waste of time."[36] There was no way the clergyman who unburdened himself this way to the readers of *Christianity Today* could prove whether he really spoke for "most" or not, but the structure of his lament had its own interest. People coming for counsel, he said, often didn't listen; or if they heard, often didn't understand; or if they understood, often didn't change their actions to suit. Their pastors then began to fret, feel guilty, suffer depression, to doubt themselves: Was it their fault? Were they inept? Had they not had a true calling? Why did counseling fail? Of course, pastoral ineptitude and even lack of true calling might provide the answers, but this disillusioned pastor thought not. He offered four thoughts. First, was it not true that the afflictions of people who came, in need, misery, despair, for counseling —a couple whose marriage had died, a community leader harassed by drink—were not the results of bad luck, bad parents, even sin, but of "will"? People willed their miseries for themselves, and "changing the will is hard work," much harder than pastoral counseling could afford. Then also: "Ministerial counseling is given free of charge." People therefore did not value it. Further: Ministers could be called any time, without appointments, again, to the devaluing of the process. Finally: "Counseling as we know it was not at the core of the New Testament Church." This last was hardly a reason for the failure of counseling; it simply provided evangelical—as distinguished from practical—grounds for dropping it. But supposing pastoral counseling was to be maintained. How would these problems be met? Should ministers charge? insist upon keeping nights and weekends, holidays and vacations, inviolate? undertake the kind of long, regular, expensive analysis adapted to affect "will"? These were not plausible. But as compared to men, women were not devalued by not being paid for their work; being always available precisely expressed a normative womanhood; and was it not possible that the "will" which resisted counseling might be at least in part provoked to resist by another will, and that a counselor who did not raise a confrontation of wills might have less of a problem?

Naturally, this prospect could be interpreted ironically from another angle: "Sexism causes work done by women to be devalued in society; when large numbers of them enter a field, the men tend to leave. . . . The entrance of large numbers of women into ordained ministry may cause it to become a 'female profession' like nursing or primary school teaching."[37] But if sexism ruled, how could women be pouring into the ministry if it was, in fact, a "largely male caste system"? The explanation was that its gates had been opened from within: ". . . already associated with the private sphere and with feminine culture characteristics of being loving and kind . . . ," already feminized, in short, the ministry might easily become "female." The transformation would feed on itself, while, fortuitously, being fed by the outside force on economics: "budget cuts leave the largely white, male tenured faculty as the righteous remnant. . . . Seminaries may become obsolete. . . . Churches may find it cheaper to provide training schools for women like those for nurses or secretaries. . . ." The irony at work here was mostly that facing feminism, for despite the assignment of this scenario to "sexism," even its feminist author could not resist noting the fulfillment of some feminist ideals: "This development might, however, have a side benefit: an ever-increasing erosion of clergy status would diminish the line of separation between clergy and laity." Still further irony suggested that women in the ministry would most deeply suit the evangelicals themselves, more than the old mainline liberal denominations. As younger evangelical scholars got beyond the clutch of loyalty to the old fundamentalists and realized that the pursuit of "inerrant" Scripture threatened "the power of the Holy Spirit," they would be free to connect with evangelical feminism's center: "Whenever women have moved into visible church leadership, the relative importance of Scripture and tradition has been reduced and the legitimacy of personal religious experience has been enhanced. . . . Although there is not a direct correlation between the women's movement and the charismatic renewal, both developments challenge traditional sources of religious authority and open up possibilities for new forms of leadership."[38]

Of course, the charismatics at Kansas City had not been all women, or in majority women. Yet, with its emphasis upon personal experience and upon healing, charismatic evangelicalism spoke directly to the evolution of the evangelical tradition as a whole toward service "to the individual, not the denomination." By comparison with Roberts's huge institutions, recapitulating and exaggerating all that was hierarchial, bureaucratic, centralized, all that tended to generate specialized medicine rather than holistic medicine, scientific care rather than person-centered care, all that had facilitated masculine competitions and masculine hegemony, a ministry of women would far more nearly fulfill evangelicalism's own deepest commitment, even as it might confront feminism with irony.

A "female ministry" would also prove compatible with deep dynamics—not structures—underlying American religious history generally. A Gallup Poll of 1978 nicely caught this long tradition in its latest stage.[39] Sixty million adult Americans, it appeared—40 percent of the total—were "unchurched." How had a generation of widespread evangelism missed them? No people in the whole world were witness to more religious activity; was this population testimony to some basic defect in evangelism? But perhaps they had not been overlooked: these "unchurched" millions "believed" the same things that the "churched" did, it appeared, and in about the same high proportions. But the same point might be made in reverse: while 86 percent of the unchurched declared that the individual should arrive at his/her "beliefs" independently of churches and synagogues, so did not less than 76 percent of the churched. So exactly what was the challenge to evangelism? Many—a quarter—even said they had the experience of being born-again. Who were these millions? The proportion among them who were young was higher than for the population as a whole, as were the proportion who were unmarried and the proportion who were male; predictably, then, also, were the proportion who were "mobile" as to residence. Unmarried young men on the move: who would evangelize them? Surely not women ministers in the church. Once Dwight Moody may have, but in 1976 the world open to such young men had changed. Other polls indicated that 6 million adult Americans practiced TM—Transcendental Meditation, not many fewer practiced yoga, and a heavy proportion of both were under twenty-five, probably a majority of them men.[40] The ranks of Hare Krishna were open; books of Ayn Rand and Robert Ringer were available, as was the toughening of ego, self, mind, and soul in the $250 course of training in Werner Erhard's est. There was, of course, place for young women, too, in these, as with the Reverend Sun Myung Moon and a whole display of communes, communities, communalities, farms, collectives, cooperatives, collaboratives, families, workshops, sisterhoods; and the case might have been defended that by 1976, for the first time in American history, large numbers of unmarried young women would also lead "unchurched" lives, much as had—and did—their brothers. This time, perhaps, the implacable rise of individualism, from hidden springs, like groundwater, would dissolve the old foundations. The 1978 poll indicated that despite the persistence of high rates of membership and of belief, those affirming the "importance" of religion in their daily lives were declining: 75 percent in 1952, 70 percent in 1965, 53 percent in 1978.[41]

Was there a logic for the refreshening of religion by means of a female ministry? Certainly, focused on pastoral counseling, healing, and therapy, perfecting rites and symbols of solace, nurture, and regeneration, female-ministered churches with their "holistic" and "person-centered" approach would offer far more formidable challenges to orthodox bureaucratic medicine than mere spiritual healing did. Meanwhile, shrunken in membership, specializing in only one dimension of religious experience, they could contribute to the recognition that other kinds of religious expression were important, basic, "normal." Innovative and entrepreneurial, the healthy and vital young, no longer in need of mother-nurture, not yet in need of mother-healing, would be freed to give unambiguously religious form to their demands upon the dead, bureaucratic, command-oriented structures of that "secular" America of corporations, government, unions, schools, and media that alarmed both "humanists" and "evangelicals" alike. Their missions, communes, retreats, hermitages, pilgrimages, would no longer be condescended to as mere "cults," "fringes," or even "healthy stages" on life's way to adjustment.[42] In other words, female-ministered "churches" might liberate the practice of male-led utopias.

Would the evangelical churches open themselves to this logic, or at least succumb to it? Would the inert but heavy weight of patriarchalism they carried from the past—manifest in such stigmata of the traditional male ministry as the calls for submission to "inerrant" authority (rather than to "experience"), the calls for moral "leadership," and the hopes for a "spread" of the gospel—continue to seem a treasure or be recognized as a burden? So long as evangelicals suffered from the need to feel superior to the mainline churches, and thus to pursue "growth" as the plainest evidence, in a democratic society, for that superiority, they could not evolve. But Billy Graham's foundering with Nixon suggested the end of something. Oral Roberts's assimilation of spiritual healing into a civic welfare culture suggested new processes of acculturation at work within and upon the old separated folk. And Jimmy Carter's refusal to offer crusade suggested the spread not of gospel but of realism. Were his policies "Niebuhrian" or merely expedient, confused, weak? Whichever, win or lose, Carter, the only evangelical among major candidates, exposed the cries for "leadership" to his right—Reagan, Connally—and to his left—Kennedy—as functions of weakness, not of strength. Perhaps the issue for evangelicalism, whether it would persist in its triumphalistic impulses, would be settled where old-time evangelical leaders themselves had no intention of letting it be settled: among women. Would the anti-feminist evangelicals promoting "total joy" in wife- and motherhood prove up to inventing ever more refined techniques of self-persuasion? And would evangelical wives and mothers be persuaded? It seemed likely that evangelical women, just as "mainline" women, would recognize that feminism provided support for more than abortion and lesbianism, and, most of all, could be enlisted for protection of motherhood and children. Then the idea that there ought to be churches that did what good mothers did would take hold among them as well. Then evangelical manhood might realize in turn that just as it was crippling to go on tied to mother, so it was crippling to go on tied to "our kind of people." As New York's horsecars, in the heterogeneousness of their passengers, were emblematic, as Henry James, Sr., thought, of the "sabbath of eternity," churches, too, even as they provided passage, might suggest the salvation to be found in leaving safe havens.[43]

RELIGIOUS RIGHT AND WRONGS

IN THE nineteen-eighties, evangelical fires of the seventies burned themselves out. Charismatic healing withdrew into its endemic obscurity. No more collective ecstasies such as that in Kansas City in 1976 were scheduled. Holy tongues spoke to private audiences. Yet what was left behind was not ashes. It was politics. The campaigns of Ronald Reagan exhibited a fusion of religion and politics unprecedented in modern American history. Lavalike, it threatened to consume old landmarks, both political and religious. The basic form of the religion in this fusion was not evangelical but fundamentalist. At its best, evangelicalism ached for the heart open to the energies of grace. The Moral Majority had no need to open its heart; its heart was already filled. The urge of fundamentalism was to be right. To be right was to be righteous, and to be righteous was to be privileged to repel and assail the unrighteous. The America surrounding the Moral Majority was not suffused with God's grace but sullied by "liberalism," "secular humanism," Satan. Ronald Reagan had spent his manhood warning the righteous of the evils rising around them. By the time they met, in 1980, man and movement were, in their fundamentals, at one.

Already in decline, the teaching of positive thinking would have no place in the politics of fundamentalism. Whether supply-side economics could reconstruct some of the basic conditions under which the popular psychology of mind cure and positive thinking flourished was another question. I shall return to it later on. But the contributions of the religious Right to the campaigns of Ronald Reagan were exercises in authority, not psychological self-manipulation, in tribalism, not individualism. Of course, new voices of positive thinking were still to be heard. Certain ecosystems seemed almost designed to sustain them, magic kingdoms echoing positive thinking's own need to take for granted the security and prosperity of the culture around it.

Catherine Ponder, described by some as "the Norman Vincent Peale among lady ministers," found her way to California by the eighties.[1] Ponder had served in Unity Church pulpits since 1956. Personal vicissitudes had drawn her to Texas; there, widowed a second time, she once again had to support herself. She later moved to Palm Desert, California, where she founded her new "global" ministry. Ponder's notable contribution to the literature of positive thinking, in explication of her conviction that the "Bible is the greatest textbook on prosperity ever written," was to produce a series of books on "Bible millionaires," including one on Joshua, one on Moses, and one on "the millionaire from Nazareth." In endless anecdotal snippets, she related mind cure's efficacy for more than just paying bills: for protection against mugging, for clairvoyance at cards, for melting away fat. Ponder ignored those impulses in Christian Science and other mind-cure groups toward de-masculinizing, possibly androgynizing, even feminizing God. All her references to God were consistently as Father. This may have registered some anxiety at the certainty of Supply. In the most heartfelt chapter she added in 1985 to her long tract, *The Dynamic Laws of Prosperity*, first issued in 1965, she discussed tithing. Giving one's tenth, she wrote, promoted circulation as against congestion, impelled money to flow and grow rather than stagnate. The Old Testament Jews had learned this lesson: when their billionaire, Solomon, had begun to tighten up, poverty and exile had not been far behind. And, she noted, one should tithe on one's gross, not just on one's net. We can only guess whether in the propinquity of the Global Ministry in modest Palm Desert to the secular glitter of Croesuslike Palm Springs there was ache, if not resentment.

But positive thinking was still capable of promoting big-time success. In Garden Grove, California, Robert Schuller not only built his fabulous, multimillion-dollar Crystal Cathedral—"larger than Notre Dame"—but beamed out his television show, "Hour of Power." Sometimes lumped in with other successful television preachers, such as Oral Roberts, Jimmy Swaggert, Pat Robertson, James Robison and Jerry Falwell, Schuller was quite unlike the others theologically. Having once been part of Norman Vincent Peale's own church in New York City, Schuller had started his "Positive Thinking Center" in Garden Grove as a young minister in 1954. His television success was based on a steady clientele: even as the evangelical TV preachers experienced some decline in their audiences beginning in the late seventies, Schuller's numbers held up, at somewhere around one and a quarter million homes. Schuller spent no time in Manichean assaults on "secular humanism," "liberalism" and moral decline. Subtracting even the minimal structure lent Peale's methods by Smiley Blanton's psychiatry, Schuller ignored boundaries between unconscious, subconscious, superconscious, etc., in favor simply of "God's Power Within You" activated by "possibility perspectives." Getting rid of "impossibility thinking" cleared the mind for being positive. Schuller could hardly fail to realize that in booming Orange County many in his flock did not need to be told how to become wealthy. Now and then he included in his own endless anecdotes reference to the sad fate of some successful men: "All of these men learned well the art of making money, but not one of them learned how to live."[2] Still, it was not as though the audience tuned in to "Hour of Power" needed to learn how to spend its money. The Southern California way of life took care of that. The Crystal Cathedral manifested the glory of prosperity.

Farther south, in sunny San Diego, Terry Cole-Whittaker brought the human potential movement into a Religious Science pulpit.[3] Soon she established her own Terry Cole-Whittaker ministries funded through classes, church collection plates and a TV show. "The Rev. Terry is the evangelist of the yuppies. Bubbly, bouncy and relentlessly upbeat, she preaches a gospel of 'happiness now' to her congregation of young, urban professionals. Wealth is good, not bad. Money is only an energy flow." "'Our ministry isn't into sin, guilt, disease, pain or hunger,'" she explained. As ever, local pastors of the old denominations complained: "'She has distorted the Christian message. . . . She doesn't believe in sin. So there is no need for Jesus Christ.'" To objections that her secret was simply to tell everyone they're wonderful, Rev. Terry had the obvious response: "'Of course I tell people they're wonderful. . . . It's true!'" Her own capacity for hope could be read in her own life: after four divorces she hadn't given up. "'I'm going to keep doing it until I get it right.'" By 1987 Cole-Whittaker, in workshops expounding "the Unfolding Female Master," appeared to be moving toward a more gender-inflected evangel.

Of course Ponder, Schuller and Cole-Whittaker registered only one dimension in Southern California culture. Rev. Fred Schwarz's Christian Anti-Communism Crusade had scorched through the region not too many years before, Orange County had sent a John Birch Society member to Congress, and there too Ronald Reagan had first whetted his speech on the dangers threatening freedom in America. Would Schuller's flock vote for Reagan as President? Ponder's? Cole-Whittaker's? The sheer massiveness of Mr. Reagan's majorities south of the Tehachapis would seem to say so. Yet the point of fusion between political and religious Right would not be—could not be—in California. The Moral Majority arose in an America that regarded California with ambivalence and had had no chance to practice mind cure and positive thinking.

The conversion of evangelical religion into fundamentalism and politics entailed spiritual crisis nowhere more poignant than where evangelicalism itself had held most promise, that is, among Southern Baptists.[4] Traditionally given to local autonomies, congregationalism and an open approach to the Bible, Southern Baptists since the war had been showing symptoms of evolution into a standard denominationalism. With Southern Theological Seminary in Louisville as their headquarters, *Christianity Today* their magazine, Billy Graham their charismatic hero, a postwar generation of new leaders had sought escape from the rigidities and negativism of the fundamentalism of the twenties, freedom from sterile debates over biblical "inerrancy" and "infallibility," outreach, cautious but firm, to matters of social justice and ethical honor. They were making progress by the late sixties and seventies. Reaction followed. One of the moderates described the reaction as that of clergy (and laymen) from small one-church towns, "afraid of living in a society where their church is not the only institution," afraid of cities, afraid of science, afraid of pluralism. But the opponents of modernization had more going for them than simple nostalgia. By 1980 a onetime president of the Southern Baptist Convention, Rev. Jimmy Allen, was warning against capitulation to "right-wing politics and sword-rattling jingoism."[5] The rising Baptist Right had outside support—big-time money and big-time politics. Slowly but surely, Baptist moderates lost their control within the denomination; by 1986 their new fundamentalist opponents had drawn within reach of taking over the seminaries and agencies and even pulpits of the church; Ronald Reagan sent them a message of congratulations.

The struggle among Southern Baptists had come to involve far more than who would control denominational seminaries and machinery. In effect, the Baptist fundamentalists, opposed to the "liberals," had been tempted by an offer of power in a national alliance, and they had succumbed. Their tempter was Jerry Falwell. In his early years as one of the thriving new television evangelists, Falwell held to the old fundamentalist "separatism," which most emphatically had rejected politics for concentration on the Word, a tradition basic to old-fashioned Southern Baptism. In 1979 Falwell changed his mind. He had waited long enough, he said, for someone else to "lead the way out of the wilderness."[6] Finally, he decided, he had to. He started Moral Majority. Moral Majority was to be a nonpartisan political organization, a "special interest group providing a voice for a return to sanity in these United States of America." From the start it worked against the reelection of the evangelical, born-again Baptist already in the White House and for the nomination, then the election of Ronald Reagan.

Falwell also abandoned another of his religious convictions for the sake of politics. Late in the nineteenth century various English Biblicists had invented a new scheme for history. Drawing—imaginatively—on the books of Daniel and Revelation, they declared that God had arranged history into discrete epochs known as "dispensations."[7] The dispensation in which mankind subsisted at present was scheduled for a spectacular end: first, eligible Christians would be plucked away from earth to safety in a "rapture"; second, Satanic forces would engage in an annihilatory war in which Jews would be massacred; third, following this "tribulation," Christ would return to earth as general of the raptured Christians behind him, who would proceed to destroy God's enemies in the battle of Armageddon; finally, the new dispensation would begin a thousand years of Christian peace (in which Jews lucky enough to have survived might, converted to Christianity, share too). It seems fair to say that historical analysis has not yet discovered the sociopsychological correlates of belief in these views. Presumably so extreme a devaluation of the present should imply extreme disinheritance and hopelessness, but this has not been remotely demonstrated of the rhapsodic premillennial dispensationalists, certainly not of Jerry Falwell. The most operational meaning of the belief seems to be Falwell's reported response to the prospect of nuclear war: the prospect did not alarm him, he said, for he knew he would not be there. As critics have noted, this outlook was notable at the least for its lack of love, a traditional component of piety in liberal Protestantism. In any case, the marching orders for Moral Majority, Inc., did not contain a breath of rapture. Moral Majority had gone over to a pressing concern for this earth, a determined care for the immediate future. In standard theological terms, it had converted from "pre-" to "post-" millennialism. Whereas Falwell openly conceded his change of belief about entering politics, he never discussed what had happened to the rapture. It is by no means clear that any political pressure to quench it had come to be directed at him. Good report had it that the candidate, in his amiable way, more than once had traded thoughts about Armageddon with his clerical supporters.[8] Yet, whatever the record of hidden beliefs might one day prove to be, it seems quite clear that from 1979 the plan of the political preachers did not include much preoccupation with the date of the coming rapture, tribulation, holocaust, Armageddon and intercession. They hoped for a Republican victory and an America dominated by the Moral Majority.

After the election, Falwell boasted: "I think that these Christian people came out of the pews into the polls and caused the avalanche."[9] Reasons abounded why he—and others—might think so. A "Washington for Jesus" rally in April had set a tone for the campaign. Falwell and other TV preachers had had free access at the Republican convention in Detroit. The candidate went to Dallas immediately after the convention to tell right-wing preachers at a "National Affairs Briefing" that, while he knew they could not endorse him, he could endorse them. The campaign's technicians of mass mobilization, Paul Weyrich, Richard Viguerie and Howard Phillips, themselves right-wing Catholics, all took pains to coordinate with the Moral Majority. This was not a normal campaign's solicitude for every preacher, priest and rabbi. Reagan and his operatives conspicuously snubbed mainline clergy, "National Council of Churches Protestants," explicitly attacked by Falwell for supporting "every kind of left-wing program imaginable."[10]

Nevertheless, as election analysis has shown, Falwell's claim was far from the truth.[11] First, there was no avalanche: Reagan won just over 50% of the vote. Second, support for Reagan from Moral Majority voters did not stand out from his support among others. Not even the startling defeat of several liberal senators targeted by the Moral Majority proved to be due to Christian Right votes: analysis showed that support for these men had declined on a much broader basis. Soon, confirmation of these findings would appear in the elections of 1982 when the Christian Right failed in most of its targeted races. Election analysis has led to a consensus: the election of 1980 was lost, not won, Jimmy Carter's bare 40% registering an irresistible sense of the failure of his presidency. Perhaps the last previous such result had been nearly half a century before, in 1932, when Ronald Reagan himself cast his first vote, for Franklin Roosevelt, in an election that was mostly a judgment against Herbert Hoover.

Reagan's first term hardly began to fulfill fantasies of power within the new religious Right. Along with foreign policy, economic issues were given first priority by the White House. The political reasons were obvious: Reagan's election had been owed as much to the high inflation and high interest rates under the Carter administration as to anything else. Besides, it was probable that, in the White House, ideology put economics first, with the President's sweeping "supply side" tax bill. Finally, it was not at all clear that the President's men, including James Baker and Edwin Meese, had not concluded on the basis of analysis that they owed little to the Moral Majority. At all events, spokesmen for the religious Right were soon voicing impatience at the administration's delay in addressing their "social issues." James Robison, the Dallas-based national TV evangelist, wondered if it was not time for the administration to "take a little heat" on the moral, social issues. Even one of the mass-mail technicians, Paul Weyrich, judged that the new men in the White House did not understand voters motivated by non-economic issues.[12]

None of this prevented the religious Right from treating 1984 as a year of jubilee, however.[13] Reagan and his operatives collaborated. Falwell, who had emerged as by far the most conspicuous of the right-wing TV preachers, was given the platform at the Republican convention in Miami to hail the President as "God's instrument in rebuilding America." One of the most hard-shell of all the old "inerrantist" fundamentalists, Rev. W. A. Criswell, heavily subsidized by Texas oil money, delivered the convention's concluding prayer. Walter Mondale's classic "social gospel" Protestantism, dedicated to charity, love and justice, was simply submerged in a stigmatization of the Democratic party as not only a congeries of special economic interests but, in political convert

Jeane Kirkpatrick's words, "San Francisco Democrats," a congeries of special moral interests, those of permissiveness, feminism, abortion, homosexuality, a nuclear freeze, "secular humanism."

This shaping of the campaign into moral and quasi-religious terms suited the President and his political operatives. It was likely from the start that Reagan was guaranteed overwhelming reelection on economic grounds alone. A painful recession in 1982–83 had not been blamed on him; it seemed the price to be paid to wring out inflation. Inflation had come down, startlingly; interest rates had come way down; the high unemployment of the recession had come down. Various less vivid things deeply troubled some economists: unprecedented deficit, as far as the eye could see; unprecedented trade imbalances; accelerating collapse of old basic industries; spreading "structural" (that is, "permanent") unemployment in various ghettoized groups, etc. But these premonitions hardly weighed against the actual experience of a return, by the summer of 1984, of what felt like good times again. Of course the President did not hesitate to hail his economic successes, just as he held economic failure to Jimmy Carter's account in 1980. But a campaign on straightforward economic grounds was not enough. In Reagan's own long pursuit of the presidency, he had never dealt with economics. His theme had always been the moral threat to America.[14] It had been simply his good luck to find serious economic disorders to his benefit when he finally won his prize in Detroit in 1980. At that time, large numbers of voters who voted for him were uneasy about Reagan both as to foreign affairs and as to his views on the moral issues. Ironically, such voters had been reassured by 1984: he had not proved more than rhetorically extreme in foreign affairs; he had not pressed for constitutional amendments on the moral issues. But if this restraint had proceeded from sensible political prudence, the campaign showed that Reagan was not interested simply in eight years in office.

Search for the roots of Reagan's moral vision of the world has dwelt upon his combat with Communists during his terms as head of the Screen Actors Guild in Hollywood. Others have suggested his identification with his chosen profession itself, inducing an inability to distinguish himself from his roles in movies. Still others have preferred rather to stress his acculturation in the local world of small-town Protestantism in pre-depression Illinois.[15] None of these lack merit. Yet they fail to effect closure on Ronald Reagan the individual. Anti-Communist combats, movie illusions, village tribalism each contained many potentials for development. Rarely do they impel presidential quests. Speculation might suggest one self-image continuous from youth to the White House, Reagan's service during several summers of his young manhood as a lifeguard at Lowell Park on the banks of the Rock River near his hometown, Dixon. Analysis of Reagan's movie roles might or might not reveal some emphasis upon themes of rescue, but of course Reagan's movie roles were not his to choose. He did choose to save the Screen Actors Guild. Then, by the late nineteen-fifties, Reagan began his career as a public speaker offering one basic speech, with one basic theme, the danger in which America found itself, with one clear subtheme, his own readiness to save it. Just what this danger was was never as simple as the dark waters of the Rock River. Communism was the obvious choice, but Reagan's own success in the SAG implied that Communists were not really reliable as a long-term threat to America. The crash of Joseph McCarthy's campaign in the mid-fifties confirmed that. Something more pervasive, if possibly more diffuse and elusive, was needed. The hero-president who had saved America in Reagan's own youth, Franklin Roosevelt, had had a clear danger to save it from, the depression. But America seemed prosperous when Reagan set out in the last years of the Eisenhower administration on his search.

We await further analysis to better understand just why Reagan solved his problem by identifying "government" as the danger to America. Certainly his basic competition as national lifesaver had come to be the government since Franklin Roosevelt's time. It was the federal government that presided over pensions for the old, extended welfare to the needy, rescued farmers crushed in world markets, headed off collisions of class, sheltered precious environments against local insult, and, of course, guaranteed the nation's security in a dangerous world. To say that in attacking all these (except the last) Reagan was attacking the New Deal, hence his own spiritual father, President Roosevelt, would be to impose, not justify, a psychoanalytic assessment. Yet little is clearer than the contrast between Roosevelt's and Reagan's own profits from life-saving. While local newspapers kept his score, adding up more than seventy-one rescues before he quit in 1932, at the age of twenty-one, Reagan's successes in pulling people from the Rock River had no "political" effect. His beneficiaries did not accumulate into supporters. Once rescued, they went their way.

This was the model Reagan pursued as President. Dismantling the agencies of government would rescue people from their entanglements and dependencies and leave them free to go their way on their own. Again, the roots of this preference in culture and psychology remain to be understood. Moreover, to the extent that it can be read as a "refusal" of power, a rejection of acting as authority and leader and father, it must be inspected as a possible disguise for quite contrary purposes. Thus, Reagan's attack on government help for Americans at home went hand-in-hand with his attack on government as having failed in protecting all Americans from world Communism. Along with his slashing of the domestic budget he proceeded with an immense increase in military spending. Yet, the anxieties widespread in 1980 over his bellicosity had been allayed by 1984 with good reason. Not only had he not entered upon gross reckless adventures. He had, presumably, revealed his own deepest attachment, through the mislabeled "Star Wars" vision, not to apocalyptic battles, let alone Armageddon, but to a withdrawal of the nation from conflict behind an invulnerable shield, a vision of course familiar enough in the isolationist politics of Midwestern Protestant Republicanism of the nineteen-thirties. Whether the confusions of White House foreign policy in 1986–87 confirm this assessment, that in foreign policy too Mr. Reagan's deepest impulse was toward rescue and disengagement, can hardly be claimed. But certainly one cannot, on the other hand, simply assume that Reaganite foreign policy expressed what its domestic policy repressed.

The danger posed to America in "government" was that people saved by government lost themselves. People rescued by government found their lives thereafter entangled and dependent on government, an experience as true of Illinois farmers as of black welfare mothers. The good lifeguard ought take no responsibility for the lives of those he rescued. Reagan's impulses toward free trade and a laissez-faire market were most likely deep and heartfelt. Not a vision of social order but a vision of human personality, a vision of a kind of individual psychology, unified his political imagination. Basically, it was a vision of energy.

Perhaps the fullest ideological exposition of Reaganism appeared in 1981, in George Gilder's *Wealth and Poverty*. While a defense of the great tax cut and supply-side economics, *Wealth and Poverty* went far beyond that. It celebrated capitalism generally as a system inducing the maximum of human endeavor, enterprise, imagination, creativity. Capitalism was validated as a psychology even more than as an economy. While Gilder explicated his own ideas—obviously heavily indebted to an array of weightier predecessors—and not the collected speeches of Ronald Reagan, his tract meshed with the President's career. The profession of acting had structural affinities with capitalism as Gilder expounded it. Capitalism incited, drew on and depended on men's capacity to imagine the as-yet-unborn, to think up new methods, new products, new needs, new ways of living. Capitalism incited new kinds of people. With his own involvement with radio, movies, TV, Reagan himself radiated readiness for futures uncontained in the past. For all his youth in a culture simpler than that over which he presided, he was not primarily a prophet of nostalgia. This is where he failed to satisfy those for whom a true "conservatism" was first of all defense of the past. His ready welcome to technological solutions to problems of politics and diplomacy was that of a man untroubled that technology had long ago come to undermine every kind of past.

Here also was located the essential linkage between the new religious Right's moral issues and economic Reaganism. Sexual permissiveness, abortion, prayerless schools, indeed "pluralism" itself all appeared to constitute indulgence rather than challenge. They registered life in a mode of consumption, hedonism, ease, addiction, rather than of production, endurance, striving, fitness. Whether Reagan himself understood the symbolic nature of these issues is not clear. The predictable results of seeking literal re-criminalization of abortion were dismal. Reintroduction of prayer in schools promised only endless legal bickering. And so on. Reagan's careful abstention from pressing for actual legislation suggested that he was aware. On the other hand, he may—ironically enough—have hoped for change through appointments to the courts. In any case, the linkage between economy and morality followed not from political expediency but from his whole record. People were to be rescued, then left alone.

Perhaps it was here that the new religious Right was itself least well prepared and most vulnerable. Its own political agenda persistently and consistently omitted economic themes. Yet the whole movement depended on oceans of money.[16] The TV congregations themselves were tirelessly pressed for contributions. Money poured to the TV ministries and to their attached political organizations from traditional right-wing sources in the Southwest and California. Quite in accord with a familiar American pathos, this symbiosis between preacher and money inevitably led to scandal. Oral Roberts's plea for contributions to save him from being taken by God was one. The farce of Jim and Tammy Bakker was another. A movement as prone as this to self-mockery was no sound basis for political majority-building.

But the deeper problem for the new religious Right was that it had induced hostility within the religious community itself. While the mainline Protestants accused by the TV preachers of surrender to secular humanism lacked means to defend themselves effectively, they were unlikely to be absorbed by fundamentalism. Yet any new political majority for conservatism needed them. While "evangelical Catholics" of the Right might be finding com-

mon ground on abortion with New Right Protestants, Catholics'
real future depended on the vast ferment within the church itself,
a veritable rising of lay and national convictions demanding reform in the Roman Catholic church. A new political conservatism
could not build just on fundamentalist Catholics. The growing
morally independent Catholics were deeply involved in the economic issues of Reaganism. Jews too had much at issue among
themselves, first, how to keep favor for Israel in American foreign
policy, second, how to keep Israel from alienating not only American foreign policy but American Jews in their traditional social
liberalism. Just as some fundamentalist Catholics struck hands with
once anti-Catholic Protestant fundamentalists, so too some Jews
saw in the dispensationalists' delight in Israel as proof of the imminence of the rapture reason to accept fundamentalists' support
despite plain signs that the anti-Semitism endemic in folk fundamentalism remained alive.

Stresses and antagonisms at work in these divisions would no
doubt tend to be eased to the extent that prosperity resumed.
Yet prosperity could not restore what had once seemed evident,
namely, a link between national affluence and a certain kind of
moral character, best seen in Midwestern Protestant Republicanism. Gilder had unflinchingly touched the most sensitive places
here. By 1986 it seemed quite clear that any return to approximately trustworthy prosperity in the United States would require
the full—or nearly full—employment of women. Women's employment had followed from powerful changes in the economic marketplace far more than from ideological feminism. Yet the New
Right could not resist responding to the new gender conditions
in ideological and moral terms. The "San Francisco Democrats"
were stigmatized as "anti-family" for urging measures of help for
all sorts of people without family support, notably single mothers.
In his tract, Gilder, using logic from evolutionary biology, insisted
that men needed the responsibility of family to discipline their
energies.[17] Without that, sexuality itself would become anarchic,
debilitating rather than inspiriting. Yet the New Right, whether
purely economic or integrated with religion, had no restoration to

offer. Indeed, as deficits grew, and as the administration repelled serious reductions in spending on arms, the prospect grew that more and more individuals, especially women, whether unmarried with children, divorced, old and alone, or caught in some other circumstance, would be left to the erratic mercies of private charity. Opposition to an Equal Rights Amendment was not going to restore the kind of gender world still evoked by New Right ideologists such as Mrs. Phyllis Schlafly, defending every wife's right to full support from an ex-husband. The constituencies for the TV ministers, one might guess, still imagined that the permissiveness which, as secular humanism, terrified them flourished only out there, among other people, on other television networks. Even they might begin to suspect the truth as Jim and Tammy's story came to them on their own channels.

The popular psychology of positive thinking had flourished among people able, for reasons of culture and politics, to imagine that the only thing wrong with their lives was within themselves. If they could learn how to manage their own consciousness according to the techniques of mind cure, the world outside would prove positive in its response. Of course this world was always that of the United States, not of mankind, but the sense of God's abundance waiting only to be received into mind had always taken for granted the greater readiness of Americans, and, hence, America, for such grace. The New Right of Ronald Reagan had no way to restore the old economy and its world. Steel mills would not refire their hearths. Japanese cars and computers would not retreat. Indeed, a whole new "third" world of enterprise was flooding in. Everybody would have to work in America, harder, for less, including women. Stronger means than positive-thinking self-inspiration were needed.

By no means did the landslide of 1984 carry within itself the logic of this stronger response. On the contrary. Narrow election analysis, not ideological debate, revealed what could well prove to be the most stubborn barrier to a new Moral Majority. George McGovern was less popular among white Southerners in 1972 than was Walter Mondale in 1984, but it was in 1984 that the Republican party's long-time Southern strategy finally broke through.[18] In 1972 many white Southerners, as yet unready to vote Republican, had gone to George Wallace. But no major group voted more heavily for Ronald Reagan in 1984 than white Southerners. What did this have to do with the religious Right, with the hostages crisis, or with inflation? The social reality underlying this vote could be seen in its obverse, the overwhelming vote for Mondale among blacks, South and North. The psychological reality could be glimpsed in a further differential: just as white Southern men voted more heavily for Reagan than did white Southern women, so too did black women vote more heavily for Mondale than did black men. In effect, the Republican campaign of 1984 cashed in on a goal of every national GOP campaign since Goldwater's (except Ford's in 1968), to exploit the continuing resistance among white Southerners to racial equality. The President's own protestations of goodwill did not matter. In view of his merited reputation as a "great communicator," neither blacks nor Southern whites were likely to have misunderstood him. He had made himself clear. So far as the religious Right was concerned, racist voting evoked the saddest part of their own cultural heritage. At no point had the evangelical ferment among blacks been gathered into the new religious Right's organizations. The obvious Southern cast to most of the TV preachers left a clear inference. The Reagan administration's own policies had been tireless: they would attack all previous efforts—such as affirmative action, busing, tax disallowances and the like—at dismantling racist structures, and then propose no new efforts of their own.[19] Nowhere else was it so determined to end subsidies. Tax benefits and social security for the middle classes remained untouchable; farm subsidies actually grew; numberless trade protections continued in force for manufacturers; blacks alone were offered the pure market.

The political calculation on which this policy was based was obvious: Republicans had nothing to lose, much to gain, whereas for the Democratic party to become the sole advocate for blacks was to leave it vulnerable to retrograde attitudes not only in the South but everywhere white flight had already demonstrated the persistence of racist feelings. Here the tension between religious and political Right would remain beyond resolution. The religious Right could not long remain complacent with the party's coded language without eventually promoting conflict. Mind-cure and positive-thinking adepts had commonly simply ignored race. If one could make out the persistence behind their views of one strain or another of standard racism, this did not inflect their teachings. Positive thinkers were even capable of picking up on postwar liberalism. Thus, at his Crystal Palace in Garden Grove, Robert Schuller could warn of the inconsistency of "prejudice" with the Possibility Thinking of Supersuccessful Persons: "So release your mind from indoctrinated prejudices. . . ."[20] But the new religious Right was conspicuously Southern and white, and the ideology it had been handed by the political Right served all-too-conveniently to excuse it from any further examination of its own soul. As for any future for reform through positive thinking, from the start it had relied upon remaining anesthetized to social and economic reality. While the Reagan administration's determined effort to re-induce such anesthesia on race—as on poverty, health, education, crime, drugs and every other realm unlikely to generate free-market solutions—had had success, only a greater success than it had yet been able to achieve economically promised to prolong it.

Back in 1966, a young progressive Republican, in despair at the capture of his party by fanatic right-wing "party crashers," thought of Ronald Reagan as only a still more extreme embodiment of fantasy, delusion and futility:

> Reality is to be shut out altogether as the GOP eschews the problematical and mentally taxing world of politics for the more glamorous, exhilarating, free-floating world of entertainment. This is the home of the pop-politician, ruggedly handsome, blond, alliterative, Ronald Reagan—the party's hope to usurp reality with the fading world of the class-B movie.[21]

Ronald Reagan had not changed by 1980. He still insisted that all answers to great problems were simple; no need for mental taxation either. He still promulgated worlds of fantasy—Star Wars, an America without racial tensions, an America where it was always morning (with an occasional high noon with the Russians). But Reagan's new appeal drew not on the eagerness of millions of Americans to join in on his fantasies, but on the congruence of his broadest themes with basic structures in American history. Hence George Gilder, the young progressive Republican of 1966, found himself in 1981 a spokesman for the movie star he had scorned. Reagan had been saved from himself by the circumstances of his political victories. The priority given the economy forced postponement of the social issues, hence postponement of the bitter, irresolvable conflicts that awaited on each of them. But these social issues were peripheral to Reagan's broadest theme, the status of government.

Unlike France, Sweden, Germany, Russia and any number of other nations, the United States had not grown up around a state. Government really had been a secondary force in American culture. Reliance upon the federal government in wars had always been followed by repudiation of any idea of perpetuating wartime agencies into peace. Jealousy of the federal government had never produced dominant state governments either. "States' rights" had always meant little government. Not even the first and greatest proponent of federal strength, Alexander Hamilton, had really visualized a European-style state. Hamilton had simply argued that the greatest stimulus to private energy would not emerge until industry had risen to rival agriculture, and that, he believed, would not happen without deliberate stimulus by the state. Alexis de Tocqueville's analysis of the liberation of imaginative energy in America assigned it to social conditions, especially "equality" (by which of course he meant equality of opportunity), not to the national state. Henry Adams's sketch of the awakening of democratic energy in 1800 attributed it entirely to the "American idea," that same equality of opportunity, and in no way to the state.[22]

Political history since 1945 tells us that this tradition had by no means been undermined or dispelled by the New Deal and the war. The New Deal had been accepted as a necessary intervention to save the economy from collapse; government had led the war effort as it had all wars. While the Democratic party had benefited from its tenure through both epics, it carried with it into the postwar era the danger of trying to repeat its successes when such successes were no longer called for.[23] Of course it had never broken into the core of perdurable old Protestant Republicanism. The Republican minority had always held to the anti-government faith. The main body of Northern Democrats too, notably urban Catholics of several ethnic origins, had every intention of winning freedom for their own enterprise. Their interest in government was purely expedient. Reaching out for still more people in need, extending the roster of those deserving the helping hand of the government, searching for more poor people, Democratic politicians made themselves less, not more, attractive to their increasingly successful onetime constituents. Once Democrats themselves, through their own failures at government, seemed to have become complicit in the economic staggers of the late seventies, they had completed their own unmasking. Besides, no postwar Democrat of high political stature ever tried to generate a philosophy of the state on which the party might stand, not Harry Truman, not Adlai Stevenson, not John F. Kennedy. The Great Society advanced by Lyndon Johnson simply extrapolated from New Deal efforts to help those in need; it did not attempt to claim for the state primary activities of economy and culture. Even those few theorists on the party's left who imagined some kind of "countervailing power" for the state fell far short of concocting Hegelian, European-style duties for the state. In short, the Democratic party itself never tried to supersede the long historic aversion to "guvmint."

By 1984, heirs of the Democratic party's left who still urged government as the agency for recovery and stability came to seem mere ideologues, their politics as abstract as visions of a "democratic socialist America." The way was open to stigmatize them as prophets of a false religion, "secular humanism." The absurdity of that accusation did not demonstrate absurdity in the evocation of a tradition of private enterprise. Reagan's own ideological extremisms could fade without leaching strength from his general theme: Americans never had been and had not remotely become people who wanted to be saved by the state. Indeed, in the years since 1945 they had learned many reasons to be suspicious of the state. That the Democratic party could not digest this suspicion meant that it would find vent in the Republican.

The long tradition evoked by Mr. Reagan included far more than just aversion to the state. The positive energies released in the economy, symbiotically intensified by unhesitating embrace of technological innovation, had made for an "individualism" that radiated out far beyond the precincts of the economy. Ralph Waldo Emerson spiritualized it into the vision of a "new man." But limits, clearly explained by Alexis de Tocqueville in 1835, had always been installed on this exercise of individual energy. Free enterprise was not to prevail in matters sexual. Individualism was not to prevail where life depended on sex. The correct social order here was always plain: every man had a wife, every woman a husband, all children grew up in a stable family. In not a breath or a plank in a platform had the postwar Democrats repudiated this consensus, but as, by 1980, it was obvious that, compared to the normative order prescribed in the old republic, sexual disorder had come to spread, fearfully so in some precincts, it was hardly surprising to find sexual issues becoming political. The right wing's preference for ascribing this disorder to the irresponsibilities and immoralities and even malignities of secular humanism once more perfectly manifested its social anesthesia and amnesia. But criticism of the absurdity of the Right's diagnosis did not consist of a successful prescription in itself. Certainly most of the disorder of families, homes and sexuality of the 1980s had deep sources in drastic economic change, not in some ideology of liberal permissiveness. But the likelihood that the right's supply-side formulas would only more sharply divide a minority prosperous enough to buy its own moral order from a growing majority with dwindling resources again did not constitute a policy for

Democrats. "Family values" did not constitute an impediment to politics addressed to the realities of the eighties, and until such politics could be composed, those who denigrated the cry for family values purely as obscurantist and retrograde would only further seem to show they had lost touch with American history.

Finally, religion, narrowly defined, had not ceased to be precious in postwar America. The grasp for political power by the religious Right quite naturally provoked opposition, but rejection of its right to do so misconstrued American history. Separation of church and state never had meant seclusion of religion to purely private life. More decisively, separation of church and state, with its ban on any establishment of religion, had carried the positive meaning that Americans were free to invent new theologies, new churches, new religions. This fertility of invention was not some principle laid down in the Constitution but a fact of American life. Historians could deplore the reasons for some of these inventions, shake their heads in amazement at others, but the church life of Americans had been volatile. The rise of the religious Right in the nineteen-sixties, seventies and eighties remained in this tradition. The tendency of the old mainline Protestant denominations to elide into a kind of tolerant indistinguishability, climaxed organizationally in a National Council of Churches with few grass roots, had been a late, and by no means a dialectically inevitable process. There was little that was fresh and vitalizing about still another conglomerate even under the rubric of ecumenism. Perhaps the greatest irony of the old mainstream denominations was their success in helping multitudes of individuals realize they did not really need churches or even "religion" at all in order to lead orderly and exciting lives. But for those who still did, this kind of ebbing within the mainline denominations left them vulnerable. Religious life in America had periodically manifested that kind of popular, even "populist" faith often exalted by European anticlericals eager to undermine their own ponderous state churches. The religious Right evinced numerous signs of such a popular, populist energy.

The New Right's congruence with deep structures in American

history of course did not guarantee its success. Were it to be linked with a new epoch of affluence and economic expansion, its chances would be indefinitely improved. Yet, as of late 1987, such an epoch hardly seemed assured. In January 1981, at his inaugural, Ronald Reagan had, in a mode familiar to conservative Republicans since Calvin Coolidge, expatiated upon the wickedness of federal debt. He had deplored ransoming the future for present gratification. He had rejected asking the children of today to pay their parents' bills tomorrow. By 1987 he had run up more deficits than all previous administrations put together. They were still increasing, not decreasing. A nation with a positive trade balance had become a nation running annual trade imbalances never before imagined. Determined to rescue the nation from perils posed by the Soviet Union, a country with which the United States had never been at war, Reagan had seen vast assets being turned over to the two nations, Japan and Germany, against whom he had fought in wartime Hollywood.

Few economists argued that the debts and deficits would not have to be paid for sooner or later, one way or another. But there was a lot of difference between sooner and later, between some ways and others. The most conspicuous fact seemed to be the emergence of a world market and a world economy in which imbalances within the United States were absorbed. Indeed, American debts and deficits may have paid for the remarkable growth of many newly developing nations. The resources for weathering through even unprecedented problems of debt and deficit may have come to be far greater than conventional economic reckoning had realized. Reaganite wishfulness did have a handhold.

Should simple wishfulness for a return to the long American boom, last clearly manifest in the hegemonic dominance still enjoyed by the United States in the nineteen-fifties be gratified, then the conditions for a real revival of the traditions of popular psychology examined in this book would also return. Inevitably, once again, large numbers of individuals would find that, despite their birthright to prosperity, they themselves had not, somehow, come to join the affluent. Once again they would be responsive to the argument that the fault lay in themselves. They would listen with hopes to teachers of techniques for better self-management. They would invade themselves with self-hypnotic formulas. They would anesthetize themselves against politics. They would take for granted that attuning themselves to the American market was equivalent to being in tune with the infinite. By no means was the religious Right immune to such wishfulness. In 1983, as its contribution to "The Year of the Bible"—proclaimed by Mr. Reagan— the Georgia-based right-wing Arthur S. DeMoss Foundation published a little spiritual manual entitled *Power for Living*. With its testimonies to peace of mind from famous athletes and to economic success from eminent executives, with its promises of solutions to every problem of "family, work, money, fear, pain, and many other topics," with its recitation of miracles of health, its guarantees of triumph over feelings of inferiority, inadequacy and worry generally, and in its very title, the little tract echoed a hundred texts of mind cure.

But not even the most determined true believers in supply-side economics believed in simple restoration of the fifties. Whether the bill for debts and deficits would be presented to the next President, or might be strung out over decades deep into the next century, whether the struggle for competitive survival in the new world markets would require the sacrifice of a whole generation of union members and farmers or was compatible with some degree of protection, the American economy was going to be strikingly different in ways already clear, and in others yet untold. Women were not going to leave the marketplace. Foreign productivity would continue to threaten American producers. Blacks would not stop bringing every enclave of racial privilege under pressure. The high cost of the medical and legal professions would—if not sooner, then later—eventually be recognized as a luxury the nation could not afford. The bill for the aged would soar, inducing tensions between age cohorts. The bill for education would soar, inducing further tensions between age cohorts. The bill for suburban and exurban living would soar and induce tensions between communities. In general, the long neglect of social costs in American culture would exact a reckoning. The focus of positive thinking in self-reform for individual gain would obviously not be adapted to such a new era. In such a new era, themes of discipline, work and self-denial would be more relevant. A politics based, not on coalitions of self-interest, but on appeals to abstract values might seem more relevant. Was the new politics of the religious Right, then, better adapted to serve, after all?

Construed socially rather than theologically, the new religious Right had little to offer such a new era. Based on a population that was itself experiencing a rise from relative deprivation to relative affluence, it was hardly likely to commend a lowering of expectations to its flocks. Ronald Reagan's own favored anecdotes demonstrating government's iniquity stressed government's extraction of money from the worthy. The worthy were always assumed to be well provided with the money. When, added to this, the new religious Right enjoyed links with truly rich men in the standard political Right, not simply general prosperity but big money could be seen to have a basic place in the religious Right's conception of values. No sacrifice would ever be asked of the billionaires of the Southwest and California. Indeed, as disenchantment with Mr. Reagan set in on the political Right, not on account of social issues but on account of arms control and Central American peace plans, right-wing organizations began to outpace the Republican party itself in funds received from big money on the right. Here was a heritage not yet reconciled to the New Deal in American history, hardly likely to be persuaded by new religious urgings.

But the relevance of the religious Right to the emergent new economic issues depended finally on theology. The 1983 tract *Power for Living,* while reaching out to claim economic rewards for its evangel, was not really a mind-cure tract. It intended instead to harness personal success to its standard fundamentalist thesis. In the process it revealed not so much differences from positive thinking as what positive thinking had repressed. The heart of fundamentalism was of course its attitude toward authority. It granted complete authority over the mind to an outside power. So did positive thinking. Fundamentalism's outside authority was the Bible, inerrant, complete, all-sufficient for all human need. Positive thinking's was a psychology of automanipulation. Neither could abide a relationship of self to outer reality in which the self remained a project, in process, engaged in unfinishable evolution. Both recoiled from opening the self to new life not already guaranteed to fit neatly in the old. Inevitably, this meant a mystified idea of God. *Power for Living* registered the religious Right's basic unreadiness to grant God true sovereignty, most strikingly in its explicit evocation of "Satan" as "our enemy." Satan of course took one form as the nation's enemy, although one of the evidences for this cited in *Power for Living* carried curious implications about God's favorite nation. In 1945, it seemed, several young scientists caught in the war prayed "to learn where God would have them flee," to Russia or to America. These were the German space scientists, and their prayers were answered, happily for America: "The Germans voted to bring their awesome knowledge to the nation *under God,* undergirded by the Bible." Why had not God delivered this awesome knowledge to his chosen nation directly? Minds given to such an analysis of history would not be supple in meeting less Manichean challenges of the new economy. Satan's most compelling locus, however, was, as Tim LaHaye's best-selling *The Struggle for the Mind* (cited in *Power for Living* as one of its sources) had spelled out: "humanist" temptations in America itself. Indeed, Satan's whole reason for being was to tempt man—as he had tempted Eve—to develop an "independent" world view, independent, that is, of God's. That God may not have had a world view but, instead, was engaged in generating worlds to be viewed was a possibility closed to fundamentalism. Indeed, Biblicism's basic psychology undermined independence even in viewing one's own self, let alone the world. "Becoming a Christian doesn't make your problems disappear, but does bring them into focus. . . . [You] become confident in the fact that God has solutions for your every problem. Watching his creative solutions to your problems actually increases your joy in being a Christian."[24] Rather than becoming the responsible center of one's own life, one learned by Bible reading to become the spectator of one's own life.

Here was fundamentalism's basic affinity with positive thinking. The life of positive thinking was far more stressful than fundamentalism's: it required constant repetition of its spirit lifters, constant alertness against impossibility perspectives, constant monitoring of rebellions of body and mind against control. Fundamentalism more readily promised joy as a consequence of its reliance on an historic book rather than on autohypnotic technique. But neither invited the individual to suspend wishes for wealth and security in favor of an objective lust for reality. If the enonomic and social conditions awaiting politics in the nineteen-nineties were to make such objectivity and lust essential, then neither the new religious Right nor its pale predecessor had a great future. Ronald Reagan's presidency would fade into an embarrassing curiosity.

NOTES

PREFACE

1. Wilfred Cantwell Smith, "Religion as Symbolism," *Propaedia, Encyclopedia Britannica* (Chicago: 1975), p. 498.

INTRODUCTION

1. "The Religion of Healthy-Mindedness" in William James, *The Varieties of Religious Experience* (New York: Modern Library, n.d.).
2. "Religion and Secular Culture" (1929) in *The Protestant Era* (Chicago: University of Chicago Press, 1946), p. 133.
3. *Philosophical Sketches* (Baltimore: Johns Hopkins Press, 1962).
4. *Los Angeles Times,* May 18, 1964, p. 35.

CHAPTER I: THE DISCOVERY OF THE "NERVOUS AMERICAN"

1. George Beard, *American Nervousness* (New York: G. P. Putnam's Sons, 1881), p. vi.
2. See especially Chapter XIII, *Democracy in America*, Bk. II, Vol. II.
3. Beard, op. cit., p. 5.
4. Ibid., p. 10.
5. Ibid., pp. 98–99.
6. Ibid., p. 120.
7. Ibid., p. 345.
8. Herbert Goldhamer and Andrew Marshall, *Psychoses and Civilization* (Glencoe, Ill.: The Free Press, 1953).

CHAPTER II: NEW SHELTERS FOR TROUBLED SOULS

1. Annie Payson Call, *Nerves and the War* (Boston: Little, Brown & Co., 1918), pp. 171 ff.
2. *The Quimby Manuscripts* . . . , ed. by Horatio Dresser (New York: Thomas Y. Crowell Co., 1921), 2nd ed., comprise the basic materials on Quimby.
3. Paul Tyner's "The Metaphysical Movement" in *American Monthly Review of Reviews*, March 25, 1902, pp. 312–20, is an interesting early discussion.
4. Horatio Dresser, *A History of the New Thought Movement* (New York: Thomas Y. Crowell Co., 1919). William Walker Atkinson, *The Message of New Thought* (Holyoke, Mass.: E. L. Towne, 1911) is by a Chicago businessman-yogi.
5. Charles Braden, *Spirits in Rebellion* (Dallas: Southern Methodist Uni-

versity Press, 1963) is a scholarly study of New Thought intrigued with its Eastern aspects.

6. Edwin F. Dakin, *Mrs. Eddy* (New York: Blue Ribbon Books, 1930), p. 3.

7. Norman Beasley, *The Cross and the Crown: The History of Christian Science* (New York: Duell, Sloan & Pearce, 1953) is a useful study.

8. Charles Braden, *Christian Science Today* (Dallas: Southern Methodist University Press, 1958) covers the last fifty years, including schisms.

9. No such library has been written of Unity as of New Thought and Christian Science history. James D. Freeman, *The Story of Unity* (Lee's Summit, Mo.: Unity School of Christianity, 1954) is a short "official" sketch.

10. Freeman, ibid., p. 138.

11. No one comprehensive list of such writers exists. Tyner mentions many, as does R. B. Allen in "New Thought," *Encyclopedia of Religion and Ethics*. F. L. Mott, *History of American Magazines* (Cambridge, Mass.: Harvard University Press, 1957), Vol. IV, discusses papers. Dresser, op. cit., mentions many. For modern writers nothing substitutes for certain bookstores.

CHAPTER III: THE TROUBLED SOULS OF FEMALES

1. Annie Payson Call, *Power through Repose* (Boston: Little, Brown & Co., 1911), p. 57.

2. For the following discussion of women, citation should be made to the magazines of the time—*Century, Forum*, especially *Harper's*. No good books have been written on my theme.

3. Emma Willard, "An Address to the Public" (1819) in *The Faith of Our Fathers*, ed. by I. Mark and E. L. Schwab (New York: Alfred A. Knopf, 1952), pp. 201–2.

4. Beatrice Hofstadter, "Popular Culture and the Romantic Heroine," *American Scholar*, Winter 1960–61, p. 98 ff. See also an intriguing literary study, W. Wasserstrom, *Heiress of All the Ages: Sex and Sentiment in the Genteel Tradition* (Minneapolis: University of Minnesota Press, 1959).

CHAPTER IV: PASTORS AND DOCTORS WHO DIDN'T HELP

1. William James, *The Varieties of Religious Experience* (New York: Modern Library, n.d.), p. 110.

2. As an interesting record of the practice of "healing" in evangelical revival circles, see A. W. Tozer, *Wingspread: Albert B. Simpson— A Study in Spiritual Altitude* (Harrisburg, Pa.: Christian Publications Incorporated, 1943). Simpson was leader of the Evangelical Missionary Alliance, founded in 1887, for thirty years, practicing divine healing along with other pentecostals.

3. Leslie Weatherhead, *Psychology, Religion and Healing* (New York: Abingdon Press, 1952) and John T. McNeill, *A History of the Cure of Souls* (New York: Harper and Brothers, 1951) help open up this territory, though Weatherhead is better on Great Britain than on America.

4. As background for this complicated story, see Richard H. Shryock, *The Development of Modern Medicine* (New York: Alfred A. Knopf, 1947) and *Medicine and Society in America, 1660–1860* (New York: New York University Press, 1960).

5. For some popular medicines, especially pertinent to women, see Jean Burton, *Lydia Pinkham Is Her Name* (New York: Farrar, Straus & Co., 1949); Robert C. Washburn, *The Life and Times of Lydia Pinkham* (New York: G. P. Putnam's Sons, 1931); Stewart Holbrook, *The Golden Age of Quackery* (New York: The Macmillan Co., 1959).

6. Alfred Lief, *The Commonsense Psychiatry of Dr. Adolph Meyer* (New York: McGraw-Hill Book Co., 1948) offers many glimpses into the changing scene of psychiatry. Clifford Beers, *A Mind That Found Itself* (New York: Longmans, Green & Co., 1908) is an important landmark.

CHAPTER V: THE THEOLOGY OF MIND CURE

1. Arlo Bates, *The Puritan* (Boston: Houghton Mifflin Co., 1898), p. 17.

2. Several scholars have studied the theology of the mind-cure churches: G. G. Atkins, *Modern Religious Cults and Movements* (New York: Fleming H. Revell Co., 1923) (critical); J. K. Van Baalen, *The Chaos of Cults* (Grand Rapids, Mich.: Wm. B. Eerdmans Publishing Co., 1938) (harshly critical); Elmer Clark, *The Small Sects in America* (Nashville, Tenn.: Abingdon Press, 1937) (neutral); Charles Braden, *These Also Believe* (New York: The Macmillan Co. 1949) (determinedly fair-minded).

3. Charles Fillmore, *The Science of Being and Christian Healing* (Kansas City, Mo.: Unity School of Christianity, 1910), p. 90.

4. H. Emilie Cady, *Lessons in Truth* (Lee's Summit, Mo.: Unity School of Christianity, 1955), pp. 65–66.

5. Norman Vincent Peale, *You Can Win* (Nashville, Tenn.: Abingdon Press, 1938), p. 79.

6. Ralph Waldo Trine, *In Tune with the Infinite* (New York: Thomas Y. Crowell Co., 1898), p. 176.

7. Ralph Waldo Emerson, "Nature," *Complete Works,* Century ed. (Boston: Houghton Mifflin Co., 1903), Vol. I, pp. 64, 40.

8. Emerson, "Fate," op. cit., Vol. VI, pp. 32, 47.

9. Emerson, "Nature," op. cit., p. 10.

10. Frederick Bailes, *Your Mind Can Heal You* (New York: Dodd, Mead & Co., 1941), p. 102.

CHAPTER VI: THE PSYCHOLOGY OF MIND CURE

1. William James, *The Varieties of Religious Experience* (New York: Modern Library, n.d.), p. 113.
2. Ibid., p. 228.
3. Ibid., p. 230.
4. Ibid., pp. 501, 505.
5. Ibid., p. 503.
6. Ibid., p. 206.
7. Ibid., p. 473.
8. *The Quimby Manuscripts . . .* , ed. by Horatio Dresser (New York: Thomas Y. Crowell Co., 1921), 2nd ed., *passim*.
9. Charles Fillmore, *The Science of Being and Christian Healing* (Kansas City, Mo.: Unity School of Christianity, 1910), p. 8.
10. Mary Baker Eddy, *Science and Health, with Key to the Scriptures* (Boston: Allison V. Stewart, 1906), pp. 376, 374.
11. James, op. cit., p. 473.
12. Henry Wood, *Ideal Suggestion through Mental Photography, A Restorative System for Home and Private Use* (Boston: Lee and Shepherd, 1893).
13. Fillmore, op. cit., Preface.
14. Ibid., pp. 27, 82, 98, 127, 138.
15. Eddy, op. cit., p. 349.
16. Mary Baker Eddy, *Rudimental Divine Science* (Boston: Allison V. Stewart, 1909), p. 15.
17. Robert Peel, *Christian Science: Its Encounter with American Culture* (New York: Henry Holt & Co., 1958), pp. 110–11.
18. James, op. cit., p. 113.

CHAPTER VII: THE PHYSIOLOGY OF FAITH AND FEAR

1. Richard Cabot, "One-Hundred Christian Science Cases," *McClure's Magazine*, August 1908.
2. Walter Cannon, "'Voodoo' Death," *American Anthropologist*, 1942, Vol. XLIV, pp. 169–81.
3. George Dearborn, *The Influence of Joy* (Boston: Little, Brown & Co., 1916), p. 197.
4. Felix Deutsch, *On the Mysterious Leap from the Mind to the Body* (New York: International Universities Press, 1959).
5. William Sadler, *Worry and Nervousness; or The Science of Self-Mastery* (Chicago: A. C. McClurg Co., 1915), pp. 48, 50, 38.
6. Ibid., p. 277.
7. Ibid., pp. 293–94.
8. James van Buskirk, *Religion, Healing and Health* (New York: The Macmillan Co., 1952).
9. William James, "The Energies of Men," *Memories and Studies* (New York: Longmans, Green & Co., 1911).

10. William James, *The Varieties of Religious Experience* (New York: Modern Library, n.d.), p. 94. For a doctor's confirmation, see G. Canby Robinson, *The Patient as a Person* (New York: The Commonwealth Fund, 1939).

CHAPTER VIII: POLITICAL SCIENCE

1. Mark Twain, *Christian Science* (New York: Harper and Brothers, 1907), p. 75.
2. H. Emilie Cady, *Lessons in Truth* (Lee's Summit, Mo.: Unity School of Christianity, 1955), p. 28.
3. Mary Baker Eddy, *Science and Health, with Key to the Scriptures* (Boston: Allison V. Stewart, 1906), p. 96.
4. Henry Wood, *The Political Science of Humanism* (Boston: Lee and Shepherd, 1901), pp. 118, 227, 64, 75, 141.
5. Ibid., pp. 285, 286.
6. Ibid., p. 295.
7. Henry Wood, *Ideal Suggestion through Mental Photography, A Restorative System for Home and Private Use* (Boston: Lee and Shepherd, 1893), p. 58.
8. Ibid., p. 60.
9. Ibid., p. 49.
10. Ibid., p. 126.
11. Ibid., pp. 156, 144, 158, 116.
12. Ralph Waldo Trine, *The Land of Living Men* (Boston: Thomas Y. Crowell Co., 1910), pp. 9, 143, 182.
13. Ibid., p. 144.
14. Ibid., p. 49.
15. Ibid., p. 271.

CHAPTER IX: IMPERSONAL PERSONS

1. Mary Baker Eddy, *No and Yes* (Boston: Allison V. Stewart, 1908), pp. 19–20.
2. Ernest Holmes, *The Science of the Mind* (New York: Robert M. McBride & Co., 1938), p. 362.
3. "Ideal suggestion contains no possible element of personality. . . . It has often been observed that even in the most careful and conscientious mental or spiritual treatments, there is the possibility of an unconscious, though unwished for, personal element. . . . Ideal suggestion presents no possibility of any such unconscious complication." Henry Wood, *Ideal Suggestion through Mental Photography, A Restorative System for Home and Private Use* (Boston: Lee and Shepherd, 1893), pp. 102–3.
4. Julia Seton, *The Science of Success* (New York: E. J. Clode, 1914), pp. 112, 116.
5. Walter Devoe, *Healing Currents from the Battery of Life* (Chicago: College of Freedom, 1904), pp. 81, 84.

6. Charles Fillmore, *Christian Healing* (Kansas City, Mo.: Unity School of Christianity, 1957), rev. ed., pp. 111–12, 115–16.

7. Ibid., p. 137.

8. Horatio Dresser, *A History of the New Thought Movement* (New York: Thomas Y. Crowell Co., 1919), p. 306 ff.

9. Mary Baker Eddy, *Science and Health, with Key to the Scriptures* (Boston: Allison V. Stewart, 1906), pp. 61–62, 64; two other female statements: Julia Seton, *Marriage* (New York: E. J. Clode, 1914) and Elizabeth Towne, *Happiness and Marriage* (Holyoke, Mass.: E. L. Towne, 1904).

10. Fillmore, *The Science of Being and Christian Healing* (Kansas City, Mo.: Unity School of Christianity, 1910), p. 193.

11. Fillmore, *The Twelve Powers of Men* (Lee's Summit, Mo.: Unity School of Christianity, 1930), p. 167.

12. Seton, op. cit., p. 48.

13. Fillmore, *Christian Healing*, p. 116.

CHAPTER X: MIND CURE AS PATHOS

1. Mark Twain, *Christian Science* (New York: Harper and Brothers, 1907), pp. 268–69.

2. Charles Fillmore, *The Science of Being and Christian Healing* (Kansas City, Mo.: Unity School of Christianity, 1910), p. 137.

3. A. C. de Tocqueville, *Democracy in America*, Vol. II, Bk. I, Ch. 7.

4. William R. Taylor, *Cavalier and Yankee* (New York: George Braziller, 1961).

CHAPTER XI: THE HOUSE THAT TITANS BUILT

1. This discussion does not invoke the debate between Max Weber and Richard Tawney. Tawney's argument that one-to-one correlations between "the Protestant ethic" and "the spirit of capitalism" both include and exclude too much has been strengthened recently by the Swedish scholar Kurt Samuelsson's *Religion and Economic Action* (New York: Basic Books, 1961). Still, Weber's effort to discern implications for economic behavior in styles of character justified in religious terms remains as a touchstone.

2. Edward Kirkland, *Dream and Thought in the Business Community, 1860–1900* (Ithaca, N.Y.: Cornell University Press, 1956).

3. Max Weber, *The Protestant Ethic and the Spirit of Capitalism* (New York: Charles Scribner's Sons, 1950), p. 181.

4. Ralph Waldo Emerson, "Fate," *Complete Works*, Century ed. (Boston: Houghton Mifflin Co., 1903), Vol. VI, p. 9.

5. Among many, two discussions: A. W. Griswold, *The American Cult of Success* (Baltimore: Johns Hopkins University Press, 1934) and Irvin Wyllie, *The Self-Made Man in America* (New Brunswick, N.J.: Rutgers University Press, 1954).

6. George Fitzhugh, *Cannibals All*, ed. by C. Vann Woodward (Cambridge, Mass.: Belknap Press, 1960), p. 218.

7. Ibid., pp. xxxviii–xxxix.
8. Orestes Brownson, *The American Republic* (New York: O'Shea, 1866) and *Works*, coll. and arr. by H. F. Brownson (Detroit: Henry F. Brownson, n.d.).
9. Fitzhugh, op. cit., p. 131.
10. Ibid., p. 199.
11. Henry Nash Smith, *Virgin Land* (New York: Vintage Books, 1957).

CHAPTER XII: LONGING FOR HARMONY

1. Josiah Strong, *Expansion* (New York: Baker and Taylor, 1900), p. 80.
2. Josiah Strong, *Our Country*, ed. by J. Herbst (Cambridge, Mass.: Belknap Press, 1963), pp. 224–25.
3. Ibid., p. 147.
4. Strong, *Expansion*, p. 103.
5. Andrew Carnegie, "Wealth," *North American Review*, June 1889. Reprinted in *Democracy and the Gospel of Wealth*, ed. by Gail Kennedy (Boston: D. C. Heath & Co., 1949), p. 7.
6. Ibid., p. 8.
7. Ibid., p. 7.
8. Sigmund Diamond, *The Reputation of the American Businessman* (Cambridge, Mass.: Harvard University Press, 1955).
9. Expanded into a book by W. J. Ghent, *Our Benevolent Feudalism* (New York: The Macmillan Co., 1902).
10. Quoted from a letter of July 17, 1902, by W. J. Ghent in "George Baer," *Dictionary of American Biography* (New York: Charles Scribner's Sons, 1958), Vol. I, p. 490.
11. In discussion of a paper by Charles Ellwood, "Religion and Democracy" in *American Sociological Society*, 1919, Vol. XIV, p. 317.
12. See my discussion in *The Protestant Search for Political Realism, 1919–1941* (Berkeley: University of California Press, 1960).
13. Judson Grenier, "Muckraking and the Muckrakers," *Journalism Quarterly*, Autumn 1960, Vol. XXX.
14. Woodrow Wilson, *Personal Papers*, Vol. II, pp. 431–32, from a speech at the Annual Banquet of the Economic Club in New York, May 23, 1912.
15. Charles Forcey, *The Crossroads of Liberalism* (New York: Oxford University Press, 1961).

CHAPTER XIII: SPIRITUAL AUTOMATION, OLD STYLE

1. Albert Shaw, *The Outlook for the Average Man* (New York: The Macmillan Co., 1907).
2. Frank Haddock, *The Power of Will* (Auburndale, Mass.: Powerbook Library, 1907), p. v.
3. Ibid., pp. x, xi.
4. Ibid., p. 163.

5. Orestes Swett Marden, *Every Man a King, or Might in Mind Mastery* (New York: Thomas Y. Crowell Co., 1906).

6. Emile Coué, *Self-Mastery through Conscious Auto-Suggestion* (New York: Malkan Publishing Co., 1922), pp. 13, 25, 37.

7. Napoleon Hill, *Think and Grow Rich* (Greenwich, Conn.: Fawcett Publications, 1961), p. 15.

8. Ibid., p. 71.

9. Ibid., p. 67.

10. Claude Bristol, *The Magic of Believing* (Englewood Cliffs, N.J.: Prentice-Hall, 1948), p. 11.

11. *100 Stories of Business Success* by the Editors of *Fortune Magazine* (New York: Simon & Schuster, 1954), Preface.

12. *The Art of Success* by the Editors of *Fortune Magazine* (Philadelphia: J. B. Lippincott Co., 1956), p. viii.

CHAPTER XIV: SPIRITUAL AUTOMATION, NEW STYLE

1. Bruce Barton, *The Man Nobody Knows* (Indianapolis: The Bobbs-Merrill Co., 1925); *The Book Nobody Knows* (Indianapolis: The Bobbs-Merrill Co., 1926).

2. Dale Carnegie, *Public Speaking and Influencing Men in Business* (New York: Association Press, 1932), originally published in 1926 as *Public Speaking: A Practical Course for the Businessman.*

3. Dale Carnegie, *How to Win Friends and Influence People* (New York: Simon & Schuster, 1936), p. 58.

4. Ibid., pp. 37, 67–68, 102.

5. Thorstein Veblen, *The Theory of Business Enterprise* (New York: Charles Scribner's Sons, 1904).

6. Elton Mayo, *The Human Problems of an Industrial Civilization* (New York: The Macmillan Co., 1934) contains his main statement.

7. Solomon Barkin, "A Trade Unionist Appraises Management Personnel Philosophy" in *Human Relations for Management*, ed. by E. C. Bursk (New York: Harper and Brothers, 1956), pp. 361–72.

8. O. A. Ohmann, "Skyhooks—Monday through Friday" in Bursk, op. cit., p. 115.

9. A. Collier, "Business Leadership and a Creative Society" in Bursk, op. cit., p. 115. See also on the main theme, Alfred Marrow, *Making Management Human* (New York: McGraw-Hill Book Co., 1957).

10. See Martin Gross, *The Brain Watchers* (New York: Random House, 1962).

CHAPTER XV: THE DIVINE ECONOMY

1. Ralph Waldo Trine, *The Power That Wins* (Indianapolis: The Bobbs-Merrill Co., 1928), p. 5.

2. Ibid., pp. 18–19.

3. Ibid., pp. 50, 52.

4. Ibid., p. 119.

5. Ibid., p. 127.
6. Ibid., p. 73.
7. Ibid., p. 89.
8. Ibid., p. 161.
9. E. L. Towne, *Practical Methods for Self-Development* (Holyoke, Mass.: E. L. Towne, 1904), pp. 31–33.
10. Herbert W. Eustace, *Christian Science, Its Clear, Correct Teaching* (Berkeley, Calif.: Lederer, Street, 1934), p. xxi.
11. Ibid., pp. 226–27.
12. Ibid., pp. 222–25.
13. Charles Fillmore, *Prosperity* (Lee's Summit, Mo.: Unity School of Christianity, 1936), p. 60.
14. Ibid., p. 88.
15. Ibid., pp. 88–89.
16. Ibid., p. 31.
17. Ibid., pp. 93, 167–68.
18. Ibid., pp. 126, 147, 164.
19. Ibid., pp. 18, 32, 80. Napoleon Hill criticized ". . . the popular belief that riches come only to those who work hard and long. When you begin to think and grow rich, you will observe that riches begin with a state of mind, with definiteness of purpose, with little or no hard work," in his *Think and Grow Rich* (Greenwich, Conn.: Fawcett Publications, 1961), p. 22. *Cf.* also, Hanna Jacob Doumette, *Petitions Celestial* (Santa Monica, Calif.: Sun Publishing Co., 1932), Ch. V, "The Gospel of Prosperity": "I do not labor. My activity is universally adjusted. . . . I am not subject to money, nor do I slave for its possession. . . . When it is required, money is provided to serve my purpose. . . . I do not struggle for a living." Pp. 39, 44.
20. Fillmore, op. cit., p. 23.
21. Ibid., p. 127.
22. Ibid., p. 110.
23. Ibid., p. 82.
24. Ibid., p. 90.
25. Ibid., p. 81.
26. Joseph Murphy, *How to Attract Money* (San Gabriel, Calif.: Willing Publishing Co., 1955), p. 31.
27. Ibid., pp. 25–26.
28. Ibid., pp. 46–56.
29. Ibid., pp. 73–74.
30. Ibid., p. 16.
31. Ibid., p. 35.

CHAPTER XVI: THE EMPTY ADVENTURE

1. On this assumption, see Gibson Winter, *The Suburban Captivity of the Churches* (Garden City, N.Y.: Doubleday & Co., 1961).

2. Harry Emerson Fosdick, *The Living of These Days* (New York: Harper and Brothers, 1956) is his autobiography, giving details on his life.

3. Harry Emerson Fosdick, *On Being a Real Person* (New York: Harper and Brothers, 1943), pp. 11–12.

4. Harry Emerson Fosdick, *Twelve Tests of Character* (New York: Association Press, 1922), p. 3.

5. Harry Emerson Fosdick, *Adventurous Religion* (New York: Harper and Brothers, 1926), p. 240 and *passim*.

6. Fosdick, *The Living of These Days*, p. 214.

7. Fosdick, *Adventurous Religion*, p. 264.

8. Harry Emerson Fosdick, *The Hope of the World* (New York: Harper and Brothers, 1933), p. 1.

CHAPTER XVII: THE TWENTIES: ADVENTURES IGNORED

1. In a rather vast literature, the writings of Judge Ben Lindsey and the sociologist Ernest Groves might be suggested as openers.

2. The publications of the Religious Education Association, an organization strongly influenced by John Dewey, are helpful here.

3. William McLoughlin, *Modern Revivalism* (New York: The Ronald Press Co., 1959).

CHAPTER XVIII: THE DEPRESSION: CONFUSION OF SOULS

1. I have explored New Deal–Protestant social gospel relations more fully in *The Protestant Search for Political Realism, 1919–1941* (Berkeley: University of California Press, 1960).

CHAPTER XIX: MORE DEPRESSION: A RELIGION PRESCRIBED

1. Henry C. Link, *The Return to Religion* (New York: The Macmillan Co., 1936), p. 12.

2. Ibid., pp. 169, 79.

3. Ibid., p. 18.

4. Ibid., p. 19.

5. Ibid., p. 135.

6. Ibid., pp. 5–6.

7. Ibid., p. 58.

8. Ibid., p. 57.

9. Ibid., p. 62.

10. Ibid., p. 101.

CHAPTER XX: PSYCHOLOGY IN THE AIR

1. L. Gilbert Little, *Nervous Christians* (Lincoln, Neb.: Back to the Bible Publishing Co., 1956), p. 102.

2. See E. Worcester, S. McComb, and I. Coriat, *Religion and Medicine* (New York: Moffett, Yard, 1908); E. Worcester and S. McComb, *Body, Mind and Spirit* (Boston: Marshall Jones, 1931); E. Worcester, *Life's Adventure* (New York: Charles Scribner's Sons, 1932).

3. For a discussion of findings, see William Oursler, *The Healing Power of Faith* (New York: Hawthorne Books, 1957), p. 340 ff.
4. See *Religion and Health*, ed. by Simon Doniger (New York: Association Press, 1958), and *Healing: Human and Divine*, ed. by Simon Doniger (New York: Association Press, 1957), among others.
5. Among the multitude of books on modern psychosomatic medicine: Helen Flanders Dunbar, *Mind and Body: Psychosomatic Medicine* (New York: Random House, 1947); Edward Weiss and O. S. English, *Psychosomatic Medicine* (Philadelphia: W. B. Saunders Co., 1943).
6. Marcus Bach, *They Have Found a Faith* (Indianapolis: The Bobbs-Merrill Co., 1946) and *The Will to Believe* (New York: Prentice-Hall, 1955), and Oursler, op. cit. See also Wade H. Boggs, Jr., *Faith Healing and the Christian Faith* (Richmond, Va.: John Knox Press, 1955) for a sharp attack, and A. Graham Iken, *New Concepts of Healing* (New York: Association Press, 1956) for a more sophisticated review of the churches.
7. Curtis Cole, "God and Success," *The Atlantic Monthly*, April 1957.
8. C. R. Brown, *Faith and Health* (New York: Thomas Y. Crowell Co., 1910), p. 150.
9. See Leonard Gross, *God and Freud* (New York: David McKay Co., 1959), p. 11 and *passim*, for an uncritical popular survey.
10. L. Linn and L. Schwarz, *Psychiatry and Religious Experience* (New York: Random House, 1958).
11. Cyril Richardson in *Religion and Health*, ed. by Simon Doniger (New York: Association Press, 1958), pp. 59–60.
12. Gotthard Booth in ibid., p. 65.
13. See James van Buskirk, *Religion, Healing and Health* (New York: The Macmillan Co., 1952) for a hopeful survey, sympathetic to Norman Vincent Peale among others.

CHAPTER XXI: POSITIVE DIVINE PSYCHOLOGY
1. Many biographical details are available in a laudatory biography by Arthur Gordon, *Norman Vincent Peale: Minister to Millions* (New York: Prentice-Hall, 1958).
2. Norman Vincent Peale, *The Art of Living* (New York: Permabooks, 1949), p. 25.
3. Ibid., p. 152.
4. Ibid., p. 69.
5. Ibid., p. 184.
6. Norman Vincent Peale, *You Can Win* (New York: Abingdon Press, 1938), p. 13.
7. Ibid., p. 120.
8. Ibid., pp. 150–51.
9. Norman Vincent Peale, *Inspiring Messages for Daily Living* (New York: Prentice-Hall, 1950–55), p. 127.

10. Norman Vincent Peale, *The Power of Positive Thinking* (New York: Prentice-Hall, 1952), p. 212.
11. Peale, *The Art of Living*, pp. 13–14.
12. Norman Vincent Peale and Smiley Blanton, *The Art of Real Happiness* (New York: Prentice-Hall, 1950), p. 3.
13. Peale, *The Art of Living*, p. 25.
14. Norman Vincent Peale, *Stay Alive All Your Life* (New York: Prentice-Hall, 1957), p. 252.
15. Norman Vincent Peale and Smiley Blanton, *Faith Is the Answer* (New York: Abingdon Press, 1940), p. 49.
16. Ibid., p. 48.
17. Ibid., p. 49.
18. Ibid., p. 91.
19. Ibid., pp. 49–50.
20. Peale, *Stay Alive All Your Life*, p. 252.

CHAPTER XXII: POSITIVE PSYCHOLOGY—NEGATIVE PEOPLE
1. Smiley Blanton, *Love or Perish* (New York: Simon & Schuster, 1956), p. 9. Published in England by The World's Work (1913) Ltd. Used with permission.
2. Ibid., p. 103.
3. Ibid., p. 114.
4. Ibid., pp. 139, 145.
5. Ibid., p. 144.
6. Ibid., pp. 194–95.
7. John Maynard Keynes, *Essays in Persuasion* (New York: Harcourt, Brace & Co., 1932), pp. 366–67.
8. Norman Vincent Peale, *The Power of Positive Thinking* (New York: Prentice-Hall, 1952), p. 116.
9. Blanton, op. cit., p. 209.
10. Norman Vincent Peale, *The Art of Real Happiness* (New York: Prentice-Hall, 1950), pp. 15–16. Norman Vincent Peale and Smiley Blanton, *Faith Is the Answer* (New York: Abingdon Press, 1940), p. 132.
11. Norman Vincent Peale, *Stay Alive All Your Life* (New York: Prentice-Hall, 1957), pp. 146, 161.
12. Peale, *The Power of Positive Thinking*, p. 106.

CHAPTER XXIII: SOCIAL ANESTHESIA
1. Norman Vincent Peale, *The Art of Living* (Garden City, N.Y.: Garden City Books, 1937), pp. 185, 134.
2. Arthur Gordon, *Norman Vincent Peale: Minister to Millions* (New York: Prentice-Hall, 1958), p. 226.
3. James Fifield, Jr., *The Single Path* (New York: Prentice-Hall, 1957), p. 221.
4. Ibid., p. 91.

5. Norman Vincent Peale, *You Can Win* (New York: Abingdon Press, 1938), pp. 13–14.
6. The New York *Times*, September 19, 1960.
7. "Can Protestantism Be Saved?" *Reader's Digest*, September 1962, pp. 49–54. That Peale was in fact self-consciously trying to accommodate his "image" his next title showed: *The Tough-Minded Optimist* (New York: Prentice-Hall, 1961).

CHAPTER XXIV: THE BIBLE VERSUS PSYCHOLOGY

1. L. Gilbert Little, *Nervous Christians* (Lincoln, Neb.: Back to the Bible Publishing Co., 1956), p. 10.
2. Ibid., p. 102.
3. Ibid., p. 53.
4. Ibid., p. 43.
5. Ibid., p. 21.
6. Ibid., p. 36.
7. Anton Boisen, *Religion in Crisis and Custom* (New York: Harper and Brothers, 1955), Ch. IV.
8. Charles Allen, *God's Psychiatry* (Westwood, N.J.: Fleming H. Revell Co., 1953).
9. Howard E. Kershner, *God, Gold and Government* (New York: Prentice-Hall, 1957), p. 29.
10. Rollo May, *The Art of Counseling* (New York: Abingdon Press, 1939), p. 218.
11. Ibid., p. 223.
12. Ibid., p. 216.
13. James Bissett Pratt, *The Psychology of Religious Belief* (New York: The Macmillan Co., 1907).
14. May, op. cit., p. 222.

CHAPTER XXV: THE PROBLEM OF GUILT

1. O. Hobart Mowrer, *The Crisis in Psychiatry and Religion* (New York: D. Van Nostrand Co., 1961), p. 60.
2. Ibid., p. 165.
3. Ibid., p. 138.
4. Ibid., p. 51; Szasz's major statement: *Pain and Pleasure* (New York: Basic Books, 1957).
5. Mowrer, op. cit., p. 230.
6. Ibid., p. 122.
7. Ibid., p. 147.
8. Ibid., p. 230.
9. Ibid., p. 143.
10. Ibid., p. 239.
11. Ibid., p. 45.
12. Ibid., p. 215.
13. Ibid., p. 215.
14. Ibid., p. 33.

CHAPTER XXVI: PSYCHOLOGY VERSUS PEACE OF MIND
1. A. H. Maslow, "Personality Problems and Personality Growth" in *The Self,* ed. by Clark Moustakas (New York: Harper and Brothers, 1956), p. 242.
2. Kurt Goldstein, "The So-Called Drives," ibid., pp. 15–24.
3. Maslow, op. cit.
4. William James, "Is Life Worth Living?" *The Will to Believe, Human Immortality and Other Essays* (New York: Dover Publications, 1956), pp. 61–62.
5. William James, "Human Immortality," ibid., p. 69.
6. William James, "The Importance of Individuals," ibid., pp. 261–62.
7. Maslow, op. cit., pp. 236–37.
8. John G. McKenzie, *Nervous Disorders and Religion* (New York: Collier Books, 1957).
9. H. M. Lynd, *On Shame and the Search for Identity* (New York: Harcourt, Brace & Co., 1958).

POSTSCRIPT I: WILLIAM JAMES AS THE AUTHORITY
1. William James, *The Varieties of Religious Experience* (New York: Modern Library, n.d.), p. 100.
2. Ibid., p. 101.
3. Ibid., p. 102.
4. Ibid., p. 106.
5. Ibid., p. 112.
6. Ibid., p. 82.
7. Letter to Mrs. James in *The Letters of William James* (Boston: Atlantic, 1920), Vol. II, pp. 75–78.
8. Anton Boisen, *Religion in Crisis and Custom* (New York: Harper and Brothers, 1955), Ch. IV.
9. James, op. cit., p. 87.
10. Nigel Bruce, "A New Copernicus?" in *Freud and the 20th Century,* ed. by B. Nelson (New York: Meridian Books, 1957).
11. Bertrand Russell, *The Conquest of Happiness* (New York: Signet Books, 1951), p. 14.
12. Ibid., p. 15.
13. Ibid., p. 90.
14. James, *The Will to Believe, Human Immortality and other Essays* (New York: Dover Publications, 1956), p. x.

POSTSCRIPT II: MIND CURE AMONG CATHOLICS AND JEWS
1. Morris Lichtenstein, *Joy of Life* (New York: Society of Jewish Science, 1938), p. 342.
2. Ibid., pp. 331–32, 342.
3. Joshua Loth Liebman, *Peace of Mind* (New York: Simon & Schuster, 1946), pp. 135, 137, 136, 64.
4. Louis Binstock, *The Power of Faith* (New York: Prentice-Hall, 1952), p. 4.

5. Will Herberg, *Protestant, Catholic, Jew* (Garden City, N.Y.: Doubleday & Co., 1955), p. 294.
6. Fulton J. Sheen, *Peace of Soul* (New York: McGraw-Hill Book Co., 1949), pp. 6, 7.
7. Ibid., p. 1.
8. Ibid., p. 270.
9. Ibid., p. 270.
10. Ibid., pp. 289–90.
11. James Keller, *You Can Change the World* (New York: Signet Books, 1950), p. vi.
12. Ibid., p. 30.
13. Ibid., p. vi.
14. Ibid., p. 28.
15. Ibid., p. 28.
16. Ibid., p. 28.
17. Ibid., p. 27.

A RECKONING FOR 1980: EVANGELICALISM: THE OLD-TIME POSITIVE RELIGION?

1. David Kucharsky, "The Year of the Evangelical," *Christianity Today*, October 22, 1976, pp. 12–13; Garry Wills, *The New York Times*, August 1, 1976; *Time*, September 27, 1976; *Newsweek*, October 25, 1976; George H. Gallup, *The Gallup Poll—Public Opinion 1972–1977*, II (Wilmington: Scholarly Resources, 1978), pp. 859–62. On Gallup's personal views, "Evangelical America," *Christianity Today*, October 8, 1976, p. 52; CBS-TV added its coverage in 1977, with a Bill Moyers Special.
2. *1977 Yearbook of American and Canadian Churches* (Nashville: Abingdon, 1978); Dean R. Hoge and David A. Roozen, eds., *Understanding Church Growth and Decline, 1950–1978* (New York: Pilgrim, 1979) draws on fifty years of data on the mainline denominations; Donald W. Dayton, "The Holiness and Pentecostal Churches: Emerging from Cultural Isolation," *Christian Century*, August 15–22, 1979, pp. 786–92 is a broad discussion.
3. Peter Wagner, "How 'Christian' Is America?" *Christianity Today*, December 3, 1976, pp. 12–16.
4. Graham was apparently the first to try to blame Watergate on liberalism and "situation ethics"; even *Time*, June 10, 1974, p. 18, commented that he was "groping wildly." See Erwin Lutzer, "Watergate Ethics," *Christianity Today*, September 13, 1974, pp. 26–27, for an attempt to defend Graham. John A. Huffman, "Biblical Lessons from Watergate," *Christianity Today*, March 15, 1974, pp. 8–12, after blaming "secular pragmatism" for Watergate, then complained of a "double standard" applied to Mr. Nixon. David M. Howard, "Nixon's Watergate—Man's Depravity," *Christianity Today*, June 3, 1977, pp. 12–14, registered shock that those once shocked at Nixon should now be shocked at Carter's avowals of human weakness.

5. Albert Mendendez, *Religion at the Polls* (Philadelphia: Westminster, 1977), chapter 8 and elsewhere, rehearses the data.
6. Timothy L. Smith, "A 'Fortress Mentality': Shackling the Spirit's Power—An Interview with Timothy L. Smith," *Christianity Today*, November 19, 1976, p. 26.
7. For instance: Donald B. Kraybill, *Our Star-Spangled Faith* (Scottsdale, Pa.: Herald Press, 1976), argues that nations are not objects of God's favor. Kenneth S. Kantzer, "Evangelicals and the Inerrancy Question," *Christianity Today*, April 21, 1978, pp. 17–21, resembled many others in wishing to be neither "optimistic" nor "pessimistic" about the meaning of the evangelical surge. Evangelicals appeared not to be familiar with the cycle theory of the historian William McLoughlin, according to which a "Fourth Great Awakening" was already under way: McLoughlin, *Revivals, Awakenings, and Reform* (Chicago: University of Chicago Press, 1978). Kantzer, however, felt the historian Sidney Ahlstrom overly "pessimistic" in postulating an end to four hundred years of evangelical Christianity's hegemony.
8. Harold Lindsell, *The Battle for the Bible* (Grand Rapids, Mich.: Eerdmans, 1976), was a leading manifesto; Carl F. H. Henry, *Evangelicals in Search of Identity* (Waco, Texas: Word Books, 1976), exhibited some of the same self-consciousness. The extreme sensitivity invested in the problem was nicely exposed in three articles by Henry, "Those Incomprehensible British Fundamentalists," *Christianity Today*, June 2, June 23, and July 21, 1978, devoted to answering James Barr, *Fundamentalism* (Philadelphia: Westminster, 1978), in which Barr, a British evangelical scholar, sought to extricate evangelicalism from what he regarded as obscurantist old Biblicism. A similar sensitivity appeared in American evangelicals' reaction to German evangelicals, such as Helmut Thielicke and Jürgen Moltmann: see John W. Montgomery, "Thielicke on Trial," *Christianity Today*, March 24, 1978, and Thielicke's somewhat scornful reply, "A Response from Helmut Thielicke," *Christianity Today*, June 23, 1978, p. 26.
9. Donald Dayton, *Discovering Our Evangelical Heritage* (New York: Harper & Row, 1976); a predecessor to this kind of study was Timothy Smith, *Revivalism and Social Reform* (New York: Abingdon, 1957). Avoiding an older kind of celebratory piety, newer evangelical scholars were reappropriating American history as a meaningful story: Mark Noll, *Christians in the American Revolution* (Grand Rapids, Mich.: Eerdmans, 1977); Nathan Hatch, *The Sacred Cause of Liberty: Republican Thought and the Millenium in Revolutionary New England* (New Haven: Yale University Press, 1977); and John Woodbridge, Mark Noll, and Nathan Hatch, *The Gospel in America: Themes in the Story of America's Evangelicals* (Grand Rapids, Mich.: Eerdmans, 1978). Naturally, all such works, imputing "meaning" to history, aroused tension with evangelical emphasis upon Scripture as the sole source of meaning; sometimes the solution was to let some parts of history have meaning but not others; see notes 13 and 33.

10. Dean M. Kelley, *Why Conservative Churches Are Growing* (New York: Harper & Row, 1972); for a criticism of Kelley's argument, see Carl S. Dudley, "Measuring Church Growth," *Christian Century,* June 6–13, 1979, pp. 635–39.

11. David Kucharsky, *The Man from Plains: The Mind and Spirit of Jimmy Carter* (New York: Harper & Row, 1976); Tom Collins, *The Search for Jimmy Carter* (Waco, Texas: Word Books, 1976); Howard Norton and Bob Slosser, *The Miracle of Jimmy Carter* (Plainfield, N. J.: Logos, 1976); Niels Nielsen, Jr., *The Religion of President Carter* (Nashville: Nelson, 1977).

12. Peter Meyer, *James Earl Carter: The Man and the Myth* (Mission, Kansas: Sheed, Andrews & McMeel, 1978), is a journalist's review of criticisms of Carter.

13. Jesse Jackson, "You Can Pray If You Want To—An Interview with Jesse Jackson," *Christianity Today,* August 12, 1977, pp. 12–16. Jackson attributed the refusal of some white evangelicals to accept him as an evangelical to their suspicion of his social activism; the deeper issue appeared at a workshop on "black theology," in the words of one participant, a Dallas pastor: "If the Bible message and blackness bump heads, blackness must go. . . . The basis of authority for truth must shift from black culture to biblical declarations." Roger Koskela, "The NBEA; When the Bible Bumps Blackness," *Christianity Today,* May 6, 1977, p. 58. The same myth, that evangelical views of the Bible did not proceed from the white male culture of middle-class scholars in, say, Oklahoma, was held against "feminist" evangelicalism as well; see note 33. For the myth applied to Carter: John W. Montgomery, "Will an Evangelical President Usher in the Millenium?" *Christianity Today,* October 22, 1976, pp. 65–66.

14. "If I Were President," *Christianity Today,* January 7, 1977, pp. 26–27.

15. Lausanne quoted, Klaus Blockmühl, "On Wealth and Stewardship," *Christianity Today,* June 23, 1978, p. 48; Ronald J. Sider, *Rich Christians in an Age of Hunger* (Downer's Grove, Ill.: Intervarsity, 1977); Richard Quebedeaux, *The Worldly Evangelicals,* Part III, "The Young Evangelical Left" (New York: Harper & Row, 1978), discusses the ESA. For a discussion of the new evangelicals at an earlier point, see William G. McLoughlin, "Is There a Third Force in Christiandom?" in *Religion in America* edited by William G. McLoughlin and Robert N. Bellah (Boston: Houghton-Mifflin, 1968), pp. 45–72. "The new evangelicals are the spiritual hardcore of the radical right"; for McLoughlin's reply to objections to this view, see note 32, loc. cit., p. 71.

16. On the election of 1960, Menendez, op. cit., and on Catholics in 1976, Menendez, "Bibliography," op. cit., for articles on the campaign, twenty-two out of thirty-four on the Catholic vote.

17. Menendez, "Epilogue: How Carter Won," op. cit., pp. 181–205.

18. James M. Wall, "Words of Faith from Jimmy Carter," *Christian Century,* January 17, 1979, pp. 38–39.

19. Examples: Malcolm MacGregor and Stanley C. Baldwin, *Your Money Matters* (Minneapolis: Bethany Fell, 1978), and Neil Gallagher, *How to Save Money on Almost Everything* (Minneapolis: Bethany Fell, 1979). The old gospel appears to have peaked among evangelicals, just as with "liberals" such as Peale, in the mid-fifties: Oral Roberts and G. H. Montgomery, eds., *God's Formula for Success and Prosperity* (Tulsa: Oral Roberts Evangelistic Association, 1955); Gordon Lindsay, *God's Master Key to Success and Prosperity* (Dallas: Voice of Healing, 1959); and several books by the Assembly of God revivalist, influenced by Roberts and A. A. Allen. According to Roberts's wife: "Money has never been a real concern to Oral. He has always said, 'The Lord has plenty of money. The Lord needs people. If I can get the right people, the Lord will supply the money. He knows where it is"; Evelyn Roberts, *His Darling Wife, Evelyn—The Autobiography of Mrs. Oral Roberts* (New York: Dell, 1976), p. 214. Roberts, founder of The Full Gospel Businessmen's Fellowship International, did get the right people. With money problems solved, God proved available for other things: "When I'm hurrying somewhere to an appointment, I often ask the Lord to save me a parking place. . . . When I slide right into the last parking slot, I give the Lord credit. . . . He is capable of reserving parking spaces": ibid., p. 193.

20. Donald W. Dayton, "The Holiness and Pentecostal Churches," *Christian Century*, August 15–22, 1979, p. 787.

21. "Should the Church Be a Melting Pot?—An Interview with C. Peter Wagner and Ray Stedman," *Christianity Today*, August 18, 1978, pp. 11–16, with Stedman criticizing Wagner; C. Peter Wagner, *Your Church Can Be Healthy* (Glendale, Calif.: Regal Books, 1976) and *Our Kind of People* (Atlanta: John Knox, 1979) expounded both the research and the strategy for evangelism.

22. Examples: Larry Christenson, *The Christian Family* (Minneapolis: Bethany Fell, 1978) and Barbara Cook, *How to Raise Good Kids* (Minneapolis: Bethany Fell, 1978); on fathers, Gordon MacDonald, *The Effective Father* (Wheaton, Ill.: Tyndale, 1977) and Thomas Howard, "The Yoke of Fatherhood," *Christianity Today*, June 23, 1978, pp. 10–14.

23. Ed and Gaye Wheat, *Intended for Pleasure—Sex Techniques and Sexual Fulfillment in Christian Marriage* (Old Tappan, N.J.: Revell, 1976) and Tim and Beverly LaHaye, *The Act of Marriage* (Grand Rapids, Mich.: Zondervan, 1976) were the two most quoted manuals. Older notes continued to be struck: Mel White, *Lust: The Other Side of Love* (Old Tappan, N.J.: Revell, 1978) picked up on Jimmy Carter's famous *Playboy* interview; history could be reappropriated for evangelical purposes here too: Leland Ryken, "Were the Puritans Right About Sex?" *Christianity Today*, April 7, 1978, pp. 13–18.

24. Jerry Kirk, *The Homosexual Crisis in the Mainline Church* (Nashville: Nelson, 1977) nicely expressed both the evangelicals' sense of superiority and their fear. Occasionally, the distinction that homo-

sexuals ought to enjoy "all basic civil rights" without having to be admitted to the ministry occurred to some as consistent with old Baptist liberatarianism: report on a Southern Baptist "seminar," *Christianity Today*, May 5, 1978, p. 51. Tim LaHaye, *The Unhappy Gays* (Wheaton, Ill.: Tyndale, 1978) nicely illustrated how the Scriptural approach got submerged; in addition to his heterosexual fulfillment manual, LaHaye had written *Spirit-Controlled Tempera-ment* (Wheaton, Ill.: Tyndale, 1967), a mind-cure book in the old manner.

25. Carol P. McFadden, "Film: Fragments of Reality," *Christianity To-day*, November 5, 1976, p. 32; Mark Marchak, "Painting as Propa-ganda: Communist and Christian Art," *Christianity Today*, Septem-ber 22, 1978, pp. 28–29; Daniel S. Eveeritt, "Bob Dylan: Still Blowin' in the Wind," *Christianity Today*, December 3, 1976, pp. 29–30; on another performer in popular music (and friend of Dylan's), the Paul of Peter, Paul, and Mary, Cheryl Forbes, "Noel Paul Stookey Down Home," *Christianity Today*, May 5, 1978, pp. 12–17; the writers John Berryman, John Leax, "'Grace Soften My Dreams'—John Berryman," *Christianity Today*, April 1, 1977, pp. 25–26, and Annie Dillard, "A Face Aflame—An Interview with Annie Dillard," *Christianity Today*, May 5, 1978, pp. 14–19; most interest-ing of all, Duke Ellington, "Duke Ellington," *Christianity Today*, June 21, 1974, pp. 23–24: "May God help us to understand Him better in death than we did in life."

26. Ruth Carter Stapleton's books: *The Experience of Inner Healing* (Waco, Texas: Word Books, 1977) and *The Gift of Inner Healing* (Waco, Texas: Word Books, 1976); *Newsweek's* story of July 17, 1978, portrayed her in biography and within the context of the movement.

27. David E. Harrell, Jr., *All Things Are Possible—The Healing and Charismatic Revivals in Modern America* (Bloomington: Indiana University Press, 1975) is a scholarly and useful guide to individuals. James Morris, *The Preachers* (New York: St. Martin's, 1973) is a skeptical-minded study of several of the more prominent healing revivalists, including Oral Roberts.

28. Kuhlman wrote, for instance, *I Believe in Miracles* (Carmel, N.Y.: Guideposts, 1962) and *Nothing Is Impossible with God* (Englewood Cliffs, N.J.: Prentice-Hall, 1976); James Buckingham, *Daughter of Destiny: Kathryn Kuhlman* (Plainfield, N.J.: Logos, 1976), and Allen Spraggett, *Kathryn Kuhlman: The Woman Who Believes in Miracles* (New York: World, 1970), are more or less sympathetic biographies.

29. So far, Oral Roberts has written his autobiography three times: *Oral Roberts' Life Story* (Tulsa: Oral Roberts, 1952), *My Story* (Tulsa: Summit Books, 1961), and *The Call* (Garden City, N.Y.: Doubleday, 1972); his parents have written his biography once:

L. M. Roberts and Claudius Roberts, *Our Ministry and Our Son* (Tulsa: Oral Roberts, 1960); and his wife has written it once: Evelyn Roberts, op cit. Harrel and Morris discuss Roberts: see note 27. Roberts's three most important writings are his "success" tract (see note 19); his tract on healing: *If You Need Healing Do These Things* (Tulsa: Healing Waters, 1950); and his theology: *God Is a Good God* (Indianapolis: Bobbs-Merrill, 1960).

30. "We Change Churches," in Evelyn Roberts, op cit., notes reactions and offers motives.

31. The many letters: *Christianity Today*, May 15, 1978, p. 63. *Business Week*, October 31, 1977, and *Christian Century*, March 1, 1978, also discuss the economics and politics of the hospital.

32. *Time*, August 8, 1977, *Christian Century*, August 17, 1977, *America*, September 2, 1977, and *Christianity Today*, August 12, 1977, among others, reported the Kansas City meeting. Richard Quebedeaux, *The New Charismatics* (Garden City, N.Y.: Doubleday, 1977) is a useful overview.

33. Marabel Morgan, *The Total Woman* (Old Tappan, N.J.: Revell, 1975) and *Total Joy* (Old Tappan, N.J.: Revell, 1976), Maxine Hancock, *Love, Honor, and Be Free—A Christian Woman's Response to Today's Call for Liberation* (Chicago: Moody, 1975), and *Elisabeth Elliot, Let Me Be a Woman* (Wheaton, Ill.: Tyndale, 1976) all explicitly attack feminism.

34. Letha Scanzoni and Nancy Hardesty, *All We're Meant To Be: Biblical Approach to Women's Liberation* (Waco, Texas: Word Books, 1974) and Herbert J. Miles and Fern H. Miles, *Husband-Wife Equality* (Old Tappan, N.J.: Revell, 1978) are examples of evangelical feminism. For evangelicals feminism raised the same problems as black culture: in *The Worldly Evangelicals*, p. 125, Richard Quebedeaux quoted his source, an unpublished thesis by Ina J. Kau, to the effect that the "evangelical feminists" were feminists first, then "evangelical" and biblical second. When criticized at an Evangelical Women's Caucus, reported in *Christianity Today*, July 21, 1978, p. 46, Quebedeaux replied, *Christianity Today*, September 8, 1978, p. 10, that although he personally favored both feminists and evangelical feminists, he nevertheless still agreed with Kau; the obvious difficulty here for impartial history was how to concede that any evangelicals, whether feminists or anti-feminists, pro-Carter or anti-Carter, pro-sex or anti-sex, got their ideas from the Bible "first," their politics second; why blacks and evangelicals should be held to account and not, say, Graham, was not explained by evangelical historians.

35. C. H. Jacquet, "Women Ministers in 1977: A Report" (New York: National Council of Churches, 1978); Fuller Seminary Conference, "Evangelical Feminists: Ministry Is the Issue," *Christianity Today*, July 21, 1978, pp. 46–47; an editors' symposium in *Christian Century*, "How Women Clergy Are Changing the Church," *Christian Century*,

February 7–14, 1979, pp. 122–218. See Victoria Booth Demarest, *God, Woman and Ministry* (St. Petersburg, Fla.: Valkyrie, 1978), for a discussion of three generations of women ministers in the most remarkable of the non-mainline denominations.

36. J. Grant Swank, "Counseling Is a Waste of Time," *Christianity Today*, July 29, 1977, p. 27.

37. Letty M. Russell, "Clerical Ministry as a Female Profession," *Christian Century*, February 7–14, 1979, pp. 125–26; Russell expounded her views at greater length in *The Future of Partnership* (Philadelphia: Westminster, 1979), particularly chapter 6, "Flight from Ministry."

38. Barbara Brown Zikmund, "Upsetting the Assumptions," *Christian Century*, February 7–14, 1979, p. 127. *The Journal of Pastoral Care*, March 1978, was an issue devoted to experiences of women ministers; the only male contributor, from St. John's Seminary, Boston, concluded, using Freud: "A good father would never want a family of will-less children. . . . To tear away . . . big daddy god . . . will not be easy. . . . But it must be done. . . . Surely infantilism is destined to be surmounted. Men cannot remain children forever! . . ."; Raymond J. Devettere, "The Freudian Father and Christian Children," *Journal of Pastoral Care*, March 1978, pp. 52–53, quoting Freud, *The Future of an Illusion*.

39. Reported in *Christianity Today*, July 21, 1978, pp. 52–53.

40. Reported in *Christianity Today*, January 7, 1977, p. 45.

41. *Christianity Today*, July 21, 1978, pp. 52–53.

42. In Jacob Needleman and George Baker, *Understanding the New Religions* (New York: Seabury, 1978), several scholars of American religion affirm that the "new" has in fact been the normal all along; Harvey Cox, "Deep Structures in the Study of New Religions," op. cit., pp. 122–30, offers suggestions why this has been so difficult a perception to achieve. Robert Wuthnow, *Experimentation in American Religion—The New Mysticisms and Their Implications for the Churches* (Berkeley: University of California Press, 1978), in chapter 9, "The Coming of Religious Populism," sketches sociological grounds for the spreading freedom of individuals to create religion. What no doubt is of most importance are the historical grounds for our ability to see that insofar as religion testifies to the "sacred," the core of the sacred can only be the individual, as the religion-creator.

43. What some of the sociological dimensions of such a church might be, the Oakhurst Southern Baptist Church in Decatur, Georgia, might suggest: beginning in the sixties with a congregation of 700, it integrated; it gave money to hungry people on other continents; and it ordained women. True to the "homogeneous unit" theory of "growth," its membership fell to barely 250. *Christianity Today*, September 27, 1978, pp. 42–43.

RELIGIOUS RIGHT AND WRONGS

1. I have based my discussion of Ponder on Catherine Ponder, *The Dynamic Laws of Prosperity*, rev. ed. (Marina del Rey, 1985).
2. Robert H. Schuller, *Reach Out for New Life* (New York, 1977) expounds his basic views.
3. Earl C. Gottschalk, Jr., "The Rev. Terry Has a Gospel to Cheer the Me Generation," *Wall Street Journal*, August 23, 1984.
4. Among many reports: Joseph Berger, "Southern Baptists Are Facing a Schism," *New York Times*, June 15, 1986; Michael Berryhill, "The Baptist Schism," *New York Times*, June 9, 1985; for several discussions of the broader Southern religious scene, David E. Harrel, ed., *Varieties of Southern Evangelicalism* (Macon, Ga., 1981).
5. Allen quoted, "Religious-Political Drive Assailed," *New York Times*, October 25, 1980; fears, Rev. Kenneth Chafin, quoted in Joseph Berger, "Fundamentalist Chosen by Southern Baptists," *New York Times*, June 11, 1986.
6. Jerry Falwell, ed., *The Fundamentalist Phenomenon: The Resurgence of Conservative Christianity* (Garden City, 1981), p. 187.
7. Among many studies of the rapture, David MacPherson, *The Incredible Cover-Up: The True Story of the Pre-Trib Rapture* (Plainfield, N.J., 1975) has the energy of a kind of scandalized insider.
8. Grace Halsell, *Prophecy and Politics: Militant Evangelists on the Road to Nuclear War* (Westport, Conn., 1986), in "Reagan: Arming for a Real Armageddon," discusses the instances in which Reagan evinced fascination with the theme of Armageddon. For an attempt to come to grips with some of the sociopsychological dimensions of waiting for the rapture, see Grace Mojtabai, *Blessed Assurance: At Home with the Bomb in Amarillo, Texas* (Boston, 1986).
9. Quoted by Robert Zwier, "The New Christian Right and the 1980 Elections," in David G. Bromley and Anson Shupe, eds., *New Christian Politics* (Macon, Ga., 1984), p. 174.
10. Falwell, op. cit., p. 218. Erling Jorstad, *Evangelicals in the White House: The Cultural Maturation of Born Again Christianity 1960–1981* (New York, 1981), pp. 147–49, discusses the near-disaster of the Dallas meeting, where Rev. Bailey Smith explained that God Almighty did not hear the prayers of Jews; Reagan had to note carefully later that his attachment was to "Judeo-Christian" values.
11. In addition to Zwier, loc. cit., see Richard V. Pierard and James L. Wright, "The Moral Majority in Indiana," in Bromley and Shupe, op. cit., for meticulous analyses of the 1980 vote. Both James Davison Hunter, *American Evangelicalism: Conservative Religion and the Quandary of Modernity* (New Brunswick, 1983) and the contributors to Robert C. Liebman and Robert Wuthnow, eds., *The New Christian Right: Mobilization and Legitimation* (New York, 1983) offer elaborate correlations of religion with demographics and politics, particularly as to the "social issues."

12. Adam Clymer, "Right Wing Seeks a Shift by Reagan," *New York Times,* September 6, 1981, for Robison and Weyrich.

13. Ch. 5, "Social Forces and the Vote," in Paul R. Abramson, John H. Aldrich and David W. Rohde, *Change and Continuity in the 1984 Elections* (Washington, D.C., 1986), offers elaborate correlations between voting and religion, notably religion identified by class.

14. Paul D. Erickson, *Reagan Speaks: The Making of an American Myth* (New York, 1985) reveals, through analysis of rhetoric, Reagan's basic mind-set.

15. Among many: Michael Paul Rogin, "*Ronald Reagan, The Movie and Other Episodes in Political Demonology* (Berkeley, 1986) stresses Hollywood; Garry Wills, *Reagan's America: Innocents at Home* (Garden City, 1987) stresses Illinois.

16. Thomas Ferguson and Joel Rogers, *Right Turn: The Decline of the Democrats and The Future of American Politics* (New York, 1986), p. 91; n. 23, 24, & 25 on p. 246 and elsewhere note specific cases of bankrolling the religious Right by right-wing big money.

17. George Gilder, *Sexual Suicide* (New York, 1973) had been his first assault on new gender ideologies; Gilder, *Naked Nomads: Unmarried Men in America* (New York, 1974) had followed it up with a survey of the woes of bachelors and bachelorhood.

18. Abramson, Aldrich and Rohde, loc. cit., pp. 134–38 on the voting by race.

19. An interesting anticipation of the Reagan policy on race: George Gilder, *Visible Man: A True Story of Post-Racist America* (New York, 1978).

20. Schuller, op. cit., p. 21.

21. George Gilder and Bruce K. Chapman, *The Party That Lost Its Head* (New York, 1966), p. 5.

22. Hamilton's link between industrialization and imagination is to be found in his "Report on Manufactures." Tocqueville's analysis appears in *Democracy in America,* J. P. Mayer, ed. (Garden City, 1969), pp. 400–7, 546, 553 and numerous other places. Adams's views appear in *The United States in 1800* (Ithaca, 1955), pp. 114, 115, 125 and elsewhere.

23. For a rather different argument about the Democratic party, denying the reality of a broad movement of opinion to the right, and assigning responsibility for conservative triumph instead to the Democratic party's own subordination to various "capital-intensive" and "multinationally oriented" big business interests, see Ferguson and Rogers, op. cit., which sees the religious Right as essentially a creature of economic interest. In Carol Flake, *Redemptorama: Culture, Politics, and the New Evangelicalism* (Garden City, 1984), in many ways the most stimulating of all discussions about the religious Right, considerable attention is paid to linkages between religion and capitalism, in a spirit quite different from Gilder's.

24. *Power for Living* (Atlanta, 1983), Germans, p. 34; independent view, p. 124; watching God, p. 99.

INDEX

Adams, Henry, 26, 156, 385
Adams, John Quincy, 133
Agassiz, Louis, 29
Agnostics, 130–31, 243–44
Agrarian myth, 137–38
Agrarian outlook, 158–59
Alger, Horatio, 134, 182
Alienation, 153–55; in sex, 82
Allen, James, 43
Allen, Rev. Charles, 293
Allen, Rev. Jimmy, 372
"American" depth psychology, 87
American Psychiatric Association, 69
Animal magnetism, 68. *See also*
    Hypnotism
Anti-Semitism, 381
Aquinas, St. Thomas, 273, 331
Armageddon, 373–74
Art, 227–28, 349–50
Art of Success, The, 175–76
Assemblies of God, 354
Atkins, Gaius Glenn, 255
Atkinson, William W., 167
Atlas, Charles, 166–67
Augustine, St., 279
Authority: of Calvinism, 54; con-
    flict in, 248–49; democratized,
    224–26; in fundamentalism, 368, 392

Bach, Marcus, 44, 255
Bachofen, J. J., 82
Baer, George F., 151
Bailes, Frederick, 44, 81
Baker, George, 240–41
Baker, James, 375
Bakker, Jim, 380, 382
Bakker, Tammy, 380, 382
Baptists. *See* Southern Baptists
Barlow, Joel, 182–83
Barton, Bruce, 182
Barton, Bruce, *The Man Nobody
    Knows*, 177–80
Bates, Arlo, *The Puritan*, 74
Beard, Dr. George: cited by Freud,
    28–29; diagnosis of, 21–31, 117–
    18; vision of, 28
Beard, Dr. George, *American Ner-
    vousness*, 22: cure in, 28; pes-
    simism in, 26–27
Beecher, Catherine, 52–53
Beecher, Henry Ward, 55–56, 134;
    consciousness and, 84; as liberal, 178
Behaviorism of Link, 243–49
Bible: dispensationists and, 373;

prosperity in, 369–70; psychiatry
    of, 293–95; psychology vs., 290–
    95; scholars of, 92; Year of, 390
Bicentennial Year 1976, 336–37
Binstock, Louis, 327–30
Birth control, 221
Black Muslims, 241
Blacks, *See* Negroes; Racism
Blake, William, 84
Blanton, Dr. Smiley, 259–75, 370;
    clinic of (*see* Religio-Psychiatric
    Clinic); as collaborator, 256–58,
    263; faith and, 276–77
Blanton, Dr. Smiley, *Love or
    Perish*, 269–73
Blizzard, Samuel, 252
Boehme, Kate A., 43
Boisen, Rev. Anton, 251–52, 300;
    on schizophrenia, 292, 320
Bonhoeffer, Dietrich von, 290
Bonnell, John S., 255
Booth, Dr. Gotthard, 258
"Boston craze," 35
Braden, Charles, 255
Bristol, Claude, *The Magic of
    Believing*, 170
Brown, Charles R., 256
Brown, Norman O., *Life Against
    Death*, 305
Brownson, Orestes, 136–37, 301–2
Buckley, Pastor James, 98
Bushnell, Horace, 55–56, 224
Businessmen: anxious, 130–32;
    apathy of, 171–75; as heroes,
    129–41, 181–83; model, 177–80;
    paternalism of, 147–51; specula-
    tors, 138–41. *See also* Management

Cabot, Dr. Richard, 95, 251
Cady, H. Emilie, 41, 73, 78, 104
California, evangelists in, 369–71
Call, Annie Payson: diagnosis of,
    46–47; names "sham emotions,"
    59; principle of, 246; sustained,
    98; works of, 32–33
Calvin, John, 218
Calvinism: authority of, 54; early,
    84; flaw in, 77; piety of, 61, 64
Cannon, Walter B., 95–98, 254
Capitalism, 379
Carnegie, Andrew, 131, 167; life of,
    147–51; Schwab and, 181;
    "secret" of, 169
Carnegie, Dale, 17, 180–88, 271,

About The Author

Donald Meyer is professor of history and American studies and Walter Crowell Professor of the Social Sciences at Wesleyan University. Born in Lincoln, Nebraska, he attended Deep Springs College in California, received his B.A. from the University of Chicago in 1947, and his Ph.D. from Harvard University in 1953. Before coming to Wesleyan University in 1967, he taught at Harvard University, as an instructor, from 1953 to 1955 and at UCLA from 1955 to 1967. Meyer is the author also of *The Protestant Search for Political Realism* and *Sex and Power* (Wesleyan 1987). His home is in East Haddam, Connecticut.